STUDIES IN MODERN HISTORY
General Editor : L. B. NAMIER, Professor of Mode
History, University of Manchester

ENGLAND UNDER GEORGE I

ENGLAND UNDER GEORGE I

THE
QUADRUPLE ALLIANCE

BY

WOLFGANG MICHAEL

PH.D. (BERLIN); HON. LL.D. (EDIN.); PROFESSOR EMERITUS OF WEST
EUROPEAN HISTORY, UNIVERSITY OF FREIBURG (BREISGAU)

TRANSLATED AND ADAPTED FROM THE GERMAN

BY

Annemarie MacGregor, Dr. Phil. (Freiburg)
and
George E. MacGregor, B.A. (Lond.)

MACMILLAN AND CO., LIMITED
ST. MARTIN'S STREET, LONDON
1939

COPYRIGHT

PRINTED IN GREAT BRITAIN
BY R. & R. CLARK, LIMITED, EDINBURGH

CONTENTS

CHAPTER I

CHAPTER IX

CHAPTER X

CHAPTER XI

CHAPTER XII

CHAPTER I

WHIG AND TORY

THE first volume of this work traces the growth of British power and the course of internal affairs beyond the Jacobite Rising and the Septennial Act, to the dismissal of Townshend and Walpole, when Whig unity collapsed. The great problem which faced the Whigs in the years 1717–1720 was how to remain in office, how to govern at all against the opposition of their old opponents, Tories and Jacobites, aided by a section of their own party, which included some of their most gifted leaders. They made great efforts, showed real inventiveness. Certain schemes, seemingly of national importance, which historians have hitherto taken as genuine, were put forward merely for party ends ; and this struggle, in which the Government was at length defeated, influenced all internal policy.

Stanhope's ingenuity, which astonished everybody, had in a few years regained for England the position held in the time of William III and of Marlborough. But the contrast between foreign and internal policy is striking ; since the days of Charles II there had existed two classes of Englishmen, mutually hostile and suspicious, who called themselves Whigs and Tories. Well-meaning people expressed the hope that parties would disappear, but meant the political extinction of their opponents ; this hope was of course vain.

The party leaders, however, were practical politicians. " I have had frequent opportunity of conversing with people of the first condition," wrote Defoe ; " no one (worthy to be thought a statesman) has really been either Whig or Tory, or governed in the least by the principles of such, according to the common accepion of them." [1]

[1] W. Lee, *Daniel Defoe. His Life and Recently Discovered Writings* (1869), vol. ii. p. 37.

Scarcely any Englishmen were able to appreciate the parties at their true value : they were themselves Whig or Tory, and all writings on the subject were polemical. " The Whigs ", said the Tories in 1710, " have sacrificed English property and manhood in the Emperor's cause." " We have been sold to the French ", said the Whigs in 1713. Even so thoughtful a writer as Lord Cowper felt bound, in his " Impartial History of Parties ", written for George I, to recommend the Whigs as the only possible party for office.[1]

The first to give the world a historical appreciation of the parties was the Huguenot writer Rapin-Thoyras, who came to England when the struggle between Whigs and Tories was becoming a decisive factor in public life. The problems involved interested him so keenly that he undertook a detailed examination of their origin and character. His *Dissertation sur les Whigs et les Tories*, published in 1717, caused a considerable stir, not least in England, where no such analysis of the parties had ever been attempted, and where so many who called themselves Whigs or Tories had no clear conception of what their party really stood for. But despite his efforts to be impartial, even Rapin-Thoyras shows a certain preference for the Whigs, though he advises their Nonconformist wing not to attack the Episcopal Church too violently. As a Protestant and a foreigner, he found that in England Church differences were much too strongly emphasized. In Episcopalians and Presbyterians, who, after all, differed so little in their dogma,

[1] Material for studying the character of the parties about 1714 is copious in the literature of the time, e.g. Swift, Defoe, Bolingbroke, Davenant, Burnet, Lady Cowper, Saussure, etc. (besides published letters). Writings directly on the subject : J. Swift, *The Public Spirit of the Whigs* (London, 1714) ; *Examiner*, Nos. 33, 37 (London, 1710–1711) ; *Some Reasons . . . . in a Letter to a Whig Lord* (London, 1712) ; Davenant, *The True Picture of a Modern Whig* (1701) (*Works*, iv.) ; J. Toland, *The Art of governing by Parties* (London, 1701) ; Cowper, " An Impartial History of Parties " (in J. Campbell, *Lives of the Lord Chancellors*, vol. iv. (1846) p. 421 *seq.*) ; Rapin, *Dissertation sur les Whigs et les Tories* (1717). No less important are the unpublished diplomatic correspondences of the time, especially the reports of the Prussian Resident, Bonet (Prussian State Archives, Berlin), and of the Austrian, Hoffmann (Vienna Archives). Recent works include : Cooke, *History of Party* (1836), vol. i. ; Delbrück, " Whigs und Tories " in *Historische und politische Aufsätze*, II. ; F. Salomon, *William Pitt* (1901), vol. i. p. 47 *seq.*; C. B. R. Kent, *The Early History of the Tories* (1908) ; Lord, " Development of Parties under Queen Anne," *Transact. of the Roy. Hist. Soc.*, N.S. XIV. 1900).

he sees merely Protestants who should join forces for their common defence against Popery.

From the origin of the Whigs and Tories in the Civil War came the political doctrines with which they were credited, and which were long considered their essence. The Tories were supposed to hold that " kingly power is by the law of God, so it has no inferior law to limit it " ; [1] and the logical conclusion was the doctrine of passive obedience to the King. The Whigs, as successors of the Roundheads, felt themselves the defenders of liberty, a liberty which, if need arose, must be upheld even by opposing force to the Crown. For a few generations "Passive Obedience" and " Resistance " were current slogans. As late as 1729 a Frenchman travelling in England was given this explanation of the difference between the Whigs and Tories, and reproduced it in his letters ; he also repeated faithfully the mutual reproaches of the two parties. " The Whigs ", he said, " accuse their opponents of wishing to establish despotism, thus making the King a tyrant and his subjects slaves " ; the Tories declare that Whigs " are real Republicans desirous of taking all authority and power from the Sovereign, leaving him no more rights than are allowed to a Doge of Venice ".[2]

Swift, a prominent Tory, deals in the *Examiner* [3] with the doctrine of passive obedience and its true meaning. He says that the Whigs accuse the Tories of believing that

a King holding his power only from God, is only answerable to him : that such a King is above all law ; that the cruellest tyrant must be submitted to in all things ; and if his commands be ever so unlawful, you must . . . not use any other weapons but prayers and tears . . . you are still to wish him a long, prosperous reign, and to be patient under all his cruelties, with the same resignation as under a plague or a famine ; because to resist him, would be to resist God, in the person of his vicegerent. . . . All laws made to limit him signify nothing, although passed by his own consent, if he thinks fit to break them. God will indeed call him to a severe account ; but the whole people, united to a man, cannot presume to hold his hands, or offer him the least active disobedience : the people were certainly created for him, and not he for the people. His next heir . . . although

---

[1] *Patriarcha or the Natural Power of Kings,* by Sir Robert Filmer (London, 1680), p. 77 *seq.*

[2] De Saussure, *A Foreign View of England in the Reigns of George I and George II,* ed. by van Muyden (London, 1902), p. 347 *seq.*

[3] No. 33 ; *Works,* ed. W. Scott (1814), vol. iv. p. 44 *seq.*

a fool or a madman, has a divine indefeasible right to succeed him . . .
although he should kill his father upon the throne. . . . But whosoever
sits on the throne without this title, though ever so peaceably, and by
consent of former kings and parliaments, is a usurper, while there is
anywhere in the world another person, who has a nearer hereditary
right ; and the whole kingdom lies under mortal sin, till that heir be
restored, because he has a divine title, which no human law can
defeat.

In this unpleasant picture of absolute monarchy Swift does
not imply that the Whigs seriously supposed the Tories to hold
these views ; but that the Whigs again and again, in a thousand
papers and pamphlets, alleged these to be the Tories' undoubted
principles, and that this was what the clergy taught from the
pulpit. Such misrepresentation Swift contrasts with the doctrine
of passive obedience, as really professed and practised, due only
to the legislative power, whatever its form : in England to the
King or Queen, together with the Lords and Commons of the
Kingdom. The executive part of this power was solely entrusted
to the Prince,

who, in administering those laws, ought to be no more resisted, than
the legislative power itself. But they [the Tories] do not conceive the
same absolute passive obedience to be due to a limited prince's
commands, when they are directly contrary to the laws he has consented to, and sworn to maintain. . . . If an arbitrary king of England
should send his officers to seize my lands or goods against law, I can
lawfully resist them. The ministers, by whom he acts, are liable to
prosecution and impeachment, although his own person be sacred.
But, if he interpose royal authority to support their insolence, I see no
remedy, until it grows a general grievance . . . ; after which, it becomes
a case of necessity ; and then, I suppose, a free people may assert
their own rights, yet without any violation to the person or lawful
power of the prince. But, although the Tories allow all this, and
did justify it by the share they had in the Revolution ; yet they see
no reason for entering upon so ungrateful a subject, or raising controversies upon it, as if we were in daily apprehensions of tyranny . . .
while we have so many laws of late years made to limit the prerogative. . . . As to the succession, the Tories think an hereditary right
to be the best in its own nature, and most agreeable to our old constitution ; yet . . . they allow it to be defeasible by act of parliament ; and so is Magna Charta too, if the legislature think fit.

In reality the old theories, which had governed Tory thinking,
had faded considerably. In the Restoration the loyal Cavaliers

were doubtless the prime movers, but the Roundheads lent their
aid. The Revolution of 1688 also sprang from an agreement of the
two parties ; in it the theoretical standpoint of the Tories was
shaken, for on this occasion they themselves denied their traditional principles. So it was in the Hanoverian Succession, for the
principle of legitimacy was far more seriously attainted by the
notorious passing over of 57 more direct heirs, than by calling
William of Orange to the throne. In the Act of Settlement of
1701 it was the Tories who had introduced those limitations of
the royal power which the Whigs accepted only to avoid endanger-
ing the whole affair. After this it was no longer possible to call
the Tories unconditional supporters of passive obedience and
legitimacy, for they had in practice given up the Kingship by
Divine Right.

They accepted William III and George I from sheer embarrassment ; they obeyed these princes because, and perhaps only as
long as, grounds existed which prevented the rule of the legitimate
dynasty. They invoked from Tudor days the old distinction
between King de jure and King de facto : the former must suffer
that for the time being they should obey the latter. But thus it
was only a conditional subjection, a limited obedience, a recognition
that might be withdrawn. This was felt by the Hanoverians, and
they had less confidence in the Tories, who accepted them half-
heartedly, than in the Whigs, whose only hope lay in the Protestant
Succession, and who now could claim to be the more loyal party.
For the Whigs could easily refute the accusation that they wished
to establish a republic — people thought of something like the
Commonwealth — or to set up an electoral monarchy. They
merely wished to remain true to the principles of the Revolution
of 1688 ; the privileges of Parliament were for them sacred ; and
it was on these that the Hanoverian Succession rested.

Extreme views were still held by certain groups on either side.
The Tories spoke of the protagonists of absolutism as " High
Flyers ". But these were now few, and though they included
men of high position, only the support of the Sovereign could have
given them weight. Of still less importance was the republican
wing of the Whigs, for the great mass of the people favoured the
monarchy. Consequently moderate Tories and moderate Whigs
both accepted the Constitution, the Tories emphasizing the rights of
the Crown, the Whigs the privileges of Parliament. Occasionally

writers even discussed the fusion of the two groups, which would
have been possible had it been a mere question of politics.

Religious differences continued sharply to divide Whigs and
Tories. The old quarrels of the days of Charles I and Cromwell
had not lost their force. To belong to the Established Church was
a mark of the Tories, who called themselves the " Church of
England " or simply the " Church " party.[1] The Dissenters on
the other hand, *i.e.* Nonconformists, Presbyterians, and members
of all sects, stood by the Whigs. As the great majority (according
to Miège [2] two-thirds of the nation) were members of the Established Church, it might look as though the Tories had a considerable preponderance. But then the Anglicans were divided into
High Churchmen and Low Churchmen. Like Archbishop Laud,
the former were unwilling to give up any ceremonial ; the latter
cared less for forms, stood for toleration, and wanted to give equal
rights to the Protestant confession outside the Church of England.
They formed a broad middle party between High Churchmen and
Nonconformists.

In a diplomatic report of 1715 [3] the priests were called the
trumpeters of the Tories, whose strength and weakness alike lay
in their close union with the Established Church. They could rely
on having the majority of the people on their side whenever they
could come forward as the defenders of the Elizabethan Church ;
and they had therefore a marked tendency to give an ecclesiastical
complexion to every question, in order to carry their point. By
this means, in 1710, Sacheverell's campaign defeated the Whigs ;
and the threatening cry of " Church in danger " rang out again
when George I, after his accession, did not take his Anglican duties
seriously enough for the High Tories. To many the cry seemed to
augur a Tory reaction ; but then the Jacobite Rising of 1715, with
its demonstrations of loyalty from both camps, not only confirmed
the Hanoverians on the throne, but also assured Whig supremacy
once more : for as soon as the people felt the Established Church
to be safe, the Tory programme lost the best part of its appeal.

The leaders of the Whigs knew from bitter experience how the

---

[1] Cf., *e.g.*, Portland MSS. (Hist. MSS. Comm.), vol. v. pp. 404, 660.

[2] G. Miège, *The Present State of Great Britain* (London, 1707), Part I,
ch. xi. p. 232.

[3] Bonet, June 3/14, 1715, Prussian State Archives.

raising of ecclesiastical questions could work their ruin : so they avoided such problems as long as possible. The Earl of Nottingham, a former Tory, was their counsellor. Their Church policy in the first years of George I simply maintained the *status quo*. Under Charles II the Act of Conformity had admitted to office only those who could show a certificate that they had taken Communion according to the rites of the Anglican Church. But the object was not fully attained, the exclusion of Dissenters was not effectual ; for the practice of occasional conformity had become prevalent. A great number of Nonconformists, with the exception of only the strictest, brought themselves to take Communion at least once in the Episcopal Church, in order to obtain the required certificate. To stop this practice the Tories, at the height of their power during the last years of Queen Anne, had passed an Act against occasional conformity. For a time the Whig Government of George I merely winked at offences against this Act, without repealing it.

The struggle between the parties was by no means confined to Parliament, nor was popular support permanently on the one side or the other. Certain sections of the people, Tory in Church questions, sided with the Whigs in matters concerning industry and commerce, and again turned Tory when royal prerogative was in question. Even leading statesmen and authors changed sides, not only from egoistic motives. Godolphin and Marlborough were first Tories, then Whigs. Nottingham passed from the Tory camp to the Whigs, but converted them to his opinions on Church policy. Daniel Defoe, the great Dissenter who had stood in the stocks because of his famous pamphlet *The Shortest Way with the Dissenters*, and who had supported Marlborough's war policy, fought after 1710 in the cause of Sir Robert Harley and his Tory ministry.

Such vacillations sometimes led to sharp changes in the country's policy. In the *volte-face* of 1710 and in the Treaty of Utrecht the Tories had been helped by Whigs whose earlier zeal for the war had been considerably cooled.[1] But even before the text of the treaties became public, they returned to their old party. Further, other circumstances such as the decision about the commercial treaty with France, the uncertainty of the Succession, the fear

[1] Bolingbroke, *Letter to Sir William Wyndham* (London, 1717), p. 28 *seq.*

that the ministry was working for the Pretender, caused the so-called Hanoverian Tories to unite with the Whigs — giving rise to talk of a Whig revival even in the days of Anne,[1] and making the collapse of the Tories seem inevitable even without the change of ruler which was imminent.

The great majority of the country population, freeholders, lesser nobility and gentry (but not the great nobles) belonged to the Tories, who therefore became the defenders of the landed interests. In writings of the time " Tory party " and " landed interest " were almost synonyms.[2] In 1713 a Tory minister, the Earl of Oxford, gave the London envoy of the Elector of Hanover, Baron Grote, certain guiding principles for the conduct of the heir,[3] intended to open his eyes to the serious results of an alliance with the Whigs. Clergy and landowners, the true supporters of the throne, must not be given the impression that he would ally himself with their opponents. The witty author of the tale of John Bull was sure that his readers would not misunderstand him when he depicted the Tory success in the election of 1710 as a marriage between John Bull and a virtuous lady from the country nobility.

If the mass of the country people, the " landed interest ", formed the main army of the Tories, the " moneyed interest " the world of business, of industry, and foreign trade, the East India Company and other big companies, the Bank of England and the Stock Exchange were the circles and interests that supported the Whigs. Their numbers included most of the State's creditors ; for since England under William III had embarked on the policy of Continental wars, there had grown that enormous public debt, which by the end of the war of the Spanish Succession had reached nearly fifty million pounds sterling. In Tory eyes

---

[1] " Le traité de commerce et l'affermissement de la succession protestante a été une résurrection pour ce Parti, qui pourra influer dans les élections prochaines ", Bonet, July 10/21, 1714, Prussian State Archives.

[2] Cf. Swift, Letter to a Whig Lord (Works), ed. W. Scott (1814), vol. iv. p. 260. "Now it has been the old complaint of your party that the body of country gentlemen always leaned too much (since the Revolution) to the Tory side." Vide also " The Public Spirit of the Whigs ", ibid. p. 423 ; and Bolingbroke, l.c. p. 20.

[3] R. Pauli, " Aktenstücke zur Thronbesteigung des Welfenhauses in England ", Zeitschrift des hist. Vereins f. Niedersachsen (1883), p. 18 seq.

this monstrous public debt was a national misfortune, the source
of the ever-increasing taxation, which they found especially oppres-
sive because the land tax, instituted to carry on the war, was
collected mainly from their class. The Whigs looked on this public
debt with equanimity, for it offered them a good investment.

The war of the Spanish Succession had been begun for the
commercial greatness of England, for the maintenance and
improvement of overseas trade. Whig circles reaped the benefit.
From the public debt they drew further profit. They became more
and more the real war party. The " landed interest " soon looked
at the war askance : they had to pay for it, and gained nothing.
They felt that the honour and advantage of the nation had been
cared for sufficiently, and that the continuation of the struggle
could only benefit England's allies. This was announced by Tory
politicians in their speeches ; it was repeated in a spate of Tory
writings. The rising of the " landed interest " against Whig policy
won its victory in 1710. When Queen Anne seemed to intend a
change in her ministry, the Bank of England had deputed some
of its members to represent against the change,[1] but in vain.
This Tory victory found its fullest expression in the Treaty of
Utrecht.

Thus the different aims of their foreign policy formed another
distinction between the parties. In 1714 the Tories were considered
accomplices of France, the Whigs friends of Holland, of the
Emperor, in short, of the Alliance of 1701. These friendships
were mutual. Foreign Powers could not but realize that the
stability of their relations with England must suffer from the
existence of these parties, and that treaties with this country
would always be unreliable, because every change of Government
must endanger them ; [2] but as things stood, they had to take sides.
The dispatches of the Austrian envoy, Hoffmann, often sounded as
if a Whig had written them ; the reports of the French diplomats
spoke the language of the Tories.

One feels tempted to substitute the designation of Town and
Country for Whigs and Tories; it is, however, difficult to draw
so sharp a distinction. The merchants, growing in wealth and
importance, were not content with increasing their trade, extending

[1] Bolingbroke, *l.c.* p. 27.
[2] Bonet, Feb. 4/15, 1715, Prussian State Archives.

their business, buying Government stock : they acquired country seats not solely in search of country air, but, as true parvenus, to force their way into the best circles, to mix with the landed gentry, if possible even with the nobility. A peerage was the proudest goal of successful plebeians. On the other side the great country families no longer refused to take part in the profitable business of the City. A directorship of the Bank of England or the East India Company was no dishonour to the man of high birth, but a source of profit ; it could brighten again the paling glory of his name. Even rich City marriages were not scorned. The dividing line between Tories and Whigs was by no means rigid.

Contemporaries tried to discern party characteristics in the manner and behaviour of individual members. The Tory is proud and haughty, treats the Whig with contempt and, when in power, with harshness. He feels himself the representative of the Estab- lished Church, and is as unwilling to allow equal rights to the opponent who does not belong to the Church, as the Roman Catholic to the Protestant in a Catholic country. As far as he can, he refuses office as well as freedom of conscience to the Non- conformist. As the landowning class the Tories are cautious in their private affairs, disinclined for innovations, in short, conserva- tive. But not so in politics. There they are impulsive, rough, quick to attack, not so much from inclination as from necessity : for once they are at the helm, the extremists in Church and politics soon set the tone. Then the party knows that it will not have the mass of the nation behind it for long, that it must press on and make use of the favourable moments, as for instance at the time of the Treaty of Utrecht.

The impression given by the Whigs is quite different. In private life they are bold, enterprising, and shrewd business men, who stake much for profit. Business occupies their minds so completely that their opponents consider that their only aim is to get what they can, no matter how. Once they had principles, but the modern Whig belongs to the party only for what he can get out of it. He wants to have financial dealings with the Govern ment, and to control the Bank of England and the East India Company ; to grow rich by trading in shares and Government stock, not caring whether he run the nation over head and ears in debt ; he wants " to keep his coach and six and to laugh to see gallant fellows, colonels and admirals, trudging afoot in the dirt ".[1]

This picture is of course prejudiced ; the Whigs in their strivings were really working for the greatness of the nation through industry, trade, and far-sighted finance : they were building modern England. In politics, they were cautious and moderate. This clever moderation together with their successes in foreign policy, and with the great progress in material development, explains how they were able to remain in power for decades.

But despite all differences the parties were agreed on one point : to gain and to retain power was the aim of both. Government posts were tempting. Under William and Anne neither party succeeded in filling all posts with its own members. But in 1714 the Whigs, after getting all civil posts into their hands, even succeeded in removing the Tory officers from the army, replacing them with trustworthy members of their own party.[2]

Out of the struggle of principles grew a struggle for power. But the parties were no longer their old selves. Each accused its opponent of gross egoism. " Prithee," says the Whig in a Tory satire, " what is the nation to us, provided our friends get into power, and are in a condition to make us thrive ? If you talk or think of the publick-good, you will never become a right Modern Whig." [3] The same reproach was made against the Tories. No one believed in their sincerity when they spoke of danger to the Church. " This is only the war-cry with which they attack the Whigs, for in this country the controversies only change their names, but fundamentally the struggle is always for office." [4] William III is supposed to have said that he would soon reconcile the two parties if only he had offices enough to distribute.[5] Rapin too observes that we should not be deceived by their big words.[6]

But very seldom does anyone discern the egoism of his own party. Only the high-minded, who had reached peace and quiet, could form a thought like that expressed by Bolingbroke in exile : " I am afraid ", he confessed, " that we came to Court in the same

---

[1] Davenant, *The True Picture of a Modern Whig* (*Works*), vol. iv. p. 151.
[2] Hoffmann, Jan. 29, 1715, Vienna Archives.
[3] Davenant, *l.c.* vol. iv. p. 30.
[4] Bonet, Sept. 23/Oct. 4, 1715, Prussian State Archives.
[5] Cf. Rapin, *Dissertation*, p. 101.　　　　　[6] *Ibid.* p. 100.

dispositions as all parties have done ; that the principal spring
of our actions was to have the government of the State in our
hands ; that our principal views were the conservation of this
power, great employments, and great opportunities of rewarding
those who had helped to raise us ".[1]

[1] Bolingbroke, *l.c.* p. 19.

CHAPTER II

THE SPLIT IN THE WHIG PARTY AND THE QUARREL
IN THE ROYAL FAMILY

FOR a long time the attitude of the Crown towards the Whigs and Tories remained undecided ; nor could the theorists of the Constitution, historical and political writers, yet give any definite advice. The keen rivalry of the parties might well have led to an increase of royal power. Opinions on the subject of Crown and parties varied from time to time. The earlier writers, who had seen the growth of Whigs and Tories, considered the parties an unqualified misfortune for the nation. Bishop Burnet disliked their very names.[1] In his Memorial on the constitution, composed in 1703 for the information of the Electress Sophia, he complains that " for the last four years of King Charles II the Crown may properly be said to have been head of a party ".[2]

Still more sharply did John Toland, the deistic author, express his dislike of party government in an essay on the subject which he sent to King William in 1701.[3] " Of all the plagues which have infested this nation since the death of Queen Elizabeth, none has spread the contagion wider, or brought us nearer to utter ruin, than the implacable animosity of contending partys." [4] They were set on foot by the first Stuart, and brought to perfection under Charles II, who was really to blame. His attempts to establish popery and slavery in England were disastrous. " High and Low Churchmen, Conformists and fanaticks, Whigs and Tories, loyalists and rebels, Patriots and Courtiers, with the like opprobrious nick-

[1] " Terms that I have spoken much against, and have ever hated." (*History of My Own Time* (1734), vol. ii. p. 4.)
[2] G. Burnet, *A Memorial offered to the Princess Sophia, containing a Delineation of the Constitution and Policy of England* (1815), p. 59.
[3] *The Art of Governing by Partys* (London, 1701).
[4] *Ibid.* p. 7.

13

names, are the abominable fruits of his Policy." [1]   But now that they are there with their irreconcilable animosities, what is the King to do ?

A King can never lessen himself more than by heading of a party ; for thereby he becomes only the King of a faction, and ceases to be the common Father of his People. If he is visibly partial to one party, and confers on them only all places of honor and profit, he naturally makes the other party hate him, who . . . will be incessantly laboring to destroy him as their enemy and oppressor. The matter is still worse, if . . . he's actually govern'd himself by a party ; for they care not in what dishonorable, difficult, or desperate attempts they involve him to gratify their revenge on the other side. . . . But the worst of all is, when he not only chuses to govern by a party, but is given to changing sides as he finds it to make for his turn. . . . Then all the Administration grows unsteady, councils uncertain, no union at home, less credit abroad, and a general slackness in execution. [2]

Toland praised William III for having till then received the good men of all parties into equal favour : "he loves not to govern by parties, but rather when his Ministers form themselves into parties, he'll have nothing to do with them any longer ".[3] The aim of policy must be the complete abolition of that fatal animosity between Whigs and Tories, though for him "there can be no balancing in preferring a Whig to a Tory ; that is a free Government to Arbitrary Power, the Protestant Religion to Popery, England to France, and . . . King William to King James ".[4]

This ideal, however, receded further and further as the political importance of the parties steadily grew. War and party politics were the two main factors in Queen Anne's reign, and it became clear that in these struggles the Crown could not stand aloof. So it was with a changed outlook that English statesmen and Hanoverian diplomats welcomed George I and tried to explain to him what the parties were. Particularly noteworthy is "An Impartial History of Parties", written for the King, before his arrival, by Lord Cowper, the great expert on the English Constitution, and a member of the Regency.[5]

[1] *The Art of Governing by Partys*, pp. 9-10.   [2] *Ibid*. p. 41.
[3] *Ibid*. p. 49.   [4] *Ibid*. p. 54.
[5] Printed in J. Campbell, *Lives of the Chancellors* (1846), vol. iv. p. 421 *seq*. Compare author's notes, p. 347.

Cowper no longer uses the strong terms employed by Toland ; he shows tact, finesse, and experience, and is moderate in his judgments, but he is not as impartial as he would like to appear. " To do them right, both are sincerely for the Monarchy of Great Britain and the Church of England. . . . The Tories accuse the others of being inclined to set up a commonwealth, and the Whigs them of a design to introduce Popery, or at least to bring the Church of England nearer to that of Rome." Both accusations Cowper considers wrong. When he mentions the Act of Settlement of 1701, the Tories appear as the party most ready to reduce the prerogative of the Crown. This was the very contrary of the generally accepted view. He still implies that George I would do better to put his faith in the Whigs, as it was impossible to govern with both parties ; though " whichsoever party shall have the lower degree of your Majesty's trust, it ought nevertheless to be used by those in power with very great tenderness and affection while obedient to your Majesty and the laws, and . . . should . . . be admitted to a fair share of . . . places and employments of trust. . . ."

These ideas were familiar to George I at his accession, and guided him in choosing his officers of state. He bestowed the important places on Whigs, but offered some minor offices to Tories ; so the Whigs felt that the King's inclination was to have a mixture of the two parties,[1] and their leaders, Marlborough, Townshend, and Halifax, who each hoped to rise to the highest places, tried to win a following among the Tories. Thus on the accession of the Hanoverians the principle of party government was not yet established. The régime became completely Whig only because the Tories themselves refused to take the small share of places offered them.[2]

In spite of a violent Tory propaganda the elections for the new Parliament gave the Government a large majority.[3] The victory had been expected, because the elections of 1710 had seemed to prove the theory of Cowper

that the parties are so near an equality, and the generality of the world so much in love with the advantages a King of Britain has to bestow, without the least exceeding the bounds of law, that 'tis wholly in

[1] *Letters and Works of Lady Mary Wortley Montagu* (1887), vol. i. p. 15.
[2] Cf. vol. i. p. 90.
[3] Cf. vol. i. p. 115 *seq.*

your Majesty's power, by showing your favour in due time (before the elections) to one or other of them, to give which of them you please a clear majority in all succeeding parliaments.[1]

Similarly Burnet :

It is an observation obvious enough, that where a nation of people is divided into factions, and the crown or government taken in with one side : that side shall in few years' time become superior and carry it all before them.[2]

Rapin studied the question even more closely :

Everybody that is in the least acquainted with England, must know how much influence the Court has in elections. . . . One of the parties is no sooner got into the Ministry, but they procure the Lieutenancies of the Counties, and all the places in the gift of the Court for persons that are devoted to their interests. Afterwards they call a new Parliament. Then besides the money, which the Ministry privately distributes, those that are in authority in the cities, towns, and counties, use all their credit and cunning, to get members elected that may favour the Court, and give its party the superiority of voices in the House of Commons. We may make judgement of the effects of these intrigues from this one consideration, that a Tory Ministry may almost constantly depend upon getting a Tory Parliament, and a Whig Ministry a Whig Parliament.[3]

The ministry, however, did not trust this principle : " As the Cabinet, so the Parliament ". To avoid the uncertainties of a new election, which under the Triennial Act was due in 1718, they chose as early as 1716 to pass the Septennial Act, and to accord it validity for the existing Parliament. The next election, with its excitements and dangers, was thus postponed till 1722 ; and in 1719 the Government even considered introducing legislation to postpone it still further.[4]

A foreign King could not expect to be more successful than his predecessors in uniting both parties for the common weal. But as it was now his fate to rule with one party only, he should have been quite sure of its loyalty. George I, however, was unable

[1] " An Impartial History of Parties ", printed in Campbell, *Lives of the Chancellors* (1846), vol. iv. pp. 428-9.

[2] *A Memorial offered to the Princess Sophia, containing a Delineation of the Constitution and Policy of England* (1815), p. 57.

[3] Rapin-Thoyras, *Dissertation sur les Whigs et les Tories*.

[4] Cf. pp. 290-2.

to control and discipline the Whigs sufficiently to prevent their internal dissensions, which led to a fatal split. George I must be blamed for the confusion at home, because from the start he worked with zeal on questions of foreign policy, but understood and cared little for home questions. The lack of royal control allowed the importance of the parties to grow steadily, and the system of one party in power and the other in opposition was slowly evolving. Curiously enough, Robert Walpole, the very statesman who first based his Government on this principle, was now for some years the stormy petrel of party politics, as though wishing to prove to his countrymen the disastrous effects of dissension within the party. His constant opposition made him so unbearable to the ministers that in October, 1715, they had to take him into the Cabinet.

In April, 1717, Walpole, Townshend, and others were relieved of office,[1] and Sunderland, Stanhope, and Cadogan gained such exclusive control that people spoke of the " Triumvirate ". Stanhope was unquestionably the most important of them ; after his outstanding successes in foreign politics it would have been hard to remove him. His successes as Foreign Minister were overshadowed only after 1721 by those of Walpole in home affairs. Cadogan may have been a gifted general, and diplomatic, but he cannot be compared with either Marlborough or Stanhope. Sunderland, son of the capable and intriguing adviser of William III, enjoyed more esteem among his contemporaries than was perhaps his due, because of his pride and self-assurance. When, during the next years, he was at the head of the State, and was considered its " First Minister ", he failed in everything. The control of foreign policy remained, fortunately, with Stanhope. In home affairs Sunderland was the originator of that hardy and incautious South Sea plan which led to one of the worst catastrophes that ever befell English business.

Sunderland himself had had much to do with the Tories, and his dreams of a mixed ministry disturbed the Whig character of the Government. Those who sought a broad English ministry must have looked upon Sunderland as their man ; yet in practice he only lost a number of Whig supporters, some of the best among them, without winning the Tories.

Since George I had thrown himself completely into the arms of

[1] Cf. vol. i. p. 328 *seq.*

the Whigs,[1] they felt that some of them might oppose him, and that if Whig opposed Whig, he would have to await patiently the victory of the stronger. When some of their most gifted members had left or been driven from office, men of lesser ability had to be promoted. Stanhope, who temporarily assumed the post of First Lord of the Treasury vacated by Walpole, was anything but an astute financier. Addison, the famous author, was a poor Secretary of State. Even the language of his diplomatic correspondence was considered far inferior to that of his witty essays in the *Spectator*. Fortunately the experienced Cowper at least was induced to remain Lord Chancellor.

The Duke of Devonshire could not be kept as President of the Privy Council, despite all efforts of the King, who kept him in audience for an hour. Devonshire begged time for reflection, then went to the Prince of Wales, who advised him to give up his office. The King was deeply offended.

But most serious for George I, both then and subsequently, was the loss of Robert Walpole, whose resignation gave the King the impression that he had been left in the lurch.[2] A few weeks later Nicholas Lechmere, the Solicitor-General, " animadverted upon such of the members as had lately resigned their places, as if they intended to distress the King's affairs ". Walpole replied that " persons who had accepted places in the government had often been reflected on for carrying on designs and acting contrary to the interest of the country : but that he had never heard a man found fault with for laying down one of the most profitable places in the Kingdom. . . . The tenour of his conduct should shew that he never intended to make the King uneasy or to embarrass his affairs." [3]

Walpole soon gave up this loyal attitude. The long-cherished hope of the Tories, that sooner or later a section of the Whigs would join them in Opposition, was nearing fulfilment. On one occasion, before an important Parliamentary decision, the Tories under Bromley and the backsliding Whigs under Walpole tried to concert their opposition.[4] But though Walpole expected a defeat for the

---

[1] Bonet, Jan. 31/Feb. 11, 1717, Prussian State Archives, contrasts George's attitude with that of William III and Anne : " . . . *ils ont toujours laissé une porte ouverte à l'un, au lieu qu'à présent on la ferme aux Tories pour toujours* ".
[2] Cf. vol. i. p. 331.   [3] *Parl. Hist.* vol. vii. p. 449.
[4] Bonet, April 16/27, 1717, Prussian State Archives.

Government, their plan failed at the eleventh hour : for he only wished to make amendments, while the Tories wished to defeat the Government Bill altogether. Walpole's friends had to vote with the Government, which gained a majority of twenty-one votes. But the position of the ministers remained as critical as ever.

The Whigs who had gone out of office now became keen opponents of their former colleagues. The party doctrine that linked them with the governing Whigs was not strong enough to prevent them from joining the Tories and Jacobites. They branded every possible Government measure as harmful and mistaken, and played the devil's advocate. Like many politicians, they followed their personal line, and failed to support either the policy of their party or the national interest.

Such behaviour brought confusion to the party and to its supporters. These had been taught to consider Walpole and Townshend as much the apostles of their own political ideas as Stanhope. Now they saw that it was possible to be a true Whig and yet oppose this Government, and they had to decide who should be trusted to defend Whig principles. So the party was split, and a strong section of the Whigs went into opposition, led in the Lords by Townshend and in the Commons by Walpole.

The position of the ministry was the more difficult because the burden of business rested almost entirely on the shoulders of Stanhope and Sunderland. " It is quite impossible ", writes Hoffmann, " that two ministers alone, and be they ever so capable and industrious, should in the long run manage the whole administration in a kingdom so divided by factions."

It was against General Cadogan that the first big attack was made with intent to overthrow the Government. Impeachment of high officials was not uncommon. Ministers and generals had to be prepared for it, if they had powerful opponents in the country or in Parliament. Marlborough and Walpole had both been impeached. Embezzlement of public money, profit at the expense of the State, were the usual accusations which, in that complicated financial system, were easy to make and as hard to prove or to refute. Cadogan was accused of having exaggerated the charge of transportation of the six thousand Dutch troops who helped to suppress the rebellion in Scotland. In addition the Opposition planned an Address of the House of Commons which would ask that the King relieve Cadogan of all his offices, and thank the Earl of Argyle publicly for the suppression of the Scottish Revolt. This expression of thanks would have been a personal affront to the King, as Argyle was the favourite of the Prince of Wales. With so much accomplished, they might even have brought about the fall of Stanhope and Sunderland.

At the Commons' debate on the affair of the Dutch troops,[1] four hundred members were present, a remarkable contrast with the usually poor attendance. When the debate opened it was noticed that Tories and discontented Whigs were in the majority. Though the Government were defeated, after an hour's debate, in the attempt to bring up a different subject, contrary to order, the delay enabled their absent friends to come to the House. According to the paper laid before the House, Cadogan's transportation of the Dutchmen to England cost £11,000; their transport back under Pulteney cost only £3000.[2] Pulteney showed " that there had been great sums of money embezzled ", but " he could not fix the fraud upon any body ".

Mr. Robert Walpole supported Mr. Pulteney's charge with much vehemence, and at two different times, spoke near the space of two hours, and strained his voice to that degree, that he was taken with a violent bleeding at the nose, which obliged him to go out of the House ; but came back before the question was put. The main stress of his reasoning was, that by the papers that had been read, there was an apparent fraud ; though he could not say, but that it might afterwards appear otherwise ; and he could not tell, but that the Lord Cadogan might produce other evidence to prove his innocence.[3]

Shoulder to shoulder with Walpole stood the Tories, whose chief speaker was the notoriously Jacobite Shippen. Although Stanhope and Craggs, and still more effectively Lechmere, as far as can be judged by reports, spoke for Cadogan, Stanhope's final motion, that in order to let the business drop the chairman leave the chair, was carried in the affirmative by only 204 against 194.[4]

One hundred and twenty Whigs voted against the Government,[5] of whom thirty-two held office. If these are considered

---

[1] *Parl. Hist.* vol. vii. pp. 466-8. Cf. also Bonet, June 7/18, 1717.

[2] *Stuart Papers*, vol. iv. p. 356. Hoffmann's Report of June 15, 1717 (N.S.), gives £3600 and £1200.

[3] *Parl. Hist.* vol. vii. p. 467.   [4] *Ibid.* p. 468.

[5] Bonet, June 7/18, 1717, Prussian State Archives.

as chance allies of Walpole, there were still about ninety " dissatisfied " Whigs ; the Tories had only 74 votes, the Government 294 loyal Whigs. On other occasions the relative strength of the parties was different ; what it would have been if ever all 558 members had been present, no one can tell, but it is certainly no exaggeration to estimate Walpole's following in the Commons at over one hundred. For the present the fall of the Government was averted, but its insecurity in face of such an Opposition was evident.

About this time the imprisonment of the Earl of Oxford, who had been two years in the Tower, once again attracted the attention of the public.[1] He lacked little but his freedom, it is true ; he could receive his friends, kept up a lively correspondence, and took a full part in all political activities, great and small. He was in contact with the Pretender James III and with James' Secretary of State, the Earl of Mar ; he was said to have influence in France, and was in constant connexion with the Jacobites in England. Oxford's part in the tortuous intrigues, the plots, and conspiracies of the Jacobites, recalls vaguely the days of the royal prisoner of Fotheringay, though, owing to his natural indolence and instability, he could not attain her tragic greatness.

The Government had always hoped that this distinguished and awkward prisoner would make his escape, like Bolingbroke and Ormonde before him. The King is said to have sent a person of quality to him, offering him his freedom if only he promised to retire to the country and not meddle in politics.

Lord Oxford clapped on his hat and said, " My Lord, you see the cock of my hat on this side . . . if the Court would but ask me to turn my hat to the other side, and assure me I should have my liberty for it, I would not do it. I shall, with the grace of God, stand my trial. . . . I have had time enough to prepare myself. You shall find I have the constitution of England and the administration of the late Queen to vindicate." [2]

On May 22, 1717 (O.S.), the Earl of Oxford caused a petition to be presented to the House of Lords praying that his imprisonment might not be indefinite.[3] The time was cleverly chosen, for

---

[1] Cf. the Reports of foreign ambassadors, which supplement the printed sources.   [2] *Stuart Papers*, vol. v. p. 541.

[3] Rapin-Thoyras, *Impartial History of England*, completed by Tindal, vol. v. p. 95 *seq.*

the storm raised by the Treaty of Utrecht had abated, and the split in the Whig party had reduced the number of his accusers. First it was insisted on the Earl's behalf that the impeachment was destroyed, since he was not brought to his trial the same session in which he was impeached. A Committee was appointed, and it found that several members of the Secret Committee which began the prosecution were absent or looked coldly upon the matter. The main question was whether Robert Walpole should be chairman again. Despite some opposition he was appointed, because the Government hoped that this would lose him the friendship of the Tories and lower his influence in Parliament. But though he still expressed the conviction that the Tory minister had betrayed the nation, he generally avoided meetings of the Committee and had to be replaced in the chair.

On June 24 the Lord High Steward, with the peers, passed to the court prepared for them in Westminster Hall, when the Commons were present as a Committee of the Whole House, their managers coming first. The King, the Prince and Princess of Wales were seated in boxes : as were the rest of the royal family, and the foreign ministers. All things being prepared, the Earl of Oxford, who had been brought from the Tower by water to Westminster, was conducted to the bar by the deputy-lieutenant of the Tower, having the axe carried before him by the gentleman-jailor of the Tower, who stood with it on the left hand of the prisoner with the edge turned from him. Then the twenty-two articles of impeachment were read, with the Earl's answer, and the replication of the Commons. After which Lord Cowper, acting as Lord High Steward on the King's request, addressed the prisoner and the Commons. Mr. Hampden then made a long speech to justify the impeachment. But as Sir Joseph Jekyll stood up in order to make good the first article, Lord Harcourt signified to the Lords, that, before the managers proceeded further, he had a motion to make, and they adjourned to their own House, and the Commons returned to theirs.

As soon as the peers were come to their House, the Lord Harcourt represented that the going through all the articles of impeachment would take up a great deal of time to little purpose ; for if the Commons would make good the two articles for high treason, the Earl of Oxford would forfeit both life and estate, and there would be an end of the matter ; whereas the proceeding

in the method the Commons proposed, would draw the trial
into a prodigious length, but only convict the prisoner of minor
charges.

To prove high treason seemed impossible even to Oxford's
opponents. So it may have been the aim of the Government to
turn Lord Oxford's trial to high crimes and misdemeanours, for
which they could "imprison him for a certain time in some
remote out-of-the-way place to be free of the mischief they know
he could do them by his working, were he at liberty ".[1] When
Harcourt's motion was debated in the House of Lords, both Tories
and dissatisfied Whigs supported it ; the Government party,
especially Sunderland and Cadogan, opposed.

But the motion was adopted by eighty-eight votes to fifty-six.
The Commons, where the ministers still held a majority, objected,
and they delivered a paper containing their reasons, to which the
Lords replied with a similar paper. Upon this the Commons
desired a Free Conference, which the Lords refused. After this
irritating game had lasted some days, the Lords proceeded to the
formalities of judicature. They returned to Westminster Hall
and ordered the Earl to be brought to the Bar. The Court called
for the accusers to appear, and waited in silence for a quarter of
an hour. Nobody came. So the Lords adjourned to their House,
where they decided that the Earl should be acquitted ; and,
having returned to the Hall, they all gave their votes that he
should be discharged. It was observed that about thirty Whig
Lords retired before the peers went for the last time to the Hall,
so only just over a hundred recorded their votes. Through the
hatred of the Whigs Oxford was still forbidden the Court, and
he was excluded from the Act of Grace which had been promised
in the King's Speech. There remained the possibility of a new
trial, based on part of the remaining articles of the impeachment,
particularly those concerning Spain, the Assiento, and the
Exchequer. But Oxford was not worried, for he knew as well
as everybody else that the threatened proceedings would never
be started.

" Whereby this notorious miscreant has escaped his due
punishment ", comments the Imperial envoy. Oxford was
received with great acclamation by the public ; he mixed assidu-
ously with his compeers, and attended the meetings of the House

---

[1] Cf. *Stuart Papers*, vol. iv. pp. 429, 437.

of Lords ; but he no longer played a leading part in politics.
Because he had not fled two years earlier, his fortune had not been
confiscated, and he could devote himself to books, fine bindings,
and to his collection of manuscripts (to-day a valuable part of
the manuscript section in the British Museum).

The confusion amongst the parties became disastrous only
when the Opposition found a recognized leader in the Prince of
Wales. For almost three years the King jealously tried to suppress his heir, while the Prince tried to escape the tutelage of his
royal father, and to win the hearts of the people by his affability.
Such conflicts were not uncommon in the princely houses of the
time, and recall the quarrels between Frederick the Great and
his father. They were largely due to the doctrine of absolute power
of the monarch, who expected unquestioning obedience from his
children as well as from his subjects.

The quarrel that in 1716 preceded the King's journey to
Hanover had been successfully glossed over. The Prince assumed
the Regency, though only with considerable restrictions ; he
took up his duties keenly, attended Cabinet meetings regularly,
and in other circumstances could have expected the highest praise
from the King. But the mistrustful father had arranged that
Sunderland, Bothmer, and Stephen Poyntz, Stanhope's confidant,
should send him secret information about his son's conduct.[1]
In their letters the Prince's zeal was represented as unseemly
ambition, culpable self-assertion, and striving after popularity.[2]

George I, on his return, did not hide his displeasure ; and the
Prince complained of the slander against him, blaming particularly
Sunderland, who had even made a special journey to Hanover.
When Sunderland and Stanhope came one day to the Prince's
Levée, they did not get so much as a glance from him. Hoffmann
congratulated them jokingly on this reception, and they declared
in a rage that they would not come again in a hurry. None the
less the proud Lord Sunderland brought himself three days later
to ask the Prince of Wales for another audience. But the Prince
sent an answer that he could do without his visit, unless he were
bringing a message from the King. The Duke of Devonshire,

---

[1] Cf. Coxe, *Robert Walpole*, vol. ii. *passim* ; for what follows see especially
Bonet's Reports (Prussian State Archives), and Hoffmann's Reports (Vienna
Archives).

[2] Cf. Vol. i. p. 223.

though he had just joined the Opposition Whigs, tried to reconcile father and son, or rather the Prince and Sunderland ; but the Prince demanded that the minister should formally declare his assertion, that the Prince of Wales had wanted to put his authority above that of the King, to be untrue. Sunderland was not prepared for such a humiliation, and the attempt failed.

From now on the Court of George I and that of the Prince of Wales were like two enemy camps. According to a foreign ambassador, there were always many more at the Prince's Court than at the King's, as the number of the dissatisfied is always greater than that of the satisfied. George I, much as he disliked it, tried by condescension to rival his son's popularity ; in October 1717 he went to Newmarket Races, and from there to Cambridge, where he received Addresses and answered them graciously. He dined with the dons, and went on foot from one famous College to another, praising their beauty. At the same time the Prince of Wales was received in the theatre of Lincoln's Inn Fields, the house of the Tories, as it was called, with endless acclamation, and in a Prologue the theatre was said to owe its existence to royal favour. But more serious were the Prince's political activities, his sympathy with the Opposition, and his cold reserve towards the followers of the King.

The difference between the King and the Prince became an open scandal when a child of the Prince was to be baptized.[1] Even when it was born, the coolness between George I and his son had been obvious. The Prince sent one of his chamberlains to Hampton Court with the news, without writing a word to his father, who came a week later to congratulate the mother ; the Prince did not appear. He soon found that a Prince of Wales had not the same rights over his children as other fathers : he wanted to christen the boy Louis, but the name had unpleasant associations with France and Louis XIV. So he had to call his son by the good Guelph name of George William.

When the god-parents had to be chosen, the King decided that he would be the first godfather ; the Prince wished to add his uncle, who was Duke of York and Bishop of Osnabrück, with the Margrave of Anspach, and his sister, the Queen of Prussia. George I decided, on the advice of his ministers, that, according

[1] Cf. Tindal, *Continuation*, vol. v. p. 550; Reports of Bonet, Hoffmann, Pendtenriedter, and other ambassadors ; *Stuart Papers*, vol. v. pp. 272-5.

to tradition, the Duke of Newcastle as the Lord Chamberlain, and the Duchess of St. Albans as First Lady of Honour to the Princess, should be god-parents. The Prince desired that they should at least act only as proxy for the princely god-parents he had chosen, but the King would not listen to this compromise.

The Prince had to submit to his father's pleasure, which the Lord Chamberlain had conveyed to him in a way not so respectful as could have been wished. After the baptism he took Newcastle by the arm, and in his bad English whispered threateningly : " Rascal, I find you out ". Newcastle understood : " I fight you ", and supposed the Prince wanted to fight a duel. He went immediately to his friend Stanhope, with him to Sunderland, who was at his daughter's wedding, and then to Bernstorff. But they could only suggest putting the matter before the King himself. George I was furious, but avoided any hasty decision. He took the then unusual step of calling a Cabinet Council, at which he is reported to have said that had he been in Hanover he would have known what to do ; but as he had come here to govern by the laws of the country, he desired their advice in this important affair.[1] Three members of the Cabinet were sent to the Prince, to know if he admitted the facts given by Newcastle. When one of them said he was sorry that the Duke of Newcastle had incurred His Royal Highness' displeasure, but that what he had done in the matter was purely in obedience to His Majesty's commands, the Prince replied that he did not believe one word he said. On this the King wrote with his own hand an order to him to remain in his apartment till he should know his pleasure further. For a few days the heir to the throne was prisoner in the Palace of St. James, with a Yeoman of the Guard at the door, who denied access to all but the Prince's servants. Meanwhile the Prince wrote a letter to the King, full of the most respectful expressions, but in the tone of one who was convinced he had acted as he should. As he received no answer, he promised in a second letter not to show his ill-feeling towards Newcastle, but even this brought no answer. After four days' confinement, the ministers suggested that its continuance might be looked upon as an infringement of Habeas Corpus, and as a wrong done to the most distinguished member of the House of Lords. The Prince was therefore ordered to leave the Palace ; he expressed his submission

[1] Cf. *Stuart Papers*, vol. v. pp. 273-5.

in a third letter.[1] The Princess decided to go with him, though the children had to stay.

They withdrew for a time to the home of the Earl of Grantham, chamberlain to the Princess; but after the first attempts at reconciliation had failed, they bought a house in Leicester Square, where by January 1718 their Court was meeting every day, despite the King's order that all persons who should go to see the Prince and Princess of Wales should forbear coming into His Majesty's presence.[2] It became the social centre of the Opposition, where Townshend, Walpole, Spencer Compton, the Speaker of the Commons, and the Tory leaders met.

To win public opinion, the Prince had those letters printed which he had written to the King from his imprisonment.[3] To please the Tories, he and the Princess took Communion at the Parish Church of St. James—where they had to listen to the text: " Now I say, that the heir, as long as he is a child, differeth nothing from a servant, tho' he be lord of all; but is under tutors and governors, until the time appointed of the father ".[4]

The Jacobites were at least as elated as the Opposition at the breach in the royal family. " You may imagine ", writes a contemporary, " how uppish the Jacobites are upon this disaster, and it must be owned they never had so much reason ".[5]

An official account of the events was handed to the diplomatic corps in London and to the British ambassadors abroad; this made a good impression everywhere but in France, where the scandal had appeared in a worse light even than in England; but here too the affair was soon forgotten. George I's reputation abroad was so little affected that only a few months later Stanhope was able to complete the Quadruple Alliance.

Meanwhile the King was doing his utmost to humiliate his son. He even thought of asking Parliament to give him control of the Prince's household and income. A letter of Charles I seemed to justify such action; but then it was shown that the privilege of appointing his own household was given to the Prince of Wales

---

[1] For all three letters see Appendix I.

[2] Cf. *Parl. Hist.*, vol. vii. p. 500.

[3] His assertion that the publication was not his doing is highly improbable, and not believed by the King. Cf. Hoffmann, Dec. 24, 1717, Vienna Archives.

[4] Gal. iv. 1.   [5] *Stuart Papers*, vol. v. p. 274.

by his letters patent, and was inalienable. The mistake was avoided, but the Prince, who knew his rights better, was jubilant. Next the King created his eldest grandson, who was living in Hanover, Duke of Gloucester, and informed the Prince of Wales that he expected him to give up £40,000 of his income, which totalled £100,000, for the education of his children. The Prince, who knew that his father would never bring a second heir into the kingdom, assured him that he wished nothing better than to have his eldest son finish his education in England, and that as soon as the boy came over he would supply whatever was needed to keep him as befitted his rank.

By a decision of the High Court the education of the grand-children was entirely put in the King's hands; the three little Princesses remained at the Palace, not because he loved them, but to punish the recalcitrant father; George William, the innocent object of the quarrel, died shortly afterwards.

Many stories, which do little honour to either side, can be gleaned from the diplomatic correspondence of the time. George I was too hard of heart to allow the three little Princesses to visit their parents without his permission, for which the parents were too proud to ask. For a long while their mother could not bring herself to go to St. James' House, and it was three months before she saw her children. " We've such a good father and such a good mother," said one of the little Princesses, " and yet we are orphans." When asked if her grandfather never visited them, " Oh no," she replied, " he doesn't love us enough for that." After the King had been told of this, he came and spent a whole hour with them, and continued his visits. At length their mother visited them, but when the King was unexpectedly announced, mother and children fled together to the next room. A few weeks later she was meeting the King, only apparently by accident, really in the hope of bringing about a reconciliation, for which, however, George I had no desire. Even when the Prince of Wales in July again offered his submission, George, finding he was at last master in his own Court, imposed conditions that the Prince found too humiliating. By November all hopes of a reconciliation had been given up, and the separation of the two Courts ceased to be a subject of conversation.

The Whigs in power, but divided among themselves; the

Tories in bitter opposition ; a serious quarrel in the royal family ;
friction and difficulties in many other quarters — here are the
chief factors in English political life for some years to come. The
wearying, irritating struggle that faced both King and ministers
obstructed their work at home and abroad, in peace and in war, in
temporal and in spiritual matters.

CHAPTER III

THE minds of Englishmen were influenced during this period by
no other writer more strongly than by Shaftesbury.[1] Grandson
of the Shaftesbury of Charles II's Cabal, his health kept him from
acquiring similar fame in politics ; but intellectually he was far
superior, and he may be said to have founded moral philosophy.
Though he died in 1713, his ideas remained in vogue for several
decades.

Shaftesbury had been brought up in the teachings of Locke,
and was more familiar with the writings and works of art of the
ancients than were most men of his time. Yet as a thinker he
went his own way. Locke had definitely denied the existence of
innate ideas, and in this way he undermined the very conception
of morality and virtue. " Virtue is praised everywhere, not because
it is innate, but because it is useful : amongst different men, the
words virtue and sin stand for different things." [2]

Shaftesbury maintained that the conception of virtue was
innate, and that every rational creature had a sense of right and
wrong : " To deserve the name of good and virtuous, a creature
must have all his inclinations and affections . . . agreeing with the
good of his kind, or of that system in which he is included, and
of which he constitutes a part. To stand thus well affected, and
to have one's affections right and intire, not only in respect of
one's self, but of society, and the publick : this is rectitude,

---

[1] Cf. Leslie Stephen, *History of English Thought in the Eighteenth Century*
(2nd edition, 1881) ; H. Hettner, *Geschichte der englischen Literatur, 1660–
1770* (7th edition, 1913) ; W. Windelband, *Geschichte der neueren Philosophie*,
I. (2nd edition, 1899).

[2] Locke, *An Essay concerning Human Understanding*, Book I, ch. iii.
§§ 6 and 19.

integrity, or virtue ".[1] The opposite is corruption and vice. " To
be well affected towards the publick interest and one's own, is
not only consistent, but inseparable : the moral rectitude or
virtue must accordingly be the advantage, and vice the injury
and disadvantage of every creature." [2] Since man is by nature
good, vice and depravity come only from the lack of natural
inclinations, and from the excessive growth of selfish or quite
unnatural impulses. " Thus the wisdom of what rules . . . in
nature, had made it . . . that virtue, which of all excellencys
and beautys is the chief, and most amiable ; that which is the
prop and ornament of human affairs . . . that by which countrys,
as well as private familys, flourish and are happy . . . is that
by which alone man can be happy." [3]

Shaftesbury concludes that neither the hope of temporal
advantages, nor the weak and uncertain belief in a future reward
and punishment, must be the motive to goodness. Only he who
can like or affect good for its own sake is in some degree good and
virtuous. But the rationalist writers drew from his theories the
conclusion that the aim of virtue was personal happiness, which
eudaemonism was first contradicted by Kant.

Many writers were inspired by Shaftesbury's praise of virtue ;
through the moralizing periodicals his ideas became the standard
by which everyday life was judged. Daniel Defoe founded this
literary genre ; from 1704 till 1713 he edited the *Review*, a
periodical intended " to set the affairs of Europe into a clearer
light ". Since he knew how little the public cared for the many
political " Mercuries " which had been appearing since the seventeenth century, he introduced the " Scandal Club ", with its
informal discussions on religion and morals, learning and fiction
and love-affairs ; virtue was praised, vice and folly condemned.
But despite the brilliance and versatility of the author, who had
himself written the five thousand pages of the *Review*, it was too
solid to hold the general public. It was left to his imitators to
strike upon the light conversational tone.

From April 12, 1709, Richard Steele produced the *Tatler* three
times a week, writing under the pseudonym of Isaac Bickerstaff,
already used by Swift ; here Bickerstaff is represented as a somewhat

[1] Shaftesbury, " Enquiry concerning Virtue ", *Characteristicks* (1738),
vol. ii. pp. 42-4.

[2] *Ibid.* p. 77.   [3] *Ibid.* p. 175 *seq.*

garrulous old gentleman who comes into contact with people of all stations, and feels he must pass on for the benefit of his readers all the news he hears. He talks of all human frailties, vices, and follies ; the coquette, the shrew, and the dangers that threaten female honour are his favourite themes. Pompous Latin quotations prepare the readers for the moral, and the *celebrare domestica facta* of No. 41 might almost be the motto of the whole journal. Politics and great events which could not be explained to the ordinary man in terms of morality slowly gave way to the commonplace. About Malplaquet there is nothing but an obviously fictitious and comic " Original Letter of the Mareschal Boufflers to the French King." [1]

Since no one was personally exposed, the readers were more amused than offended by the bantering criticisms. Gay liked the *Tatler* because it was the first to disapprove the fashionable vices, and because Bickerstaff ventured to praise the married estate, to assert that devotion and virtue were necessary to the character of a fine gentleman, and " to tell the town that they were a parcel of fops, fools, and vain coquettes ; but in such a manner as even pleased them, and made them more than half-inclined to believe that he spoke truth." [2]

Steele was in deadly earnest with his criticisms. When subsequently the *Tatler* appeared in book form, he wrote in the introduction : " The general purpose of this paper is to expose the false arts of life, to pull off the disguises of cunning, vanity, and affectation, and to recommend a general simplicity in our dress, in our discourse, and in our behaviour ". In the final number of January 2, 1711, he added with satisfaction : " The general purpose of the whole has been to recommend truth, innocence, honour and virtue as the chief ornaments of life ".

Addison and Swift both helped in producing the *Tatler*. Without naming Addison, Steele modestly declared that " the most approved pieces in it were written by . . . a person who is too fondly my friend ever to own them ". The English essay as an artistic form is indeed Addison's creation, and in the articles of the *Spectator*, which he published with Steele's aid two months after the last *Tatler*, his gifts find their fullest expression. As poet, dramatist, or politician, he would have been forgotten ; but the

---

[1] *Tatler*, No. 77.

[2] Aitken, *Richard Steele*, vol. i. pp. 253-4.

lively essays of the *Spectator* have kept his name alive till the present day.

The *Tatler* was superseded by the *Spectator* because the possibilities of Bickerstaff's entertaining stories became too limited. He was replaced by the " Spectator " and his famous circle of six companions, of whom the best known are Sir Roger de Coverley, William Honeycomb, and the member of the Inner Temple. Within this novelistic frame the reader is made familiar with each character ; and before the journal is given up, in December 1712, they retire one by one from the scene.

In style the *Spectator* is superior to the *Tatler*, in content it is more varied. It appeared every day with essays about public affairs or private life, art or literature, music or the theatre. On Monday the subject might be the definition of beauty, on Tuesday the Italian Opera would be ridiculed, on Wednesday the artificiality of French taste in gardens was discussed. Taste in art was still largely under French influence, though a tendency to give all artistic creations a national form was gaining strength. The *Spectator* was a true mirror of current opinion, reflecting everybody's likes and dislikes ; but it never gave offence, as it carefully avoided questions of religion and politics which divided the nation. Even the articles about God and Providence, published in the Saturday edition for Sunday reading, were so general and free from controversial questions that Anglicans and Dissenters, the orthodox and the freethinkers, were equally satisfied. Praise of the English Constitution or minor criticisms of Louis XIV were sure of universal approval. Contemporaries thought the influence of both *Tatler* and *Spectator* to be immense : " All the pulpit discourses of a year scarce produced half the good as flowed from the *Spectator* of a day " ; [1] but they were probably more successful in amusing than in reforming society.

Addison and Steele produced a third moralizing periodical, the *Guardian*, but were no longer as keen at this work. Steele was becoming more interested in politics ; he tried to make the *Guardian* a Whig journal in opposition to the leading Tory paper, Swift's *Examiner* ; when, as a result, it lasted only from May till October 1713, he devoted himself completely to politics. Addison revived the *Spectator* in 1714, avoiding all political questions, and almost stripping it of its novelistic form ; but within six months

---

[1] Aitken, *l.c.* vol. i. p. 314.

the journal disappeared again, and Addison took office with the Whigs under George I. The day of the moralizing journal was over in England, though the *Tatler* and *Spectator* were translated and imitated abroad.[1] The *Freeholder*, which Addison founded in December 1715, to win the hearts of the people for the Hanoverians, contained scarcely an article which was not purely political. " I shall do all in my power ", he wrote, " to recommend a good cause, which indeed requires no more than barely to explain what it is." [2]

For some years the praise of virtue and morals had been considered the highest theme of all literature ; so it was a great surprise when Bernard de Mandeville, a Dutch doctor who had spent his life in England and wrote perfect English, proclaimed the contrary in neat, expressive prose and witty doggerel verse. He was familiar with current English ideas, yet as a foreigner was not quite under their spell.

In 1705 there appeared " The grumbling hive of knaves turn'd honest ". It is a mock poem about human society in the guise of a beehive, and is intended to refute Shaftesbury's theory of virtue. The author simplifies his task by not bothering about the actual habits of these clever insects, depicting them as purely human. He apologizes for doing so :

> Which, since their language is unknown,
> Must be call'd, as we do our own.

The bees had the best government, for :

> They were no slaves to tyranny,
> Nor rul'd by wild democracy ;
> But kings, that could not wrong, because
> Their power was circumscrib'd by laws.

Then he speaks of lawyers, officials, physicians, priests, even of navigation and trade, which completely destroys the picture of the beehive. Mandeville describes a national community just as it appears in the eyes of a pessimist. There were diligent people and lazy ones ; and the sluggards knew only too well how to profit from the work of the others. The lawyer's art " was raising feuds and splitting cases ". " Physicians valued fame and wealth above the drooping patients' health." Among the priests some

---

[1] In Germany by the end of the century there were more than five hundred similar journals, but none of them as good as their English models.

[2] *Freeholder*, No. 1.

few were learned and eloquent, but whilst these holy drudges
starved, some lazy ones, for which they served, indulged their ease,
with all the graces of health and plenty in their faces. The Kings
were cheated by their ministers. Justice herself was bribed with
gold, she checked only the desperate and the poor, and secured
the rich and great. But though

> Thus ev'ry part was full of vice,
> Yet the whole mass a Paradise.
>
> .   .   .   .
>
> The worst of all the multitude
> Did something for the common good
>
> .   .   .   .
>
> This, as in musick harmony,
> Made jarrings in the main agree. . . .

Avarice was slave to prodigality. Luxury employed a million of
the poor. Vanity, folly, fickleness in fashions was made the very
wheel that turned the trade. And yet the grumbling brutes were
not content. At every ill success they cursed the politicians, cried
" Damn the cheat ", and would, though conscious of their own
faults, not bear them in others. In the end all the rogues cried
brazenly, " Good gods, had we but honesty ! " Mercury smiled
at the impudence, and others called it want of sense. But Jove,
out of indignation, granted them their request. And lo ! a sudden
alteration took place. As nobody did any wrong, no quarrel
ensued. There was no more need for lawyers, and with inkhorns
by their sides they trooped off. Justice herself in her chariot
disappeared in the air with her train of smiths, gaolers, turnkeys,
assistants, serjeants, and bums. Few physicians, few priests
officiated piously ; ministers and thousands of officers became
dispensable and had to go. No more force abroad, no more luxury.
The big country houses were sold. The price of land and houses
fell. Those who remained could not maintain themselves against
the insults of numerous foes, whom they valiantly opposed.

> Harden'd with toils and exercise,
> They counted ease itself a vice ;
> Which so improv'd their temperance,
> That, to avoid extravagance,
> They flew into a hollow tree,
> Blest with content and honesty.

A nation that wants to live in splendour, says " The Moral "

at the end, needs great vices as well as virtues. Trying to revive
a golden age of honesty would mean to renounce all progress, all
the " world's conveniences ".

In 1714 a new enlarged edition appeared under the title : *The
Fable of the Bees : or, Private Vices, Publick Benefits* ; and it begins
with a promising discussion on the origin of virtue.

The chief thing . . . which lawgivers, and other wise men, that
have laboured for the establishment of society, have endeavour'd,
has been to make the people they were to govern believe that it was
more beneficial for every body to conquer than indulge his appetites,
and much better to mind the publick than what seem'd his private
interest. . . . Those that have undertaken to civilize mankind . . .
being unable to give so many real rewards as would satisfy all persons
for every individual action, they were forced to contrive an imaginary
one . . . observing that none were . . . so savage as not to be
charmed with praise . . . justly concluded, that flattery must be
the most powerful argument that could be used to human creatures.
Making use of this bewitching engine, they extoll'd the excellency
of our nature above other animals . . . they began to instruct [men]
in the notions of honour and shame, representing the one as the worst
of all evils, and the other as the highest good to which mortals could
aspire ; which being done, they laid before them how unbecoming it
was the dignity of such sublime creatures to be solicitous about
gratifying those appetites which they had in common with brutes.

As it was very difficult wholly to subdue them, the conquest of
them was glorious.

. . . they divided the whole species in two classes. . . . The one consisted of abject, low-minded people, that . . . were wholly incapable of
self-denial, and . . . had no higher aim than their private advantage.
. . . But the other class was made up of lofty high-spirited creatures,
that . . . aim'd at no less than the publick welfare, and the conquest
of their own passions.

.   .   .   .   .   .

[They call everything] which, without regard to the publick, man
should commit to gratify any of his appetites, Vice . . . and give
the name of Virtue to every performance, by which man, contrary to
the impulse of nature, should endeavour the benefit of others. . . .

It is visible then, that it was not any heathen religion or other
idolatrous superstition, that first put Man upon crossing his appetites
. . . but the skilful management of wary politicians. . . .

In 1729 the *Fable* was further enlarged by a second part,

consisting of six dialogues. In these Horatio is the typical admirer of Shaftesbury, who cannot understand that Cleomenes is so impressed with *The Fable of the Bees.* Shaftesbury's theories are correctly expounded by Horatio, but of course refuted by Cleomenes, who takes the opportunity to discuss at length the great problems of society, State, and religion.

Mandeville always keeps in mind his opposition to Shaftesbury and the moral philosophy of the day. As a man who has to work hard for his living, he attacks the aristocratic philosopher's life and teachings.

A man that has been brought up in ease and affluence . . . may form fine notions of the social virtues, and the contempt of death. But should he be asked why having this intrepidity . . . he did not follow arms when his country was involved in war ; or when he saw the nation daily robb'd by those at the helm, why did he not make use of all his friends and interest to be a Lord Treasurer ; that by his integrity and wise management he might restore the publick credit ; that boasted middle way and the calm virtue recommended in the *Characteristicks* are good for nothing but to breed drones, but they would never fit him for labour and assiduity, or stir him up to great achievements and perilous undertakings.

Though the essence of Mandeville's philosophy is *laisser-faire* in social matters, many felt that his theory was not unreasonable ; and he himself tried to argue away the unpleasant side of it by saying he had only intended to show : " that private vices by the dextrous management of a skilful politician, may be turn'd into publick benefits ". But still the followers of Shaftesbury — William Law, Hutcheson, and Berkeley, Hume and Adam Smith among them — rained attacks on Mandeville's cynicism from 1724 till the end of the century. The notoriety of the book earned it enemies even on the Continent.

In an age which raised virtue above all things, religion could no longer maintain its old authority, but ranked below virtue :

Virtue is really something in itself, and in the nature of things : not arbitrary or factitious, not constituted from without, or dependent on custom, fancy or will ; not even on the Supreme Will itself, which can no way govern it ; but being necessarily good, is govern'd by it, and ever uniform with it.[1]

[1] Shaftesbury, " The Moralists, a Philosophical Rhapsody ", *Character-isticks* (1738), vol. ii. p. 267.

The end of religion is to render us more perfect and accomplished in all moral dutys and performancys.[1]

This rather dull conception of religion almost turns it into a mere charity institution ; yet there cannot be virtue without religion, for " the perfection and height of virtue must be owing to the belief of a God ".[2] In this point Shaftesbury agrees with the religious philosophy of the day, since both religion and virtue " consist in doing good actions, or in a disposition to do them. . . ." If you would know any man's affections towards God, consult his behaviour towards men. Though his professions be ever so voluminous, though his zeal be ever so noisy, though he believes by the lump and swallows creeds by dozens ; yet if he is immoral, he is worse than an infidel.[3]

Another trend of philosophical thought was Deism, which sought to explain Christianity by reason. It developed inside the Anglican Church without leading to the formation of a new sect ; and it owed its growth at least in part to the progress of science in the seventeenth century. Herbert of Cherbury (1583–1648) has been called the father of English Deism, though he died long before the controversy began. Locke belongs only partially to the new school of thought ; in his *Essay concerning Human Understanding*, and in his book *The Reasonableness of Christianity*, he retains a divine revelation, but he leaves man his faculties " to judge of his inspirations, whether they be of divine origin or no . . . reason must be our last judge and guide in everything ".[4] But as Locke refuses to give up his belief in miracles, which he considers a peculiar manifestation of God, he cannot be said to have attacked either Church or religion.

For the Deists, reason alone can supply the explanation of religion. John Toland's treatise, *Christianity not Mysterious* (1696), is in title little different from Locke's *Reasonableness of Christianity* (1695), but though Toland frequently uses Locke's ideas, he arrives at very different conclusions. He admits no contradiction between knowledge and faith.

---

[1] " Enquiry concerning Virtue ", *Characteristicks* (1738), vol. ii. p. 88.
[2] *Ibid.* p. 76.
[3] *The Independent Whig* (London, 1721), p. 193.
[4] Essay IV, 19, § 14.

As we never have a full conception of whatever things we know, no Christian Doctrine, no more than any ordinary piece of nature, can be reputed a mystery because we have not an adequate or complete idea of whatever belongs to it. That what is revealed in religion must and may be as easily comprehended and found as consistent with our common notions, as what we know of wood and stone.[1]

Later, in his *Pantheisticon* (1720), he admits that the differentiation of natural religion from revealed religion creates the basis of the contrast between esoteric and exoteric doctrine.

Toland is not a great philosopher, but he gave expression to the ideas that were current among the educated, who believed that God had manifested himself clearly enough in nature. For the masses there remained the traditional Christianity.

By reducing the miraculous in religion to the plane of reason, faith was rendered meaningless and superfluous. Religious people felt hurt in their most sacred feelings, and the clergy saw their position threatened. The lower House of Convocation declared Toland's book heretical, though their decision was not confirmed by the upper House ; and it was burnt by the common hangman. From the pulpit the public was everywhere warned against Toland and his treatise. One Irish lord declared he would no longer go to Church, for where Jesus Christ used to be preached he now heard only the name of John Toland.

From now on the tenets of Deism determined the thoughts of the period. From putting traditional religion to the test of reason, people advanced to proclaiming a natural religion, based on the universal belief in divine guidance ; everyone had to decide for himself what was the relation between the two. Later it was denied that there was any opposition between them.

Nor have I patience to hear the name of deist (the highest of all names) decry'd, and set in opposition to Christianity. As if our religion was a kind of magick, which depended not on the belief of a single Supreme Being.[2]

Finally, the superiority of natural religion was expressly proclaimed by Matthew Tindal in his *Christianity as Old as the Creation* (1730). According to him the natural religion is perfect; revelation can add nothing to, and detract nothing from it. As far as

---

[1] Toland, *Christianity not Mysterious,* p. 80.
[2] Shaftesbury, *Characteristicks,* p. 209.

Christianity is in harmony with natural religion, it may be said to be as old as creation ; therefore it ceases to be a historic entity, and becomes merely one aspect of infinite reason. The deists confused their conviction of the existence of a God, based on mere reason, with man's natural desire for religion, and saw in the varied forms of positive religions not an expression of the thoughts of different epochs and peoples, but only the accessories with which the clergy had blurred the knowledge of God in order to lead and cheat the masses more easily. Their attempt to shake off the shackles in which Europe had lain for centuries, led to the assertion of a permanent right to freedom of thought. In 1713 Anthony Collins published a *Discourse on Freethinking* which upheld it as the only cure for superstition ; and the name of freethinker came to be applied to all those who refused to have their intellect hemmed in by traditional barriers. The noisy proclamation of deism created that opposition to Church and religion which was peculiar to the rationalism of the eighteenth century, and which led to the odious cult of Reason in the French Revolution.

Deism and freethinking have always been associated with Freemasonry.[1] The degree of relationship has been exaggerated ; but without it English Freemasonry would have lacked the power to win members in every country of Europe.

The masonic movement developed out of the medieval guild of masons, in which master, journeyman, and apprentice used to form close bodies. These groups, and then their meetings, came to be called " lodges ", the name applied to masons' huts from the end of the thirteenth century. Outsiders were accepted from the seventeenth century under the title " gentleman masons " ; by the beginning of the eighteenth century these " speculatives " outnumbered the " operatives " in the lodge at York, and gradually the name freemason, which had been used only for leading and skilled artisans, replaced that of mason.

The earliest extant minutes in England date from the eighteenth century ; some earlier information comes from Scotland. In 1717 four London lodges are said to have inaugurated a Grand Lodge,

---

[1] For what follows cf. W. Begemann, *Vorgeschichte und Anfänge der Freimauerei in England* (Berlin, 1909–1910) ; and *Vorgeschichte und Anfänge der Freimauerei in Irland* (1911) ; *Historische Zeitschrift*, 109, p. 454.

with the ambitious idea of constituting themselves a governing
body for the movement ; and this unconfirmed event is usually
considered the beginning of modern Freemasonry in England and
abroad. Several hundred, perhaps a thousand, members, belonged
to it, with a Grand Master at their head. In 1721 this position was
occupied by no less a man than the Duke of Montagu ; and a
newspaper reported that the Prince of Wales was shortly to become
a Freemason. Records still say nothing of any wish to form a
universal fraternity, but there is much pompous, solemn talk of
the high ideals they decide to practice. By naively innocent falsi-
fication of history, they lay claim to the greatest thinkers and the
highest thoughts of the past. The dedication of a work written in
1722 for all Freemasons, and evidently by a Freemason,[1] hails
them as fit companions of the greatest kings. The famous *Book
of Constitutions* of 1723 took the history of Freemasonry back to
the creation, with Adam and his sons as the first Lodge.[2] Grand
Master Moses is recorded to have " often marshalled the Israelites
into a regular and general lodge, whilst in the wilderness ". Such
interpretations are possible to those who, like the Rev. James
Anderson, Junior Grand Warden and author of the historical
portion of the *Book of Constitutions*, recognize no difference between
Freemasonry and the art of building.

The establishment of the Grand Lodge in London was followed
by the gradual spread of the Company in England and throughout
the world. The Mother Grand Lodge of England carried on no
propaganda, but simply issued warrants for the constitution or
affiliation of lodges elsewhere. By 1731 there were twenty-two
lodges in England ; others followed abroad. Though its structure
was loose, a Company that spread over countries and continents
was a great worry to governments, but still more to the Church.

The close link with Deism is obvious from the work published
in 1722, which says that religion is the law of nature, that is the
law of God, for God is nature.[3] According to the *Book of Constitutions*, the Freemason must not be an atheist, but should only
acknowledge the religion common to all men. It was this spirit
of rationalism, urging Freemasons to strive for a freer humanity,
to attack prejudice, and to encourage all that was ideal, which

[1] Cf. Begemann, *Freimauerei in England,* vol. ii. p. 80 *seq.*
[2] *Ibid.* p. 154 *seq.*
[3] *Ibid.* p. 86.

drew the foremost men of the world, among them Goethe and
Frederick the Great, into the Company.

Amongst the many and often ephemeral pamphlets and journals
of the day, which repeatedly raised questions of morals and religion,
the work of Daniel Defoe deserves further attention. With all
his versatility,[1] he constantly returns to the subject of man's
relation to God, religion and Church, writing at times with quiet
objectivity, at others with the subtlest irony. When his *Shortest
Way with Dissenters* appeared in 1702, recommending in the tone
of a High-Flyer that the State should treat Dissenters as Louis XIV
had treated the Huguenots, there were High Churchmen who at
first found the advice excellent. When the author was punished
for his satire, he was fêted in the stocks and crowned with flowers.
    Defoe had enjoyed the favour of William III, in whose defence
he had written *The True-born Englishman*. After William's death
he supported first the Whigs, and later on Oxford's peace policy,
though without fully becoming a Tory. He composed lengthy
tracts supporting the Peace of Utrecht, and the subsequent
commercial agreement with France, which he himself had opposed
at first. Before Queen Anne's death he wrote the ironical *Reasons
against the Succession of the House of Hanover* (1713), and other
similar pamphlets.
    In 1714 Defoe still showed his loyalty to Oxford in the *Secret
History of the White Staff*, which is certainly his work ;[2] but he
began to write for the Whigs once more, now that they were back
in power. For such a change of front Defoe had always an extenuat-
ing formula ; but when in 1715 he formally entered the service
of George I, the world did not know it, and continued to believe
for a century and a half that from now onwards he had written
nothing political. To-day we know that he had become the literary
collaborator of the Government, and that he was writing against
the Jacobites and for the Septennial Bill, among other work.[3]
    Defoe's most famous work is *The Life and Strange Surprizing
Adventures of Robinson Crusoe*, in which his " agreeableness of

---

[1] Cf. the list of 254 works by Defoe given in W. Lee, *Daniel Defoe. His
Life and Recently Discovered Writings* (1869), vol. i. p. xxvii *seq.*
[2] Cf. W. Lee, *l.c.* vol. i. p. 240 ; W. Michael, " Das Urbild John Bulls ",
Historische Zeitschrift, 100, p. 254.
[3] Cf. W. Lee, *l.c.* vol. i. Introd. p. viii *seq.*

style and manner, the little art he is truly master of, of forging a story, and imposing it on the world for truth ",[1] had an extraordinary success. The story was suggested by the adventures of Alexander Selkirk, a Scottish sailor who, after quarrelling with his captain, voluntarily deserted the ship at the island of Juan Fernandez in the Pacific, and lived there alone for over four years. In 1711 he returned to London, where his strange fate was much discussed. With only a few weapons and implements he had built huts and gained his food; his only companions had been goats and cats; prayer and reading the Bible had made him a better Christian. Steele went to see him, and depicted his lonely life in the *Englishman*. Daniel Defoe made use of the same material, but only as a frame for his own ideas. He shows how an ordinary man can, when left with only a few simple tools and the knowledge he may have, use the resources of the mind to triumph over the forces of nature. By reflection and diligence Robinson Crusoe teaches himself crafts that he had seen but never practised before. In a place hidden from the eyes of possible foes, he builds himself a comfortable well-fortified dwelling. The story of his patience and success sounds like a hymn to the victory of civilization over nature.

The peculiar charm of the book depends not on the exciting career of the hero, but on the insight with which his feelings are put before the reader, who is so convinced of the psychological truth of the tale that he lives through all Robinson's sensations, his fears and joys, his worries great and small. The moral is the more effective because it appears as a conclusion drawn by Robinson himself, who, despite all his adversities, again and again speaks in praise of being content.

Much of what Robinson says at first recalls rather the Deist or contemporary writer of moralizing works than the Christian or the Dissenter. His approach to God is personal and rational. The pious thoughts suggested by his miraculous escape, by the many pieces of fortune which enabled him to survive, and by the horrors of an earthquake, are soon forgotten. But gradually he begins to feel that his troubles are the just punishment of God for having ignored his father's advice, and a short prayer escapes his lips. Through his close contact with nature he comes to believe in the presence of a Power that has created everything and governs

[1] Cf. W. Lee, *l.c.* vol. i. p. 282.

everything. Inevitably natural religion fills the soul of the man who is left to himself.

It would seem that Robinson is one of the great mass who are not yet ripe for a religion of reason : for from an abstract sense of natural religion he advances to positive Christianity, praying and reading his Bible ; he longs to be saved, not as before from his solitude, but from the burden of sin. The anniversary of his ship-wreck becomes a day of fasting, to be spent in penitence and in prayer for mercy. In the felicity of his new religious conviction, he prefers his solitude to the company of men.

The first two parts of *Robinson Crusoe* appeared in 1719 ; in a third part, the *Serious Reflections* (1720), Defoe adds a theoretical exposition of the ideas implicit in the first two parts. He puts forward the two propositions, that through Providence the eternal God guides the whole world, which he has created by His power ; and that this Providence manifests a particular care over, and concern in, the governing and directing man, the best and last created being on earth. According to Defoe, natural religion proves the first, revealed religion proves the second thesis beyond all contradiction.[1]

In direct contrast to *Gulliver's Travels*, the other world-famous book of this period, *Robinson Crusoe* is entirely non-political. It deals with the universal and eternal problems of human life, which are as interesting to-day as two hundred years ago. What Robinson relates in the second part about the conditions in his island, now inhabited by Englishmen, Spaniards, and natives, with Robinson at their head as the owner of a proprietary colony, is nothing but the sequel to ideas contained in the first part. In describing the type of State they developed, there is no criticism of any form of government, and no one could feel offended.

As a Dissenter, Defoe must naturally have believed in religious tolerance. In the second part there appears a French Catholic priest who, ignoring differences of sect, tries to teach the inhabitants of Robinson's island a simple, Christian respect for God. In the *Serious Reflections*, Defoe, speaking of the various sects in England, hopes that " how many several ways soever we choose to walk towards Heaven, we should all meet there at last ".[2]

The success of *Robinson Crusoe* was such that not even all the

[1] *Serious Reflections*, in Hazlitt's *Works of Daniel Defoe* (1841), p. 57.
[2] *Ibid.* p. 50.

criticisms hurled against it, and the exposure of certain improbabilities in the tale, could seriously affect it. One of its critics says himself that " there is not an old woman that can go to the price of it, but buys the *Life and Adventures* and leaves it as a legacy . . . to her posterity ".[1] Abroad, the book was admired, translated, and, during a few decades, imitated. No less a man than Rousseau has emphasized its eternal value when he required that Émile's library should for a long time be composed of one book only, *Robinson Crusoe*.[2]

[1] See W. Lee, *l.c.* vol. i. p. 298.
[2] Rousseau, *Émile*, Book III, translated by W. H. Payne (London, 1903), p. 162.

CHAPTER IV

THE VICTORY OF WHIGGISM IN CHURCH POLICY [1]

In 1717 the Bangorian Controversy caused a considerable stir among clergy and laymen. Benjamin Hoadly, a freethinking clergyman, who some years previously had preached against Passive Obedience and Non-resistance and had made a name for himself as an opponent of the High Church, had been in 1715 advanced by George I to the See of Bangor. Hoadly accepted the office, conferred purely as a mark of favour, and remained in London. In 1716 he wrote *A Preservative against the Principles and Practices of the Non-jurors*. A still greater sensation was caused by a sermon on the text "My kingdom is not of this world ",[2] delivered before the King on March 31, 1717. Hoadly inferred that no human authority could replace that of the divine founder of Christianity ; therefore the Church could not have absolute authority. The priesthood had no supernatural power to forgive sins, to dispense grace, or to refuse salvation. For what the priests did was only the work of man ; the Apostles may have possessed these miraculous powers, but they could not transfer them to their successors. Quite logically Hoadly later said that the Eucharist was nothing but a piece of symbolism to commemorate Jesus.

The sermon was printed, and irritated the Church-minded all the more as the King was said to have ordered its publication.[3] The emphasis of Hoadly's argument lay on the word "absolute ",

[1] Cf. C. J. Abbey and J. H. Overton, *The English Church in the Eighteenth Century* (ed. 1896) ; John Stoughton, *History of Religion in England*, vol. vi. ; *The Church in the Georgian Era* (ed. 1881) ; F. W. Wilson, *The Importance of the Reign of Queen Anne in English Church History* (1911) ; H. S. Skeats, *History of the Free Churches of England* (ed. 1891).

[2] St. John xviii. 36.

[3] Bonet, May 7/18, 1717, Prussian State Archives.

and his opponents wrongly accused him of denying the Church any authority.   Nevertheless he seemed to relegate Church and clergy to a human level, as he had done earlier with Kingship by Divine Right.

His views tended to blur the difference between English and German Protestantism, and were taken alternately for the ideas of Latitudinarians and of Deists. It was unheard of that a Bishop of the Anglican Church, particularly as he was in favour with the King, should express these opinions, which logically must have made the laws against Dissenters seem meaningless.   Thus the controversy over the interpretation of a text became a struggle for the old position of the Anglican Church and of its members within the State.

Public interest in the controversy was such that dealings were held up on the Stock Exchange and many shops were closed.[1] In the literary storm that followed, at least seventy-four tracts are said to have been published within the first month.   Defoe was one of those who took up their pens ; he slyly assumed the tone of a Quaker who hailed Hoadly's sermon as the enunciation of Truth, and innocently admonished the Bishop to lay down the insignia of office and to join the Society of those whose principles he professed.

The lower House of Convocation now began an examination that could only end with the condemnation of the Bishop of Bangor, which would have been tantamount to condemning the religious views of George I and his ministry.   They appointed a committee of six of their members which drew up a Representation, " in which both the Preservative and Sermon were censured, as tending

" ' (1) To subvert all government and discipline in the Church of Christ, and to reduce his kingdom to a state of anarchy and confusion.

" ' (2) To impugn and impeach the regal supremacy in causes ecclesiastical, and the authority of the legislature, to inforce obedience in matters of religion by civil sanctions.' " [2]

---

[1] Cf. Leslie Stephen, *Hist. of English Thought in the Eighteenth Century* (ed. 1881), vol. ii. p. 156.

[2] Cf. *Parl. Hist.* vol. vii. p. 453.

The whole House approved of the Report, but before they could submit it to the Bishops, the Government put a stop to the proceedings by a prorogation to November 19, and thus silenced the protests of the High Church clergy.[1] A Member of Parliament remarked mockingly " that the King having ordered his ministers to disband part of the army, they had, by mistake, disbanded the convocation ".[2]

This prorogation was a turning-point in Church history ; its constant renewal made it practically equivalent to dissolution, and for more than one hundred and thirty-five years Convocation was not again summoned. The reasons for this development went deeper than the Bangorian Controversy — George I's ministry was determined to do something for its political friends, the Dissenters, but could only overcome the inevitable resistance of the clergy by disposing of Convocation.

The political significance of the Government's action became obvious when it was moved in the House of Commons that Dr. Snape, one of the first to attack Hoadly's sermon, " be desired to preach before the House at St. Margaret's, Westminster ".[3] The Opposition intended to avenge on the floor of the House the Whigs' victory over Convocation ; only this motive could have placed Robert Walpole and his brother Horace on the side of the High Churchmen. The motion was carried ; and as Dr. Snape exercised some moderation in his sermon, the Opposition were next day, in a sitting sparsely attended by Government supporters, able to carry a vote of thanks, and a request that the sermon be printed.[4]

George I was in a difficult position.[5] Legally he himself had to belong to the Church of England, which he had solemnly promised to protect in his Coronation Oath. On the advice of Nottingham, who had gone from the Tories to the Whigs, he had agreed to observe the Tory point of view in Church matters, and assured the Church that it had nothing to fear.[6] He was constantly reminded of that promise by the mistrustful vigilance of the Anglicans.

---

[1] The course of events is recorded in various ways, but Bonet's Report (May 14/25, 1717, Prussian State Archives) seems to clear it up.

[2] *Parl. Hist.* vol. vii. p. 452.   [3] *Ibid.* p. 452.   [4] *Ibid.* p. 466.

[5] Cf. Bonet, April 5/16, 1717, Prussian State Archives.

[6] Instruction to Bothmer, Sept. 25, 1714, Hanover Archives.

On the other side the Nonconformists were demanding more than freedom of religion. They had long been allowed to hold their own services; and George I, on his first appearance before the Privy Council, promised to support and maintain the Churches of England and Scotland, " without the least impairing the toleration allowed by law to protestant dissenters ".[1] These included Presbyterians and Independents, Baptists and Quakers. A contemporary estimated the number of Free Churches in England and Wales at no less than one thousand one hundred and fifty in 1715–1716, Middlesex (with London) having more than any other county. But there is evidence that this list is imperfect; a modern writer estimates that there were one thousand five hundred.[2] The Nonconformists were so numerous, and their claims to George I's gratitude so strong,[3] for having unwaveringly supported the Protestant Succession, that it would have been impossible to exclude them from all office. In some counties their exclusion would have meant taking doubtful elements, sometimes even Jacobites, to be Sheriffs, Justices of the Peace, Mayors, and other officials responsible for the maintenance of public order.[4]

They now claimed the civil rights enjoyed by the Anglicans. On principle they demanded the repeal of the Test Act of 1673, that imposed conformity on all officials, though they did not expect success in such an extreme demand. Their efforts were concentrated on the repeal of the Act of 1711, which forbade the " occasional conformity " by means of which they notoriously evaded the Test Act, and on the repeal of the still-born but hateful Schism Act (1714). By this Act Queen Anne's Tory Government had hoped to win the youth of England for Anglicanism by forbidding Nonconformists to have schools or to teach anything more than reading and writing.

Even before the death of Anne the Dissenters, deeply perturbed by the laws of 1711 and 1714, had sent a deputation to Hanover with their complaints, which they would continue to bear if they could expect to be relieved from their burdens when

---

[1] *Parl. Hist.* vol. vii. p. 18.

[2] Cf. Skeats, *History of the Free Churches of England*, p. 225.

[3] Cf. *Lay Conformity justified, in a Dialogue between a Gentleman of the Town in Communion with the Church of England, and his Dissenting Friend in the Country* (London, ed. 1716), p. 51; also John Toland, *The State Anatomy of Great Britain* (London, 1717).

[4] Bonet, April 5/16, 1717, Prussian State Archives.

the Succession took place. The Elector assured them he would
have the laws repealed, and since his accession had often renewed
his promise, but always put them off till a more favourable
occasion.[1]

In *The case of the Protestant Dissenters in England fairly stated*
(1715), the repeal of these laws was demanded as much in the
interest of the King as of the Dissenters. This pamphlet was
followed by many others,[2] and the agitation led to a meeting in
the Rose Inn, near Temple Bar, on March 26, 1717, at which over
two hundred Members of Parliament discussed the introduction
of a Bill to repeal the laws.[3] Among others Lord Molesworth and
Richard Steele declared that since these laws against the Dissenters
had only been made because they supported the Protestant
Succession, the King must be willing to revoke them. But this
was the moment of the crisis caused by the split in the Whig party,
and Mr. Tufnel, who was in touch with ministerial opinion,
recommended that the matter be postponed. It was decided to
collect further information ; six or seven Bishops apparently said
they would not oppose repeal, and at another meeting in April [4]
it seemed definite that a Bill would be introduced.

However, the violence of the Bangorian Controversy made
ministers feel that the time was inopportune for a politico-religious
Bill ; and at the same time the Anglicans began an agitation
against repeal.[5] Twenty-one Bishops met at Canterbury, and sent
the Bishop of Carlisle with a humble message to the King, that
they would be unanimous against a Bill which threatened the
safety of the Anglican Church. But the ministers were able to
draw some of these Bishops over to their side. In October 1717,
the claims of the Dissenters were helped by the conversion to
Roman Catholicism of the Electoral Prince of Saxony following
the conversion of his father, the King of Poland. The whole
Protestant world was worried ; Bonet called the attention of
ministers to the dangers which seemed to demand the unity of

---

[1] Bonet, Dec. 26, 1718/Jan. 6, 1719, Prussian State Archives.
[2] See Skeats, *l.c.* p. 227.
[3] Tindal (Rapin, *Hist. of England continued*) (1747), vol. iv. pt. ii. p. 524.
[4] Bonet, April 5/16, 1717, Prussian State Archives.
[5] For what follows cf. Bonet's Reports in the Prussian State Archives,
also Hoffmann's Reports, Vienna Archives ; *Parl. Hist.* vol. vii. pp. 502-4 ;
Tindal, vol. iv. pt. ii. p. 552 ; *Portland MSS.*, vol. v. p. 541 ; *Stuart Papers*,
vol. v. p. 258.

all Protestants. But the English, with their scanty understanding of Continental affairs, could not see the importance of the argument.

At the opening of the next session of Parliament, however, the King's Speech noted that " the common enemies of our Religion are . . . endeavouring to undermine and weaken it, both at home and abroad ". The King therefore wished that " all those who are friends to our present happy establishment, might unanimously concur in some proper method for the greater strengthening of the Protestant Interest : of which, as the Church of England is unquestionably the main support and bulwark, so will she reap the principal benefit of every advantage accruing by the union and mutual charity of all Protestants ".[1] From now on " Strengthening of the Protestant Interest ", a phrase that recalls Cromwell's Protestant policy, was the formula used to explain the Government's friendly treatment of Dissenters.

In reply to the King's Speech the House of Lords welcomed the intention to strengthen Protestantism *as far as may be* — a small addition that suggested their doubts. In the Commons, the dissatisfied Whigs so much forgot their party principles as to oppose the cause of the Dissenters ; Walpole himself spoke for the Tory motion to add the words " as far as the laws now in force will permit ". Though this brief and subtle amendment was rejected, it foreshadowed difficulties for the Government's policy of friendliness to the Dissenters. The Tories called up their absent members from the country ; nervous people thought the Crown in great danger. Even the thoughtful Bonet wrote that the execution of the ministerial plan would mean throwing the brand of discord into the country.

So the plan was dropped, and the Dissenters were again put off with promises. The ministers had announced it so ostentatiously that their shameful retreat was a triumph for the Opposition. But during the next year the prestige of the Government rose high with the conclusion of the Quadruple Alliance and the naval victory of Cape Passaro, and the ministers felt their position strong enough to give effect to their old promise despite Tories and dissatisfied Whigs. It was one of the cases where foreign affairs had an obvious influence on home politics.

On December 13, 1718, to the surprise of many, Lord Stanhope offered in the House of Lords a Bill for the repeal of the Occasional

[1] *Parl. Hist.* vol. vii. p. 502.

Conformity and Schism Acts, entitled " An Act for strengthening the Protestant interest in these kingdoms ".[1] After the first reading, Lord Stanhope moved that the Bill be read a second time ; this occasioned a long debate, in which the Duke of Devonshire, a dissatisfied Whig, suggested that it was irregular to bring in a Bill of so great consequence without previously acquainting the House. But he was readily answered by Lord Stanhope, " that his Grace had forgot that about two years before he brought in himself, in the same manner, a bill of much greater consequence ", namely, the Septennial Bill. The Earl of Nottingham, the author of the Occasional Conformity Bill, said mockingly " That the Church of England is certainly the happiest church in the world, since even the greatest contradictions contribute to her support : For nothing could be more contradictory than a bill which is said to be calculated to strengthen the Protestant Interest, and the Church of England, and which at the same time repeals two acts that were made for her further security ". The Earl of Ilay said that in his opinion the Bill " broke the Pacta Conventa of the treaty of Union . . . and that he was apprehensive, that if the Articles of the Union were broke with respect to one Church, it might afterwards be a precedent to break them with respect to the others ". The opponents of the Government tried to put off the second reading to a long day ; the Court party was unwilling to let the affair cool, by adjourning it so long. Finally, the second reading was fixed for December 18.

Accordingly five days later the Bill was read a second time, and a motion was made for committing it to a committee of the whole House ; in the debate the Earl of Cholmondeley suggested that, before they proceeded any further in an affair wherein the Church was so nearly concerned, he thought it very proper to have, in the first place, the opinion of the Bishops. This being unanimously assented to, the Archbishop of Canterbury stood up and declared that the Acts which by this Bill were to be repealed, were the main bulwarks and supports of the Established Church ; that he had all imaginable tenderness for all the well-meaning conscientious Dissenters, but he could not forbear saying, that some amongst them made a wrong use of the favour and indulgence shown them. The Archbishop of York urged in particular the

---

[1] Cf. *Parl. Hist.* vol. vii. p. 567 *seq.* ; this is complemented by Bonet, Prussian State Archives, and Hoffmann, Vienna Archives.

danger of trusting the Dissenters, the open and avowed enemies of the Church, with power and authority.

The Bishops, however, were divided. Hoadly, who spoke next, said that he had always endeavoured to bring over the Dissenters ; but that he ever was of opinion that gentle means were the most effectual for that purpose. He endeavoured to show the unreasonableness and ill policy of imposing religious tests as a qualification for civil or military employments, which abridged men of their natural rights ; and that by admitting the principles of self-defence and self-preservation in matters of religion, all the persecutions of the Heathens against the Christians, and even the popish inquisition, may be justified. This enunciation of the principle of toleration already suggests the age of rationalism. The Bishop of Rochester, Francis Atterbury, who was a leader of the Jacobites, and later hero and martyr of a big Stuart plot, declared that this Bill was levelled against the Church of Scotland, as well as against the Church of England : for which reason he hoped those peers who represented the nobility of Scotland would be against this Bill.

Of eight Bishops who spoke, four were in favour of the Bill and four against. It may be true that some of the former were influenced by hopes of advancement. It is also alleged that an uncle of the Bishop of Lincoln, rich, without children, and a Dissenter, came to him and told him that if he did not vote for the Bill he must expect nothing from him.[1] Be that as it may, the divergence of opinion among the Bishops made it impossible for anyone to assert that the Bill threatened the existence of the Church.

Lord Lansdowne, one of the twelve Tories who had been created peers in 1711, is said to have delivered an expressive and curious philippic against the Dissenters. He was more poet than politician, his tirade so full of polished rhetoric, his attack on the Bishops so violent, that it can hardly have been spoken in the form now known, but must be considered an excellent literary statement of the point of view adopted by the opponents of the Dissenters.[2]

---

[1] *Portland MSS.*, vol. vii. p. 247.

[2] The tirade appeared in pamphlet form under the title *The genuine Speech of the Lord L——ne against Repealing the Occasional and Schism Bills* (London, 1719). It has been adopted verbatim by the *Parl. Hist., q.v.* vol. vii. p. 576 *seq.*

I always understood that the toleration was meant as an ease to tender consciences, and not an indulgence to hardened ones. The act to prevent Occasional Conformity corrects only a particular crime of particular men ; it concerns no other set of Dissenters, but those followers of Judas, who came to the Lord's Supper to sell and betray him. . . . It is very surprizing to hear the merit of Dissenters so highly extolled and magnified within these walls ; for who is he amongst us, that cannot tell of some ancestor either sequestered or murdered by them. It is notoriously known, that they brought the Royal Martyr to the block ; but to extenuate that guilt in favour of the Presbyterians, it seems to be insinuated by a very learned lord, that they performed good offices at last, and were instruments of the Restoration. . . . To restore themselves, not him (the King), to dominion, was their only aim . . . but that the monarchy was restored free and independent, the Church re-established pure and undefiled, was no thanks to the Presbyterians. . . .

The Roman Catholics and Dissenters have been mentioned in the debate upon the same level. . . . But if we may compare them with the Dissenters . . . the Catholics . . . have infinitely the advantage. . . . To whom do we owe our present security in the Protestant establishment, but to the most potent, the most arbitrary, the most famous for persecution of all the Popish powers . . . France, Savoy and the Emperor ? And have not the ministers, one after another, assured us, that these mortal enemies to our souls in another world, are our only guarantees for our salvation in this ?

Several more peers attacked the Bill violently ; Sunderland and Cowper even became insulting to each other. One of the clauses omitted as derogatory to the Test and Corporation Acts, would have allowed that if an Anglican clergyman refused Communion to a Dissenter, and this refusal were testified by two witnesses, the duty of taking Communion would thereby be fulfilled, and the man entitled to assume office.[1] If records are correct, it was Cowper who brought about the defeat of this clause.

Another remarkable episode in the debate was Lord Nottingham's motion for an amendment, that no one should be admitted into any place without subscribing to the Articles of Faith, particularly that relating to the divinity of our Saviour. This was meant as a blow at the growth of Socinianism, and seemed most opportune because of recent events in Exeter that were being much discussed. A preacher had denied the divinity of Christ from the pulpit. In

[1] Cf. Chammorel to Dubois, Jan. 2, 1719, Aff. étr. Corr. Pol. Angl. 322 (Paris).

a subsequent meeting a formal vote was taken, whether this dogma
was to be retained or not. Sixteen had denied, and thirty-two
affirmed Christ's divinity. Nottingham's motion was taken very
seriously in the House of Lords, and strongly supported both by
the opponents of the Bill, and by a number of others who considered such a confession of positive Christianity to be an essential
qualification for office ; it was only defeated by four votes. The
Bill itself was adopted by fifty-five votes against thirty-three. It
was remarked that the Prince of Wales, instead of withdrawing
before the vote as was his wont, voted in person against the
Government. He evidently wished to show all the world his zeal
for the Established Church, and his disapproval of his father's Church
policy.

There is no proper record of the Commons' debate on the Bill
on January 7, 1719, since " excepting His Royal Highness the
Prince of Wales, and some noble peers, no strangers were this day
admitted into the House ".[1] The Tories, as High Church party,
were united against the Bill. Thomas Hanmer, the last Speaker
of the House of Commons before Queen Anne's death, and William
Shippen, the notorious Jacobite, were among those who made
successful speeches ; but, as often at this time, it was Robert
Walpole, the Whig, who took the Government more severely to
task than any Tory dared to do. With his forceful dialectic he
managed to explain away the contradiction between his previous
opposition to the Bill against Occasional Conformity and his present
opposition to its repeal. Previously, he said, he had supposed
the Bill was a prelude to legislation that would destroy toleration
completely ; he could then no more have approved that, than he
now could approve the intended evasion of the Test Act, which
was still evident despite the dropping of the clause that explicitly
stated this aim. This would seriously disturb the nation, which
would be afraid of a repetition of the policy that led to the fall of
James II. It was really the Tory cry of " Church in danger "
that Walpole was hurling at the Government and at Parliament.
Then he went on to spiteful remarks about the late Lord Sunderland, father of the present minister, about the disastrous advice
he had given to James II, about the treachery of the secret
relations he had entertained with the Prince of Orange in order
to remain the first man in the State. He ironically denied that he

[1] See *Parl. Hist.* vol. vii. p. 584, note.

was drawing comparisons. Finally, he even dared to add that it was a consolation to have an heir to the throne who had shown that the aversion from the Anglican Church was not hereditary in the royal family.

Had anyone else launched so rash an attack, he would have been severely punished by the House itself. Hoffmann[1] considered that Walpole deserved to be sent to the Tower and expelled from Parliament. But not even the best friends of the Government dared propose such action. The speech, however, only displayed the factiousness of his opposition, without changing the fate of the Bill. It is said that he later regretted it ;[2] yet possibly this support of Anglicanism may have helped to ease his relations with the Established Church, and to make the Bishops loyal supporters of Crown and Government in the days of his ministry.

The same day the Bill was adopted by the Commons by 243 votes to 202. The Dissenters still hoped for the repeal of the Test Act,[3] but in vain — Communion at least once according to Anglican rites remained the condition of office. Only in the nineteenth century was the Test Act formally repealed, though it had long been a dead letter. The quarrel between Anglicans and Nonconformists continued, though it lost much of its bitterness. In the same year, 1719, appeared a pamphlet called *The Independent Whig* ; its two authors, Gordon and Trenchard, attacked indiscriminately Established Church and clergy, all political decisions of the last twenty years, and all governments since William III.[4] The pamphlet must have been very successful, for it encouraged the authors to publish under the same title a journal which was to continue the fight against the Episcopal Church, " to illustrate the beauty of Christianity, by exposing the deformity of Priestcraft . . . [and to] show what a Babel they had built upon the foundations of Christ and his Apostles ".[5] The clergy are said to

---

[1] Jan. 20, 1719, Vienna Archives.

[2] Belsham, *Memoirs of the Kings of Great Britain of the House of Brunswick-Lüneburg* (1793), vol. i. p. 184.

[3] Bonet, Jan. 20/31, 1719/20, Prussian State Archives.

[4] The pamphlet is not to be found in the British Museum, but its contents can be approximately deduced from a reply : *The Characters of two Independent Whigs, viz. T. H. of the North, and Squire T. . . . of the West* (London, 1720).

[5] *The Independent Whig*, Wed. Jan. 27, 1720 (ed. in book form, London, 1721), p. 9 *seq.*

be foes to truth, liberty, and virtue. Honesty and knowledge are
the essential talents required for the ministry ; the man endowed
with them and with the Grace of God is, without the consent of
any Bishop, entitled to be a pastor in the Scripture sense of the
word.[1] Morality and Virtue are more highly esteemed than Faith
and Religion,[2] showing that the Dissenters now take their intel-
lectual weapons from the armoury of the Moralists and Deists.
The Independent Whig frequently recalls the tone of Shaftesbury
or of Hoadly.

In April 1719 occurred an incident indicative of the changed
relationship between the Roman Catholic Church and the State,
which was now having to make concessions to the right as well
as to the left. Craggs, as Secretary of State, read to the French
chargé d'affaires, Destouches, the King's Speech by which George I
was shortly to close the session of Parliament. It was usual for
His Majesty on such occasions to praise the zeal of his legislature
by emphasizing the significance of one of its most important Acts.
This time he was to speak about the recent Act for strengthening
the Protestant interest ; but the phrases chosen were such that
the Frenchman immediately felt them to be insulting to the
Roman Catholic religion, and urged their omission. He found it
natural that the necessity of unity among the Protestant Powers
should be mentioned. But there was no need to add that only
from this union could they hope for the utter destruction of the
papacy, to which end the King and nation and the two Houses
ought to work together and without pause. Destouches asked
Craggs " if he did not feel the effect that would be produced by
such invective, used in a speech where mention was made of the
close understanding between France and Great Britain ; and if
Cardinal Alberoni and all the Spanish emissaries would not find
in it a spacious excuse for attacking His Royal Highness (the Duke
of Orleans), and discrediting him among Catholic Princes and
peoples ".[3] Craggs agreed, even saying he had foreseen some such
effect, and the passage was suppressed.

---

[1] *Ibid.* Mar. 23, 1720 (book form), p. 67 *seq.*
[2] *Ibid.* July 13, 1720 (book form), p. 193 *seq.*
[3] Destouches to Dubois, April 16/27, 1719, Aff. étr. 323. The story must
be true, for Dubois wrote two days before the speech was read, and is correct
in what he mentions of the content.

It seemed as if the Roman Catholics were also to benefit from the spirit of toleration; they no longer were a danger to the Established Church, but the severe laws against them still remained in force. In the days of Elizabeth the English Church had been finally established, and successfully defended against the Roman Catholic Powers abroad. After the struggle against Philip II and the defeat of the Armada came the century of the Stuarts, when Rome hoped to impose a counter-reformation from above. After the Restoration, Roman Catholic hopes centred in the children of Charles I. They staked everything for Charles II, and counted on his gratitude. In the Declaration of Breda Charles II had declared for the principle of religious freedom, as long as it did not disturb the peace of the country; he had twice used his prerogative to make Declarations of Indulgence, but had been forced to revoke them. There were even direct negotiations with the Pope and with Louis XIV for making Roman Catholicism the state religion in England.

Charles II found himself impotent against the storms of indignation he roused in the people and in Parliament. After 1675 the Catholics placed their hopes in Charles' brother, the Duke of York. There followed the critical years during which only the life of Charles II prevented the accession of a Roman Catholic to the throne. Efforts to exclude the Duke of York from the Succession were unavailing, and as James II he appeared to use every means to regain England for Roman Catholicism. The attempt cost him his throne. The accession of the Protestant William of Orange and the Act of Succession in 1701 showed how determined were people and Parliament never to have another Roman Catholic sovereign. From now on the Catholic danger could not come from the crown, but only from the banished Stuarts; for George I, whose reign depended on the Protestant Succession, it would have been suicidal to favour Roman Catholicism.

Now that the Roman Catholics were no longer feared, they were no longer hated. There were probably only some 25,000 [1] of them, most numerous in Lancashire, Staffordshire, and Essex; they

---

[1] Guy Miège, *Geist- und weltlicher Staat von Grossbritannien und Irland* (Leipzig, 1718), p. 578. Miège suggests that there was scarcely one Roman Catholic in two hundred of the population; and Cunningham, in *Growth of English Industry and Commerce in Modern Times* (1903), p. 935, estimates the population about 1720 at five and a half millions.

included several leading families. But their position was more unsafe than that of Dissenters or of Jews ; the severe penal laws against them, made harsher under William III, had not been relaxed ; only recently the conduct of schools and teaching had been forbidden them on pain of imprisonment, and legally their children could not inherit their landed property before taking the Oath of Supremacy and Allegiance. In peaceful times they had not much to fear ; they could quietly hold their services and most Roman Catholic nobles even had their family chaplains.[1] But as soon as there was any suspicion of their conspiring against the Government, their life and property were in danger. By a law of William III any priest when officiating risked imprisonment for life. Bonaventure Giffard, under James II first Vicar Apostolic of the Midland district and Bishop *in partibus*, was on the fall of the Stuarts held captive for two years. On his liberation he remained in London, where within five months he had to change his lodgings fourteen times and, having been in prison three times, " daily expected a fourth prison to end his life in ".[2]

A reconciliation between the English Roman Catholics and the Government was sought by Abbé Strickland. As a Roman Catholic priest of English extraction, yet brought up in France and a Doctor of the Sorbonne, not a subject of George I and yet a true admirer of English government, he was the born mediator in this conflict. He was favoured by the noblest of English Roman Catholic families, who had so far refused the Oath of Allegiance to George I, hoping for the restoration of the Stuarts. After the rising of 1715 had failed, they were disappointed with the Pretender and thought it wiser to deserve the mild treatment they had enjoyed in peaceful times by becoming loyal subjects. But they had first to get the Pope's consent to their taking the Oath of Allegiance. Clement XI was for a time inclined to acquiesce. Strickland went to Rome to negotiate in 1718,[3] and the College of Cardinals had already decided to consent and to announce their decision through the Papal Nuncio in Brussels.

Suddenly the Pope altered his attitude. The conflict between England and Spain was becoming more serious, as the Spanish

---

[1] Hoffmann, Dec. 12, 1719, Vienna Archives.   [2] *D.N.B.* vol. xxi. p. 291.
[3] For what follows cf. Strickland's Memorial delivered in Vienna in Jan. 1719. A copy exists among the St. Saphorin documents in the Hanover Archives.

fleet had been destroyed off Sicily, and war seemed inevitable. Spain, like every opponent of England in those days, adopted the cause of the Pretender. Clement XI immediately recalled to mind the protection that the Papal Curia had already given to the Stuart cause; and when James Edward himself appeared in Rome, he found the Pope ready to collect money for him and to help in other ways. Strickland's prospects seemed to vanish when the Pope, instead of sending instructions to the Nuncio in Brussels, appointed Cardinal Gualterio, the Pretender's representative in Rome, to be Protector of England. James Edward was given permission to choose and nominate the Irish bishops.

Strickland left Rome, disappointed but not despairing. Only now does he appear to have entered into close relations with the English Government, which had realized the importance of securing the loyalty of its Roman Catholic subjects for the critical days to come. The ministers wanted to strengthen their position in the war against Spain and to diminish the Jacobite danger; so they gladly accepted his proposal to approach Rome through the Court of Vienna, just as two years earlier the Pope had used Viennese influence to help the English Catholics.

In January 1719 Strickland went to Vienna. In a letter from Craggs [1] he was recommended as a man of high standing, of talent and knowledge. He called on St. Saphorin, the British Ambassador, who was sceptical of the result, but hoped at least that, once in Rome, Strickland might find an opportunity to prevent the marriage of the Pretender with the Princess Sobieski, which just then was being widely discussed. At Court he was well received by the Emperor and by the Austrian ministers, to whom he explained the purpose of his mission in a memorial. St. Saphorin gave him his full support, and expounded the position of the English Roman Catholics to Prince Eugene and Court Sinzendorff. If the penal laws were strictly applied, in six years there would be less than two thousand Roman Catholics in England. It was in the Emperor's own interest to co-operate in making a milder application of those laws possible. St. Saphorin even asked that the Emperor should use his influence in Rome to have Strickland appointed Archbishop *in partibus*.[2]

---

[1] Dated July 30, 1718, but delivered only in Jan. 1719, Hanover Archives.

[2] St. Saphorin to Sinzendorff, Feb. 8, 1719; to Stanhope, Feb. 8, Feb. 18, 1719, Hanover Archives.

The Emperor was willing to mediate, and accordingly sent an Instruction to Count Gallas, his representative in the Curia. At the same time the Nuncio in Vienna received a Papal Brief which required him to ask the Emperor's intercession on behalf of the Irish Catholics ; so the Abbé and the Nuncio could discuss the interests of their respective protégés.

On March 1, 1719, St. Saphorin reported that Strickland had left Vienna satisfied ; on May 20, he had heard nothing further from him, but had learnt that Count Gallas had, in spite of his efforts, not even received an answer from the Pope. On June 3 he knew that Rome had sent *des réponses dilatoires* — and therewith the matter was at an end. At the beginning of July Strickland was back in London.

St. Saphorin, who expected this result from the beginning, had recommended the use of force. He wanted to remind the Pope that at any time his Civita Vecchia could be destroyed by the cannons of the British Mediterranean fleet. Stanhope seems to be of similar opinion when he writes : [1] " Once the matter is under way, the King will use every appropriate means to overcome the resistance of the Papal Curia ". In June 1719 the King's private secretary, Robethon, believed the ministers still determined to enforce their rights with His Holiness as soon as Admiral Byng's hands were free.[2] Had this been done, after Strickland had left Rome and the Sobieski affair was settled, it would have looked like a brutal act of revenge.

Strickland's plan was not dropped, but the Government tried to reach its objective in a different way.[3] In return for a promise to apply the penal laws more mildly against the English Roman Catholics, these were to support the demands to be made in Rome. In June and July 1719 Craggs and Strickland several times conferred with three prominent representatives of the English Catholics, the Duke of Norfolk, Lord Waldegrave, and Charles Howard. They were handed a paper, probably composed by Strickland, which contained a basis of agreement.[4]

[1] To St. Saphorin, Feb. 4, 1719, Hanover Archives.
[2] Robethon to St. Saphorin, June 21, 1719, Hanover Archives.
[3] For what follows cf. State Papers relating to Great Britain and Ireland, S.P. 43/57.
[4] Lord Mahon, in his *History of England*, ed. 1853, vol. ii. App. pp. lxxvii-lxxviii, reproduces most of this paper, but what he says about it is not altogether correct.

In order to put the Roman Catholics in a way of deserving some share in the mercy and protection of the government, it is required that some of the most considerable depute a proper person with a letter to the Pope, to inform him that whereas they must be otherwise utterly ruined, they may yet obtain some liberty and security for their religion upon four conditions, all in his own power, and evidently consistent with the Roman Catholic principles.

I. It is required that he order his former decree about the oath of allegiance . . . to be published and executed by proper delegates. . . .

II. That he take from Cardinal Gualterio . . . the title and office of Protector of England. . . .

III. That he revoke the indult granted the Pretender for the nomination of Irish Bishops. . . .

IV. That any person hereafter employed in the mission shall immediately be revoked and called away *bonâ fide* upon information of any offence by him given to the government. . . .

As any delays or tergiversation in coming into these measures can never be coloured with any pretence of conscience or religion, so if any should be made by persons obstinately disaffected to the government, they would have no means left to secure the peace of the realm, but in the real and full execution of the penal laws, and more particularly of the act for transferring the rights of succession of the next Protestant heir, the immediate heir not conforming at the age of eighteen. . . .

But 'tis hoped that the Roman Catholics, by a ready concurrence in what is equally their duty and their interest, will make it practicable for a mild Government to treat 'em with moderation and lenity, if they endeavour to deserve it as well as other Dissenters.

If these conditions were accepted, the consent of eight leading Catholics, four nobles, and four gentry, was to be won. Letters with their signatures were to be sent to the Pope, and also to the Emperor as mediator.

In the lively discussions on these questions Norfolk and Waldegrave were several times on the point of agreeing, but Charles Howard always objected. The letters were written and one afternoon it was even thought that the signatures would be appended ; but during the conference " Charles Howard and the Duke withdrew several times into the back room to consult, where no doubt the former got the better again of the latter, for they determined at last not to sign, and so left Dr. Strickland ".[1]

[1] Craggs to Stanhope, July 7, 1719, S.P. 43/57.

Negotiations ceased ; Norfolk expressed his regret to Craggs and hoped that they would later be resumed with better success. But for a long time there was no further question of an agreement with the Roman Catholics.

Strickland was so angry over the final collapse of his cherished plan that he asked the sadly disappointed ministers to mete out harsher treatment to the Roman Catholics. Some of their leaders were to be arrested, the unfortunate Giffard to be imprisoned once more. However, the Government soon realized that such persecution was useless, and that to make martyrs of the Roman Catholics was not in the interest of the State ; the penal laws against them were applied as mildly as before.

Strickland had failed because the English State, with its Established Church and Protestant Monarchy, was confronted with an utterly strange world which it could not assimilate. The toleration of the Whig ministers had been activated not by philosophical ideas like Deism, but by political considerations only. After Strickland's failure they were only too ready to blame the Prince of Wales and his followers, who had always caused them the greatest difficulties in home and foreign affairs. The Roman Catholics had certainly been told by someone that the fall of the ministry was imminent, and warned not to build on sinking ground.

The legal position of the Jews in England was as bad as that of the Roman Catholics.[1] Since their expulsion in the thirteenth century under Edward I they had not been legally permitted to live in the country, and the severe penal laws against them had remained in force. The Jewish visitor to England was to wear a yellow badge that he might always be recognized ; to convert a Christian to Jewry was a capital offence ; Jews might not take oath on the Bible ; the property of a Jewish widow was to be administered by the Crown.

These laws, however, had long been a dead letter. The Puritans had favoured the admission of the people of the Old Testament ;[2] Cromwell saw how these well-to-do and experienced merchants might help England's commercial life, and he promised them his

---

[1] Cf. K. H. Schaible, *Die Juden in England vom achten Jahrhundert bis zur Gegenwart* (1890) ; *Jewish Encyclopaedia* (1903), vol. v. art. " England ".

[2] Cf. W. Michael, *Cromwell*, vol. ii. p. 91 *seq.*, p. 211.

protection, though the opposition of Churchmen and the jealousy
of other merchants made further action impossible. A Dutch
Rabbi, Menasseh ben Israel, came to England to prepare a new
home for his co-religionists, many of whom saw in Cromwell the
promised Messiah. Though there was no mass immigration, a
large number must have come. In 1657, two years after Menasseh's
arrival, they bought a cemetery, in 1662 they already possessed a
synagogue — for after the Restoration they were still tolerated.
Under James II the tax on foreigners which they had to pay was
for a time remitted, and this cost the Treasury £10,000.[1] Since
those days their numbers constantly increased. At first they were
mostly Portuguese Jews, but after the accession of the Hanoverians
many came from Germany.[2] In 1718 they possessed in London
a most beautiful synagogue,[3] in 1729 they had a second.[4] An Act
of Parliament of 1723 allowed them to acquire property.

Their influence was most marked in the business world. The
various restrictions imposed upon them could not prevent the
growth of their wealth or of their influence in the City. The
Mendes da Costas of the seventeenth century and Sampson
Gideon, Walpole's friend, made themselves famous as financiers.[5]
Besides great and small transactions as brokers and intermediaries,
the Jews began to take an increasingly important part in overseas
trade. They could share in Joint Stock Companies, but at first
they seem to have been excluded from the Regulated Companies ; [6]
in the eighteenth century they took active part in both. Much
can be learned from the writings of those who saw in the rise of
the Jews an injury to the English merchant class.[7]

[The Jews], by insinuating and settling themselves in great trading
ports, and in our American plantations, corresponding chiefly with one
another, do thereby raise great estates, insomuch, as they are now
become the great remitters of money on the exchange, to the great
detriment of our English merchants.[8]

The Jews, by their corrupted charms and secret intrigues . . . do

---

[1] Cf. Schaible, *l.c.* p. 60.   [2] *Ibid.* p. 76.
[3] G. Miège, *l.c.* p. 577.
[4] Saussure, *A Foreign View of England in the Reigns of George I and
George II*, ed. van Muyden (London, 1902), p. 329.
[5] Cf. W. Sombart, *Die Juden und das Wirtschaftsleben* (1911), p. 55 *seq.*
[6] Cf. Cunningham, *Growth of English Industry and Commerce in Modern
Times* (1903), p. 327.
[7] *Ibid.* p. 326.   [8] *Somers Tracts*, vol. xi. p. 617.

boldly presume to . . . engross the principal part of our trade, as some say, in the East India, African, Hudson's Bay, and Hamburgh Society. The Jews have engrossed the Portugal and Barbary trade to themselves and have bid very fair for the Spanish, they have out- done our English merchants and have got into their hands the trade of Barbadoes and Jamaica, whereby they have . . . driven all the course of our exchange and merchandize before them.[1]

Despite the patent exaggeration in these descriptions, there can be no doubt that from now on the Jewish element played an important part in English business life. So it is not surprising if distinguished Jewish families were accepted into higher society. In 1720 all the nobility and gentry were invited to a Jew's wedding in the City. The Prince of Wales honoured it with his presence, his consort sent an excuse to the bride, she being with child.[2] Learned Jews made a name for themselves ; [3] the doctor and mathematician, Jacob Sarmento, was made a Fellow of the Royal Society in 1730 ; some were noted for their patronage of art and music, and it has even been said that Handel took the subjects of his oratorios from the Old Testament in order to please his Jewish patrons.

Early in the Hanoverian dynasty the Established Church had already lost its unchallenged position, though it had surrendered none of its privileges. Views had changed : Dissenters were no longer looked upon as the iconoclast Puritans of the seventeenth century, or Catholicism as popish idolatry which it was intended to force upon the English people. Owing to the Protestant Succession and the relaxing of religious tensions, Dissenters and Roman Catholics were no longer a danger. Besides, the rationalistic ideas of the age, which examined religion in the light of reason and condemned persecution, often influenced the Government's Church policy. Yet these ideas could not lead to general religious tolerance and the complete equality of the different churches, because they had not sufficiently influenced the masses. The Government could risk being tolerant in practice only, and had to retain the legal restrictions on Dissenters, Roman Catholics, and Jews.

[1] *A Historical and Law Treatise against the Jews and Judaism* (1721).
[2] *Portland MSS.*, vol. v. p. 602.
[3] Cf. Schaible, *l.c.* p. 66.

CHAPTER V

THE Quadruple Alliance was intended to revise the map of Europe and to realize the European Balance of Power. England held a dominant position, and was able to compel France to continue, in conjunction with Austria, the policy of Utrecht, which had been begun by Louis XIV under the same pressure. That England also wished, through the Quadruple Alliance, to give the law to the world, is shown by an otherwise unimportant episode during the negotiations for the Alliance.

In the spring of 1718, when England and France were trying to win Austria's adherence to the Triple Alliance, a plan which had been drawn up in England and approved in Paris was sent to Vienna.[1] After accepting it in principle, the Austrian ministers objected to the Preamble, in which it was implied that the three Western Powers had made themselves arbiters of the conditions necessary for peace in Europe. The Preamble contained examples to prove that this was only a repetition of a practice found in earlier treaties ; for instance, the Triple Alliance of 1668 had tried to impose its will on Spain. Count Sinzendorff raised the matter with the two British diplomats charged with the negotiations.

We cannot prevent you, in the treaty you make with France and Holland, from introducing any motives you find fitting ; but all these motives must in no circumstances be included in the treaty that the Emperor accepts, because firstly . . . it might be supposed it was fear that made the Emperor agree, and secondly, the Emperor will never allow anything in a treaty that he signs which would make it seem that he approves the habit, lately adopted by certain European

---

[1] *Projet du Traité entre leurs Majestés Britannique et Très-Chrétienne et les Seigneurs États-Généraux pour la paix entre l'Empereur et le Roi d'Espagne, et entre l'Empereur et le Roi de Sicile*, S.P. 80/36. Cf. Appendix 2.

powers, of determining the fate of others when they believe that their own advantage demands it.

In the heated discussion that followed, the Austrians showed themselves very sensitive about the Preamble, for which they reproached the English at every opportunity.[1]

As the Emperor had accepted the Alliance in principle, the English Government did not think it worth while to press the Preamble, which was replaced by one so meaningless that it could offend nobody. Though they pointed out that these motives had been specially mentioned in order to draw the Dutch into the Alliance, they now said that the value of the agreement was so evident that a long explanation of its motives was unnecessary.[2]

In the third secret article, which dealt with the subjugation by force if necessary of the Kings of Spain and Sicily, a reference to precedents was also omitted at the wish of the Austrians. The right of the Great Powers to impose their will on others was rejected in principle, though allowed against Spain and Sicily.[3]

Hope of reaching a peaceful understanding with Spain had almost vanished after Stanhope's unsuccessful journey to Spain, and the English victory gained off Cape Passaro before war had even been declared. On his way home Stanhope discussed the projected plan of campaign with ministers in Paris, though he felt some doubts about the loyalty of a country that had for thirty years been the enemy of England, and in which the majority still hated the English and disliked a war against the nephew of Louis XIV.

Philip, Duke of Orleans, Regent for Louis XV, was bound with England by ties of mutual interest. But though he had signed the Quadruple Alliance, he did not turn a deaf ear to its opponents, for he was a vacillating character whose main aim was to possess power and to give the impression of independence of action. Whoever wanted to influence him had to be circumspect. He often promoted talented men of humble birth, like Dubois and John Law, because he felt oppressed by the greatness of the last reign and liked to break away from the old traditions.

---

[1] Relation des conférences . . . Vienna, May 22, 1718, S.P. 80/36.

[2] Cf. a document in French, dated Londres mai 30/juin 10, 1718, inscribed on the back : " Remarks on the alterations made in the Treaty at the Imperial Court ", S.P. 80/36.

[3] Cf. Přibram, *Oesterreichische Staatsverträge*, England, vol. i. p. 366.

Villars and Huxelles, the old opponents of England, were still at the head of military and foreign affairs. Though they had voted for the Quadruple Alliance, they now did all they could to prevent the war, to estrange the Regent from his allies, and to make him come to terms with Spain. One day, after the Regent had spent three hours in his closet with Stanhope and Stair, Villars ventured the remark that he had never heard of a prince negotiating with two ministers of the same foreign state at the same time.

The English and Austrian Governments had long wished to free the Regent of such influences. They looked upon every strengthening of his position as their own gain. When by a sort of *coup d'état* he silenced the opposition of the Parliament of Paris to his financial policy, it was said that George I was more pleased with this news than with the victory of Cape Passaro. But it was more important to break the opposition to the Regent's foreign policy, and to this end Dubois, who had conducted the negotiations in Hanover in 1716, had arranged the Triple Alliance in 1717, and signed the Quadruple Alliance in London in 1718, seemed the right man to put at the head of foreign affairs.

Guillaume Dubois was a man of modest manner and unbounded ambition. His success was due to adroitness, sagacity, and pene-tration, and to the clever way he handled men. " He is wonder-fully alert," wrote Craggs during the negotiations for the Quadruple Alliance, " as soon as he picks up a bit of news he dispatches a courier . . . were I to hide a thing from him to-day, all that would happen would be that he has means to know it to-morrow, and he would have a thousand suspicions to boot." [1]

As soon as Dubois had returned to Paris after signing the Quadruple Alliance, he and Stair arranged to work for the abolition of the Councils of War and of Foreign Affairs, which were to be replaced by Secretaries of State. In his first tentative suggestions to the Regent, Stair avoided mentioning Dubois' name, as this would have done him no good. When the Regent replied proudly that he, like Richelieu, wished to be the only one who knew all the secrets of foreign policy, Stair did not contradict him, but suggested he ought to have someone on whom he could rely implicitly. Stair's move was supported by others ; and by

[1] Graham, *Annals and Correspondence of the Earl of Stair* (1875), vol. ii. p. 368.

September 6, 1718, he was able to draw a promise from the Regent that Huxelles would soon be dismissed. Next day the same assurance was given to the Imperial envoy, Count Königsegg. On September 10 Stanhope arrived from Spain, and stayed longer than intended in Paris, as the Regent suggested there might be agreeable news to carry back to London.[1] The two English diplomats worked together for Dubois' promotion, and put forward testimonials from London and Vienna. Dubois himself remained in the background, only taking care that a flattering letter he had received from Craggs came to the Regent's notice. On September 24 the Councils were replaced by secretaryships with Dubois as Secretary for Foreign Affairs.[2] With the eclipse of Huxelles and Villars, France's European policy became for a long time dependent on that of England, and only regained its independence under Fleury in the thirties. Dubois, in gratitude, wrote to Stair and Stanhope that he would use his position " *pour l'intérêt commun de nos maîtres* ". England could count on his services as long as he could rely on English support.

War could still be avoided if, as a result of Passaro, Spain agreed to submit to the Quadruple Alliance. Colonel Stanhope, together with his French colleague, Nancré, had just gone to the Escorial when news of the victory reached them. As yet no one in the palace had heard of it. They informed Alberoni of what had happened, instead of the King, and hoped to hear from him what course they should take ; Alberoni asked Nancré alone to come to him that evening and give him further details. He showed himself grateful for their tact, but declared he was sure that even after this misfortune the King would never abandon the Sicilian enterprise, nor recall one man of the troops he had there.[3]

Spain's attitude after Passaro long remained obscure. Alberoni probably had no intention of submitting to the terms of the Quadruple Alliance. This curious man, an upstart from Italy, had quickly made himself at home in his Spanish surroundings, where

---

[1] Stanhope to Craggs, Sept. 14, 1718, S.P. 78/162.

[2] Based particularly on the following in S.P. 78/162: Stair to Craggs, Aug. 20, 29 ; Sept. 4, 7, 1718 ; St. Saphorin to Stair, Aug. 22, 1718 ; Stair and Stanhope to Craggs, Sept. 14, 25, 1718 ; Dubois to Stair, Sept. 25, 1718. Cf. also Wiesener, *Le Régent, l'abbé Dubois et les Anglais*, vol. ii. p. 261 *seq.*

[3] W. Stanhope to Craggs, Sept. 12, 1718, S.P. 94/88.

his inventive mind was always busy finding clever ways of dealing with his opponents. Ignoring the Treaty of Utrecht, he was trying to recreate Spain's lost political importance. He thought he could use everyone, from Turkey to Scotland, to forward his policy. For contemporaries he was the embodiment of European unrest, and they considered his fall an essential condition for peace. Yet at times he wished to avoid conflicts, and even seemed unwilling to carry out the warlike intentions of Philip V and Elizabeth.

With Alberoni's approval [1] Colonel Stanhope avoided the Spanish Court. The belongings of English merchants in Spain were seized ; this was contrary to treaty stipulations, which required six months' warning,[2] but was evidently no surprise, as the merchants had removed their most valuable possessions to places of safety.[3] Even the English residents were kept prisoners in their homes, with Spanish soldiers at the door. Those vessels that had escaped at Passaro were used to seize forcibly, and not without bloodshed, the English vessels in Spanish ports or even, when opportunity offered, on the high seas.[4] Letters of marque were issued, and soon there was a regular hunt of English merchant vessels on both sides of the Atlantic. The English ambassador in Madrid was only waiting for his letter of recall, in order to leave Spanish territory.

But as long as Nancré remained at the Spanish Court and con-tinued negotiations with Alberoni, the break between Spain and the Powers of the Quadruple Alliance was not complete. The Cardinal was in no hurry, for since Turkey had now made peace with Austria, he was hoping for help from the north. In the summer of 1718 the Tsar and Charles XII were negotiating for a permanent peace ; Alberoni had visions of a strong Northern League, in which Russia, Sweden, and Prussia would fight beside Spain against George I. In September it was the common talk of Paris that the fleets of Moscow and Sweden had actually joined and had taken a great number of Tories aboard bound on some expedi-tion against the King of England. Alberoni could not disguise from Lord Stanhope, during his visit to Spain, the hope of this

---

[1] W. Stanhope to Lord Stanhope, Sept. 26, 1718, with the enclosure, Nancré to W. Stanhope, Sept. 25, 1718, S.P. 94/88.

[2] Craggs to Stair, Oct. 14, 1718, S.P. 104/30.

[3] W. Stanhope to Craggs, Aug. 28, 1718, S.P. 94/88.

[4] W. Stanhope to Lord Stanhope, Sept. 26, 1718, S.P. 94/88.

help from the north [1] against the terms of " *ce vilain et détestable traité* ".[2]

But the conferences between Peter the Great and Charles XII were broken off, and the Tsar even sought a *rapprochement* with England. A note was submitted by the Russian resident in London, full of expressions of friendship, which put forward Peter's wish for a defensive and even an offensive alliance with George I.[3] The English ministers, though not quite sure that the offer was sincere, felt they ought to follow up the proposal and send an envoy to St. Petersburg.[4] So this other great resource of the Cardinal also proved abortive.

In these circumstances the Cardinal, though not a real apostle of peace, did sincerely desire it. Day after day he sat for hours with Nancré and Daubenton, the King's confessor, wondering how to make Philip change his mind, and considering what offers the allies could, for the cause of peace, make to Spain, and above all what they would do for Queen Elizabeth.

It was the Queen herself who determined the issue. She is said to have thought the Powers in the Quadruple Alliance cared more for the welfare of her children than for her own. If, as might be expected, her husband should die soon, her own lot was uncertain, and it did not help much that her children had prospects of succeeding to Italian states. She hated a treaty which brought her nothing. As she had thought of spending her widowhood in Sicily or Sardinia, these new acquisitions must be kept, and so now " *the Termagant* " pressed Philip to go to war. On October 19, Alberoni thought he had won the King for peace ; but next morning the King showed that he was bent on war. " The confessional ", Daubenton remarked, " had this time proved unequal to the alcove." [5]

Alberoni's attitude now changed, he became as proud and haughty as before, and he devoted himself heart and soul to the diplomatic and military preparation of the war. Indeed, his position at Court and his own security made this necessary. Whether he was carrying out his own policy or only that of the Queen, the

---

[1] Stanhope to Craggs, Paris, Sept. 14, 1718, S.P. 78/162.

[2] Stair to Stanhope, Nov. 3, 1718, S.P. 78/162. Cf. Alberoni's letter to the Duke of Parma, quoted Bourgeois, *Le Secret des Farnèse*, p. 331.

[3] Lord Stanhope to Colonel Stanhope, Sept. 12, 1718, S.P. 78/162.

[4] Stanhope to Norris, Oct. 5, 1718, S.P. 104/122.

[5] Stair to Craggs, Nov. 8, 1718, S.P. 78/162. Cf. Bourgeois, *Le Secret des Farnèse*, p. 332.

statesmen of the Quadruple Alliance were determined that this firebrand, with his naval expeditions, his diplomatic tricks, and his conspiracies, must be removed if the peace of Europe were to be assured.

When on October 19 Nancré was received for the last time by the King and Queen, he saw a malicious smile on the Queen's face. This smile, Alberoni told him afterwards, reflected the triumph that Elizabeth Farnèse had won over him, the Cardinal, during the night.[1]

The breach between Spain and the Western Powers was now complete. In London the Spanish ambassador, Monteleone, had used the last weeks of his stay in the attempt to weaken the position of the English Government at home. He wrote and published a letter to Craggs complaining of the illegal action of the English fleet.[2] Craggs retorted [3] that Byng had given the Spanish admiral a perfectly correct warning that force would be used if he did not cease his warlike activities. Reference was also made to the piratical acts of the last year in the Mediterranean, in which the Spaniards had forced English captains to help in the transport of the Sicilian and Sardinian expedition, and cut off their ears if they were recalcitrant. Craggs' reply was not published, the English Government declaring to the representatives of friendly Powers that they did not care to follow the evil example of an appeal to the people.[4] Monteleone even had the honour of dining with the King before returning to Spain, and was allowed to take leave of the three little Princesses and the English and German ministers, but not of the Prince and Princess of Wales. A royal yacht was placed at his disposal ; and he on his side undertook to return to England if Colonel Stanhope were prevented from leaving Spain.[5]

People and Parliament had to be won for the now inevitable war, for though the Sovereign had the sole right of declaring war, only Parliament could grant the supplies. The Spanish Court was firmly persuaded that the British Parliament would never be brought to

---

[1] Stair to Craggs, Nov. 8, 1718, S.P. 78/162. Cf. Bourgeois, *Le Secret des Farnèse*, p. 332.

[2] Monteleone to Craggs, Aug. 25/Sept. 5, 1718.

[3] Craggs to Monteleone, Sept. 4, 1718, S.P. 104/255.

[4] Hoffmann's Report of Sept. 20, 1718, Vienna Archives.

[5] Bonet's Report of Oct. 17/28, 1718, Prussian State Archives ; Hoffmann's Report of Oct. 21, 1718, Vienna Archives ; Craggs to W. Stanhope, Oct. 6, 1718, S.P. 104/138.

support the war.[1] In England everybody thought first of the profitable trade with Spain and her colonies. The ministers' task was not
eased when the victory off Passaro, instead of arousing patriotic
enthusiasm, was interpreted more as a service to the Emperor,
Charles VI, than as an English victory over a growing maritime
rival.

The Parliamentary campaign began through the Government
section of the press. Daniel Defoe treated the question from every
angle. In a special pamphlet he pointed out that by the terms of
alliance it was England's duty to take up arms in defence of the
Italian provinces of Austria ; [2] but far more effective was an article
published in November 1718, in the *Whitehall Evening Post*, which
he himself had founded shortly before. He appealed to the English
mind by treating the problem simply from the point of view of
English interests, particularly commercial interests. The struggle
against Catholicism and the duty of helping the Emperor, which
Defoe had considered so important, are here definitely subordinated
to the purely English view :

> That there is a necessity for Great Britain to exert herself in timely
> preventing the growing exorbitance of the Spanish power. . . . That
> 'tis nonsense to talk of this war from religious amusements, that it is
> carried on between Popish Powers, who we ought to let . . . dash
> themselves to pieces one against another, that the Protestant Powers
> may . . . pull them all down at last, and bury them in the ruins of
> the *Whore of Babylon*, etc. When Europe is engaged in a religious
> war . . . these things will be seasonable enough . . . this is a war
> of civil interest, not religious. . . .
>
> . . . It is a malicious mistake to say, that Great Britain is *an
> auxiliary* in this war . . . our concern in it is infinitely more than that
> of the Emperor. . . . It is not of a thousandth part of the consequence
> to the House of Austria who possesses the kingdom of Sicily, the
> harbour of Cagliari, the Vare of Messina or the Gulph of Naples, *as
> it is to us*. The Emperor would be Emperor, and a most potent,
> powerful Prince, though he had not a foot of ground in Italy. . . .
> If the present (Spanish) King sets up for a superiority of his marine
> power . . . Sicily, in such a hand, would be like a chain drawn cross
> the mouth of the Levant Seas. . . .
>
> Great Britain cannot acquiesce in letting Spain possess Sicily,
> without giving up her trade to Turkey and to the Gulph of Venice
> . . . her trade to Zant for currants, to Gallipoli for oyl, to Messina

---

[1] W. Stanhope to Craggs, Oct. 31, 1718, S.P. 94/88.
[2] *The Case of the War in Italy stated.* See Lee, *Defoe*, vol. i. p. 277.

and Naples for silk, and in a word . . . her whole commerce of the Mediterranean.

. . . How long (shall we) be able to . . . carry on our navigation and commerce with our own people at Jamaica, Barbadoes, etc., if the naval strength of Spain be suffer'd to grow to such an immoderate and monstrous pitch.[1]

Only a few months later Defoe was minimizing the military strength of Spain and the dangers of the coming struggle. It is true that Alberoni's prospects had received a severe blow by the death of Charles XII, but now Defoe had only scorn and mockery for the enemy. " What is Spain ", he exclaimed, " surrounded with the armies of France, the navy of England, the victorious troops of the Emperor ? " With each of her three opponents superior to her, for Spain to stand out is " nothing but a State lunacy, an infatuation beyond what was ever seen before (the holding out of *Jerusalem* against the *Romans* excepted) ".[2]

Parliament was much more sensitive to the opinion of leading commercial circles than to the press. In September 1718 the Government received a long document entitled *A State of the difficulties which the South Sea Company labour under, and in which they pray to be redressed.*[3] Its twenty-five articles contain an exposition of the difficulties of trade with the Spanish colonies, especially in the Assiento, and a request that the King should convey their complaints, to which many more could be added, to the Spanish Government. The whole document had, of course, been engineered by the ministers. They would have liked the City of London to express its thanks to the King for his advancement of the country's commercial interests ; but the City was not in the right mood, and refused to thank the King for having ruined its trade. However, the Government hoped that a good impression would be made by two other Addresses, one of them from the East India Company.[4] This thanked the King for suppressing, by means of English diplomacy in Vienna, the troublesome competition carried on by English merchants from Ostend, under the Emperor's flag. No one at that time saw how important this Belgian–East Indian trade would become, or what diplomatic difficulties would arise from it.

[1] See Lee, *l.c.* vol. ii. p. 79 *seq.* [2] *Ibid.* p. 92 *seq.*
[3] B.M. Add. MSS. 25562.
[4] Bonet's Report of Nov. 11/22, 1718, Prussian State Archives.

As both the conclusion of the Quadruple Alliance and the breach with Spain had to be mentioned in the King's Speech at the opening of the new session of Parliament, the Government hoped to win the substantial support of both Houses, and to be sure that the necessary supplies would be voted. The King's Speech was written by Stanhope, submitted to the other ministers for examination, then translated into French for the King, who gave it his approval. The day before Parliament opened it was shown to some of the Government's friends in both Houses, together with the text of the Addresses which the Government wished to be sent to the King.[1]

The Speech was a masterpiece of political exposition, in which the development of the conflict with Spain was told straightforwardly and yet not without rhetorical effect. It was claimed that in the Quadruple Alliance better conditions had been stipulated for Philip of Spain than had been insisted upon in his behalf even at the Treaty of Utrecht.

But the war in Hungary, which by our mediation is since happily ended, having tempted the court of Spain unjustly to attack the Emperor, and the hopes they have since conceived of raising disturbances in Great Britain, France, and elsewhere, having encouraged them to believe, that we should not be able to act in pursuance of our treaties . . . they have not only persisted in such a notorious violation of the public peace and tranquillity, but have rejected all our amicable proposals and have broke through their most solemn engagements for the security of our commerce.

To vindicate therefore the faith of our former treaties, as well as to maintain those which we lately made, and to protect and defend the trade of my subjects . . . it became necessary for our naval forces to check their progress. . . . The court of Spain . . . has lately given orders at all the ports of Spain and of the West Indies, to fit out privateers, and to take our ships.

I am persuaded that a British parliament will enable me to resent such treatment as becomes us : and it is with pleasure that I can assure you of the ready and friendly resolutions of our good brother, the Regent of France, to concur and join with me in the most vigorous measures. . . .

There never was a time when your unanimity, your vigour, and dispatch, were more necessary to so many good ends, as those we have now in view. I have done my part. It remains with you to give the last finishing to this great work.[2]

---

[1] *Ibid.*   [2] *Parl. Hist.* vol. vii. p. 557 *seq.*

These words, while they emphasized the King's right to decide on peace and war, called strongly for the support of Parliament by stressing the national aspect of the situation. The Speech also referred to a very considerable reduction of the land forces; and said that the naval force, together with that of the allies, would soon put a happy end to the troubles. In view of the general dislike of the standing army, these references could not but make a favourable impression.

But no King's Speech, however brilliant, could guarantee a Government victory in the debates on the Addresses.[1] The ministry, convinced that their own future and that of the Quadruple Alliance was in the balance, did their utmost to influence Members of Parliament personally. They were full of promises, hinted that unpopular plans of the Government would be dropped, that nothing more would be heard of attempts to reconcile the Prince and the King, or of forbidding trade with Sweden, and that the repeal of the Act against Occasional Conformity was not under consideration.[2]

The ministers even went as far as sounding all " susceptible " members, both Whigs and Tories. Their number was considerable, for many of the gentry found it difficult to live in London on the income from their estates. The Government spent large sums, and as a result even Jacobites were heard to say that the quarrel with Spain was a vital interest of the nation. Only the dissatisfied Whigs were immune from such bribery, but without the full support of Tories and Jacobites they would not be able to defeat the Government. Craggs declared cheerfully that " if the Cardinal depends on assistance from the Parliament, he will read such an address as will make him stare ".[3]

After the reading of the King's Speech on November 11, 1718, the Addresses gave rise to heated debates in both Houses. Both sides knew that the Emperor in Vienna, the Regent in Paris, and Alberoni in Madrid were following the proceedings with bated breath. The Opposition particularly objected to congratulating His Majesty on the success of his naval forces, as their attack appeared to be a serious breach of the laws of nations. The Earl of Orford thundered that he would rather have his tongue torn out

---

[1] For what follows cf. *Parl. Hist.* vol. vii. p. 557 *seq.*; and the diplomatic correspondence of the time.

[2] This implied promise was broken within a few weeks. Cf. p. 51 *seq.*

[3] Craggs to Stair, Nov. 3, 1718, S.P. 104/30.

than approve a policy, the aims of which he could not understand, but which would land the nation in a war with Spain. He and the other dissatisfied Whigs did not see that they were now condemning a policy they had recently supported. Townshend spoke three times in his attempt to have the Address rejected. Even the incorruptible Cowper, who since he had produced the Memorial concerning the parties had been on good terms with George I, and who only six months earlier had sat as Lord Chancellor in the council that was negotiating the Quadruple Alliance, now spoke against the Address. Still more surprising to foreign observers was the behaviour of Lord Lansdowne, a Gentleman of the Bedchamber. After accompanying the King to and from Parliament in the state coach, he returned to vote against the Address.

The House of Lords was won to the Government's point of view by a speech from Lord Stanhope. He outlined once again the history of the conflict with Spain, and recounted his own journey to France and across the Pyrenees, to prove that the Government had done everything possible for peace. He went on proudly to say that it was high time for Great Britain to check the growth of the naval power of Spain, in order to protect and secure the trade of British subjects, which had been violently oppressed by the Spaniards. In reply to a request that Byng's instructions might be laid before the House, Stanhope answered with more vehemence than honesty that

with relation to Sir George Byng's instructions . . . His Majesty had acted by the advice of his Privy Council ; that he was one of that number . . . that he doubted not, but . . . these measures would be approved of by all true Englishmen ; and that he was ready to answer for them with his head.[1]

This speech made a great impression on the whole assembly, and the Address was carried by eighty-three voices against fifty.

In the proposed Address of Thanks from the Commons, the House was not only to approve what had been done, but also to promise the King that it would " support him, in the most vigorous and effectual manner, in such farther measures as His Majesty shall judge necessary . . . to check the growth of that naval power, which must otherwise prove dangerous to the trade of three Kingdoms, and to the repose of Europe ". Since copies of several

[1] *Parl. Hist.* vol. vii. p. 561.

treaties, including the Quadruple Alliance, had been presented to the House at the last moment and in Latin, the Opposition alleged that it was unparliamentary and unprecedented to approve a thing before it had been fully and maturely examined. Walpole, after declaring that he was thoroughly convinced of His Majesty's great care for the general peace of Europe and the interest of Great Britain, went on :

that the giving sanction, in the manner proposed, to the late measures, could have no other view, than to screen ministers, who were conscious of having done something amiss, and who, having begun a war against Spain, would now make it the parliament's war : concluding that instead of an entire satisfaction, they ought to shew their entire dis-satisfaction with a conduct that was contrary to the laws of nations, and a breach of solemn treaties.

For Stanhope's journeys he had nothing but scorn, calling the minister a knight-errant of the Emperor, as Bolingbroke had been for Louis XIV. The excess of his spitefulness defeated its own ends, and the Jacobites greeted him mockingly as a worthy friend and ally.

The Government's case was presented with great tact and eloquence by Craggs. He had been appointed Secretary of State, in succession to Addison, by Stanhope and Sunderland, who saw in him a powerful exponent of their policy in the Commons. Mr. Craggs gave an account of diplomatic events since the Alliance of May 1716, with the Emperor, which, as he reminded the House, Mr. Walpole himself had signed. This document was still the basis of English policy. At the same time, His Majesty had sincerely desired to maintain friendship with Spain. In order to add weight to his endeavours for restoring the tranquillity of Europe, His Majesty had acquainted the Commons, towards the end of the last session, that he intended to employ a naval force when it should be neces-sary ; whereupon this House had unanimously resolved to return His Majesty their thanks for his unwearied endeavours, and had assured him of vigorous support. Craggs purposely omitted to say that Walpole had even then objected to an Address which he said had all the air of a declaration of war against Spain. Craggs con-cluded that since this Address a war with Spain could not be called the War of the Ministers, but rather the War of Parliament ; and that the Spaniards had put themselves completely in the wrong by haughtily rejecting His Majesty's repeated amicable proposals, and by inflicting the heaviest hardships and difficulties on the trade of British subjects.

Walpole rose again to emphasize that he distinguished between His Majesty and his ministers. The threat of an impeachment was implicit, but he was seeking in particular to avoid damaging his reputation with George I — for his opposition undoubtedly sprang from a burning desire to replace Sunderland, Stanhope, and Craggs with his own friends.

Craggs readily admitted of the distinction between the King and his ministers ; and owned that ministers were not infallible, but was positive that nothing had been done which was not consistent with the faith of treaties, and the honour and interests of the nation. For his own part he was ready to undergo the severest examination, whenever the House should think fit to enquire into the conduct of the ministry.

The Address was carried by a majority of sixty or sixty-one votes. Walpole had not made himself popular. The friends of the Government made fun of him. " Let us curb our emotions," St. Saphorin wrote from Vienna, " for when we give way to them we fall into follies and excess."

The Commons would have granted even more than the Government asked. For 1719, 13,500 sailors were allowed for the sea service and 12,435 men for the land service. This low figure for the army would reassure the public, which might be afraid that British troops would be used for a campaign in Spain. The necessary grants amounted to two and a quarter million pounds, and were to be raised by a land tax, the malt tax, and a lottery. A far more serious sacrifice for the nation was the interruption of trade with Spain.

It was not till five weeks later, on December 17, that the declaration of war was proclaimed in London. A procession, like that seen at the proclamation of George I, with the Kings-of-Arms at the head, moved through the streets. Four times they stopped and read the declaration, which skilfully presented anew the arguments used in Parliament. It also pointed out that the Jacobites were being supported by the Spanish Government, for Colonel Stanhope had received news that the Duke of Ormonde was daily expected in Madrid.[1] The declaration did not meet with the same acclamation as when war was declared against France in the two

[1] W. Stanhope to Craggs, Bayonne, Nov. 26, 1718, S.P. 94/88.

former reigns, for the war of the Quadruple Alliance was never as popular as the wars against Louis XIV.[1]

When the King's Message on declaring war with Spain was read in Parliament, only the Earl of Nottingham objected, suggesting that they must have time to consider whether the step was consonant to the treaties.[2] Stanhope retorted that all the members had had five weeks to examine them. The same afternoon the Lords *in corpore* presented their Address of Thanks to the King, who interrupted his meal to receive them. In the Commons the opposition to the proposed Address was much stronger. Some members alleged that they believed the grievances complained of by our merchants might have been redressed in an amicable manner. This was refuted by Colonel Stanhope, who told the House that to this end he had presented at least five-and-twenty memorials to the Spanish Court without any success. Paul Methuen, who had himself been an ambassador in Spain and was now an ally of Walpole, accounted for the dilatoriness of the Court of Madrid by the different regulations and judicatories in the several kingdoms, provinces, and ports of Spain. Shippen again insinuated that this war seemed to be calculated for another meridian. An attack by Walpole was countered by a clever speech from Craggs. After the previous decisions of the Commons opposition was not only unpatriotic, but was pointless; and the Address was approved by a majority of seventy-one votes.

Meanwhile the English ministers were impatiently awaiting France's declaration of war. They had praised the Regent's good faith in Parliament, and now did not know how to explain the delay.[3] Lord Stair had come to an agreement with the Regent that if England did not declare war before December 8 (O.S.), France would follow within a week. But Dubois now asked for fourteen days for the necessary preparations; so the English Government thought it advisable to postpone their own declaration a little.

---

[1] Tindal, *Continuation*, p. 581.

[2] For the following cf. *Parl. Hist.* vol. vii. p. 581 *seq.*; Nottingham's name is given in a Report of Hoffmann, and in Limier, *Mémoires du règne de Georges I* (The Hague, 1729).

[3] For the following account see Stair to Craggs, Nov. 29, Dec. 5, 10, 14, 24, 1718, Jan. 3, 7, 1719, S.P. 78/162; Jan. 13, 1719, S.P. 78/163; Stair to Dubois, Dec. 4, 1718, S.P. 78/162; Dubois to Stair, Dec. 5, 1718, S.P. 78/162; Craggs to Stair, Nov. 13, 27, 29, Dec. 8, 18, 25, 29, 1718, Jan. 5, 1719, S.P. 104/30.

Stair almost doubted Dubois' sincerity, but it appears that Orleans and Dubois wished first to lay bare the machinations of the Spanish party in France.

The intrigues against the Regent had not ceased with Dubois' promotion. The Government had long known of a plot that had been brewing among Princes of the Blood, but had only become important when it gained the cognizance of the Spanish Court.[1] An impulsive, ambitious Princess, the Duchess of Maine, was the soul of the enterprise, and the Spanish ambassador, Prince Cellamare, her ally. Their aims were to capture the Duke of Orleans and proclaim Philip V Regent, at the same time appointing someone to act for him, or summoning the États Généraux. Alberoni took up the project with his usual enthusiasm. He realized that nothing could be done without Spanish troops, who would not yet be able to leave Sicily, so he had to delay the *coup*, while keeping up the spirits of his friends in France.

The Cellamare conspiracy had not advanced beyond the stage of a Court intrigue before it was betrayed. Dubois, whose attention had been called to it by Stanhope, had been watching its development for months. As there was no immediate danger, he could await the most suitable moment to crush his enemies. That moment had come when, on the point of declaring war on Spain, he could stir public opinion against the ruthless plotting of enemies at home and their alliance with the ambassador of a foreign Power. Orleans would crown the success of his own policy by appearing as the saviour of the State. With all the necessary proofs in their hands, the French Government could deal with Prince Cellamare as England had dealt with Gyllenborg a year previously. The diplomatic world was once again filled with excitement; like the Gyllenborg case, that of Cellamare has a place in the history of international law.[2]

In December 1718 the Spanish ambassador was arrested, his papers searched, and he himself was put across the frontier with due decorum. The Regent immediately published two letters from Cellamare to Alberoni,[3] which disclosed the plans of the conspirators. Soon afterwards a letter from Alberoni was intercepted

---

[1] On the Cellamare conspiracy cf. Baudrillart, *Philippe V et la Cour de France*, vol. ii. p. 326 *seq.*

[2] It is usual, but wrong, to see a difference between the two cases.

[3] See Limier, *l.c.* vol. iii. p. 198 *seq.* and p. 202 *seq.*

in which he exhorted his ambassador to fire every mine. The breach with Spain was now inevitable. The great mass of the French people took the side of the Regent, whose position was greatly strengthened. The conspiracy was so opportune for the heads of the Quadruple Alliance that Robert Walpole asserted that the English ministers had prompted the Regent to these measures in order to make it easier for him to go to war.

At last, on January 9, 1719, the French declaration of war was published together with another manifesto.[1] Both were lengthy documents in language so forceful that London and Vienna were delighted. The declaration of war described French policy towards Spain since Utrecht, recounted the efforts made for the maintenance of peace, and finished by reminding the public of the Cellamare conspiracy. Great care was taken to distinguish between the Spanish King and his minister. Philip was the dupe, Alberoni the culprit. It was he who had prevented Spain's adhesion to the Quadruple Alliance, and now he was threatening France with conspiracy, rebellion, and civil war. Truth and fiction were closely interwoven in the attempt to make the war against the grandson of Louis XIV acceptable to the French people.

The Spanish Government also appealed to the French people, claiming that they were fighting not against France but against the Duke of Orleans, who had usurped the office of Regent which should have belonged to Philip V. With this fiction Philip even hoped to disarm the French troops and win them to his side should they be sent against him. In the most effective of his declarations, addressed to the Three Estates in France, Philip spoke as a Frenchman and a Prince of the House of Bourbon.[2] He would never forget what he owed to the land of his birth and of his education, nor that the French had sacrificed life and property to set the crown of Spain upon his head. Their Government was said to be dependent on England for their foreign policy, and on the point of assisting the Emperor to the universal monarchy, whilst internal affairs were subordinated to the greed of the Regent, whose one aim was to win the crown for himself. After all peaceful negotiations had failed, he, Philip, would march into France, but he could give his word as a king that he came only to fulfil the true will of the French people.

While Philip and Orleans were attacking each other in their

---

[1] See Limier, *l.c.* vol. iii. p. 234 *seq.*

[2] The content is given at length by Baudrillart, *l.c.* vol. ii. p. 357 *seq.*

manifestos, and England was pressing for the early commencement of hostilities, France made a last attempt to avoid the war.[1] Nancré, who had returned from Spain, opened a correspondence with Alberoni, but with equal stubbornness France demanded that Spain should accept the terms of the Quadruple Alliance, and Spain that France should withdraw from it. Alberoni wrote that the King of Spain would rather perish than submit to coercion by the enemy ; he, the minister, only regretted that there would develop a personal war between the two princes. The sole result of these negotiations was irritation in England. The British Government complained bitterly that France's one-sided and secretive procedure endangered all that had been gained from their mutual treaties, all their hopes for the future, and would create a very bad impression in Vienna. Dubois then, with an air of innocence, showed them the letters that had been exchanged, and only asked that the one from Alberoni with the phrase " *guerre personnelle entre les deux princes* " should not be published, as it might create a bad impression in France.

The friendship between England and France was also disturbed by incidents due to Lord Stair's proud demeanour at the French Court. Dubois, who as son of a mere apothecary was especially sensitive, had repeatedly complained of Stair's unbearable arrogance ; that his services in the cause of the Anglo-French alliance gave him no right to behave in France as he was doing ; and that he was going further in his demands than his Government required, apparently to show his zeal and efficiency in London. The British Government offered to recall Stair ; but Dubois did not wish them to go so far. He only asked to be informed what demands Stair had been instructed to make.[2]

A month later, in February 1719, Stair was appointed envoy extraordinary. With the splendour of his carriages, of his horses, of his liveries, he tried to surpass the pomp that was customary on such occasions.[3] To his disappointment he was not allowed to drive into the Cour Royale eight-in-hand, but had to unharness six of his horses. He was all the more anxious to preserve his dignity

---

[1] Cf. Wiesener, *Le Régent, l'abbé Dubois et les Anglais*, vol. iii. p. 42 *seq.*

[2] Destouches to Dubois, Jan. 9, 1719, Dubois to Craggs, Jan. 16, 1719, Aff. étr. Corr. Pol. Angl. 322. Craggs' answer in Wiesener, *l.c.* vol. iii. p. 28 *seq.*

[3] Bonet, Jan. 16/27, 1719, writes : " *il a reçu trois fois l'argent destiné à cela* " (*l'entrée publique*), Prussian State Archives.

in exchanging visits with the members of the Court, especially with
the Princes of the Blood. A *contretemps* between him and the Duke
of Chatres, son of the Regent, was happily settled by the quick
intervention of the Regent. A more serious quarrel arose when the
Ambassador's visit was being returned by the Prince of Conti.[1]
The Prince had received Stair in the vestibule of his home, but
expected the representative of the King of England to come out
and meet him at the door of his carriage. Stair replied indignantly
that he would never do such a thing without the express order of
his King, and the Prince drove away without having seen the
Ambassador.

The whole diplomatic corps was in commotion. The Imperial,
the Dutch, the Sardinian, and the Portuguese Ambassadors all
justified their colleague by declaring solemnly in identical letters [2]
that it was the unquestionable will of their masters that they should
be on the same footing as the Princes of the Blood. But the Regent,
much as he desired England's friendship, could not afford to offend
the Princes. He complained at the English Court, and Dubois
wrote that the incident with my Lord Stair " is going to destroy
everything unless the King of Great Britain finds a prompt remedy ".[3]
Stair and Dubois, after discussing the matter confidentially, tried to
look as if it were not serious, and even laughed as they parted.
But a solution had not been found. Stair said he could of course
ask to be recalled ; but he was told by the French that such a
remedy would be worse than the trouble itself.

The next step lay with England. George I was very displeased
with his Ambassador, and his ministers were particularly anxious
not to offend the Regent at the moment. Their letters show them
almost in despair over this ridiculous question of form : " The day
before yesterday we had a long scribble from Dubois ", " You can't
imagine how worked up he is ", " he is determined that we shall
yield ", " we shall really have to call a Council of State ".[4] If Stair
had not immediately sounded the alarm amongst all the other
ambassadors, he could simply have been ordered to comply with

[1] For what follows see letters from Stair, Mar. 1, 4, 12, 26, 29, Apr. 22,
29, 1719, S.P. 78/163 ; Craggs to Stair, Mar. 9, 16, 24, 26, Apr. 9, 16, 28,
1719 (O.S.), S.P. 104/30.

[2] All of Mar. 4, 1719, S.P. 78/163.

[3] Dubois to Craggs, Mar. 8. 1719, Stowe Coll. 247, B.M.

[4] Cf. Letters from Schaub and Robethon to St. Saphorin, Mar. 1719,
Hanover Archives.

the French demand. To get out of their dilemma the British Government politely requested the Regent to be judge, as he knew best what was compatible with the dignity of the British Ambassador. At last Lord Stair found an imaginary precedent in an earlier declaration of the Imperial Ambassador, by virtue of which he was able to honour the Prince of Conti in the manner demanded. The British Government had saved the Quadruple Alliance, and maintained their lead in matters of policy by giving way in a small matter of form.

Though the British and French Governments made various treaties for the sake of peace during the decades after the death of Louis XIV, the artificiality of their alliance flashed out from time to time. The peoples understood nothing of this policy, and only felt the differences of national character and interests ; so they continued to hate and despise each other. This weakened the Governments' confidence in each other, as they always had to be prepared for a sudden reversal of policy.

After France's pledge at Utrecht to destroy the harbour of Dunkirk, there were frequent disputes over French attempts to evade their obligations.[1] These had been settled in the Triple Alliance of 1717, and Anglo-French co-operation had since been strengthened by the Quadruple Alliance. But in the summer of 1719 England was again disturbed by activity in the harbour of Dunkirk.[2] It was evidently intended to reconstruct a waterway of moderate breadth, that would connect Dunkirk with the Bergues canal, some miles to the south. The French declared the works to be a mere *rigole* for drainage, without however deceiving Colonel Lascelles, the English expert in Dunkirk.[3]

I cannot forbear smiling at their little Rigole . . . the truth is, the Rigole (if it must be so called) is the whole breadth of the canal, in the place where the sluice was, and is near forty foot wide, upon which they work continually, even on Sunday and Hollidays. If they have no design (as they pretend) of bringing in such vessels as can pass the sluice, why are they at the expense of making two turning bridges ? [4]

[1] Cf. Vol. I. pp. 134-5.

[2] Cf. Wiesener, *l.c.* vol. iii. p. 158 *seq.*

[3] The assertion in the *D.N.B.* vol. xxxii. p. 157, that Lascelles was employed in Dunkirk till 1716, and not again till 1720, is inaccurate.

[4] Lascelles to Armstrong, Aug. 20, 1719, S.P. 104/30.

The British Government instructed Stair to speak to the Duke of Orleans about the matter. The Regent answered that he knew nothing of the work, which would be stopped immediately. As the work continued, Stair handed Dubois a diplomatic note in strong terms, saying that on this point there could be no *complaisance*. Again and again Stair was reminded to show no *complaisance*,[1] for France's infringement of the Treaty of Utrecht was the more grave as it affected her closest ally.

Really it is a very melancholy consideration, that at a time when we live with them in the strictest amity we cannot obtain the honest plain execution of a treaty which admits of no evasions.[2]

Stair's representations did not have immediate result, and he repeated them verbally and in writing. At last Dubois answered on September 9 : the Regent's order, which had incomprehensibly been ignored, should be renewed ; the channel would be reduced to a mere *rigole*, so narrow that there would not be room for a sloop to pass.[3] Stair was inclined to accept this reply, but not so the Lords Justices who were now exercising the Regency in London. Stair was instructed to demand the total demolition of even the *rigole*, and to accept no compromise. Evidently France gave way to the firm demands of her ally, for Dunkirk disappeared for some years from diplomatic correspondence. An English engineer remained on the spot ;[4] yet though France did not dare to turn the harbour into a naval base, she did enough there to make the English feel unsafe despite all treaties.

Hardly was one difficulty overcome before another arose. A French company had been founded with a capital of fifty million of stocks, for fishing on the coasts of Nova Scotia and the sand-banks of North America.[5] This was considered an infringement of English rights. There were also tedious and unprofitable negotiations about the frontiers of English and French colonies on the American mainland. At the same time the French occupied Santa Lucia, an island near Barbados, to which England herself raised

[1] Cf. Craggs to Stair, Aug. 31, 1719, S.P. 104/30.
[2] Craggs to Stair, Oct. 12, 1719, S.P. 104/31.
[3] Dubois to Stair, Sept. 9, 1719, S.P. 78/165.
[4] Craggs to Sutton, July 7, 1720, S.P. 78/168.
[5] Stair to Stanhope, Nov. 7, 1719, S.P. 78/165.

older claims. The question was frequently discussed by Dubois and Stair, but without result. More serious was the British complaint that British " rebels ", *i.e.* Jacobites, could not only travel freely through France but even settle there.

These difficulties could have been overcome but for the anti-English tendency within the French Government which was linked with the rise of John Law. This Scotsman, with his golden promises and his vast plans for all branches of French economy, could only succeed if he drove English competition completely from the field. In provocative speeches Law boasted how thoroughly he would do this. Later the Regent had to make him *contrôleur général des finances*, though he declared that vanity and boundless ambition had turned his head.[1] Law was spoken of as *Premier Ministre*, and his growing influence at the French Court threatened both relations with England and the whole policy of the Quadruple Alliance. Above all, Dubois' position was endangered, so he tried by all means to render it more secure from the accidents of fortune and the humour of the Regent. Like Richelieu and Mazarin, Dubois was in the Church ; he felt that if he could only become a Cardinal, his political power would be such that Law would not be able to oust him. As early as December 1718 Stair wrote that " the Cardinal's hat has completely turned the head of our poor friend the Abbé ".[2] As Law's position at Court grew stronger, so too did Dubois' longing for the purple. He would not ask the Regent directly for his help, for he always wished to appear modest and disinterested, and let his friends act on his behalf. In 1719 the matter was frequently discussed in the letters of Stair and St. Saphorin. From Hanover Stanhope sent a surprising letter to Stair, in which he wrote with great seriousness that he had had the idea that Dubois ought to be made a Cardinal ; Vienna had already agreed, so it was now for the Regent to do his share. As the Allies were just going to bring down one Cardinal and deprive him of his insignia, what could be more natural than that they should try to advance another ? But Dubois himself must not hear of the matter, for it would offend his delicacy of feeling if ever the House of Austria were brought to work in his interest.[3]

[1] (*Hardwicke*) *State Papers*, vol. ii. p. 602.
[2] Stair to Stanhope, Dec. 4, 1718, S.P. 78/162.
[3] Stanhope to Stair, June 16, 1719, S.P. 78/164.

But in a second letter Stanhope explained that the first was written to be shown to the Regent if Stair found it convenient and " if the Abbé approved of it ".[1] Stair was afraid that the Regent would never be brought to agree to the plan, as he would think the Abbé might be too independent and make too great a figure if he had that hat upon his head.[2] So the Abbé's hopes remained unfulfilled but alive.

Our poor friend, the Abbé, is, by turns, all fire and all ice, one day flying in the air, and the next grovelling in dust ; one day open and frank, and the next day dark and mysterious. Sometimes he thinks I have too much power with the Regent and endeavours to break off my seeing him in private and, at other times, he desires I should have credit, and desires the Regent should hear me, and listen to me.[3]

The Abbé's position was still precarious, and he was dependent on good relations with England to render it secure.

England's domineering attitude towards France is clearly illustrated in a conversation between Craggs and Destouches, the French Ambassador in London. At the end of March 1719, Craggs, as Secretary of State, was explaining the English view of the international situation [4] in his skilful and temperamental manner, fully intending that all he said should be conveyed to the Regent and Dubois. He pointed out that the Duke of Orleans ought not to bargain with King Philip, but ought to send his armies into Spain, where Alberoni, encouraged by France's hesitations, was growing bolder and bolder. " Where would we have been ", he asked, " if we had shown Spain the like consideration ? " They realized the difficulties caused by the *malintentionnés*. But they were astonished that the French still harboured their old prejudice, and the strange idea that they and the English were natural enemies. Could they not understand that as long as France was only seeking peaceful recovery without disturbing the peace of Europe, the English were perforce her best and most useful friends ?

Craggs then protested against the accusation that England was partial to the Emperor. True, Charles VI was her old Ally, and it was not in her interest to break with him ; but she was very firm

---

[1] Stanhope to Stair, June 17, 1719, S.P. 78/164.
[2] Stair to Craggs, July 8, 1719, (*Hardwicke*) *State Papers*, vol. ii. p. 580.
[3] Dubois to Craggs, Mar. 8, 1719, Stowe Coll. 247, B.M.
[4] Destouches to Dubois, Mar. 28, 1719, Aff. étr. 323.

when it seemed that he was carrying his pretentions too far. Was it not England who drove him to accept the clause of the three months asked for by the Dutch, and the new postponement of the disposition of the reversions ? " If France wishes ", Craggs concluded, " that we should draw away from the Emperor enough to satisfy her, she must put herself in such a position that she will never need the support of that prince ; that is to say, by honestly giving up the old system,[1] she must convince us that she intends to remain within her boundaries, and she must ally herself more and more closely with us."

France's subordination to England is shown still more clearly by the plan of campaign which was put forward by Stanhope and accepted without question by the French. As early as September 1718, Stanhope, during his stay in Paris, had explained his programme to the Regent and his minister. They now asked him to submit his ideas in writing. With the King's approval, Stanhope complied in the form of a letter to Dubois, dated March 30 (O.S.).[2] As he had himself commanded British forces in Spain, he could bring personal experience to bear in drawing up the plan of campaign. The Cardinal must be pressed at home, to prevent him looking abroad. His stubbornness and power could be broken by rousing both the people who had borne so unwillingly the loss of their privileges, and the nobles who were groaning under the contempt to which he had exposed them. It was what Europe would expect even if the Cardinal had not set the example himself. After all his plots against the King and the Regent, and his attempts to arm their subjects against them, their honour and their security called for strong action. An expedition was to be sent to Los Pasajes and neighbouring districts ; then His Royal Highness should divide his army into two columns, one to advance along the Basque coast, the other into Catalonia ; this would not only divide the Spanish forces, but would also bring hope of a restitution of their privileges to all the provinces bordering on the Pyrenees. At the same time His Royal Highness should declare in a manifesto that he was seeking no conquests or other acquisitions in Spain, and

---

[1] " The old system " means here the policy of Louis XIV. Later, in the forties, it came to mean the policy of coalitions against France. Cf. W. Michael, " Die englischen Koalitionsentwürfe des Jahres 1748 " (*Forschungen zur brandenburgischen und preussischen Geschichte*, vol. i. p. 527 *seq.*).

[2] *Vide* Appendix 3.

only wished to free His Catholic Majesty and his kingdoms from the oppression and tyranny of a foreign minister. As the confidence of the people might be more easily won if the King of England guaranteed their privileges as well, His Majesty offered to send a minister plenipotentiary to accompany the French Army and to join in the guarantee of the privileges wherever necessary. " The choice might fall on my cousin Stanhope, for with his knowledge of Spain he might be more suitable there than any other ; and His Majesty will send him as soon as he knows the will of His Royal Highness, from whom he is to take his instructions."

The appeal to the provinces of the north and east was only a repetition of what had been done in the War of the Spanish Succession. But the way in which the Catalans had been then left to the mercy of Philip V was no encouragement for a second rising.

While the plan of campaign was being settled, and effective collaboration between England, France, and Austria seemed assured, Holland had still not been induced to sign the Quadruple Alliance.[1] The States General had refused to join the Alliance before an agreement was reached with the Emperor about the execution of the Barrier Treaty of November 1715. This Treaty had hardly been signed when the Estates of Flanders and Brabant complained bitterly in Vienna.[2] The frontier territory ceded to Holland was the granary of Brabant ; Ostend, the only harbour left to the Emperor, was in serious danger ; Antwerp, which was paralysed by the closing of the Scheldt, was now completely encircled, and deprived of all trade ; and finally, the burdens that had been placed upon the country were unbearable. The Emperor lent a willing ear to these complaints, which gave him a right to press for fresh negotiations, though the ratifications had already been exchanged.

Prince Eugene had been appointed Governor of the Austrian Netherlands, but he never performed the duties of this office himself. Before going to Brussels his representative, the Marquis Prié, had

---

[1] Cf. Vol. I. p. 339 *seq.*

[2] Cf. *Oesterreichische Staatsverträge*, Niederlande, vol. i. (ed. Sŕbik), p. 532 *seq.* : Dollot, *Les Origines de la neutralité de la Belgique et le système de la Barrière* (1902), p. 411 ; Gachard, *Histoire de la Belgique au commencement du XVIII siècle* (1880), p. 471 *seq.*

to visit The Hague to open negotiations with the States General. The Dutch soon realized that they could not insist on the terms of the Treaty of 1715, for without certain concessions on their part Charles would hardly be brought to fulfil the heavy financial burdens laid upon him.

Prié's hopes that agreement would be reached in a few weeks were doomed to disappointment. This was evident to the English, and as their European policy meant more to them than haggling over the Barrier, they agreed that the Barrier question should be treated separately ; Prié promised that it would be done with all possible speed.[1] Meanwhile Stanhope worked for the completion of his great system and did not for the moment insist on Holland's co-operation.

The negotiations concerning the Barrier dragged on for two years and became extremely dull, as only financial questions were disputed. The Emperor pressed for a settlement, the English Ambassador received repeated orders to bring about an agreement.[2] But only on December 22, 1718, long after the Quadruple Alliance had been signed, was the new treaty concluded by plenipotentiaries of the three states. The territory ceded to the States General was reduced to a fifth of the size assigned to them in 1715, but otherwise the terms of the " great Barrier Treaty " remained unchanged.

With the agreement of 1718 the main obstacle to Holland's accession to the Quadruple Alliance seemed to have gone. The Emperor had done his share ; France and England were ever ready to make sacrifices to expedite her accession. England declared herself willing to settle an old debt of £200,000 that had been liquidated by Holland.[3] It was already being said that the town of Amsterdam and the Province of Holland had declared so decisively for the Alliance, that the matter was as good as settled ; and that some ships, laden with war material for Spain, had been detained in the harbour of Amsterdam at the last moment. Hopes rose high in London. Holland's accession to the Alliance, together with the readiness of Parliament to grant supplies, the warlike intentions of

[1] Cadogan and H. Walpole to Townshend, Oct. 9, 1716, S.P. 84/254.
[2] Instructions for Cadogan, Hampton Court, Aug. 21, 1717, and April 18, 1718, F.O. 90/32.
[3] Stanhope to St. Saphorin, Jan. 27, 1719, Hanover Archives.

France, and the news of Charles XII's death, would surely have a great effect on Spain, and might even bring her to comply before war was actually begun. For the moment the Government limited naval preparations to a minimum.[1]

However, though in January 1719 the Dutch declared in London that they were ready to join the Quadruple Alliance, they at the same time demanded three months' grace before they should declare war on Spain. This time was to be used for fresh negotiations with Spain, in hopes of avoiding the war. Further, the Dutch wished to reduce by half the number of troops they were to furnish under the clauses of the Quadruple Alliance. England and France would willingly have agreed to all this, for their only concern was that Holland should take some part. But after violent scenes between the English ministers and Pendtenriedter,[2] in which the English declared they could not possibly do without the States General, the Austrian refused to sign the agreement with Holland unless the demand for three months' grace were dropped. For with this further respite the Reversions of Tuscany, Parma and Piacenza would be kept open for Spain three months longer. When Philip V had not agreed to the terms of the Quadruple Alliance in the three months originally granted him, Vienna had felt entitled to dispose otherwise of the Italian Duchies, which would have prevented the Bourbons from gaining a foothold in Italy. A plan for a new partition of the territory was already in existence.[3]

The failure of the Emperor's attempt, thus at the eleventh hour to keep the Bourbons out of Italy, was to be the source of later complications and wars. But the Western Powers refused him their help, France because she feared an increase in the power of Austria, and England because her commercial interests might be endangered by Holland's neutrality. Holland, a declining Power, was doing her best to keep up as far as possible with England, and to avoid every conflict.

As the two Western Powers were both on the side of Holland, the Emperor had to yield. " I cannot see how the thing will turn out ", wrote Pendtenriedter,[4] and asked for new instructions, even

---

[1] Hoffmann's Reports of Dec. 30, 1718, and Jan. 13, 1719, Vienna Archives.
[2] Pendtenriedter's Reports of Jan. 27 and Feb. 14, 1719, Vienna Archives.
[3] Přibram, *Oesterreichische Staatsverträge*, England, vol. i. p. 405.
[4] Report of Feb. 14, 1719, Vienna Archives.

though the English threatened that the three months now asked for might very soon become five.

Charles VI, who knew only too well that without the help of the English fleet he could never regain Sicily, gave way to the English demand, and Pendtenriedter was instructed to sign the treaty with Holland and to make sure that the whole text of the Quadruple Alliance, including the important secret and separate articles to which the Dutch had formerly raised objections, were accepted by the States General. As for the Reversions, the Emperor was ready to yield, and he did not mean it quite seriously when he once more desired his Ambassador to do all he could to prevent the Reversions being again kept open for Spain, and not to yield " till it was to be feared that otherwise everything would be upset ".[1]

As such an attempt would have been quite useless, Pendtenriedter only demanded a written assurance that after these three months Spain should be allowed no more time, and that the Bourbons should have no farther claim on the Italian duchies. The English ministers refused, and the point was warmly debated. And so they parted in an ill humour and both went to the King, who between the English ministers and Pendtenriedter was very embarrassed. At last, in March, the English promised to give the desired assurance immediately on the signing of the treaty with Holland—but not before. It was also agreed that the Dutch must declare their adhesion within four weeks, if that were to be the starting-point of the further three months' grace for Spain.[2]

Holland now found a new cause of delay by announcing that she could not adhere to the Quadruple Alliance with its secret clauses till the ratifications of the last Barrier Treaty had been exchanged. Marquis Prié was authorized to make the exchange, but required that the States General should first join the Quadruple Alliance in London. After arguments about the sequence of these events, Lord Cadogan suggested that both transactions should be made in London at the same time, or one soon after the other, in which case the exchange of ratification should come first, as the Dutch desired. The proposal was accepted, and Prié sent Pendtenriedter the documents of ratification and the order to exchange them. The exchange

---

[1] Charles VI to Pendtenriedter, Feb. 15 and Mar. 7, 1719, Vienna Archives.

[2] Pendtenriedter's Reports from Mar. 7 to Mar. 28, 1719, Vienna Archives.

was made on May 11 (N.S.), 1719, between Stanhope, Pendten-riedter, and van Borssele. Pendtenriedter confined himself to a few words of advice about the political situation ; [1] but Stanhope, who had lost patience, used language which made the poor van Borssele tremble. He admitted that the Dutch were a source of embarrassment, but added that England would soon be able to do without them. Above all, Holland would not be allowed to profit from the trade with Spain to the exclusion of England.[2] This outburst was not seriously meant. Only a few days later Stanhope was trying hard to bring about the adhesion of the States General.[3]

At this time George I decided, despite all internal and external dangers, once again to spend some months in Hanover. These journeys caused not only a removal of the Court, but also the break-up of the diplomatic corps : some of its members remained in London, some accompanied the King to Hanover, and some took a holiday. The day after George's departure, Pendtenriedter followed him to The Hague ; for on May 30 the States General had decided to accept the Quadruple Alliance, including all the secret and separate articles. Just before the exodus from London it had been finally agreed that Holland's signature should be attached in The Hague.[4] Everyone thought the matter settled ; George I, anxious to reach Hanover, did not wait for the final formalities in The Hague ; Stanhope followed in the highest spirits.[5] The representatives of the four states were on the spot, their credentials in order, and everything ready for the signing.

But yet again the States General took fright at the possibility of war with Spain at the end of the three months, and suddenly refused to sign without the addition of a special article limiting their share in the campaign to a contingent of 3000 men.[6] This condition was naturally interpreted as proof that the Dutch intended, even after the three months, to take no serious part in the war, perhaps no part at all. The representatives of England,

---

[1] Pendtenriedter, May 11, 1719, Vienna Archives.

[2] Schaub to St. Saphorin, May 12, 1719, Hanover Archives.

[3] Stanhope to St. Saphorin, May 5, 1719 (O.S.), Hanover Archives.

[4] Pendtenriedter's Report of May 22, 1719, Vienna Archives.

[5] Pendtenriedter's Report from The Hague, May 30, 1719, Vienna Archives.

[6] *Ne in omni eventu ultra tria millia militum in auxilium conferre teneantur neque ad plura vel alia obstringantur* ; Srbik, *Oesterreichische Staatsverträge, Niederlande*, vol. i. p. 642.

France and Austria would not hear of the new article ; but the Dutch stood by their *neque ad plura vel alia*.[1] No agreement was reached, and Pendtenriedter went straight to Vienna, after reporting that he himself had forced the issue, while making it appear that England and France had broken off the negotiations.[2]

The Allies were unanimous in condemning the mercenary spirit of the Dutch. From Paris Stair wrote that " The ill will of a few private individuals in the United Provinces has rendered our efforts futile ".[3] St. Saphorin in Vienna felt that the ruling classes in Holland were to blame. He wrote home that though these people called themselves the true Republicans, they had no principles at all. Under Louis XIV they were Frenchmen, under Strafford, Englishmen, now they were Spaniards. That would continue to be so till they were brought to elect a Stadtholder.[4] In London Sunderland dubbed the proceedings at The Hague the most disgraceful affair that had ever occurred in negotiations between great powers.[5] Four weeks later the Dutch Ambassador tried to remind Sunderland of the promise to settle the debt of £200,000. The English minister answered him angrily that if the Dutch imagined they could make fools of the three greatest Powers in Europe and then expect special consideration, they were just as mistaken as when they hoped they would be allowed to grab all the trade with Spain.[6]

" The Dutch are still resolutely bent not to come into the Quadruple Alliances," wrote a contemporary on June 28th, " and since promises can have no effect upon them, threats are now used. The Emperor says he will take their barrier from them, and France and England that they will seize their ships, but they seem to understand their game better than to lose it for a few hard names." [7] They knew that according to current international law England could not forbid a neutral power to trade with her enemy, except in contraband of war.[8]

[1] Cf. Sŕbik, *l.c.* p. 591.   [2] June 1, 1719, Vienna Archives.
[3] Stair to Stanhope, June 30, 1719, S.P. 78/164.
[4] St. Saphorin to Stanhope, June 18, 1719 ; to Schaub, same date, Hanover Archives.
[5] Hoffmann, June 13, 1719, Vienna Archives.
[6] Hoffmann, July 14, 1719, Vienna Archives.
[7] *Portland MSS.* vol. v. p. 587.
[8] A principle that was only dropped in the Great War.

The three allies, it is true, discussed what steps could be taken. Stanhope seriously thought of giving effect to his words. He wrote to St. Saphorin : " Perhaps we would be able to bring them quickly into line if we effectively suppressed their trade with Spain ". But it would be better if the Austrians helped by sending against the Dutch a privateering fleet from their ports in the Netherlands.[1]

This letter crossed another from St. Saphorin containing a similar proposal.[2] The Court of Vienna might well be brought to issue letters of marque, even without English participation. For the Austrians had no alliance with Holland, and their Government was decidedly annoyed with the Dutch, who had tricked them first into signing the Barrier Treaty, and then into the exchange of ratifications, under the false pretence of intending to join the Quadruple Alliance. It might even be managed that the Emperor be brought to take the initiative in asking the King's approval for the issue of letters of marque in the Austrian Netherlands.

"The Emperor won't wait to be asked twice ", was Schaub's prophecy.[3] Prince Eugene and Count Sinzendorff found the suggestion excellent, and put it immediately before the Conference of Ministers. These, too, agreed in principle, and only said that the form of the letter must be such that the privateers should not go further than was desirable. But on second thoughts the Austrians felt the enormity of the plan. Sinzendorff told St. Saphorin the Emperor would desire that England and France should give similar orders, so that he should not bring on himself alone all the ill-will of the Dutch, who were only waiting for a chance to wrest Ostend from him.[4] St. Saphorin described this as typical of the Court of Vienna : " as soon as you approach them on a matter that is of the greatest interest to themselves, they take it up only with the greatest caution ".

England and France refused to co-operate actively. The threat of privateering was intended only as a means of bringing Holland into the Quadruple Alliance ; but for Holland's own allies to engage in it might have had the most serious consequences. Moreover, though the Western Powers had worked honestly to bring Holland into the Alliance, they did not wholly object to a procrastination

---

[1] Stanhope to St. Saphorin, June 30, 1719, Hanover Archives.
[2] St. Saphorin to Stanhope, July 8, 1719, Hanover Archives.
[3] Schaub to St. Saphorin, July 7, 1719, Hanover Archives.
[4] St. Saphorin to Stanhope, July 12, 15, 1719, Hanover Archives.

that allowed Spain more time for submission, and kept open the door in Italy which the Emperor would so gladly have closed to the Bourbons. In a confidential letter to Cadogan,[1] the Secretary of State, Craggs, recommended him not to take the Dutch too much to task, not even to demand special assurances that all trade with Spain would be suppressed.

You must know that we ourselves give passes for ships to trade to Spain with our own manufactures and in the West Indies, we allow our ships and colonies to get as much as they can of their gold and silver ; it is the business of the Spaniards and not ours to prevent such a trade. . . . If they do but take effectual care to stop all contrabands we shall enquire no further . . . the Spaniards will sufficiently prevent all other trade, when the Dutch shall have declared war against them and stopped them from such things as they chiefly want.

The English searched Dutch ships when the cargo seemed suspicious, and confiscated what contraband they found.[2] But there was no more question of England's suppressing the whole of Holland's trade with Spain than of giving up her own trade on both sides of the Atlantic. When, for example, merchants interested in Jamaican trade presented a petition to the Government, they were formally permitted to carry on their profitable trade with the Spanish West Indies,[3] though the war had already begun.

[1] Craggs to Cadogan, July 28, 1719, S.P. 104/83.
[2] W. Stanhope to Craggs, Aug. 17, 1719, S.P. 94/232.
[3] Delafaye to Stanhope, June 16, 1719, S.P. 43/61.

CHAPTER VI

THE WAR AGAINST SPAIN

No war was ever begun with less enthusiasm than that of 1719. Dubois wished to limit its area and duration to a minimum ; Craggs promised that the war should be as short as could be wished. " It will be a war only in name ", Stanhope declared.[1] The people flattered themselves that a mere show of war would be enough to consolidate peace.[2] " The last act of the drama," said the Government, " and when the curtain drops Spain will be forced to sign the Quadruple Alliance." [3]

The allies never wearied of repeating that not Spain, but the wicked Cardinal Alberoni, was the enemy, till they almost believed it themselves. The overthrow of " the mad Cardinal ", " the turbulent minister ", occupied them as much as the military preparations. " As long as he retains his position, (he) will never let Europe rest ", said Dubois, who therefore wished to weaken his position by having him deprived of his ecclesiastical dignities. England, France, and Austria were to agree on a course which would bring the Pope to take away the Cardinal's hat from Alberoni, and to refuse him the Bulls for Seville.[4]

The Governments of France and England realized how unpopular the war was in the two countries. Dubois complained that with the whole of Spain, half of France had risen against the Regent, and that the war they were beginning would be like a civil war.[5] Moreover, the Jacobites in France, where they were more

---

[1] See Bourgeois, *La Diplomatie secrète au XVIIIe siècle* (n.d.), vol. iii. p. 47.
[2] Bonet, Nov. 14/25, 1718, Prussian State Archives.
[3] Bonet, Jan. 6/17, 1719, Prussian State Archives.
[4] Dubois to Destouches, Jan. 18, 1719, Aff. étr. Angl. Corr. Pol. 322.
[5] Dubois to Stanhope, Jan. 16, 1719, Aff. étr. 322.

numerous and powerful than across the Channel, would be a danger to England ; so the two Governments ought to work together the more closely.

Charles VI alone desired a vigorous campaign. His ambassador in London declared emphatically that the Spanish Bourbons must not be allowed to grow too powerful outside the Iberian peninsula, that even their power in Spain must be restricted, and their great treasures drawn from the Indies must be cut down by a reasonable division. A nominal peace should not be tolerated. In reply, Pendtenriedter received the crushing answer that the English nation had only been brought to accept the war at all by the hopes of an early peace.[1]

The parts played by the three allies resulted naturally from their positions and aims. The Emperor sought to conquer Sicily by driving out the Spanish troops there. France with her land forces was to carry the war into Spain itself. England, whose fleet under Sir George Byng was still in the Mediterranean, intended only to support operations from the sea. When the Austrians asked for British troops to be made available for the campaign in Italy, these were flatly refused.[2]

Spain's power of resistance was not to be underestimated. It was expected that, even without the forces in Sardinia and Sicily, she could send 40,000 regulars to the frontier under experienced French and Walloon officers.[3]

The supreme commander on the French side was Marshal Berwick, a natural son of James II and Arabella Churchill, who, after his father's fall, had entered the service of Louis XIV and won fame as an unbeaten general. He made his plans with the greatest care. All the passes across the Pyrenees were occupied before his army of 30,000 men crossed the frontier stream, the Bidassoa, in April 1719.[4] A number of fortresses fell in quick succession into his hands. The population of Irun had fled, but returned confidently when the French announced that they had only come to free them from the tyranny of Alberoni.[5]

---

[1] Pendtenriedter's Report of Jan. 26, 1719, Vienna Archives.
[2] Stanhope to St. Saphorin, Jan. 6, 1719, Hanover Archives.
[3] Bonet, Jan. 6/17, 1719, Prussian State Archives.
[4] Berwick, *Suite abrégée des Mémoires* (Michaud et Poujoulat, 3e sér. 8), p. 448.
[5] Stair to Craggs, Apr. 26, 1719, S.P. 78/163.

Instead of the frontier fortress of Fuenterrabia, the next objective
of the French was the port of Los Pasajes, further to the west.   The
expedition [1] against this port had first been planned in January
between Stair and the Duke of Orleans.[2]   It was known that in
this small but well-situated port Alberoni had set up all the shipyards and stores necessary for the construction and fitting out of
men-of-war.   England, anxious to prevent the reconstruction of a
strong Spanish navy, had offered that British ships should take part
in the attack ; but Berwick declared that he did not need them.[3]
England pressed for prompt execution of the plan,[4] but it was again
and again postponed.   At last a detachment of French troops under
the Marquis de Cilly entered Los Pasajes, and found six large vessels
under construction, which they burnt on the spot, together with
such stores of masts and wood as could not be shipped to Bayonne.
Two hundred Spanish soldiers and twenty officers were taken
prisoner, and a force of five hundred, coming to the town's relief
from the neighbouring garrison of San Sebastian, was driven off by
musket fire.[5]   England might well be pleased with this exploit.
Craggs wrote to Stair that " the circumstance of destroying so many
of the enemy's shipping has been very agreeable to this country ".
He asked to be given full details concerning the losses of Spanish
ships : " for such particularities will give people here a great
satisfaction ".[6]

After the easy success in Los Pasajes the plan of the French
campaign was broadened.   It had been intended to draw the mass
of the Spanish forces towards the Bidassoa by movements of troops
in that area, and then near the end of May to launch the main
attack near the Mediterranean, in Catalonia.   Here it would be easy
to bring all supplies by water from France, and the Catalans themselves would probably take up arms to regain their old privileges.
Whilst the fortresses on the coast were to be attacked by one French
force, Berwick was to march from Rousillon across the Pyrenees and

---

[1] Since Saint-Simon there has been a controversy whether the expedition
served French aims or English. Cf. Bourgeois, *l.c.* vol. iii. p. 62[4].
[2] Stair's Reports, especially that of Jan. 13, 1719, S.P. 78/163 ; Pendtenriedter's Report, Jan. 13, 1719, Vienna Archives.
[3] Stair to Craggs, Jan. 13, 1719, S.P. 78/163.
[4] Craggs to Stair, Jan. 17, 1719, S.P. 104/30.
[5] Berwick to Stair, Apr. 26, 1719, S.P. 78/163.
[6] Craggs to Stair, Apr. 28, 1719, S.P. 104/30.

to enter Spain by the valley of the Segre. His arrival would be the
signal for the Catalans to rise.

Now it was decided that the position gained at Los Pasajes
should be strengthened by the capture of Fuenterrabia. The siege,
directed by Berwick himself, made slow progress. The digging of
trenches was begun in the night of May 27 to 28, but the French
artillery, consisting of 26 cannon and 12 mortars, opened fire only
on June 9. It soon showed its insufficiency in face of the enormously
thick walls of the fortress.

On June 10 William Stanhope arrived to represent England in
the French camp. His instructions, which are not preserved, and
must be guessed from letters of contemporaries, ordered him to
assist Berwick in his negotiations with the Spanish population ;
but his main object was to keep an eye on the French Marshal
and to see that the French prosecuted the war seriously.[1] He was
the spokesman of England's maritime interests, and nearly all the
damage that was done to the Spanish naval forces was due to his
prompting.

William Stanhope was well suited to his delicate task. At 29
years of age he was well versed in warfare, and also in diplomacy,
which he had learned in Spain itself. He was known for his taci-
turnity. With skill and tact he made his suggestions in few words
and in spite of frequent differences of opinion, he avoided all serious
dissension.[2]

The Duke of Orleans, who was informed that Stanhope would
follow any directions he cared to give him, pretended to be delighted
that he had been sent, and Berwick expressed hearty approval of
Stanhope's instructions. The appearance of cordiality was carefully
preserved, but actually Stanhope's presence was most irritating to
the commander of the French army and recalls the part played by
the Dutch field deputies in the Duke of Marlborough's camp. From
Paris Berwick received instructions to be cautious : " You will
show Mr. Stanhope all due respect, but of course tell him only
what he may know without prejudice to our interests ".[3]

In the fourth week of the siege the position of the French army

[1] Pendtenriedter, Apr. 28, 1719, Vienna Archives.
[2] For what follows cf. W. Stanhope's Reports, S.P. 94/232. Also Stair's
Reports, S.P. 78/164.
[3] Lemontey, *Histoire de la Régence*, vol. i. p. 268.

outside Fuenterrabia became critical. Philip V himself, with an army said to number 9000 men on foot and 4000 on horseback, had advanced as far north as Lesaca, about 10 miles from Fuenterrabia, intending to relieve the fortress, and to march into France as soon as he had collected all his troops. In a letter to the governor that was intercepted by the French, he wrote that if he could hold out till June 18 or 19 he would be saved.

The French had lost at least 800 dead and wounded, and what was even more distressing, the same number of deserters. To keep off the enemy, Berwick had sent some troops to Navarre and was going to follow them himself, when on June 15 the lunette, probably the strongest point in the defence, was taken. Next day the town surrendered. Berwick, who had received advice that the head of the enemy's army was come to a village within two leagues of the camp, had to grant the garrison free retreat, though without drums and flags.

The consultations that followed between Berwick and Stanhope about further plans were difficult, for Berwick insisted on great moderation. He refused to march against Pamplona and the main force of the Spaniards, though this was by no means large, or to penetrate further into Castile. The reasons he gave were the difficulties of commissariat and the lack of stores ; the King of Spain would always be before him and destroy the country he was to march through. But the true and substantial reason was that he dared not venture to march so far into Spain and leave the King with the power of getting behind him, lest he should march with his army into France. Berwick decided to follow the coast westward, avoiding the main Spanish army, and to launch an attack on the stronghold of San Sebastian. Stanhope proposed, and Berwick readily agreed, that the port of Santoña, lying further west, should also be visited and treated like Los Pasajes.[1]

The tactics of avoiding the main force of the enemy were not merely due to principles of strategy. Diffidence and doubts whether his troops would fight against the grandson of Louis XIV were reducing Berwick's striking power. The mass desertions showed the influence of Philip's declarations and manifestoes.

Stanhope now suggested that the time had come to call out the Spanish provinces. The Basques were still quiet, but no doubt,

---

[1] Wiesener, in *Le Régent, l'abbé Dubois et les Anglais,* vol. iii. pp. 70-71, tries unsuccessfully to disprove the English origin of the expedition.

only because of the presence of the King and his army. The Government had restored their former privileges, and had remitted the hated Aduanas ; but they knew that this clemency would end with the war. Catalonia and Aragon were, however, patiently awaiting a call to arms. Every day envoys and messengers entered Berwick's camp, pressing him to give the word, on which the whole populace would rise. But now the French Government would not hear of encouraging revolts in Spain, lest it afterwards should render more difficult the peace which must soon come, as the position of the Spaniards in Sicily was untenable. They were simply demanding Spain's adhesion to the Quadruple Alliance, and would not assume responsibility for the restoration of the old Catalonian privileges. Besides, Berwick himself had recently subjugated these provinces for the Bourbon King of Spain and thus caused the loss of their old privileges ; and he feared what the world would say if he now called upon them to take up arms to regain these same privileges.

England was astonished at these arguments. An early peace would be best brought about by those things which made it impracticable for the enemy to carry on the war, particularly the rising of the provinces. " Besides ", wrote Craggs, " in the Regent's circumstances, who is afraid every day of a rebellion in France and irruption there from the King of Spain, the cool advice they gave him to avoid the encouraging Catalonia . . . is a depth of wisdom beyond my penetration." [1] Furthermore, such a rising would protect the rear of the French army, which could then march wherever it liked. Alberoni should not be allowed to say any more " that suppose he should be drove out of Sicily and Sardinia, and attended with other misfortunes abroad, still he could shut himself up in the continent of Spain and laugh at the Quadruple Alliance ".[2]

The English representations would not have overcome the French doubts, without the news of a Spanish victory in Sicily. Berwick declared that France must now wage war in earnest ; and the Duke of Orleans gave official approval to the plan of encouraging the Spanish provinces to rebel. As the army was in Basque territory, the first negotiations were with the Estates of Guipuzcoa in Tolosa. In their name the Alcalde of Hernani appeared before

---

[1] Craggs to Stair, June 27, 1719, S.P. 104/30. Cf. also Craggs to W. Stanhope, June 29, 1719, S.P. 104/30.

[2] Craggs to Stair, June 27, 1719, S.P. 104/30.

Berwick, who told him that the provinces could only maintain their privileges by submitting to the sovereignty of France. On August 3 the Estates came into the French camp, and Berwick assured them of France's protection. Then they were received by Stanhope, who gave a similar assurance on behalf of Great Britain. A few days later the Estates of Biscay met in Bilbao, where a French trumpeter was to call upon them to submit themselves to France ; but they required first to be assured of the fulfilment of the Guipuzcoan demands. Alava, the third Basque province, actually submitted. But these negotiations were never brought to a formal conclusion, since Dubois still hesitated to send Berwick the necessary powers to give the Basques the written guarantees they demanded. Berwick and Stanhope were in an embarrassing position. They had arranged with the representatives of Guipuzcoa that they should enumerate their demands in a Petition. When the Petition was presented, Berwick had not yet been authorized to grant its demands, and Stanhope could not act alone. To calm the Estates and to win time they decided to find fault with the form of the Petition. When Berwick was at last empowered to sign, he and Stanhope had already left because the scene of war had shifted.

After the taking of Fuenterrabia the French army besieged San Sebastian for the whole of July. Again the French artillery proved insufficient. The town capitulated on August 1, but the garrison held out in the citadel till the seventeenth. Berwick, who did not wish to push further into Spain, now decided to change the scene of operations. Meanwhile Philip remained a long while inactive in Pamplona ; then he, the Queen, and the Cardinal left. The Spanish army under Prince Pio marched into the Pyrenees as far as Roncevalles, but they neither crossed the frontier nor sought to engage the enemy ; they busied themselves with the destruction of all roads that led from the French positions into the interior of Spain.

Concurrently with the siege of San Sebastian the attack on Santoña was launched, under the personal direction of Stanhope.[1] The plan had been approved by the Regency in London, while George was in Hanover.[2] Only under pressure from Stanhope did Berwick lend some of his soldiers, declaring that it was purely in

[1] For what follows cf. W. Stanhope's Reports, especially June 21, July 20, Aug. 1, 4, 8, 11, 17, 1719, S.P. 94/232.

[2] Craggs to W. Stanhope, June 19, 1719, S.P. 43/57.

order to do a service to George I and his ministers.[1] Even in the execution of the attack the French showed so little enthusiasm that only Stanhope's dash prevented the French from giving up at the start.

On August 11 three English men-of-war, which had been on this coast for two months and had already helped in the siege of Fuenterrabia, took the expedition for Santoña on board. The little force of 750 Frenchmen, under two generals, and 300 British marines arrived on the evening of August 12 off Santoña, which contained 800 militiamen and a few invalids, but no regular soldiers. As the harbour was narrow at the entrance and had breastworks cast up from thence along the sides to the town with near 50 pieces of cannon planted upon them, it was thought advisable not to attempt going into it, but rather to endeavour to land in a bay upon the back of it. But here, too, the enemy had raised two batteries, behind which they had about 600 men drawn up to oppose a landing. The cannon of the ships fired upon them for a considerable time, as they did also upon the ships, to which they did no other damage than the tearing of two or three sails. At six o'clock they put the troops into the boats, but the great swells together with the artillery made a landing very hazardous if not impracticable. They therefore put off again and went into a bay about a mile further to west, where the sea appeared to be somewhat smoother. The enemy not expecting them in that place, they immediately landed without opposition. It was some hours before Stanhope could prevail upon the French to get into the boats to try if they could land, for the breaking of the sea so terrified them, that the two generals gave orders to their boats to return to the ships, saying it was madness to sacrifice their master's troops by attempting to land upon such a coast. Stanhope promptly jumped into the sea, telling them he was resolved to go ashore, upon which the others had to follow. They spent the night on the top of a neighbouring hill, and at the break of day on the thirteenth they marched towards Santoña. No enemy appeared, but the magistrates of the town came to render their submission. The invaders then marched through the town straight to the harbour, and destroyed all the cannon on the mole. Then the English seamen burnt completely three men-of-war and a vast quantity of the finest deal planks just come from Holland, and other naval stores. Stanhope would have

---

[1] W. Stanhope to Craggs, Aug. 11, 1719, S.P. 94/232.

liked to ship the planks to England, but the loading would have cost too much time, and the French declared they must leave at once. However, Stanhope could report triumphantly : " The Spaniards have not one single ship a-building upon this coast nearer than Cadiz, and I hope the seeing so many burnt this year in their harbours will discourage them from attempting any such thing for the future, at least during the war ".

After the fall of San Sebastian the French army left the Basque country for Catalonia, skirting the northern slopes of the Pyrenees. Stanhope's reports are dated from St. Jean de Luz, Tarbes, Toulouse, and Mont Louis. They entered Spanish territory once more in Puycerdá, and marched against the small fortress of Urgel on the Segre. Again the siege dragged, for it took weeks to bring up the necessary artillery through the dreaded passes of the Pyrenees. The citadel only fell in October 1719, by which time Berwick had already returned to France, to enter Spain a third time near the eastern coast. He came with 75 squadrons and 4 battalions, about 30,000 men ; but even with this large force he did not intend to make a grand campaign, but only to take Rosas, raze its fortifica- tions to the ground, and return to France till the following year. Even this siege was consented to by France purely to gratify the Court of England. During the winter, preparations were at last to be made for the attack on Pamplona.

On the approach of the French army the enthusiasm of the Catalans was such that it had to be restrained, lest rebellion broke out too early and resulted in a defeat by Spanish troops, before the French army could intervene. " The game seems evidently to be in our own hands," wrote Stanhope jubilantly, " if we will but play it." [1] Three or four thousand Catalans had risen, throughout the province armed bands appeared, who made raids as far as the Ebro, intercepted all that was being sent to or from Barcelona, and caught the Government reinforcements. Berwick gave orders that the rebels should be supplied with weapons and formed into battalions.

But the Catalans had never had much confidence in their French liberators, who had once been the instrument of their servitude, and who would probably abandon them again as soon as it seemed advantageous. We are fighting with the noose around our necks,

[1] W. Stanhope to Craggs, Sept. 3, 1719, S.P. 94/232.

they said. The French troops showed them little sympathy, and on every occasion they were told by officers and soldiers that they were nothing but rebels against their King, a grandson of France. It was only the promises they received from the representative of George I that made them go on.

Stanhope, as a true Whig, wished to wipe out the stain that had fallen on England's honour when the Tories under Queen Anne had sacrificed the Catalans. But even if the French had intended to keep Rosas, they would only have been master of a small corner of the country, and the rest would have been at the mercy of the numerous Spanish garrisons, in Gerona and Barcelona, in Cardona and Lerida, in Balaguer and Tarragona. Unwillingly Stanhope realized that he had to sacrifice the Catalans, and felt it would be cruel and unjust to give them further encouragement. The rebellion, as far as is known, never advanced beyond a mere start.

Even the attack which Berwick intended to launch against Rosas was a failure from the outset. The necessary artillery was to be sent by sea from France, and a squadron from Admiral Byng's fleet was to cut off the town's supplies by sea. Some weeks after the army had invested the town, but was still waiting for its artillery, a storm, the like of which was not remembered on this coast, wrecked most of the French ships. Such artillery as was saved did not seem sufficient to conquer the fortress, especially as the French camp had been heavily damaged by the stormy seas. Berwick still hesitated to withdraw, particularly as the storm had uncovered 15,000 cannon-balls on the shore, probably thrown away by the army of the Duke of Vendôme in 1697, when he marched to the siege of Barcelona. But despite this discovery the Marshal had to give up the attempt on Rosas and return with his whole force to France. Stanhope returned to England. Berwick's Spanish campaign was over, as the war was nearing its end.

The news of Berwick's successes at Fuenterrabia and San Sebastian had been received in England with the more pleasure, as his countrymen took a particular pride in the glory of an Englishman.[1] But their enthusiasm was soon cooled by the disappointments that followed.

England, which as so often had been stage managing the war from behind the scenes, found that France was not playing her rôle

[1] Craggs to W. Stanhope, June 18, 1719, S.P. 104/30.

seriously, and decided to take a more active part herself. Colonel Stanhope had not yet carried out his raid on Santoña when Lord Stair suggested from Paris [1] that a small expedition should be fitted out and sent to Galicia in the north-west of Spain. The suggestion was keenly taken up by the Regency in London. Their plan was to send two 50-gun ships to join those under Captain Johnson, already cruising off Spain's Atlantic coasts, as this would enable the English commander to control the whole of these coasts as he should judge proper. With eight or ten battalions that should be sent on transports it would be possible for him not only to destroy the shipping on the coast, but also to demolish any forts. A considerable diversion might be made, and this would facilitate the operations of the French army ; the ships and troops might assist them whenever the service should require and permit it.[2]

In Hanover, whither Stanhope had again accompanied the King, the project was considered dangerous. A recent Jacobite rising in Scotland [3] had only been suppressed with the aid of Dutch troops, and though the danger was in fact past, it formed a very reasonable argument against the expedition,[4] particularly at a time when Parliament had just fixed the army at a mere 12,000 men. Only when the Regents proposed to keep the Dutch forces in England until the return of the expedition did George agree.[5] The squadron was to be led by Admiral Mighell, and the command of the landing force was entrusted to Lord Cobham, who had fought under Marlborough, and had distinguished himself in 1708 at the siege of Lille. He had the reputation of being a dashing officer who did not hate a difficulty.[6] As an unbending Whig he had been dismissed from the army in the last years of Queen Anne, but was restored by George I and had been in Vienna as ambassador in 1714. His second in command was General George Wade, later a Field-marshal.

At first Berwick had fully approved the plan. He thought that the English soldiers, together with six Swiss battalions he had under his command, would be much more reliable than the French soldiers,

---

[1] Craggs describes himself as originator of the plan in a letter : (*Hardwicke*) *State Papers* (1778), vol. ii. p. 587. Cf. also W. Stanhope to Craggs, July 20, 1719, S.P. 94/232.

[2] Craggs to Stanhope, June 30, 1719, S.P. 43/57.

[3] Cf. chapter on the Stuart Danger, p. 199 *seq.*

[4] Stanhope to Delafaye, July 1 (O.S.), 1719, S.P. 43/2.

[5] Stanhope to Delafaye, July 14 (O.S.), 1719, S.P. 43/2.

[6] Craggs to Newcastle, Aug. 16, 1719, B.M. Add. MSS. 32686.

whose heart was not in the war. But when he decided to leave the
Basque provinces the expedition could no longer be of help to him,
at least for the current year ; so he recommended that, if the plan
were not dropped, the expedition should attack Corunna. A few
weeks later, in August, he heard that the expedition was being
prepared with the object of annoying the coasts of Spain, destroying
shipbuilding stores, and making elbow-room for him. The news
gave him little satisfaction, for he believed Corunna and Cadiz to
be the only useful objectives, and the expedition had neither the
artillery nor the time to take either town ; and to give him elbow-
room was useless since it was not the Spanish army that hindered
him in the execution of any of his designs, but the want of provisions and artillery. It seemed to him better to send 4000 men
straight to Sicily, to support the Emperor's troops there.[1] He saw
that the aims of the English and French forces were totally different,
and decided that military co-operation was impossible. Before the
English fleet appeared off the coast of Galicia he had left Basque
territory. With such dissipation of the French and English forces
there was evidently no possibility of defeating the Spaniards at
home.

The departure of Mighell's squadron from Portsmouth was held
up for a long time by the slowness with which supplies arrived ;
and then by weather which forced it to return. When it finally
reached the Spanish coast [2] it consisted of a single big ship of 70
guns, several frigates with 20 guns, and a large number of so-called
bomb vessels, carrying in all about 4500 men.

Having searched in vain for Captain Johnson, who after sailing
up and down for thirty-five days between Ortegal and Corunna
had been forced by lack of provisions to return home, Cobham
sailed on down the coast. As they passed Corunna it must have
been obvious to Admiral Mighell that his small squadron could
not force the harbour entrance, which was strongly guarded by
fortifications and batteries. So he sailed on, reaching the fortress
of Vigo, which lies a little way up the estuary of the same name,
on September 29 (O.S.). On the same evening the troops landed a
few miles below the town without difficulty, for the musquetry of

---

[1] W. Stanhope to Craggs, Aug. 20, 1719, S.P. 94/232.

[2] For what follows cf. Cobham's Reports (S.P. 94/89) ; these are of more
value than those from Admiral Mighell (the naval commander) to Delafaye.
Cf. also Byng's Reports of the same time, S.P. 42/71.

the peasants from the mountains at a great distance did not kill
a single soldier. Far more dangerous was the wine of the last
vintage. As the soldiers were accustomed only to beer, for two days
they were in a very ill condition of defence. Only with difficulty
did their officers get them in a little better order, by taking away
the wine and punishing the worst drunkards.[1] Discipline must
have been altogether in a sorry state, for according to Cobham's
report half the population had fled into Portugal, and those which
remained murdered marauders and fired from behind the rocks and
hedges upon every party that went 500 yards from the camp.
Plundering, violence and destruction lay in the trail of the English
force. Such behaviour did not conflict with the purpose of the
expedition : for, unlike Berwick, the English wished to cause a
general terror throughout the whole coast of Spain and consequently to cast an universal odium upon the Cardinal and his
administration.[2]

The little English army now took up position in front of the
town, with its left wing to the sea, and the right extending towards
the mountains.[3] At the same time detachments were sent out to
discover the strength of the enemy in the town and in the citadel.
These preparations sufficed to bring about the surrender of the
town. The gun-carriages were burned, the cannon spiked, and the
regulars retired into the citadel. Cobham garrisoned the town and
the fortress of San Sebastian with 800 men. Now the artillery
could be landed and got into position ; and the bomb vessels began
to entertain the citadel, but with little success, by reason of the
great distance and the badness of the fuses. The next day the
battery of between forty and fifty mortars, small and great, began
to fire, and continued to play for four days with great success.
The fourth day Cobham ordered further artillery to be landed and
with some cannon found in the town to be placed in battery on the
fort of San Sebastian. At the same time he sent the Governor a
summons of surrender, declaring that if he stayed till the second
battery was ready he should have no quarter. As the Governor
had the day before been carried out of the Castle wounded, the

---

[1] Wade's Report, Oct. 11, 1719, S.P. 94/89.
[2] W. Stanhope to Craggs, Sept. 3, 1719, S.P. 94/232.
[3] An official account of the taking of Vigo was printed, dated Whitehall
Oct. 22/Nov. 2, 1719 (enclosed with Hoffmann's Report of Nov. 3, 1719),
Vienna Archives.

acting Governor asked for a respite in which to ask instructions of the viceroy of the province, who was staying a few miles away at Tuy. The respite was refused and the fortress surrendered. The garrison was allowed to march out " with arms and baggage, drums beating, colours flying, their cartouches and flasks full of powder and ball in proportion ". These military honours were conceded the more readily to the Spaniards, for if they had behaved as they ought to have done, the place would probably not have been taken so quickly.[1]

The expedition could stay on where they were only if sufficient provisions could be drawn from the district. But after their first experiences the populace would not believe the declarations that no harm would be done to them. Cobham sent detachments to the neighbouring towns to demand contributions or victuals ; but they got nothing, for all the more important citizens had fled. Then places in the vicinity were plundered and destroyed ; the deserted town of Redondela, and the arsenal and the archiepiscopal palace in Pontevedra, were completely burnt down. With the advent of the October rains the troops had to be quartered in Vigo, where they were safe both from the weather and from the peasants. But the supplies on the ships were dwindling. On October 11 (O.S.) Cobham intended to stay till they heard from England whether they should abandon Vigo or garrison it ; but as it soon became evident that they could not wait so long, he gave orders to take on board all weapons and stores found in the town and to blow up the cistern and the well in the Castle. The departure on October 27 (O.S.) ended an expedition which, since Corunna was not reached, was not worth the cost.[2]

When Spain sent her expedition to Sicily, Victor Amadeus had not yet joined the Quadruple Alliance. Sardinia did not seem to him sufficient compensation for Sicily, particularly as it had just been conquered by Spain ; on the other hand he realized that, as a Spanish army of 23,000 men and 6000 cavalry had already landed in Sicily, he would inevitably lose the island either to them or to the Emperor.

[1] John Armstrong to Ch. Wills (Lt.-Gen. of the Ordnance), Oct. 11 (O.S.), 1719, S.P. 94/89.
[2] Cf. Hoffmann's similar opinion in his Report of Nov. 21, 1719, Vienna Archives.

Victor Amadeus had soon lost the sympathies of his new subjects : for he refused to make his home in Sicily, and gave all
important offices to Piedmontese, who made themselves unpopular
by unnecessary harshness. So the populace welcomed the Spanish
invaders and favoured their operations. The Piedmontese troops
were soon forced back to the east coast, and even here could not
hold out without foreign support.

In these circumstances Victor Amadeus considered accepting
the help of Charles VI, without however joining the Quadruple
Alliance. The Emperor had been willing to offer his help, although
the political attitude of Savoy was still ambiguous, in order to
prevent the whole of Sicily falling into Spanish hands. But before
negotiations could be completed, the destruction of the Spanish
fleet by the English made the Quadruple Alliance master of the
situation. Victor Amadeus had to open the citadel of Messina,
which was being attacked by the Spanish army, to the Imperial
troops who were waiting on the mainland.

The Spaniards, however, seemed determined to subdue the
whole island rapidly, and the siege of Messina made such progress
that the defenders were left no breathing-space. Even the arrival
of Imperial troops, who could now be brought over without hindrance, and even outnumbered the Piedmontese, did not give them
fresh courage. The commander, Marquis d'Andorno, began negotiations with the Spaniards in spite of protests by the Imperial general.
On September 20, 1718, the citadel was surrendered ; the garrison
was allowed to march out with military honours.[1] Vienna was
sorely disappointed. Shortly before, Prince Eugene had arranged
in conjunction with Admiral Byng that the transport of troops
from the mainland should be hastened ; and that everything should
be done to force the Spaniards to withdraw. Instead he received
the news of Messina's capitulation, which seemed to him almost
unbelievable.[2]

The jealousy and mistrust between the Imperial and the Savoyard
troops reached such a pitch that the Emperor was on the point of
conducting a campaign in Sicily without further regard for the
Piedmontese. Marshal Daun, who was directing operations from

---

[1] Cf. Hammer, *Geschichte des osmanischen Reichs*, *VI : Feldzüge des
Prinzen Eugen*, her. von der Abteilung für Kriegsgeschichte des k.k. Kriegs-
Archives, II. 9, p. 93 *seq.*

[2] *Ibid.* Milit. Corr. Nos. 23, 25.

the mainland, received instructions to regard the Piedmontese as friends, but friends that might be or become his enemies.[1] The Spaniards made the most of the situation, and with the support of the islanders made still further progress despite England's complete control of the sea.

After the fall of Messina the struggle centred round Milazzo, a stronghold on a tongue of land in the north that stretches far into the sea. Again Imperial troops that came to reinforce the Piedmontese had to put themselves under the command of the Piedmontese general. As both sides had entrenched themselves firmly, there was a long period of trench warfare in front of the fortress, which only ended when the Spaniards withdrew in the spring of 1719.

Meanwhile, on November 8, 1718, Savoy had adhered to the Quadruple Alliance in London. An agreement was reached about the exchange of Sardinia for Sicily,[2] and Victor Amadeus adopted the title of King of Sardinia. But the divisions between Charles VI and Victor Amadeus continued, as the Emperor's natural demand that the Sicilian fortresses still occupied by Piedmontese troops be forthwith handed over to him met with determined opposition from Victor Amadeus. England supported the King in his opposition, fearing that once the Emperor had received Sicily he would soon lose interest in the Quadruple Alliance, and not help with the reconquest of Sardinia.

No further actions of importance took place in the island. In a battle at Francavilla, where the Spaniards had chosen their own position, both sides claimed the victory, the Spaniards with better reason. From this time on the Imperial troops slowly improved their position, and recaptured Messina after heavy fighting. But when peace was concluded neither Sicily nor Sardinia had been completely wrested from the Spaniards.

The part played by the English fleet under Sir George Byng was of the greatest importance. The severing of all communication with Spain turned Sicily and Sardinia into besieged strongholds that became harder and harder of defence. As later with Napoleon in Egypt, so too here bravery was of no avail against the forces that drove the Spaniards to submit to the army of Charles VI,

[1] *Ibid.* p. 108.
[2] Cf. Přibram, *Oesterreichische Staatsverträge*, England, i. p. 404.

which was aided in every way, including actual military operations, by the English navy.

The instructions which Stanhope sent to Byng from Paris after his victory off Passaro remained valid for the whole duration of the war.[1] He was to continue to distress the Spaniards as much as possible, till they had declared their accession — the word *submission* was avoided — to the Quadruple Alliance. At first he was told only to attack their ships eastwards of Barcelona, but this limitation was soon dropped when the Spaniards without declaring war confiscated British goods and seized the English consuls and merchants in their ports.

When Byng cut all communications with Sicily and Sardinia, it was evident to the Spaniards that they would do best by capitulating, on terms that allowed them to bring all their troops home. But even if Charles VI and Victor Amadeus might have been brought to agree, the Western Powers would not : for these troops, the best that Spain possessed, would immediately have served against France or have made an invasion into England. Byng was frequently reminded that he must in no circumstances allow them to be sent home before Philip accepted the Quadruple Alliance, for in Sicily they were like so many hostages, and England's best security for Spain's conduct. At one time the English were afraid that the Emperor might, despite their protestations, agree to evacuate the Spaniards on his own ships. Craggs wrote to Byng saying that, in such an event, " you are, if you can, to sink every one of them to the bottom of the sea ".[2]

The Austrians were wise enough to avoid such a conflict ; for only with the protection of the English fleet could communications be maintained between the Imperial authorities in Italy and the forces in Sicily, since isolated Spanish men-of-war still existed in the Mediterranean. These Spanish vessels still managed by surprise, or by such ruses as the hoisting of the English flag when near parts of the coast held by the enemy, to give some small aid to their countrymen in Sicily or to capture occasional transports. The transports to Sicily had therefore to be protected ; and in May 1719, a small expedition which set out from Milazzo to conquer the Lipari Islands was also safely escorted on its way. Craggs assured

---

[1] Dated Paris, Sept. 19, 1718, S.P. 78/162. With this a letter to Byng, same date. Cf. also Stair to Byng, Sept. 8, 1718, S.P. 78/162.

[2] Craggs to Byng, June 29, 1719, S.P. 43/57.

Byng "that it is impossible for the Spaniards to assemble any force at sea to molest you".[1] The siege of Messina was undertaken on Byng's suggestion, and was made a success by the participation of his cannon. After the fall of the citadel celebrations were postponed till the Admiral could appear in person.[2]

In November 1718 Byng was presented with a portrait of the Emperor set in diamonds, together with a secret gratification of 100,000 francs, and the captains of his ships also received presents intended to keep alive their zeal for the Imperial cause.[3] In July 1719 Hoffmann received instructions to urge that an English squadron should winter in the Mediterranean, and thus prevent the Duke of Anjou (Philip V) from attacking Italy and the neighbouring islands again, or from sending new troops and supplies.[4] The Admiralty replied that Byng's ships were in great need of repairs, but that a sufficient number of them would remain in Sicilian waters. Soon after this the Austrians heard that preparations were being made in ports belonging to north and central Italian States, to send the Spaniards men, provisions, and ammunition. Eleven thousand men were said to have marched through Tuscany. In Vienna Sinzendorff had promptly made representations to the representatives of these States, and had even threatened the Florentine ambassador that communications by land with Leghorn would be cut. But as effective measures could only be taken with the support of the English fleet, Byng was at Austria's request instructed to keep a watchful eye on the Italian principalities. At the same time England requested the Emperor to avoid taking any decisive steps except in agreement with the allies.[5]

Finally, on March 20, 1720, the English Admiral was to have the satisfaction of bringing in person to the Imperial headquarters the news that Spain had accepted the Quadruple Alliance. Agreement between the opposing generals in Sicily on the cessation of hostilities was not easily reached. Count Mercy was instructed by the Emperor to demand that with the armistice the Spaniards should immediately evacuate the island ; and the Marquis de Lede

---

[1] *Ibid.*   [2] Hammer, *l.c.* p. 192.   [3] *Ibid.* p. 116.
[4] Charles VI to Hoffmann, July 27, 1719, Vienna Archives.
[5] Charles VI to Hoffmann, Aug. 16, 1719 ; Hoffmann's Report, Sept. 15, 1719 ; Hoffmann to Craggs, Sept. 2/13, 1719 ; Craggs to Hoffmann, Sept. 3/14, 1719, Vienna Archives.

declared he had no powers to agree to such terms. A meeting arranged by Byng was fruitless, and hostilities were renewed. It was only on May 6 that, under his guidance, the two generals signed the treaty which gave Charles VI practical possession of Sicily. Naturally it was again the English fleet which took the Piedmontese troops from Sicily to Sardinia, and then arranged for the return home of the Spanish troops from both islands. Only on August 20, when Admiral Byng left for Hanover to report the successful completion of his task, did the curtain fall upon the Mediterranean struggle.

CHAPTER VII

ALBERONI'S FALL AND THE TRIUMPH OF THE
QUADRUPLE ALLIANCE

THE allies saw in Alberoni the man who had sought to stir the
Porte, Sweden, Russia, and Prussia against the Quadruple Alliance,
and who had tried to overthrow the Governments of England and
France through conspiracies among their own subjects. The
Cardinal therefore would evidently be the first victim if Spain
were defeated ; for, in Stanhope's words :

. . . as his unbounded ambition has been the sole cause of the war
. . . if he is compelled to accept peace, he will only yield to necessity,
with the resolution to seize the first opportunity of vengeance. . . .
Any peace made by the Cardinal will be only an armistice of uncertain
duration ; nor can we depend upon any treaty, till we make it with a
Spanish minister, whose system is directly opposite.[1]

Before the war ended Alberoni tried twice to make peace without having to accept the " exécrable traité ". The Spanish success
at Francavilla had made such an impression abroad, and had been
so much exaggerated in Madrid, that it seemed peace could be made
with honour. On the suggestion of the Duke of Parma, the Marquis
Scotti was sent by the Duke to Madrid, and then went on to Paris
with proposals from the Spanish Government.[2] On August 10,
1719, he saw Dubois and the Regent in secret, telling them that
the peace plan which he was to propose was sure to satisfy the
Allies ; but that he was instructed not to reveal its details till he
had put them before the Marquis de Beretti Landi, the Spanish
ambassador in The Hague. All he required for the moment was a
passport to Holland. The French statesmen, together with Lord

---

[1] Printed in Coxe, *Kings of Spain* (1815), vol. ii. p. 365 *seq.* Cf. also
Wiesener, *Le Régent, l'abbé Dubois et les Anglais,* vol. iii. p. 122 *seq.*

[2] For Scotti's mission cf. Wiesener, *l.c.* vol. iii. ch. vi.

Stair, suspected that the Spaniards intended the issue of the passport to be interpreted as a sign that the French were willing to make peace, and that the negotiations should be carried on in the neutral territory of Holland. The Spaniards probably also expected to make an agreement with the Dutch for mutual support in the furtherance of their interests, and for certain changes in the Quadruple Alliance that would be agreeable to both States.

The French Government made no secret of their suspicions, and said that before issuing the passport they must consult England and Austria. France's allies bluntly refused to negotiate with the Marquis Scotti, as they would not consider terms of peace before Alberoni's dismissal.[1]

The secret of Scotti's peace plan had been blurted out by Beretti Landi even before Scotti had reached Paris. Philip was to give up Sicily, but was in return to keep Sardinia and to receive Gibraltar and Port Mahon, the two English bases in the Mediterranean. The Duke of Savoy, who would thus be deprived of what he had gained at Utrecht, was to be compensated elsewhere. There must have been further hints in this direction, for in England it was even suspected that Victor Amadeus himself had had a hand in the matter.[2]

Alberoni's second attempt to reach separate agreement with England shows even less political judgment than the first. The English statesmen treated his efforts with contempt. Craggs wrote to Stair :

Your Excellency must remember one Colonel Seissan, who left the French service at the siege of Tournai and has since rose to the post of Major General in that of the King of Poland. This man has, I suppose, from his acquaintance with My Lord Stanhope, myself and others of the King's servants, framed a notion, that he was a very proper person to negotiate no less a matter than a peace with Spain, and no doubt of it, according to the custom of all adventurers and projectors, had made this matter very plain and his own abilities very necessary to the disgraced Cardinal. His Emminency, who has sufficiently shown how much he delights in and depends upon extraordinary measures . . . had sent for the person out of Poland and without any other ceremony had dispatched him on board a Spanish ship with a passport for England.[3]

[1] Cf. Stair's letters in (*Hardwicke*) *State Papers*, vol. ii. pp. 584, 586 ; also Bourgeois, *Le Secret des Farnèse*, p. 365.

[2] Hoffmann's Report, Aug. 11, 1719, Vienna Archives.

[3] Craggs to Stair, Dec. 14, 1719, S.P. 104/31.

With his letter of introduction from Alberoni Seissan called upon Stanhope, hoping to negotiate with him like a diplomat. The letter naively reminded Stanhope how, as they took leave of each other in the Escorial before Stanhope left Spain, they had promised each other mutual trust when the time came to end the war.[1] Now the Cardinal wanted to take the remark literally, and asked that Stanhope should listen to the proposals Seissan was to put forward. These were more moderate than Scotti's demands, for Alberoni had meanwhile realized that he could not simply ignore the Quadruple Alliance. But he would only adhere to the Alliance on four conditions.[2] The most important was that Sardinia, Sicily, Naples, and Milan should revert to Spain if in any one of them the sovereign died without male heir. In return Seissan was to promise England free trade with Mexico, and the Emperor the marriage of the Prince of Asturias with an Archduchess.[3] But just these offers seemed suspicious in England. Craggs felt that the proposals proved " how very extravagant this priest's way of thinking has been ", and how weak his policy.[4]

When Seissan reached England his mission was already doomed to failure : for the Government had received news of Alberoni's fall. Lord Stanhope still received Seissan and accepted a copy of his proposals, answered them in writing — and that was all.[5]

Alberoni's fall [6] had been brought about by Spain's enemies. Their instruments were the Marquis Scotti, the very man who had just been acting for Alberoni ; and Lord Peterborough, the famous conqueror of Barcelona, energetic, bizarre, and full of political schemes. Though the English Government used Peterborough with great caution and frequently disowned him, he was now obviously the right man to weave a great intrigue in London, in Paris, in Parma. The Duke of Parma too, as whose consular agent Alberoni had once gone to Spain, now worked for his fall, since he had been informed in writing that there would be no peace as long as Alberoni was at the helm.

---

[1] Printed in Graham, *Annals of Stair*, vol. ii. p. 392.
[2] *Ibid.* pp. 393-4.
[3] Lemontey, *Histoire de la Régence*, vol. i. p. 278.
[4] Craggs to Stair, Dec. 14, 1719, S.P. 104/31.
[5] Stanhope to Dubois, Dec. 18, 1719 ; printed in Graham, *Annals of Stair*, vol. ii. p. 391.
[6] Cf. details in Bourgeois, *l.c.* pp. 366-91.

When Scotti returned to Madrid Alberoni was suspicious of him, and tried to keep him away from the King and Queen. But with practised duplicity Scotti pursued his intrigue ; the first lady-in-waiting conveyed a letter to the Queen, and made possible secret conversations. He convinced Elizabeth Farnèse and her husband that it would be well for their royal reputation if the whole blame for Spain's misfortune were cast upon their minister. When even their confessor declared against Alberoni, his fate was sealed. On December 5, 1719, when the King and Queen were away hunting, Alberoni received orders to leave the ministry at once, Madrid within a week, and Spain within three weeks. The King refused to see him again, and the letter the Cardinal wrote him he threw into the fire.

Furiously angry Alberoni set out for the south of France, on his way to Italy. France, England, and Austria, who were still afraid of him, gladly issued him passes through the districts occupied by their troops. " I have always heard ", Dubois remarked, " that one should build golden bridges for an enemy." [1] Philip and Elizabeth were especially afraid that the Cardinal might compromise them by his revelations. Not far from Madrid he was held up and robbed of all his papers, among them apparently a will of Philip V which would have made the Queen regent and Alberoni head of the Government.[2] A second attack on Spanish soil seems to have been really the work of robbers. The Cardinal leapt on to a horse, and forced his way sword in hand. When he had crossed the French frontier he exclaimed, " Thank Heaven, I am in a Christian land ! " To the inquisitive crowds that pressed round him he vented his scorn of the royal couple, saying that Philip was a man who only needed a confessional and a woman's loins for his happiness. The Queen, he said, had the devil in her body ; she only needed to find a man of intelligence who was also a soldier, and she would have France and Europe on the hop yet.

Alberoni was given no peace in Parma, and a case was started against him in the Curia. For a year he wandered from place to place in the Imperial territories of Northern Italy, in order to retain his liberty. But on the death of Clement XI he had to be granted safe conduct to Rome for the election of a new Pope, despite the

---

[1] Dubois to Stair, Dec. 19, 1719, S.P. 78/165.

[2] Not the will of Charles II, as Saint-Simon believed. Cf. Lemontey, *l.c.* vol. i. pp. 279-81.

trial awaiting him. Clement's successor was well inclined toward
the Cardinal, whom he allowed to settle permanently in Rome. He
regained considerable importance in the Church, but his rôle as a
temporal politician, as the firebrand of Europe, was finished. Instead, he wrote books with plans meant to bring peace between
the nations in the distant future, after a European crusade against
the infidel.[1]

Frederick the Great, like the rest of his century, believed firmly
in Alberoni's diabolic greatness : " had he been given two worlds
like ours to destroy, he would have asked for a third ". He was
indeed a powerful figure, and no one but he could have made the
world believe in a Spanish *risorgimento* in the eighteenth century.

Alberoni's fall was a European sensation. Dubois wished to be
the first to inform his friend Stanhope of the news, and sent a
special letter which Destouches, Secretary of the French Embassy
in London, was to deliver immediately, even if Stanhope were with
the King. Destouches found Stanhope and Sunderland in the
House of Lords, and had them called out. After embracing him
the ministers returned with him to the House, where Stanhope
read out the letter, adding that peace must now be near. The
Lords, and the Commons where it fell to Craggs to announce the
news, were delighted. Only Robert Walpole used the occasion for
a gibe at the Government.[2] The King of England, he said, ought
now to follow Philip's example and give the boot to the ministers
who were advising him so ill. A supporter of the Cabinet retorted
that George had done so two years earlier. The cheerful news
came very opportunely, for it served to alleviate the bad impression
caused by the serious defeat of the Government some days before
over the Peerage Bill.

Everyone confidently expected peace : for why should Alberoni
have been disgraced if Spain were not ready to accept the Quadruple Alliance ? Yet though the diplomats congratulated each
other on the Cardinal's disgrace, which " opened a new scene ",[3]
and though the Governments had very good intentions, a long

---

[1] Cf. Vestnitch, " Le Cardinal Alberoni pacifiste ", *Revue d'hist. dipl.*
(1912).
[2] Hoffmann's Report, Dec. 22, 1719, Vienna Archives.
[3] Craggs to Stair, Dec. 18, 1719, printed in Graham, *Annals of Stair*,
vol. ii. p. 124.

and thorny path lay between the cessation of hostilities and a general peace settlement. The Quadruple Alliance, which provided a programme for the reorganization of Europe, now had to show its practicability. Holland was still outside the Alliance, and unconditional submission could not be expected from Spain. Moreover, no one but a few incurable optimists in Vienna believed the plans of the Quadruple Alliance to be final ; not only had Dutch and Spanish adhesion to be won, but the details of the plan had to be discussed anew. A settlement was rendered more difficult by the petty quarrels between France and England,[1] and by the growing influence of Torcy and Law. Torcy, a man of noble birth and of more character than Dubois, wished to restore the old system of Louis XIV, and realize the saying, *il n'y a plus de Pyrénées* ; he had always been mistrusted by the English, who were afraid of a union between him and Law, which might endanger their interests at the French Court. Stair urged the Regent again and again [2] not to continue Torcy in the secret of foreign affairs, as with this knowledge he would be the only man in France capable of hurting him after the King's majority ; with the secret in his own hands, the Regent would be in the position of Richelieu, whom Louis XIII had to retain though he did not love him. The Regent listened politely, but only replied that he would give the matter his careful consideration.

Stair felt he was not equal to his present difficult task, and asked to be recalled.[3] The seriousness of the position was fully recognized in England. Just as peace with Spain was to be made, alarming news came from Stair :

> Our friend Dubois has completely surrendered to Law and made a reconciliation with Torcy, and the three have worked together with Orléans, this much is certain. I have been given the same news from another quarter, from a very good source, and with the addition that peace with Spain is about to be made in a fashion that will please neither the King nor the Emperor.[4]

In London the ministers were in confusion.[5] There were even

---

[1] Cf. above, pp. 83-87.

[2] Cf. (*Hardwicke*) *State Papers*, vol. ii. p. 595. Also Stair to Stanhope, Oct. 20, 1719, S.P. 78/165.

[3] Stair to Stanhope, Nov. 7, 1719, S.P. 78/165.

[4] Stair to Stanhope, Dec. 27, 1719, S.P. 78/165.

[5] Hoffmann, Jan. 2, 1720, Vienna Archives.

rumours that France and Spain were not only making a hurried peace, but intended to use their joint forces against England and the Emperor.[1] The first necessity was to find out where France stood, for the political labours of recent years were at stake.

Stanhope decided on another rapid trip to Paris. The Christmas recess made it easier to leave London. At the same time he thought of recalling Stair, who clearly was not the man to build up afresh good relations with France ; but it was not easy to replace him. Accordingly Stair was informed by Craggs that Earl Stanhope would come to Paris, fully instructed upon the several points contained in his dispatches. Stanhope would during the eight or ten days of his stay follow Stair's advice and instructions in the task of agreeing on terms of peace, if Spain should offer one. " He will drive straight to your home, where he will expect a bed ", Craggs added in a further letter.[2]

On January 3 (N.S.), 1720, Stanhope set out for France ; after a bad crossing, during which the ship lost its masts, he reached the French coast safely, and hastened on to his task in Paris. His first conversations with the Regent, with Dubois, and Law convinced Stanhope that there was no intention of breaking with England and of concluding a separate peace with Spain.[3] " It is impossible to talk better than they do ", he wrote home with relief. He saw that the Regent was completely master of the situation, particularly in foreign affairs. Torcy did not come into the question ; Dubois promptly sought the protection of his powerful English friend ; and John Law was soon disarmed by Stanhope's amiable flatteries.

On the all-important question of Spain the Regent declared that he would not depart from his obligations to the Allies, and would not begin separate negotiations, much less make any agreement with the Spanish Court which would be objectionable to the Allies, but that together with them he would firmly insist on the execution of the London terms. Stanhope, who did not quite trust the Regent, pointed out mercilessly all the reasons for England's

[1] Stair to Craggs, Jan. 6 (N.S.), 1720, S.P. 78/165.

[2] Graham, *Annals of Stair,* vol. ii. pp. 125-7.

[3] For what follows cf. Stanhope's Reports (S.P. 78/167) and Pendten-riedter's Reports (Vienna Archives) ; *(Hardwicke) State Papers,* vol. ii. p. 602 *seq.* ; Graham, *Annals of Stair,* vol. ii. p. 125 *seq.* and p. 411 *seq.* Also Wiesener, *l.c.* vol. iii. pp. 225-6 ; Weber, *Quadrupel-Allianz,* pp. 101-2 ; Bourgeois, *Le Secret de Dubois,* pp. 119-20.

mistrust : the Franco-Spanish negotiations, which were to be kept secret from England ; the many Jacobites living in Paris ; the declaration that France would never give up Santa Lucia ; and finally all the difficulties she had put in the way of George I's Northern policy. Each one of these facts furnished ten grounds of mistrust. The King expected to see them refuted, for only so could he really believe in the Regent's friendship. Orleans promised that he would listen to no further proposals from Spain that conflicted with the terms of the Quadruple Alliance, and that no move in this direction would be made except in full agreement with His Britannic Majesty. The Jacobites would be forced to leave immediately. As regards Santa Lucia and other outstanding questions, England would receive satisfaction.

Stanhope was not the man to be satisfied with mere assurances. He waited for the arrival of two couriers who were to bring Spain's propositions for peace. These he found extravagant, and he induced all the members of the Quadruple Alliance, which now included Savoy, to sign a joint declaration.[1] This spoke of the London Treaty as final, and recalled the agreement that, unless Spain announced her adhesion within the time allowed, the Italian Reversions would pass to others.

The Regent, in his anxiety to please Stanhope, suggested that an agent be sent to inform the Court of Madrid of the determined attitude of the Allies. As Stanhope was doubtful about sending a Frenchman, Orleans proposed that Stanhope's private secretary, Luke Schaub, who had had much experience of diplomatic negotiations, should be the agent. Stanhope was delighted, and told Pendtenriedter that if this had been the only result of his journey to Paris, it would have been worth going. He could now return to London with the certainty that France was for the present, and probably for some time to come, loyal to her Allies. For he had hinted that it would be easy for England, rather than France, to make a separate agreement with Madrid, which might include joint measures against French trade and against Law's notorious Mississippi Scheme.

Of John Law Stanhope remarked that if his successes in France endured, the power of the nation would be terrible, and greater than that of all others. But he did not take Law too seriously ; he

---

[1] Enclosed with Pendtenriedter's Report of Jan. 22, 1720, Vienna Archives.

confessed that he understood nothing of Law's financial system, and certainly could not see, from the peculiar results, either what it was based on or how long it could last.[1]

The polite treatment of Law was anathema to Stair, whom Stanhope treated with scant consideration. The Ambassador's exaggerated suspicions had almost alienated the French Government ; and angry French spirits were now appeased by Stanhope's open announcement of his imminent recall.

Spain's propositions for peace had been like the demands of a victorious power : the French were expected to evacuate the Spanish territory they had occupied, the Spanish troops in Sicily were to be transported home, and indemnities were to be paid to Spain for her losses, particularly at Passaro. She was to receive Sardinia, Gibraltar, and Port Mahon. Elizabeth's son, Don Carlos, was to receive Tuscany and Parma, not as Imperial fiefs, but as free principalities ; and he was to go immediately to Italy, to grow up amidst his future subjects. Even Sicily was to revert to Spain if the House of Savoy died out. These terms gave little prospect of Spanish submission, and made it clear that the Allies were fighting for something more than Alberoni's dismissal.

Yet on January 26, 1720, scarcely a week after Schaub's arrival in Madrid, Philip V and his minister Grimaldo signed an agreement by which Spain acceded in practice to the Quadruple Alliance, in form only to the Paris agreement of July 18, 1718, which had been signed by France and England, but not Austria.[2] As Philip only recognized Charles VI as the " Archduke ", the document speaks vaguely of a peace " between the Courts of Madrid and Vienna and the existing rulers therein " (*inter utramque Aulam Madritensem et Viennensem, et inter principes utriusque Dominationis modo Regnantes*).

It was further agreed that the formal adhesion of Spain to the Quadruple Alliance should be given at The Hague, on the still neutral territory of Holland ; and that the Spanish declaration should also apply to the London agreement of August 2, 1718 (N.S.). Thus on February 17 Spain formally and unconditionally accepted the Quadruple Alliance (*pure et plene nullaque adhibita reservatione*),

---

[1] Pendtenriedter, Jan. 22, 1720, Vienna Archives. Cf. also Weber, *Quadrupel-Allianz*, p. 101.

[2] Cf. Vol. I. p. 351.

and the great European quarrel of the last twenty years seemed buried.

The sudden change in Spain's attitude was not due merely to Schaub's brilliant diplomacy or to the firm tone of the recent Declaration from Paris ; rather it was the result of a more accommodating attitude on the part of the Allies. Shortly after Schaub's arrival, Seissan returned from London to Madrid with Stanhope's letter.[1] Stanhope, while bluntly refusing to entertain his proposals, had hinted that once Philip had accepted the Quadruple Alliance in principle, he could put forward his wishes, and England would willingly support them in the further negotiations, as far as they did not conflict with her obligations.

Spain took the hint. Immediately after signing the agreement on January 26, Grimaldo presented to the Powers a note in which he put forward a number of conditions, which were not however to be *conditiones sine quibus non*. But nothing was decided ; and even The Hague agreement of February 17 was not a final settlement. The Powers were unanimous that outstanding questions should be put before a European Congress, but a decision on the seat of the congress was not yet reached.

The attempt to solve by force the great problems left by the War of the Spanish Succession was only a partial success. The epoch of the Quadruple Alliance was followed by the age of congresses.

With Spain's submission the last reason against Holland's adhesion to the Quadruple Alliance seemed to have gone. Ever since June 1719 the three other Powers had unceasingly sought to win the Dutch, who never refused on principle, but always dragged other questions into the negotiations, particularly that of the three months' grace for Spain. The picture is always the same : Holland pressing for the Reversions to be left open to Spain, Austria trying in vain to prevent the inevitable, England and France irritated with their ally and secretly pursuing the same end as Holland. As Charles VI could not do without the English fleet, he had, in September 1719, to accept a fifth renewal of the period of grace.

The Dutch adopted a more conciliatory attitude only when Alberoni had fallen and the war was nearing its end. But the

---

[1] Stanhope to Seissan, Dec. 17/28, 1719 (enclosed with Hoffmann's Report of Jan. 2, 1719), Vienna Archives.

Powers' interest in Holland's accession was waning ; Charles VI now wished it only because he did not want to meet them as mediators in the coming congress. At the last negotiations, in the spring of 1720, Holland's intention to accede was finally brought to nought by a minority in the States General.[1] Though Spain's submission had meanwhile made these negotiations academic and provided the starting point for new ones, Holland's attitude had a bad effect on her relations with the Powers. It added to Austria's irritation over the Barrier question, which was soon further increased by the quarrel over the Ostend–East India Company. In England as in France there remained some grudge against the States General for years.[2]

A question that was hotly debated before any congress could meet was England's renunciation of Gibraltar. Cromwell had been the first to consider its acquisition, but his admirals thought the plan was not feasible.[3] With the War of the Spanish Succession the question of supremacy in the Mediterranean assumed vital importance. In 1704 Gibraltar was taken, and became a valuable base for the protection of trade. The merchants were delighted, but the strategists wanted a roomy harbour where a whole fleet could winter. In 1708 James Stanhope took Port Mahon, the port of Minorca. " England ", he declared, " ought never to part with this island, which will give the law to the Mediterranean both in time of war and peace." [4]

Minorca seems to have been more highly valued than Gibraltar, because from it the English fleet could at any moment make a flanking attack on French squadrons leaving Toulon, thus threatening both France's sea route to Italy and her immensely important Levant trade. Gibraltar was no threat to France, then England's

---

[1] For nearly 200 years historians boldly stated that Holland actually adhered to the Quadruple Alliance. The source of this error may be Tindal, *Continuation*, v. (1747), p. 565 *n.*, where Dec. 22, 1718, is given as the date of Holland's accession. Some historians give this date, but some make Holland's accession follow closely on that of Spain. The true facts are given in H. v. Srbik, *Oesterreichische Staatsverträge*, Niederlande (1912), vol. i. p. 574 *seq.* Cf. also Goslinga, *Slingelandt's Efforts towards European Peace* (1915), p. 41 [1].

[2] Polwarth and Whitworth to Newcastle, May 11, 1724, S.P. 78/174.

[3] Cf. W. Michael, *Cromwell*, vol. ii. p. 137 *seq.* ; Corbett, *England in the Mediterranean*, 1603–1713, vol. i. pp. 323 *seq.* and 333.

[4] Cf. *D.N.B.* vol. liv. Stanhope, p. 15.

chief enemy, for her ships did not need to pass through the straits ; but for England its possession insured that no other power barred her own entry into the Mediterranean. This was doubly important as long as there was real danger of union between France and Spain ; but now its possession seemed far less important than that of Minorca with its strong offensive position.

At the Peace of Utrecht England retained Gibraltar and Port Mahon, which were to be the buttresses of her position in the Mediterranean. The Spaniards did not particularly resent the loss of Minorca ; but Gibraltar in English hands, as Philip V used to say, was a thorn in the side of Spain.

According to Saint-Simon England thought as early as 1716 of renouncing Gibraltar.[1] The Marquis Louville, who as confidant of Philip V had enjoyed great influence in the Spanish capital, was sent to Madrid by the Regent with the consent of George I. He was not to breathe a word of his real mission either to the English or to the French Ambassador, much less to Queen Elizabeth or Alberoni. Only to the King in person was he to disclose the secret of his mission, which was the surrender of Gibraltar to Spain. The world, and especially the British Parliament and its parties, were to hear of nothing but the *fait accompli*. The Governor of Gibraltar would one day receive a written order from the King to hand over the fortress immediately ; he was then to move with the garrison to Tangier ; this town had been surrendered to the Moors in 1684, and it was now perhaps intended to reoccupy it. But Alberoni successfully prevented Philip from receiving Louville, who had to leave Spain without fulfilling his mission. Alberoni's suspicions had lost Spain the great opportunity of regaining Gibraltar.

Saint-Simon's story was considered a fable by the historians of the nineteenth century. Not that Louville's visit to Madrid was invented ; but the documents showed it to be one of the many intrigues which aimed at the removal of Italian influence from the Spanish Court.[2] Even if Gibraltar is not mentioned either in the documents concerning the mission or in Alberoni's letters, and though Saint-Simon's Mémoires must be taken with reserve, it is

---

[1] Cf. also the *Mémoires* of Dudos and Marmontel, dependent on those of Saint-Simon, as is shown by Lemontey, *Histoire de la Régence*, vol. i. pp. 9-11.

[2] Cf. Baudrillart, *Philippe V et la Cour de France*, vol. ii. p. 228 *seq.*; Bourgeois, *Le Secret des Farnèse*, p. 216 *seq.*

unlike him to invent a whole story. He claims to have spoken of the matter both with the Regent and with Louville. As Louville was to report on the hidden purpose of his mission in secret dispatches, the silence of the documents on the question of Gibraltar proves nothing ; and as the British Government shortly afterwards clearly intended to cede Gibraltar, there may well be some truth in Saint-Simon's story.[1]

Certainly the possession of Gibraltar and Minorca was felt to be a burden as early as 1716. Bonet reports that the cost of garrisoning them amounted to more than £89,000, without reckoning the expense of sending ships to and fro. He thought that these expenses were borne for the sake of trade ; but that once the danger of union between France and Spain was past, England would willingly barter these places for trading privileges, and that such action would be highly popular and advantageous to the Crown.[2]

In the last months of 1717, in the course of the negotiations that led to the Quadruple Alliance, Stanhope told Dubois that he was ready to cede Gibraltar in order to complete his plan, though it might cost him his head. The remark was strictly confidential, but Dubois promptly passed it on to the Regent, and the plan was kept in mind both in France and in England. It was generally said that George I had suggested it " *de son pur mouvement* ".[3]   But the King used to adopt Stanhope's opinion in questions of foreign policy ; and Stanhope, the conqueror of Minorca, had always been indifferent about Gibraltar. The plan was treated as an open secret ; indeed the French Ambassador in Madrid once asked for instructions which would empower him to make the formal offer of Gibraltar, but Dubois pointed out that there could be no question of such a document without a formal declaration from England.[4]

When Stanhope went to Spain in the summer of 1718 in a last effort to avert hostilities, Craggs wrote to him about a letter that Stanhope himself had sent to Sunderland from Paris :

I am ordered by the King to let you know that he approves of your propositions relating to Gibraltar, and in case your Excellency

---

[1] Coxe, *Kings of Spain* (1815), vol. ii. p. 329, thinks the story improbable, because he did not know that the negotiations for a *rapprochement* between England and France were already in hand.

[2] Bonet, Sept. 29/Oct. 9, 1716, Vienna Archives, *Vide* Appendix 4.

[3] Graham, *Annals of Stair*, vol. ii. p. 415.

[4] Cf. Lemontey, *Histoire de la Régence*, vol. ii. p. 395.

finds it will conclude and settle everything, you are hereby authorized to make that offer when you shall find it expedient.[1]

In Stanhope's letters, containing full accounts of his lengthy conversations with Alberoni and with the King and Queen, there is no mention of Gibraltar. But he seems none the less to have made the offer. A few months later the French declaration of war, in which all the advantages that had been offered to Spain were enumerated, stated expressly in Article 8 that France had engaged herself to obtain for Spain the return of Gibraltar.[2] This could hardly have been stated in such formal terms unless England had previously made a formal offer.

The French statement could not escape the notice of the English public, which must have been alarmed at the possibility that the King alone, by the exercise of his prerogative, might cede English possessions. Though his theoretical right to do so was unquestioned in the eighteenth century, such a loss would have roused the anger of the people against their sovereign, and might have cost a minister his head. But this would not alter the validity of what had happened,[3] and Parliament would have had to look on helplessly.

Craggs at once pointed out to the French chargé d'affaires that the Article would cause an unpleasant scene in the House of Commons. Walpole did not raise the subject himself, as he usually avoided attacking the King in person ; but Fuller, who was considered to be Walpole's tool, announced one day that he had brought to the House a lampoon called " A Manifesto on the causes of rupture between France and Spain ", in which a foreign individual took upon himself to dispose of the property of the English Crown, boasting that he had assured the restitution of Gibraltar to the King of Spain. But the House was so astonished that it remained in profound silence. None of the ten or twelve members on whose support Fuller had reckoned dared open his mouth ; and Walpole himself, who had completely forsaken his *enfant perdu*, was not even present. Thus the House passed on to the next business without paying any attention to the incident.[4]

The time had been badly chosen, for during the war the question

---

[1] Craggs to Stanhope, July 17 (N.S.), 1718, S.P. 104/138.

[2] See Dumont, viii. II. 6.

[3] On the change of view, cf. Anson, *Law and Custom of the Constitution* (3rd edition), vol. ii, pt. ii., p. 103 *seq.*

[4] Destouches to Dubois, Feb. 1, 1719, Aff. étr. 322. *Vide* Appendix 5.

could only be an academic one. But when Alberoni had fallen and
Spain's accession to the Quadruple Alliance was imminent, the
question of Gibraltar was raised again. Both England and France
appeared to be trying to win Spain to their side by separate negotiations. Stair declared that if France attempted such a thing, England
could always steal a march on her by offering Gibraltar.[1] When
Stanhope came to Paris in January 1720, Gibraltar was discussed
but nothing was settled. Shortly after, when the question became
acute, Orleans and Dubois, Stair and Pendtenriedter could not
agree whether Stanhope had promised to cede Gibraltar or not.
They had all heard his words; but Orleans and Dubois affirmed
that Stanhope had led them to assume that the King would make
no difficulties about giving up Gibraltar;[2] Pendtenriedter wrote
that he did not know what Stanhope had said to the Regent, but
that to himself the English minister had expressed grave doubts
about the matter;[3] and Stanhope emphatically denied that there
had been any talk of Gibraltar.[4]

The whole question had changed its character as soon as it
reached the public. How it was divulged is not clear; but on
January 22 (O.S) it was reported that the English Government
intended to offer Gibraltar to Spain as an inducement to peace,
and that there was already strong opposition to the plan.[5] Spain,
it was said, was in any case bent on rebuilding her fleet, and if
she possessed Gibraltar she would control the straits, making
English trade in the Mediterranean impossible except under the
protection of a powerful fleet, which would have been more costly
than the maintenance of Gibraltar. It was even suggested that as
Port Mahon could not be held if Gibraltar were lost, the position
in the Mediterranean ought rather to be strengthened by the
acquisition of Majorca.

Very soon there was no more talk of royal prerogative in the
matter. Stanhope himself told Hoffmann that Parliament must
decide. In the Commons a motion for an Address to the King was
being prepared, which would request him to keep Gibraltar in all

[1] Pendtenriedter's Report, Jan. 8, 1720, Vienna Archives.
[2] Stair to Craggs, Feb. 22, 1720; (*Hardwicke*) *State Papers*, vol. ii. p. 607.
[3] Hoffmann's Report, Mar. 6, 1720, Vienna Archives.
[4] Hoffmann's Report, Mar. 2, 1720, Vienna Archives; Craggs to Stair,
Feb. 18, 1720, in Graham, *l.c.* vol. ii. p. 416.
[5] Hoffmann's Report, Feb. 2 (N.S.), 1720, Vienna Archives.

circumstances. This would have been equivalent to a vote of censure on the Government. It was delayed only by assurances given by the ministry to individual members, that the cession of the Rock was not intended.[1] On January 25 Craggs told the Commons that he had a statement to make to the House about Gibraltar and Port Mahon, but that he would await an occasion when more members were present.[2] Later he wrote to Stair : "What I said upon this subject in the House of Commons was altogether unavoidable, since . . . without such a seasonable interposition, within less than half an hour an address to the King would have been proposed there for retaining Gibraltar, which upon all accounts it was highly necessary to prevent ".[3]

In order to test the mood of Parliament, Stanhope himself now proposed the introduction of a Bill that would permit the King to dispose of Gibraltar as seemed to him best for the country. The alarming result of this proposal is described in one of Stanhope's letters.[4]

You cannot imagine what a stir this attempt made among the public, which everywhere rose in indignation at the mere suspicion that we might in peace be deprived of this place, after so many successes in a war unjustly begun by Cardinal Alberoni. One thing that did much to inflame public opinion was a rumour spread by our adversaries that the King had given a formal engagement to surrender the place ; they thought they had in this a means of attacking the ministry. A great many pamphlets were published,[5] to rouse the public and to prepare it to undertake further campaigns rather than cede Gibraltar. It was impossible to stem the tide, and the wisest course was to drop the proposal in Parliament ; for had it been pressed, we would unquestionably have got the reverse of what we intended, and we ran the risk of seeing a Bill passed that would have tied the King's hands for ever.

For the present at least the Government were convinced that they must refuse every request to cede Gibraltar, whether made by

---

[1] Thos. Brodrick to Lord Chancellor Middleton, Jan. 24, 1720 (O.S., Feb. 4, N.S.), printed in Coxe, *Robert Walpole* (1798), vol. ii. p. 183.

[2] Hoffmann's Report of Feb. 6, 1720, Vienna Archives.

[3] Craggs to Stair, Feb. 18, 1720, S.P. 104/31. Graham, *l.c.* vol. ii. pp. 144-5, writes *reasonable* in error for *seasonable*.

[4] Stanhope to Schaub, Mar. 28, 1720, S.P. 78/167. This has been incorrectly reported by Wiesener, *l.c.* vol. iii. p. 297, writing from second-hand information.

[5] None of these seems to have been preserved.

France or by Spain, though Lord Stanhope did not accept the rebuff as final. When, after the Madrid declaration of January 26, Spain asked for Gibraltar, England refused categorically.

As for Gibraltar, much as the King of Great Britain was inclined, for the sake of avoiding war, to please the King of Spain by ceding this place for an equivalent, the events of the war and the expenses and losses that it has imposed on the subjects of His Britannic Majesty have so changed conditions that there can at present be no question of such a cession.

This answer could do little harm in Spain, as the Spanish requests were not *conditiones sine quibus non*. But in France the refusal was taken as a form of treachery on the part of an ally. Dubois' anxieties are visible in his letters to Stanhope,[1] in whom he frequently confided, and to Destouches, who was not to let any-one know of them except Lord Stanhope.[2] When in the morning of February 17 Dubois received news of England's refusal, he immediately took it to the Regent, whom it upset intensely. His honour, so he said, was besmirched in Spain and in France, he was disgraced before all Europe ; for he had been led to believe that England would cede Gibraltar, and he had been allowed to promise it to Spain ; and now he was to appear as a man who had vilely abused the trust of the King of Spain. At first the Duke of Orleans, who possessed all the pride and self-assurance of the *Roi Soleil* without his dignity and grace, reproached Dubois for having shown the King of Spain's declaration to the English and Austrian ambassadors before he had made sure of England's readiness to cede Gibraltar, adding that no one else would have been forgiven this mistake.[3] At once England's enemies at the French Court raised their heads anew. Law spoke of the coming war with England, and how people would then see the value of his system.[4] Dubois saw his policy and his position endangered, unless England came to his aid.

Neither England nor France could give way. At Dubois' request Lord Stair went to the Regent without waiting for instructions from

[1] Dubois to Stanhope, Feb. 17, 1720. See Sevelinges, *Mémoires secrets du Cardinal Dubois*, vol. i. p. 309.

[2] Dubois to Stanhope, Feb. 24, 1720. See Sevelinges, *l.c.* p. 311.

[3] Stair to Craggs, Feb. 22, 1720, S.P. 78/167.

[4] (*Hardwicke*) *State Papers*, vol. ii. p. 608.

London. He had hardly entered the room before the Regent addressed him furiously, saying that as King George had given him his word, the Regent hoped he would not break it. When Stair answered that that was before the war, Orleans replied that he had reason to believe the King at heart still felt as before. Shortly afterwards Stair received general instructions in two letters from Craggs, one French, one English.[1] The first was to be shown to the Regent, and in it there was little more than a hint at the decisive factor, public opinion :

> Son Altesse Royale fera aussi quelque attention à l'indisposition où sont les peuples du roi contre une restitution de cette nature après une guerre dont il ne leur doit revenir d'autre fruit que la paix.

The letter in English, however, was plain and emphatic :

> As well His Majesty's servants as people of all other interests and denominations in this country agree that the cession of that place would not only be a ridicule upon our successes in this war, but that the possession of it will be a great security to our trade in the Mediterranean. And therefore, tho' His Majesty were ever so much disposed to part with it, it may well be doubted whether he would have it in his power so to do.

The Regent now tried, by moving the negotiations to London, to overcome Britain's stubbornness. The two secretaries of the French Embassy, Chammorel and Destouches, were not sufficiently important to carry on such negotiations ; so the old intention of sending a new head to the Embassy, which had been vacant since Iberville left, was now executed. Count Senneterre [2] had been appointed to the Court of St. James a year earlier, but for reasons that are no longer known he had not yet assumed his duties in London. He now came armed with the fullest possible information, in a memorial even more complete than those usually issued to French ambassadors in the eighteenth century. In it all the important characters at the English Court were depicted with startling accuracy and knowledge, from George I and his son down to the King's Turkish valet. Its valuable information about the English

---

[1] Both dated Feb. 18, 1720, S.P. 104/31.

[2] It had first been intended to send the Marquis d'Allègre ; but as his wife was believed to be a friend and convinced supporter of the Pretender, he was not sent. Cf. Stair to Craggs, Jan. 22, 1719, S.P. 78/163.

and German advisers of George I, and about their mutual relations, could only have been given by Dubois, thanks to his political experience and his intimate connexion with Stanhope and Craggs.[1]

The appointment of Senneterre had all the appearance of a challenge to England. He brought a strongly worded note from the Regent to George I ;[2] and he was accompanied by one Monsieur de Plénœuf, a friend of John Law, a supporter of the " old system ", witty, full of intrigues, and an old pedant.[3] It was Plénœuf who sent John Law reports from London about the South Sea Bubble. The divisions of the French Court were thus reflected in the French Embassy in London : for Destouches was a follower and regular correspondent of Dubois ; he complained that Plénœuf knew as little of politics as of finance, and was only collecting material to " upset our system ".[4]

The English Government awaited Senneterre's arrival with mistrust and caution.[5] They intended to receive him only after hearing the Regent's reply to the letter sent to Stair, but intended for the Regent's eyes ; and if the ambassador talked too big, they would answer him in kind. Should France continue to press her demands, they would let Parliament decide on the fate of Gibraltar.

However, Senneterre's attitude was much more restrained than was expected. In his audience with the King he was moderate, and George I, as was his wont, avoided all business discussion. Stanhope admitted that any " vivacity " that appeared in the conferences with Senneterre was rather on his own side. When Senneterre pointed out that the Regent was bound by his promise to the Spaniards, Craggs replied coolly that it was the Regent's fault if he promised something which was not his to give. The Government now found it convenient to let the House of Commons, with the support of all parties, approve the motion to call up all absent Members in order to prevent, if need be, the cession of Gibraltar. Hoffmann was told that if France again asked about Gibraltar she would get the answer : " *De quoi vous mêlez-vous ?* "

Hoffmann's interest in the question of Gibraltar was not due

---

[1] Dubois to Senneterre, Apr. 13, 1719, Aff. étr. 323. See Appendix 6.
[2] Cf. Wiesener, *l.c.* vol. iii. p. 292.
[3] Cf. Wallenrodt, May 27/June 7, 1720, Prussian State Archives.
[4] Destouches to Dubois, May 13, 1720, Aff. étr. 331.
[5] For what follows cf. especially Hoffmann's Reports, Vienna Archives.

merely to curiosity or to his fears of a conflict between the two allies of Charles VI. Its cession seemed to him against the interest of Austria, as he foresaw the danger to his master's position in Italy should France and Spain be drawn together again : for then the English fleet would be the Emperor's only help.

The unfriendly reception of Senneterre was only intended to show that England would object to any pressure in the question of Gibraltar ; but it left relations with France so strained that ministers began to fear that the question was being used as a pretext for a coming change of system.[1] John Law, Torcy, and their friends were demanding war against England. In February 1720 Law asked if the messenger who was come from England had brought the cession of Gibraltar ;[2] and a week later he remarked : " The gentlemen of England must not higgle over Gibraltar. It is more than enough kindness if they are allowed to keep Port Mahon." When asked if he was really aiming at war, he replied, " I do not wish for war, but I do not fear it ".[3]

Dubois' position was growing steadily more difficult, and the only person who could save him was Lord Stanhope. In answer to his cries for help Stanhope decided to go to Paris.[4]

With Stanhope's arrival the Regent's tone concerning Gibraltar changed so completely [5] that Stanhope suspected some misunderstanding between France and Spain ; more probably the Regent's vacillating character was so influenced by Stanhope's personality that he was drawn back to the path of Anglo-French friendship.

Stanhope wrote to Schaub that he began by complaining of the attitude of Orleans and Dubois in the question of Gibraltar, which looked like the prelude to a change of system. If France continued to send couriers up and down between Paris and Madrid without informing England of the content of the dispatches, the King would be forced to begin separate negotiations with Spain and to advise his allies to do likewise. Orleans and Dubois strongly denied

---

[1] Stanhope to Schaub, Mar. 28, 1720, S.P. 78/167.

[2] Pulteney's Report, Feb. 10, 1720, S.P. 78/166.

[3] (*Hardwicke*) *State Papers*, vol. ii. p. 609.

[4] " *M. l'abbé du Bois s'est cru perdu, a crié au secours et m'a fait venir ici* " : Stanhope to St. Saphorin, Paris, Apr. 1, 1720, S.P. 78/167.

[5] For what follows cf. Stanhope's letters from Paris, S.P. 78/167 ; Chammorel to Dubois, Apr. 1 (N.S.), 1720, Aff. étr. 331 ; Hoffmann, Apr. 2 (N.S.), 1720, Vienna Archives ; Wallenrodt's Reports of Mar. 22/Apr. 2, Mar. 25/Apr. 5, Apr. 1/12, 1720, Prussian State Archives.

that they had come to any agreement whatever with Spain. Stanhope then said that he knew from a good source that some of the Regent's ministers were advising a complete change of system and even war with France's best allies. This the Regent could not deny, but he assured Stanhope that there was only one minister who was concerned with foreign affairs, that the others did not count, and that he himself was master of all. Then the Regent "listened patiently and kindly to many harsh things I told him about his own position, and that of France, about some of his ministers, and how necessary for him I believed it to be that he should cultivate the friendship of his allies if he did not wish to risk certain destruction ".[1]

It was now possible to agree on a joint policy. Both States were to send an envoy to Spain. Till Colonel Stanhope could reach Madrid Luke Schaub would represent England, and would try to obtain the evacuation of Sicily and Sardinia before the opening of the congress. Schaub was not to discuss Gibraltar before this congress ; and though the Regent would not promise the same of his envoy, he agreed that the subject should be avoided in practice. With the formal promise that neither would make definitive peace without the other, confidence was restored between the allies. Orleans and Stanhope could now discuss in calmer tones the position in the north, the value of John Law's " system ", the choice of a seat for the coming congress, and also the possibility of Dubois being made a cardinal. He had recently risen at astonishing pace from a mere abbé to be Archbishop of Cambrai, and he himself compared his career with that of St. Ambrose. Possibly even his Protestant friends could help him to the purple ; Lord Stanhope wrote to St. Saphorin that if he could secure Vienna's support for the advancement of Dubois, he would be doing his King a very real service.

Stanhope returned to London amidst general praise. Craggs wrote to him that

The difficulties you have surmounted, the good disposition you have raised and confirmed and the clear conviction you have given His Royal Highness, the Regent, that it is his interest to persevere in joint measures with the King, have established matters on that foot, which is most pleasing to His Majesty and do afford the agreeable

[1] Stanhope to Schaub, Mar. 28, 1720, S.P. 78/167.

prospect of seeing our great work completed with the same union with which it has been carried on.[1]

For the English people the question of Gibraltar was closed, even though Stanhope gave the Court of Madrid to understand that there might be some hope of future negotiations if only they let the subject drop completely for the present.

[1] Craggs to Stanhope, Mar. 24 (N.S.), 1720, S.P. 78/163.

CHAPTER VIII

FROM the expulsion of the Stuarts till the middle of the eighteenth century every enemy of England adopted the cause of the Pretender; France, Sweden, Spain, and later France again, allied themselves with him in order to win the support of a part of the British people against the Government. But the conflict between Stuarts and Hanoverians was only a side issue in the great struggles with these countries, while the wars of Succession on the Continent were inextricably linked with the main issues of the century. Had Louis XIV won the war of the Spanish Succession and made satellite states of Spain and the Netherlands, he would have outshone the Habsburgs and would have seriously damaged England's prosperity. In the war of the Austrian Succession Maria Theresa defended the power and unity of the Habsburg dominions against the last onslaught of the Bourbons.

The Stuarts represented no vital interest of the British people. Their claim was in no way connected with the development of Parliamentary government, with trade, commerce or agriculture, with the colonies or even religion. The Roman Catholics could not expect to regain their influence, for there were too few of them in England, and those in Ireland had no say even in their own affairs. The Established Church and the Nonconformists, Whigs and Tories had equally little to gain from a Stuart restoration. The Pretender's proclamations contained no programme, only empty phrases about the Usurper and the rightful King, with little that was positive; they generally dealt with England's current difficulties, which they promised to remove, and for which the House of Hanover was always made responsible. The dissolution of the Union with Scotland was only occasionally mentioned, as it might gladden Scots hearts, but would alienate the English.

This lack of ideas, this futile show of meaningless names and titles, is in striking contrast with the activity, strength, prosperity, and spirit of initiative in English life and politics. Far-sighted statesmen, like Stanhope, Craggs, and later Walpole, were steadily building up the modern British Empire, while foolish enthusiasts wanted to alter the course of history though they had nothing to offer but a fading dynastic idea represented by a thoroughly insignificant person.

In 1708, 1715, 1719, and 1745, the Stuarts made their main attempts to regain the lost throne, but the threat to England was continuous.[1] The Jacobites were a community, almost a State within the State, composed of conspirators — Englishmen, Scots, and Irishmen, at loggerheads with the existing régime or ousted by it. Of those who lived in British territory little is recorded, as they were closely watched and had to be very cautious. They were strongest in Scotland, and had a certain following in the west and north of England. Abroad they had greater freedom of action ; foreign Governments did not always hinder their activities, some even listened to their arguments, though ostensibly helping England in its constant struggle against them. On one occasion a Jacobite cipher was disclosed to the English Government by none other than the Abbé Dubois.[2]

James Edward, the Pretender,[3] who was honoured by his followers as His Majesty James III, lived under the name of the Chevalier de St. George. In outward appearance he was a true Stuart and strikingly like his father James II. The painter Kneller used to say that he more than anyone else could vouch for the genuineness of the Prince born in 1688, as he had so often studied and painted the features of the Stuarts. He and his father were tall and lean, both had a prominent chin, a wide mouth, a big nose, and a narrow oval face, made even longer by the enormous peruke. Yet in expression they were different : James II disagreeable and aloof, resolute and stubborn, his son delicate, gentle, and irresolute. Unable to distinguish essentials or to give his followers a strong

---

[1] Valuable material about the Jacobites is to be found in *The Calendar of the Stuart Papers*, vols. i.-v. (1902–1912), Historical Manuscripts Commission.

[2] Stair to Craggs, Jan. 30, 1719, S.P. 78/163.

[3] Cf. C. S. Terry, *The Chevalier de St. George* (1901) ; M. Haile, *James Francis Edward, the old Chevalier* (1907).

lead, James Edward remained inactive in the background, awaiting
opportunities, while the Jacobites worked for him. He assumed a
dignified air of patient suffering, and till his death played the rôle
of a king driven from his realms by a hostile fate, but still convinced
of his divine right. He considered himself a true Englishman ;
English was his mother tongue, though he had learnt to speak
French and Italian fluently.[1] In short, he was a true representative
of the social polish and distinction of his family.

Though he had always been a faithful Roman Catholic, yet he
was sure he understood his duties towards the Protestant people
over whom he was destined to rule, and he meant to perform these
honestly, for he remembered what had happened to his father. For
the day when fortune should call him to the throne, he had decided
on at least one point in his programme.

Who can doubt my desire [he writes] to favour the Catholics, but
who does not know that in the long run I should do them more harm
than present good by going too far. . . . I am a Catholic, but I am a
King, and subjects must be protected no matter what their religion.
I am a King, but as the Pope himself said to me, I am not an apostle,
and am not obliged to convert my subjects except by my example.[2]

He saw, too, that he must avoid the importunities of his co-
religionists :

Not all Catholics are saints, alas ! and only too many of them are
more ambitious than truly zealous . . . they would prefer never to
see me restored, than not to find themselves on my right hand and on
my left.[3]

He complains that as he would be living among Protestants, he
would have to give preference to them in distributing places and
honours. He had already dismissed all Jesuits from his entourage,
for he knew what England felt about them.

In return the Pretender expected the Protestants to appreciate
his good will and to give him their confidence. He could never see
that in the age of the Glorious Revolution and the Act of Settlement a Roman Catholic was unsuited to the British throne. During
his short kingship in 1716 he created a very bad impression by
refusing to attend a Te Deum in Perth that was being celebrated

---

[1] Cf. Dickson, *The Jacobite Attempt of 1719* (Scot. Hist. Soc. 19), App.
No. 35.

[2] *Stuart Papers*, vol. v. p. 515.   [3] *Ibid.* vol. v. p. 514.

after one of the regular Church of England services. He had no
more understanding than his father for the requirements of the
English people whom he wished to rule.

In a detailed account of his reasons he said :

> I cannot well understand why some people have laid so much
> stress on my assisting once at a *Te Deum* . . . except they think by
> it that the people will be imposed on and conclude that I am either
> a Protestant or in a fair way towards it, and in that case it cannot
> be wondered I should decline that step, in which, conscience apart,
> there would be so manifest a dissimulation. . . . I have given sufficient
> proofs of . . . the happiness they (my Protestant subjects) may
> enjoy under me . . . either they have and will receive me as a
> Catholic, or they will not. . . . It was not, I am sure, either ambition
> or the prospect of future greatness and happiness that determined me
> to this undertaking . . . their delivery was my principal object,
> towards the effecting of which, if they will not join with me, it will
> be their misfortune more than mine.[1]

Hundreds or even thousands of Jacobites living in France and
in the Netherlands were a serious threat to the British Government
mainly because they formed a widespread organization controlled
by the Duke of Mar,[2] Secretary of State, *i.e.* First Minister, to James
Edward.   In 1715, as General of the Scottish forces, he had been
defeated on Sheriffmuir ; now he was serving the Stuarts with the
pen instead of the sword.   He had not the qualities of his pre-
decessor Bolingbroke, but he was a diligent worker, who corresponded with Jacobites all over the world, and in his letters he
appears to be a devoted servant of James Edward, though his
secret aim was to win George I's favour and to forsake the Stuarts.
His political agents negotiated both openly and secretly at the
European Courts : in Madrid Sir Patrick Lawless, in Paris Arthur
Dillon, an Irishman who had won fame as a general in the French
army, in Vienna John Walkingshaw of Burrowfield, and most
important of them all, the Duke of Ormonde.

Behind the little group of ambitious men, Oxford and Bolingbroke, Mar and Ormonde, who were Jacobites only because they
could not get on with the Government of the Hanoverians, stood

---

[1] *Stuart Papers*, vol. iv. p. 11 *seq.*

[2] John Erskine, Earl of Mar, was given a patent by the Pretender
creating him Duke of Mar (Oct. 22, 1715 ; see *Stuart Papers*, vol. i. p. 455),
and was given this title in subsequent Jacobite correspondence, as th﹥
Pretender was styled James III.

the mass of those who were Jacobite by conviction. Some remained loyal to James as to a prince cheated of his inheritance ; the Scots, because he was a Stuart ; the Catholics, because he was of the right faith. Many preferred exile and loss of property to recognition of the " Elector ", the " Usurper ". They saw hope in every difficulty, real or supposed, of the Government ; they were always inclined to over-estimate their numbers in England, and to see a Jacobite in every Tory, in every opponent of the Government ; they always supposed foreign Powers ready to take up their cause. Wherever in Europe there was hostility towards, or irritation with England, the messengers of James Edward came trying to stir up a war that would bring about the downfall of George I.

While a numerous group of Jacobites followed the Pretender everywhere, a second group was to be found with the Queen Mother, Mary of Modena, in St. Germains. In 1673 she had married the Duke of York only because she was told by Louis XIV and the Pope that she could serve her religion better as Duchess of York than in a cloister. Parliament had tried to prevent the marriage ; one of the ministers advised her to return to Italy ; and the people in the street burnt a caricature of the Pope to show their displeasure at the Catholic marriage of the heir to the throne. Later, as Queen, she appeared as the embodiment of the King's Roman Catholic tendencies. When she bore him an heir, she made his downfall certain. Next, she lived thirty years in exile, and after the death of James II she divided her life between pious practices and activities on her son's behalf. One of her last cares was to win John Law, the coming man in France, for the Stuart cause.[1] It was not a great deal she could do for her son, but she took part in the Jacobite correspondence, though she declared she disliked politics. Occasionally she approached the Duke of Orleans in money matters ; the Duke had continued the large pension that had been paid her by Louis XIV, in order to influence the needy Stuarts. Because she lived near the French Court and enjoyed its respect, she seemed indispensable. Her influence on James Edward was such that Mar grew jealous and had to be appeased. James Edward was torn between the strictly Catholic course urged by the Queen Mother, and the Protestant interest now represented by Mar instead of Bolingbroke. But he thought he was going his own way, and yielding to his mother only as far as became a dutiful son.

[1] *Stuart Papers*, vol. v. p. 404.

Are not Queen Mary and I the most unhappy people of the world ?
. . . Our first view is equally my service and interest, but to see them
equally suffer, while Queen Mary has all the trouble and none of the
agreement of it, is what that very duty can never allow.[1]

After the suppression of " The 'Fifteen " and the subsequent
trials, crowds of British Jacobites left the country with the intention
of returning as soon as success seemed near.   Hundreds of them had
settled at Avignon, where James Edward had since formed his
Court.   It was a hard blow when, as a result of the Triple Alliance
of January 4, 1717, the Pretender was no longer able to live north
of the Alps.[2]   His friends thought that his voluntary departure
gave him a claim to the gratitude of France, and negotiations were
carried on to secure his financial position.   The Pope too, they felt,
would be glad if the use of force against his territory in the South
of France were avoided, and might well raise his pension, at least
to the amount received by the Swedish Queen Christina.   So James
Edward left Avignon, and in return his demands were met.   Even
his personal debts incurred at Avignon were paid by the French
Government.[3]

Since the time when it seemed likely that he would be forced to
leave Avignon, the question of his future home was much discussed.
Zweibrücken, which belonged to the King of Sweden, was mentioned,
also the dominions of the Emperor, as he had not yet joined the
policy of the Western Powers.   James Edward would have liked
best to go to Flanders, which Queen Mary, too, considered better
than Zweibrücken,[4] but the Duke of Lorraine, who was attached to
the Stuart cause and well versed in European politics, thought that
" if the Emperor were to grant an asylum it would be in his hereditary states rather than in Flanders ".[5]

John Walkingshaw of Burrowfield was sent to Vienna, under the
pseudonym of Mr. Obrian, with instructions from James Edward.[6]
He was to endeavour to get the Emperor to allow them to reside
in some place of his dominions, especially in Flanders ; by their

---

[1] Peter Knight (James III) to the Duke of Mar, *Stuart Papers*, vol. iv.
p. 393 *seq.*   The pseudonyms used in the Stuart Correspondence have been
replaced here and elsewhere by the historical names.

[2] Cf. Vol. I. p. 323.

[3] Stair to Robethon, Jan. 28, 1717, Stowe Coll. 388, ix. f. 9, B.M.

[4] *Stuart Papers*, vol. iii. p. 147.

[5] *Ibid.* p. 578.   [6] *Ibid.* pp. 192-3.

being so near England the Elector's affairs in Britain would soon be in such disorder that he would not be in a condition to give his Imperial Majesty any trouble. He was to do all he could to gain some of the ministers for James' cause, and to this end he was to use the arguments most likely to induce them to espouse it at least privately, such as the advantage to the House of Austria and the danger of the treaty between the Elector, the Regent of France, and Holland, which could only have been designed against the Emperor. Furthermore he was to inform the Imperial ministers of the aversion of the generality of the people to the Elector, and of the new causes of aversion which the present Government gave them daily by cruelties and alterations of the laws.

In spite of the existing discord between the Vienna Court and George I, Walkingshaw's mission had little success. He was not received by the ministers, and to prevent him presenting his credentials to the Emperor, it was alleged that they contained a technical error. After months of waiting he was admitted to the presence of Prince Eugene, who only told him that his stay in Vienna might do prejudice to the Emperor, and advised him to leave. He was hardly allowed to await the formal recall by his sovereign, which befitted a true diplomat.[1] Meanwhile the London Government had heard of his mission and even knew his real name and the address he used for his correspondence. Prince Eugene could honestly protest to the British Ambassador that the attitude of the Imperial Government had always been loyal ; but with less sincerity the Austrian ministers claimed that they knew nothing about this man coming by order of the Pretender.[2]

On a similar mission Carnegy had been sent to Switzerland to inquire whether Lucerne or one of the other cantons would allow James Edward to reside in its territory.[3] Already during Queen Anne's reign the possibility of his going there, should he be banned from Lorraine, had been mentioned. But now all the cantons had acknowledged George I.[4] Lucerne would not have him, because it was afraid of the Protestant cantons of Berne and Zurich, which kept up friendly relations with England. Only a few months

---

[1] *Ibid.* vol. iv. pp. 89-90.
[2] Stanyan to Stanhope, Mar. 20, Apr. 10, 21, 1717 ; Stanhope to Stanyan, Mar. 12 (O.S.), 1717, S.P. 80/34.
[3] *Stuart Papers*, vol. iii. p. 270.
[4] Hoffmann, Dec. 21, 1714, Vienna Archives.

previously George I had asked all the cantons to forbid the Pretender to travel through their territory or to stay in it. The Roman Catholic cantons had answered that to refuse the Chevalier passage was contrary to international law, and that he himself was surely not thinking of living in Switzerland. First Bellinzona, and next Altdorf were now recommended, and Carnegy had succeeded in winning the consent of the cantonal authorities when he learned from Mar that the Duke of Orleans had been obliged not to allow James Edward to stay north of the Alps.

The banned prince had to go to Italy, where the Pope was willing to receive him. In February 1717 a large party travelled across the South of France, and through frost and snow to the Mont Cenis.[1] The coaches had to be taken to pieces ; the Pretender, the Duke of Ormonde, and a few more were carried up on chairs, the others rode up on mules. Going down past Nouvallaise, which belonged to the King of Sicily, they reached Susa, and everywhere they were courteously received by royal officers.[2] The British ministers could now feel safer, since the snowy barrier of the Alps stood between them and the Pretender.

James Edward expected only his personal suite, a few people of quality, and some of his gentlemen, to follow him into his Italian exile. The others he left free to choose where they would reside. In doleful letters [3] he recommended particularly Holland and Flanders, for the Jacobites already there " do not apprehend they will be disturbed and think that any who are obliged to leave France will get a safe residence there, provided they behave discreetly in going thither privately in small companies, not many to be in one place and the people of distinction passing under other names ".[4] The fewer the Jacobites who remained in Paris and St. Germains, the better ; but most of them might at least be able to remain in France. Only the most distinguished of them could be required under the terms of the Triple Alliance to leave ; but if they lived a retired, quiet life, and not many in one place, it was likely that the British Government might not think it worth while to demand their being sent away.[5] Those who had gone to Toulouse were advised to disperse thereabout ; those at Bordeaux the Duke of

---

[1] *Stuart Papers*, vol. iii. p. 526.   [2] *Ibid.* p. 539.
[3] *E.g. Ibid.* pp. 490, 495, 502, 504, 506.
[4] *Ibid.* p. 490.   [5] *Ibid.* p. 502.

Mar asked to leave the town and the coast, and disperse themselves
up and down the country, by which they would be less liable to
observation ; he hoped they would not be molested, for this station
was the most convenient for transporting them to their own country
when the time came.[1]

The Jacobites were now most numerous in the parts of the
Continent nearest to England.   The British Government made
efforts to drive them to more distant countries, but was not always
successful.   Holland obeyed willingly, as she was on friendly terms
with England and partly dependent on her.   Though a Jacobite
agent told Prince Eugene that they did not lack friends in Holland,[2]
not much is heard of their activities in that country.

In Flanders, which had been a source of danger to the English
throne in the Wars of the Roses, the numerous Jacobites were a
more serious threat.   In 1716 and 1717 their presence was frequently
the subject of diplomatic negotiations between England and Austria.
The British resident in Brussels, Leathes, was told again and again
to watch them closely, to intercept their letters, to report on their
activities, and to send lists of their names to London.[3]   In May
1717 the British ambassador in Vienna, Abraham Stanyan, complained to Prince Eugene that in the Austrian Netherlands a great
number of rebels were obviously waiting for the Swedish invasion
in order to swarm into England ; he asked that the vice-governor,
the Marquis de Prié, should order them out of the country.[4]   After
this request had been laid before the Emperor, Stanyan was told
that any subject of the King of England whom the resident should
name, would be turned out.[5]   But apparently Prié felt this was going
too far, and suddenly the negotiations in Vienna were resumed in
quite a different tone.   The Memorial given to the British ambassador said that his demands were based on the false premise
that there were in the Netherlands a large number of British subjects known to have taken part in the Scottish rebellion.[6]   None

---

[1] *Ibid.* p. 503.

[2] *Ibid.* vol. v. p. 533.

[3] Townshend to Leathes, Feb. 21, Oct. 5, 1716 ; Sunderland to Leathes,
May 10, 17, 31, June 17, July 19, 1717, S.P. 104/16.

[4] Stanyan to Sunderland, May 8, 1717, S.P. 80/34.

[5] Marquis Rialp to Stanyan, May 22, 1717 (enclosed in Stanyan's Report
of the same date), S.P. 80/34.

[6] " Réponse donnée par M. le Marquis de Rialp, le 7 juillet, 1717,"
S.P. 80/34.

the less, the Marquis de Prié had been ordered to refuse asylum to persons of quality who were suspect to the British Government, and to let all others know that they had to refrain from any action or correspondence detrimental to England, or they would be punished according to the laws of the land. This was all that the Emperor could do ; the Dutch did not refuse hospitality to refugees, and to demand this from the Emperor was an encroachment on his sovereign rights. If, however, Leathes had occasion to suspect a particular refugee, he could put the matter before Prié.

England would not accept this refusal, particularly when Austria could not do without the help of the English fleet in the Mediterranean. When a week later Stanyan presented another Note,[1] the Austrian ministers felt relieved, for by now they were worried about the brusque tone they had adopted. Stanyan, noticing their relief, declared promptly but untruthfully that he had not sent the Austrian Memorial to London. The Note maintained that it was by no means a question only of " dissatisfied vassals of his Britannic Majesty, who had fled to the Netherlands ", but of persons convicted of high treason, who had taken up arms against their King, had wished to destroy their own country, and who, still filled with the spirit of rebellion, considered the Netherlands the best place to work out their plans. Nor should the ministers forget how painful it must be to the King that, while his other neighbours helped him in every way in dealing with the rebels, and refused them shelter, these rebels should find a safe refuge in the territories of the Emperor.

The following weeks were probably filled with correspondence between Brussels and Vienna. On September 4 Stanyan reported that Prié was to be given whatever instructions England desired.[2] The change was due not to Stanyan's arguments alone, but also to a successful Spanish attack on Sardinia, which made the support of the English fleet more than ever necessary to Austria.

From France the Jacobites were never expelled. The Court of St. Germains, which was the natural centre of Jacobite activities in France, could not be suppressed ; at most it could be kept quiet ; its constant relations with the indefatigable Jacobites in the great city of Paris could not be controlled, nor could the whole of France

---

[1] Dated July 13, 1717 ; a copy is in Stanyan's letter to Sunderland, July 14, 1717, S.P. 80/34.

[2] Stanyan's Report, Sept. 4, 1717, 80/35.

be continually searched for friends of the Stuarts. They often
became troublesome even to the Duke of Orleans, and throughout
the period 1716–1718 were the subject of negotiations between
England and France. The Earl of Stair apparently had an excellent
system of espionage, by which he always knew the abode of the
Duke of Ormonde or the Duke of Mar better than the French
authorities. With the results of his enquiries carefully written down
he frequently waited upon the Regent, demanding the expulsion
of certain refugees,[1] or complaining that Dillon, while a Lieutenant-
General in the French army, could openly act as a minister of the
Pretender. Sometimes he came on instructions from his own
Government;[2] more often on his own initiative. The Regent feigned
to be astonished and indignant that his repeated orders had been
disregarded by the rebel leaders, and promised to have them
arrested if they did not leave immediately ; all Jacobites would
be compelled to leave the country. With his gift for listening
patiently to disagreeable things and answering politely, the Regent
never wearied of renewing his promises ; but nothing was done.
At last Stair seemed to realize the hopelessness of his efforts : " The
removal of the rebels hangs just as it did, every week the Regent
tells me they shall be sent away and they still remain ".[3] Though
James Edward had been forced to go to Italy, his followers remained
behind ; Jacobitism carried on its threatening activities, secretly in
England and Scotland, far more openly in France.

James Edward not only lacked a kingdom, he lacked both
fortune and income. His main source of revenue was the pension
of 50,000 *livres* a month paid to his mother by the French Court,
and 5000 Roman crowns a quarter from the Pope.[4] The total
annual income of the Stuarts would therefore be 683,000 French
livres ; in English money, £42,000 or £43,000. From this sum,
which was not small for those days, many expenses had to be
met ; among them, large annuities to followers in distress on the
Continent. A certain Mr. Dicconson was for many years treasurer

---

[1] Stair's Reports, June 2, July 7, 1717, S.P. 78/161 ; Aug. 18, Sept. 21,
Nov. 24, 1717, S.P. 78/162 ; Apr. 16, 1718, S.P. 78/163 ; May 4, 1718,
S.P. 78/164.

[2] Craggs to Stair, Apr. 17, 1718, S.P. 104/29.

[3] Stair to Craggs, Aug. 21, 1718, S.P. 78/162.

[4] Cf. *Stuart Papers*, vol. v. p. xx *seq.*

in St. Germains, and controlled all income and expenditure.[1]   In 1718 he paid about 46,000 *livres* in annuities.   Individual names are not given, but the places to which the money was sent—12,270 *livres* to Paris, 11,905 to Bordeaux, 2405 to Holland, 5072 to Brussels, 535 to Liège, 4403 to St. Omer, 9373 distributed in St. Germains — must have been the Jacobite centres on the Continent.

Although these annuities did not absorb one tenth of the Stuart income, the conscientious treasurer declared that with so little money they could no longer be paid ; [2] but James Edward himself decided that their payment could be continued.[3]   Far more was spent on the upkeep of two courts, on the travels of political agents, and for many other purposes in different countries.   It is surprising that the Pretender still, on occasion, offered to aid friendly rulers with large sums of money.   In August 1717 it was hoped that Peter the Great and Charles XII would make a treaty of peace and then work together for the Stuart cause, their condition being the payment of £100,000 with which to make due and timely preparations.   To raise this sum by a collection from all Jacobites in Great Britain would be unsafe and subject to discovery, but it was hoped that twenty of James Edward's principal friends might raise five thousand pounds each, which would be repaid with due recompense after James' restoration.[4]   Though the plan was never carried out, it shows the Pretender's confidence in the resources and devotion of his followers at home.

On the way to the Papal States James Edward passed through Turin and met the King of Sicily ; he hoped that this prince, who had not yet accepted the Treaty of Utrecht, would become his friend.   But Victor Amadeus was too clever to espouse a cause that had so little prospect of success.   The interview was confined to an exchange of compliments, and when the Stuart came to the question of assistance he met with a curt refusal.[5]   James wrote to his mother a short, disgruntled account of the interview.   But at least his appearance and manner seem to have made a good impression on the Dowager Duchess of Savoy.   She wrote to Queen Mary that she found him handsome, and endowed with the wit, the air, and the manners which became his rank.[6]   James continued

---

[1] *Stuart Papers*, vol. iv. p. 26 *seq.* ; vol. v. p. 425 *seq.*, p. 593 *seq.*
[2] *Ibid.* vol. iv. p. 398 *seq.*   [3] *Ibid.* p. 462.
[4] *Ibid.* p. 520 *seq.*   [5] *Ibid.* p. 119.   [6] *Ibid.* p. 143.

his journey through Bologna and Imola to Pesaro, his immediate objective. Next he paid a short visit to Rome, but his friends advised him strongly not to settle there. " I wish ", wrote one of them, " there were no objection against this place's being his *séjour* for good and all, till he could go where he ought to be, for I never could be of opinion it was his interest to choose such an exile as Pesaro or Urbino in a corner of the world preferably to the place in the world where there is most correspondence with all the powers of Christendom." [1]

That James was strongly attracted by Rome, the seat of his great protector the Pope, and the eternal city of sacred memories, was quite natural. Like every traveller, he visited all the sights, studied antique and renaissance work, marvelled at the beauty of St. Peter's and of the statues on the Capitol, and was impressed by " the greatness of the old Romans and the littleness of the new ones ".[2] After a stay of a fortnight, he felt that he would need another month to see at leisure all that was to be seen. But his stay had a further purpose. He saw in private the Cardinals and all the foreign ministers except the Emperor's. The strictness of his incognito did not detract from the importance of these audiences. Then he was received by the Pope, " who ", he wrote to the Duke of Mar, " is a tall, lusty, well-looked man as you'll see for his age. I believe there may be wiser people in the world, but he has certainly very good sense, and was mighty easy with me, and kind to me. I wish you could have heard all he said to me in relation to religion, for I am sure it would have pleased you as it did me to find all my sentiments on that article confirmed by himself." [3]

But Mar disagreed. He reproached his King for going to Rome at all. Both Cardinal Gualterio, who had charge of the Pretender's affairs at the Court of Rome,[4] and Queen Mary had openly said that the prince had gone to Rome on purpose to show his great respect for the Catholic religion, and that he ardently desired to take part in the Corpus Christi procession. This might easily have revived the hardly forgotten mistrust of his Protestant friends in England and " should that happen, there may be an adieu bid to all hopes, and that demon would return seven times worse than before ".[5] Ormonde, too, wrote anxiously that " the Whigs will insinuate to the people that curiosity was only a pretence to cover

---

[1] *Ibid.* p. 285. [2] *Ibid.* p. 288 ; cf. also p. 282.
[3] *Ibid.* p. 288. [4] *Ibid.* vol. i. p. 242. [5] *Ibid.* vol. iv. p. 351.

some private bargain with the Pope to the prejudice of the Protestants ".[1] James tried to justify his actions :

My seeing the procession pass by here on Corpus Christi Day, and hearing the Pope's Mass on St. Peter's Day is but what all Protestants in the world are curious to see, and . . . they assist at them in the same manner that I did. As for any extraordinary devotion performed by me here, all the world knows that there has been nothing of it. I came . . . to satisfy my curiosity, and to speak about money, for I can assure you religion had no share in the journey.[2]

James paid a short visit to the Pope's country house at Castle Gandolfo (on the lake of St. Albans). Then on July 11, 1717, they arrived in Urbino, where James spent the winter in a spacious palace belonging to the Pope. Two centuries before, in the time of Raphael, the town had been a centre of culture and society ; now it was a forgotten village in the foothills of the Apennines. " You are in the land of the living ", James wrote to a friend in Lorraine ; " I am in a desert and between snow-covered mountains ; we only learn what happens in your countries so long afterwards that the position has often changed before we have news of it." [3]

The small group of followers that gathered round James was pompously termed the Court of Urbino. With the arrival of Mar in November 1717, Urbino became the headquarters of Jacobitism, though it was difficult to work from this remote corner. With every post, letters went to England, to France, and to the Netherlands ; with every post came news of events from the outside world. Decisions were made, instructions given, new connexions sought.

The social activities at the Court, too, benefited greatly from the presence of Mar. As a lover of art and music he had been enjoying Italian music at Venice and Bologna. Here he had some pretty good singers and instruments [4] at his disposal, and arranged small private concerts in his rooms in the palace three times a week. Lord Panmure played the bass fiddle, the Earl of Marischal the flute, and everyone gave of his best. Often the " King " looked in, and he really came to like Italian music.[5] But at other times he preferred lonely walks along the snowy paths of the Apennines.

After the Pretender's arrival in Urbino the English ministers

[1] *Stuart Papers,* p. 370.
[2] James II to the Duke of Mar, *ibid.* p. 394.
[3] *Ibid.* vol. v. p. 454.   [4] *Ibid.* p. 236.   [5] *Ibid.* p. 368.

must have felt that he was safely out of the way, but only a few weeks later a sensational incident brought him once more into the limelight. The Earl of Peterborough, whose extravagant journeys had gained him even greater notoriety in Europe than his celebrated conquest of Barcelona, had once again set out with a large retinue for Italy. He was received with military honours at Calais, stayed a while in Paris, and then continued his journey with peculiar haste.[1] No one would have suspected that the journey had other grounds than curiosity or health, had he not been followed by a crazy rumour that he intended to assassinate the Pretender. Mar did not believe that Peterborough was capable of undertaking so vile a thing.[2] Queen Mary and Dillon, too, considered that the story was hard to believe, but ought not to be neglected, so they sent an express to James. Cardinal Origo, the Legate of Bologna, informed James of an anonymous letter containing the assertion that Peterborough and a disguised monk had set out on the journey with this object.[3] After all these warnings James thought he was in real danger; when he learned that Peterborough was on papal territory at Bologna, he wrote immediately to Cardinal Origo, requesting him to arrest Peterborough with all his servants and papers. The Pope approved of all the Pretender's actions; for the person he acknowledged as King might with his full consent do exactly what he would do if he were on his throne in London with an accused criminal before him.[4] Accordingly Peterborough was arrested on September 11, 1717, and confined in Fort Urbano, where he was closely questioned, and his papers were examined. But no evidence against him could be found; he even pretended to have Jacobite sympathies. True, he had had several private audiences with George I, and had supped with him and his ladies two or three times before his departure, and he had much more money with him than was necessary.[5] Though these facts were no proof of his guilt, he was required to produce further proof of his innocence. There was much correspondence about the place and manner of his confinement. On October 15 he was allowed to leave Fort Urbano and was escorted back to Bologna with due ceremony, and he was released on parole till his innocence should be established. Meanwhile the Pope was so worried about the affair, and it had

---

[1] *Ibid.* vol. iv. pp. 510, 525. [2] *Ibid.* p. 517.
[3] F. W. Head, *The Fallen Stuarts* (1901), p. 202. [4] *Ibid.* p. 203.
[5] *Stuart Papers*, vol. v. p. 166 *seq.*, p. 574 *seq.*

caused him so much trouble that on November 14, at his request, James set Peterborough at liberty.

The English ministers were at first almost amused at the Earl's misfortune, and are said to have remarked : " Who cares for it or who will reclaim him ".[1] Soon, however, their attitude changed. People realized the affront to Parliament in the person of a member of the Upper House, and cried for revenge. Sunderland told the Austrian envoy, Hoffmann, that it was high time to settle accounts with the Pope, who had supported all enemies of England financially, had ordered days of prayer for the restoration of the Pretender, and had arrested Peterborough. Because of all this the Government had, he said, decided to bombard the Civita Vecchia and to make the vicars-general feel the arm of the law. Hoffmann, who, as representative of the Emperor, was the natural agent of Papal interests, took the opportunity thus offered to say a word for the Pope. How could they make such severe reprisals on behalf of this foolish vagabond lord ? At any rate satisfaction should be demanded first. Sunderland agreed and asked if Count Gallas, the Imperial envoy in Rome, could be entrusted with the task ; for England and Rome had no representatives accredited to each other because of the hostility of Protestant England to all that was Roman Catholic. There were English envoys in the other Italian states to smooth out difficulties ; but a conflict with the Papal Curia might easily become serious unless a friendly Power intervened.

Hoffmann felt that he could consent in the Emperor's name to Sunderland's request. Three days later he received the copy of instructions drawn up by the Secretary of State, Addison, and addressed to Count Gallas, as though he were a diplomat in the service of England.[2] He was to make five demands : the immediate liberation of the prisoner ; the declaration that the arrest had not been made on the Pope's authority ; the punishment of the Legate of Bologna ; a promise from the Pope never again to interfere in English affairs or to support the cause of the Pretender ; and finally, an assurance that he would not again permit British subjects to be molested in his territories, least of all in deference to the wishes of the Pretender. In case of refusal, a squadron of English

---

[1] *Stuart Papers*, p. 133.

[2] Addison to Gallas, Oct. 25, 1717 (enclosed with Hoffmann's Report of the same date), Vienna Archives.

warships would visit the papal coasts, " *où elle trouvera occasion de donner des marques du juste ressentiment de Sa Majesté* ".

The Emperor could hardly escape the role of mediator thus pressed upon him. Though he made a mild protest against the actual form adopted by the English, he declared that he would consider as a mark of confidence the commission thus irregularly entrusted direct to Count Gallas. He gave his envoy the desired orders, but at the same time advised the British Government to be conciliatory. Hoffmann and the Freiherr von Pendtenriedter, who had just come to London, were to remind the British ministers that the whole affair was after all due to Peterborough's notoriously restless spirit.[1] Was it not going too far, to inflict such a punishment on the Pope, who after all was revered by all Catholic powers as the visible head of the Church ?

The Emperor was playing for time, to allow the excitement in England to abate ; on December 24 Pendtenriedter could report that the heat of the ministers was cooled, and that if Gallas' report should prove reasonably satisfactory the matter would soon be dropped.

The Pope readily declared that Peterborough had not been arrested on his authority, and that the Legate of Bologna had acted without his knowledge, on a baseless suspicion. In return the British Government did not press its remaining demands, and the incident was soon closed to everyone's satisfaction.

The Jacobites in England are more difficult to trace than those abroad, for many seemingly loyal subjects, from Members of Parliament down to frequenters of the coffee-houses and inns of Fleet Street, may have been friends of the Stuarts at heart, ready to take up arms for them if there were any prospect of success. Most of them must have been Tories because of the emphasis they laid on the doctrine of divine right and passive obedience. But of the active politicians of this party only those on the extreme right wing adopted the cause of the Pretender. Their acknowledged leaders were the Earl of Oxford and the Bishop of Rochester, Francis Atterbury ; in Parliament they were followed by men like Shippen and Wyndham ; in the country a small number of people with money and influence were ready to support their aims, for which they raised considerable sums several times.

[1] Instruction for Pendtenriedter and Hoffmann, Nov. 20, 1717, Vienna Archives.

Of their leaders the Earl of Oxford was the most distinguished. In September 1716, when a Swedish invasion was to ensure the success of a Jacobite rising, Mar asked Oxford what method should be taken with the Emperor and Holland to keep them from doing mischief ; and what he would advise as to Scotland. " I beg . . . and expect . . . you will . . . give me your advice and directions in everything which you think I may have to do. I have long looked on you as a father and director in those matters." [1]

In giving his advice, Oxford tried to infect Mar with something of his own hatred of George I. In a verbal message he once suggested that if the King

come to a field battle there be always two or three hundred horse, chosen men that are hardy and bold, some of them whose relations have been put to death, if such can be found. Let those be still hovering on the wings till a proper time, and then let them pierce furiously where George is, and their orders must be to give quarter to no great man . . . for, if the King [James] be victor, this project will save him trials, which even in the most just cause are sure to create ill blood.[2]

It sounds like the watchword of the Wars of the Roses : Spare the people and slay the nobles.

Oxford, who remained in the Tower till the middle of 1717, was able to keep in touch with the outside world, but he could not influence the general public ; nor was he, even in the eyes of his friends, the man to hold the threads of a conspiracy that spread like a net over Europe. It seems that he himself once recommended Atterbury, the Bishop of Rochester, as leader of the Jacobites in England.

Francis Atterbury was a High Churchman with great gifts and enthusiasm, whose profound belief in the divine right of the Stuarts made him one of the pillars of English Jacobitism. He was dashing, ruthless, and sincere, Oxford sly and cautious ; so there was mutual distrust, jealousy, and tale-bearing, and each slandered the other's political friends. Each had his own followers : Atterbury relied especially on James Murray ; Oxford on Captain Ogilvie and his wife, and on John Menzies, the energetic and well-informed London correspondent of James III. In June 1717 Atterbury came to Oxford and asked him bluntly to discard Menzies and Ogilvie, which Oxford refused to do.[3] James and Mar tried several times to settle these petty quarrels that were damaging their cause. " 'Tis

---

[1] *Stuart Papers*, vol. ii. p. 465.   [2] *Ibid.* vol. v. p. 539.
[3] *Ibid.* p. 555.

hard ", Mar wrote to Ogilvie, " the King cannot have the liberty of employing such as he pleases for certain uses and things. That is the old St. Germains way." [1]

Significant is the complete difference of opinion on the question whether the Tories should ally themselves with the Opposition Whigs. Oxford and Menzies, who wanted it, seem to have been working chiefly for the return of the Tories to power, even if it had to be under George I. Oxford would very possibly have betrayed the Pretender if George I had given him office ; Atterbury and Murray sought nothing but the downfall of the Hanoverians.

There was one group of people whose faith in the Jacobite doctrine was evident : the Nonjurors. [2] When in 1689 the Oath of Allegiance to William and Mary was imposed on all clergymen, against the better judgment of William, eight Bishops and over four hundred others refused to take it. They went into forced retirement, and became martyrs of their convictions, though they were not expelled from the Church. Sancroft, who had been Archbishop of Canterbury, and was the first leader of the Nonjurors, was able to live as a well-to-do country gentleman on the family estate of Fressingfield in Suffolk ; but most of the others had to rely on charity. If their only principle had been adherence to their oath to James II, there would have been no more Nonjurors when those who were dismissed in 1689 were dead. But they were separated from the mass of the English clergy by the unswerving strictness of their conception of obedience to authority as required by the Bible, of passive obedience, non-resistance, and the divine right of kings.

The feelings of all mankind, they said, must be shocked by the proposition that, as soon as a king is expelled by traitors, all his servants are bound to abandon him. Would any student of the sacred writings dare to affirm that the conduct of Shimei was proposed as a pattern to be imitated, and that Barzillai, who loyally adhered to his fugitive master, was resisting the ordinance of God, and receiving to himself damnation ? [3]

---

[1] *Ibid.* p. 443.

[2] Cf. Th. Lathbury, *A History of the Nonjurors* (1845).

[3] Cf. Macaulay's exposition of the arguments used by and against Nonjurors ; *History of England from the Accession of George II* (London, 1855), vol. iii. p. 446.

Only in 1694 did the schism become real. In all form, and with due respect for the privileges of James II, they began to elect and to ordain new bishops to fill gaps that arose in their ranks, thus assuring the continuity of their own schismatic hierarchy. But in the course of time the importance of the Nonjurors decreased ; many of them, including some of the most distinguished, took the Oath of Allegiance ; they were divided into two hostile camps on questions of theology and liturgy ; and the Chevalier de St. George was an uninspiring character, whose close connexion with Rome was unpopular. The mass of the English people could not be brought to believe that Papism was not lurking behind Jacobitism ; and in the Nonjurors they saw nothing but apostates from the Church of England who were similar in aims and methods to the Jesuits, and were quietly carrying on the work of Rome.

Their power was so small that the Government took little notice of them, not even disturbing their meetings in London at which they prayed for James III as King. After the rising of 1715 they were treated a little more severely, though very few of them had actually taken part in it. Even the best known martyr of the subsequent trials, William Paul, had never before refused to take the Oath, and had had a promising clerical career. He had joined the rebels and been taken prisoner ; and only when his prayers for mercy had been refused did he adopt the attitude of the Non-jurors. He professed to be a son of the Church of England, " but I would not have you think I am a member of the schismatical Church whose Bishops set themselves up in opposition to those orthodox fathers ". [1]

Theoretically anyone suspected of sympathy with the Nonjurors had to take the Oath, and if he openly refused to take it, was to be put in prison ; but actually the Nonjurors were again left almost unmolested. Only in 1716, when their internal divisions led to stormy attacks on certain meetings,[2] did Parliament and Convoca-tion threaten to intervene ; however, common sense and the efforts of the Jacobite leaders soon restored peace. But public attention was again attracted by a controversy between the Nonjurors and the Established Church, in which both groups were divided in their opinions, and in which Benjamin Hoadly himself took part. In this controversy the Nonjurors reasserted firmly their principles,

---

[1] Lathbury, *History of the Nonjurors*, p. 250.
[2] *Stuart Papers*, vol. iii. p. 236.

which were " to oppose usurpation in Church and State, and to maintain the Christian doctrine of non-resistance to sovereign powers which are lawful ".[1]

The Nonjurors' devotion to their cause found few admirers, and the public treated their theological bickerings with indifference or contempt. Their number dwindled, for they were as shepherds without a flock. Their main support came from the Jacobite families in which they could gain a living as chaplains or tutors, just as the Roman Catholic priests did in Catholic families — and like the Roman Catholics, they came to be regarded by the mass of the people as the natural enemies of State and Church.

The hypocritical Nonjuror, who ensnares an honest country squire and for selfish and Jacobite ends abuses the hospitality shown him, is the theme of *The Nonjuror* (1717), a successful play by the poet-actor Colley Cibber. In it the priest, who recalls Molière's Tartuffe, initiates his friend in all the secrets of Nonjuror theory, which is depicted as differing from Roman Catholicism merely in outward form. " We mean to souse old Satan, and the Pope ", says the Prologue. After a conversation with his host our Tartuffe laughs cynically : " Ha ! ha ! Would it not make one smile that it should ever enter the brains of this man (who can in other points distinguish like a man) that a Protestant Church can never be secure, till it has a popish prince to defend it ? "

One conversation is particularly realistic and witty. " What say our last advices from Avignon ?." asks the Squire, and his trusty adviser serves him up excellent news. " The council has approved our scheme and press mightily for dispatch among our friends in England. The Court's extremely thronged . . . never was there such a concourse of warlike exiles."

He himself, modest Nonjuror that he was, and unworthy of such honour, had been promoted to the See of Thetford, and was now addressed by his master in private conversations as " My Lord ". In the end the scoundrel is of course unmasked, and is finally crushed by the terrible discovery that he is actually a lurking emissary of Rome, a priest in popish orders, who has several times been seen to officiate public mass in the Church of Notre Dame at Antwerp. Besides he has been known actually in arms at the first rebellious rising in Northumberland, and is therefore guilty of high treason.

[1] *Ibid.* vol. v. p. 529.

The author received £200 from George I, who attended a performance of the play, in recognition of his loyalty; and some years later he was made Poet Laureate. The numerous Jacobites in London, and even William Shippen, whom many thought to be the original of the Squire, had to bite their lips and say nothing. They became the butt of the public, which applauded the last lines of the prologue :

> Ship off, ye slaves, and seek some Passive Land
> Where tyrants after your own hearts command ;
> To your Transalpine Master's rule resort,
> And fill an empty abdicated court.
> Turn your possessions here to ready Rhino,
> And buy ye lands and lordships at Urbino.

In Scotland the name of the Stuarts still savoured of independence from England, and might at any time become the signal for a rising. In 1719 it was hoped to rouse the west of England round Bristol, but whether the hope was justified is doubtful. In the large towns like London there were occasional riots in favour of the Stuarts.

The rise and fall of Jacobite activities in England was closely bound up with political events. At the time of the rising of 1715–1716 the authorities had to take measures against numerous Jacobite demonstrations. In June 1715 a rich butcher was whipped near London because he maintained that the King had no right to the crown.[1] Bonet comments that such punishments were now more frequent, and that the people mostly sided with the offender. This mood continued well into 1716. In the summer of that year the wrath of the people vented itself on the so-called mug-houses,[2] a kind of Whig club-house, of which there were a few in London. Mobs used to appear shouting " High Church and Ormonde ! " and sometimes they managed to break in, destroy the premises, loot the cellars and drink to the health of James III.[3] Often these " mughouse riots " developed into regular affrays, for the inmates defended themselves stoutly. Once even a party of Horse Guards was called in and fired on the rioters. Till then it had been believed they

---

[1] Reports of Bonet and Hoffmann, June 1715.
[2] Cf. W. Besant, *London in the Eighteenth Century* (1902), p. 320.
[3] Tindal, *Continuation* (1747), iv. II. p. 502.

had orders that they should in no circumstances fire upon the people.[1]

Just as excitement over this was dying down, there came rumours of an imminent Swedish invasion. Even the discovery of the plan and the spectacular arrest of the Swedish ambassador did not destroy Jacobite hopes of support from the Northern Powers. Then followed the trouble with Spain. The mood of the people was shown in many little incidents that would not deserve mention were they not symbolic. In 1718 a youth of eighteen years planned to murder George I ; but he disclosed his intentions to a Nonjuring priest, who handed him over to the authorities. When he was examined by the Privy Council, the youth confessed to everything and admitted that he did not know George I at all, and had only heard good of him ; but as a usurper he was to be got out of the way. Asked who had suggested the plan, he replied that the holy books and the fine sermons on passive obedience had alone been his accomplices. In his dying speech, which, however, can hardly have been his own work, he expressed his regret at the failure of his plan, and the hope that another would be more successful. Contrary to usage, the Government tried to prevent this " dying speech " reaching the public ; but the Jacobites managed to smuggle in copies printed abroad.[2]

Despite persecution and oppression the Jacobites did all they could to influence the masses. Oxford University, the Tory strong-hold, counted many friends of the Stuarts among its members. It played a leading part in spreading Jacobite propaganda, and was once said to be more important in politics than in learning.[3] On January 30 (O.S.), 1718, the anniversary of Charles I's death, a clerical member of the University dared to say in his sermon that the blood of the royal martyr would not be expiated as long as one scion of his illustrious family had to eat the bread of exile.[4] A year later, when George I was on the Continent, the Regency decided to punish an Oxford preacher who had called the King a usurper, unless he were punished by the Vice-Chancellor of the University.[5]

---

[1] Hoffmann, Aug. 4, 1716, Vienna Archives. Cf. also Limier, *Mémoires du règne de George I* (1729), vol. ii. p. 297.

[2] Tindal, *Continuation*, iv. II. p. 555 *seq.*; Hoffmann, Feb. 11, Mar. 18, 1718, Vienna Archives ; Bonet, Jan. 31/Feb. 11, 1718, Prussian State Archives.

[3] Bonet, Oct. 7/18, 1715, Prussian State Archives.

[4] Bonet, Mar. 4/15, 1718, Prussian State Archives.

[5] Delafaye to Stanhope, June 26, 1719, S.P. 43/61.

About the same time there appeared a pamphlet, *Vox populi vox Dei*, calling upon the people to rise in a body for the Pretender.[1] The author must have created a stir, and he attracted the attention of the Regents, because he had tried to explain his Jacobite sympathies with Whig theories. He takes as his motto " *Ex ore tuo te judico* " ; and, adopting the standpoint of the Glorious Revolution, he accepts the doctrine that the source of all power is the people. The majority of the people being, so he says, Jacobite, every Whig must also be Jacobite, for it has always been a Whig principle that they should give effect to the will of the majority ; *Vox populi vox Dei*. In conclusion he puts forward three theses : (1) That every assertor of hereditary right must be a Jacobite. (2) Every Whig who makes *Vox populi* his rule of government must be so. (3) Every assertor of limited monarchy must be so, the Chevalier being endowed with all princely virtues. As frequently happened, the author was not to be found ; but the printer was arrested, found guilty of High Treason, and sent to his death, which he faced bravely.

The Jacobites also hurled poisonous abuse at the Prince of Wales. In one pamphlet he was apostrophized as " a thing they call Prince of Wales ".[2] The author had collected all the evil gossip about the heir, and the spiteful calumnies against the royal family, and added his own trimmings. Every member of the royal house was accused of the worst sins of the flesh. Signs and wonders had happened in the land to testify the wrath of heaven against this unworthy regiment. " These with that great weakness in thy head prove, that the hand of the Lord is against thee and thy house and there will not be one of thy breed left, unless thou leavest this land and content thyself with thy own as an honest man would do."

There is no lack of evidence that the Pretender had many supporters in the country, particularly among the lower classes, who always hoped to benefit from every change. A sedan-chair man once knocked at the window of the Princess of Wales and called out to her that she was no princess in this country, and that people would be happy when the true King, James III, wore the crown.[3] An Irish soldier once ran in his uniform through the streets of

---

[1] S.P. 43/61. Cf. also Hoffmann's Reports, Nov. 14, 21, 1719, Vienna Archives.

[2] Hanover Archives. A copy in writing is in S.P. 35/7. In the (still handwritten) Calendars the date 1716 ? is given.

[3] Bonet, Mar. 31/Apr. 11, 1719, Prussian State Archives.

London and proclaimed James King.[1]   The extent of popular
sympathy for the Jacobites suggests secret work on their behalf,
and gives some point to the story then current, that Cardinal
Alberoni, England's most active enemy and a man with a finger
in every pie, was not unconnected with this activity.   The ground
was certainly well prepared, had the Stuarts succeeded in making
an armed entry.   A poem apparently written in the summer of 1719,
when such an attempt was made without success, ends with the
lines :

> Happy were it for the nation
> If with evils past content
> They would make a restoration
> And the ills to come prevent.[2]

But correspondence with the Jacobites in England was difficult
to maintain, because of the watchfulness of the diplomats and
agents employed by George I's Government.   Pseudonyms, cryptic
phrases, and secret codes had to be used, and all remarks about
politics were concealed in apparently innocent personal messages.
Frederick's attachment for his beloved Patricia meant the Duke
of Mar's unswerving loyalty to James Edward.   But these methods
availed little against the peeping of the officials.   Whatever was
sent by post was opened and read.   " In this art they are skilful to
perfection. . . . And they spare no cost : there are proper officers
for every part, and there is one reader and decipherer has 500*l.* a
year pension besides other perquisites. . . . And, whenever they
let a letter pass, it is only to encourage and watch for the answer." [3]
Again and again the correspondents in England earnestly desired
" that nothing should be writ over by the post ".[4]   So all communications of importance were sent by courier, written in ordinary
English ; but even this was dangerous, and many a letter was
thrown into the Channel by the bearer, lest it be seized.[5]   Only
verbal messages were really safe.   Mrs. Ogilvie frequently travelled
to and fro between England and France, between Oxford and Mar ;
to the best of her memory she wrote down at one end what she
had received at the other.[6]   Less welcome were those would-be

---

[1] Hoffmann, July 12, 1718, Vienna Archives.

[2] Manuscript enclosure with Bonet's Reports of July 1719, Prussian
State Archives.

[3] *Stuart Papers*, vol. iv. p. 335.   [4] *Ibid*. vol. v. p. 548.

[5] *Ibid*. vol. iv. pp. 388, 402.   [6] *Ibid*. vol. v. p. 556.

·messengers from James Edward's circle, who came to England and wanted to give themselves an air by repeating casual remarks of their master as highly confidential messages, contradicting each other and causing more confusion than enlightenment.[1]

The dispatches and more explicit memorials, in which the English correspondents reviewed the general situation, are valuable as sources because of their varied contents, though they are influenced by the Jacobite bias of their authors. People like James Murray and John Menzies tried to find out what the King had said in Cabinet, how a minister had revealed to a leading Tory his despair at the hopeless situation, what was said and done in Parliament, and what the people talked about in the street. Sometimes they even gained access to diplomatic documents.[2] The quarrel between George I and the Prince of Wales, and the split in the Whig party were hailed with delight, and the danger that threatened the dynasty was greatly exaggerated. Of the friction between English and German ministers at St. James surprisingly little was said. Speculations concerning the possibility of George I abdicating were idle, but deliberations as to how long the ministers could work with the existing Parliament were more reasonable. What was said of the Government's foreign policy was almost always wrong.

The attitude of the Jacobites towards the English parties was also discussed. Had the Tories all been Jacobites, James' interest would have been to unite them with the dissatisfied Whigs in order to upset the Government and to make possible his restoration. As they were not, such a union would only have meant a change of Government without upsetting the Hanoverians. Their aim in Parliament was therefore to keep the three existing party groups as far apart as possible ; this would keep both the Government and the Opposition weak till the situation at home and abroad was favourable for a *coup*.

In July 1717 they considered that they had hitherto succeeded, and that " Mr. Shippen's services in this matter in the House of Commons can never be sufficiently acknowledged ".[3] As a Tory he opposed the Government, but he also tried to degrade King George and his family in the eyes of the people, in order to show how much better the national interests would be guarded by the Stuarts. He repeatedly mocked at the King's policy, which to him seemed

---

[1] *Stuart Papers*, pp. 537-8.   [2] Cf. *ibid.* p. 331.

[3] *Ibid.* p. 558.

" *rather calculated for the meridian of Germany than of Great Britain* ".

It is the only infelicity of his Majesty's reign, that he is unacquainted with our language and constitution ; and it is therefore the more incumbent on his British ministers to inform him, that our government does not stand on the same foundation with his German dominions, which by reason of their situation, and the nature of their constitution, are obliged to keep up armies in time of peace. Nor is it in the least to be wondered at that His Majesty, who hath spent the earlier part of his life in those dominions, should think sixteen or even 32,000 men, might be continued in so rich and powerful a nation as this is.[1]

Several times Jacobite machinations decidedly influenced the proceedings in Parliament. Lord Oxford, after his trial, assured the Pretender of his eternal gratitude for his services in this affair.[2] In 1718 James boasted of having recommended his supporters in Parliament " to hinder the sending an English squadron into the Mediterranean ", and hoped for the King of Spain's " good dispositions towards him " in return.[3]

Recognition of their folly and the necessities of life brought many exiles to ask for pardon. During the first years after " The 'Fifteen " a number of repentant Jacobites were allowed to return home. But the Government found it was letting in only untrustworthy elements ; by the end of 1718 the Cabinet Council was of opinion, " His Majesty ought to shew no further clemency. For . . . there has not been one instance of any return of gratitude or repentance, tho' there have been thousands of His Majesty's pardon and indulgence." [4]

None the less, the Government tried to win one of the Jacobite leaders by enticing offers. It would have been a triumph to rob James of his best servants. There was little hope of success with Ormonde ; but Mar was more than accessible. Though he would sometimes tell his King openly of these offers,[5] at other times, when the outlook was black, he did his best to make his peace

---

[1] *Parl. Hist.* vol. vii. p. 508 ; cf. also pp. 582, 435-6.
[2] Stair to Craggs, Mar. 11, 1719, S.P. 78/163.
[3] *Stuart Papers*, vol. v. pp. 617-8.
[4] Craggs to Stair, Dec. 29, 1718, S.P. 104/30.
[5] *Stuart Papers*, vol. iv. p. 515.

with the "Usurper". Mistrust of him is frequently visible in the Jacobite correspondence.[1] The Pretender appeared to believe firmly in his loyalty,[2] for he was never remarkable for his knowledge of men. Already in 1717, when James had to leave France, which had just concluded an alliance with England, Mar called on Stair, the British ambassador in Paris. He spoke as a Scot and an old friend, not concealing his despair of the Pretender's cause ; and he seemed inclined to come to a personal agreement with the British Government. Stair, to raise no false hopes, did not respond to the proposal ; he only used the opportunity to find out all he could about the Jacobites.

In 1719, Mar, on his way from Italy to take the waters at Bourbon, which he had heard most closely resembled those of Bath, was told that he could not cross the French frontier without a passport. He therefore applied to Stair for it ; [3] and as the Jacobites had just suffered another reverse, he also renewed his advances. He could honestly affirm that at the moment he had no designs against George I ; and, to reassure the ambassador, he could add that there was no further danger from Ormonde's expedition,[4] and that he himself was no longer in the Chevalier's service. Stair reported to London and to the King, who was in Hanover. Stanhope was ready to negotiate, but advised the greatest caution. He was not afraid of Mar himself, but of the bad impression which his pardon might make in England. He seems to have demanded Mar's unconditional submission as an essential preliminary. Stair tried to bring the two together, for he would gladly have regained for a Scottish peer the royal favour and his confiscated lands. Meanwhile the municipal council of Geneva, where Mar was waiting, held him a prisoner till the decision of the British Government was known. Stair advised Stanhope that he be allowed to proceed to Bourbon ; the restoration of his property would perhaps present difficulties, as it was a matter for Parliament ; but while at Bourbon, he could be allowed a pension from the King. " In this way you risk nothing, you will always be master of his conduct, and imperceptibly he will fall away from the Pretender and become suspect to him and his adherents ;

[1] Cf. *Lockhart Papers*, vol. ii. p. 16 *seq.*

[2] *Stuart Papers*, vol. v. p. 371.

[3] For what follows cf. (*Hardwicke*) *State Papers*, vol. ii. pp. 561-99.

[4] Cf. below, p. 189 *seq.*

gradually you will bring him to do what he would refuse if you had demanded it of him." [1]

The Government seemed willing to grant the pension, but no definite settlement was reached. Negotiations dragged on, till Mar grew suspicious. Stair pointed out that Mar would be driven again into the Pretender's arms. The Geneva Council never received the order to set him free, nor even an intimation that they should act as they thought best ; so, tired of waiting, they eventually released him. Mar, in a towering rage, returned to Italy and James. The English ministers, he said, may be capable people, but they know as little how to make proselytes as to assure themselves of their friends' loyalty. Stair felt inclined to agree with him.

The efforts of the Jacobites to win over prominent opponents were even greater. They made the mistake of believing that every outstanding politician who joined the Opposition was already one of them, or could at least be won for their good cause. Mar and his friends wished particularly to convert the chief Scottish nobles. When in spring 1717 the Duke of Argyll and his clan had fallen into disfavour at St. James, they at once sought to win over this rich and powerful group. Strangely enough even the victor of Sheriffmuir was not deaf to their offers. In a long letter to Argyll's brother, Lord Ilay, Mar depicted the world as seen through Jacobite eyes. All the conditions for the restoration of the Stuarts appear to be fulfilled. It is true that the standing army makes any rising without help from abroad impossible, but on this they can count. Russia and Sweden are just making peace, and allying themselves with the Pretender. The plan that was frustrated by the arrest of Gyllenborg will be then taken up again, " and with greater probability of success . . . almost to a certainty ".[2] France will hardly object ; Prussia may join in the project, and make Holland sit still. There is no danger from the Emperor, and the Princes of the Empire are favourable. Only distance prevents Spain and Sicily from giving active help — and so it goes on. The whole Continent is waiting impatiently for the day when James III will mount the throne of his fathers, the day for which England and Scotland are longing in their misery. Finally, high honours are offered to Argyll and Ilay if they adopt the Stuart cause. Mar felt he could safely promise Argyll the rank of Duke in England, Ilay that of Earl.

[1] Stair to Stanhope, June 17, 1719, S.P. 78/164.
[2] *Stuart Papers*, vol. iv. p. 257.

The two Scottish nobles listened to these advances, but avoided everything which might compromise them. Their communications with Mar's messengers were only oral. They declared that no consideration upon earth should prevail upon them either to serve the Elector of Hanover or the Prince ; but they were determined to act within the laws of their country.[1] They would carry on the struggle against the Government only in Parliamentary form, as they did when they spoke so violently against the impeachment of Lord Oxford.[2] They would have declared for the Pretender openly if his prospects had been really as good as Mar liked to depict them. Many others seem to have negotiated with the Jacobites, but without committing themselves. Of the Duke of Shrewsbury, who in 1714 had so successfully championed the Protestant Succession,[3] Menzies wrote to Mar that he " is right and true . . . also your real friend ". What passed between Menzies and the Duke is not known, as it could not safely be written by the common post.[4] The Jacobites may well have reckoned on the leading English Catholics ; they spoke of the Duke of Norfolk as one of themselves. On occasion their hopes would be still wilder. In July 1717 a memorial was sent by James Murray to Urbino, on the Bishop of Rochester's direction, pointing out the many difficulties of the English Government : the division between George I and his son, the disagreement among the Whigs, the attack on Cadogan by the discontented Whigs, the prosecution of Hoadly, and the proroguing of Convocation. Murray suggested that :

the management of this ministry has been such that they could not have pursued measures more for the King's [James III's] interest, if they had been in a direct design to serve him. They cannot probably stand the meeting of this Parliament another year, and, if they call a new one, there must be a new ministry of course. . . . They are men of vast ambition and no principles. . . . In this situation 'tis submitted whether an application from the King to them might not be for his service.[5]

Mar was astonished and sceptical :

I doubt much if either Cadogan, Stanhope or Sunderland can be brought to have such thoughts . . . and for Marlborough, he seems now to be out of play.[6]

---

[1] *Stuart Papers*, vol. v. p. 327.
[2] *Ibid*. vol. iv. pp. 456, 498.
[3] Cf. Vol. I. pp. 53-4.
[4] *Stuart Papers*, vol. v. p. 177.
[5] *Ibid*. p. 558.
[6] *Ibid*. vol. iv. p. 497.

But he felt that the attempt to win over one or other of the ministers could do no harm. Some weeks later he tried to tempt Cadogan by a clever and very moderate letter[1] in which he avoided all the usual phraseology of the Usurper and the rightful King. Instead he writes of " your master " and " my master ", and proposes the simplest solution to the disputed succession, that George I should renounce his new possessions, which " by the laws of God and man belong to another ". In return he promises King George the assistance of his master in acquiring such new possessions on the Continent " as would make his family more considerable than any of its neighbours . . . with a just regal title ". Cadogan did not deign to reply.

Another man whom the Jacobites dreamed of making first a Tory, then a Jacobite, was Robert Walpole, the most important member of the Opposition in Parliament. When Walpole once listened to Tory arguments, it was taken as a good beginning.[2] There was even talk of trying him by means of money,[3] and this the Pretender thought excellent. Actually his past made it difficult for Walpole to join the Tories ; " he must be a supreme ", and the Tories would never diminish themselves to work under him.[4] Even if he had become a Tory, he would have had nothing in common with the Jacobites ; his opposition to George I's ministers would never have developed into an attack on the House of Hanover.

A further plan which occupied the leading Jacobites was James Edward's marriage. His mother, his advisers, and his friends in England and abroad, all were convinced that this step was essential, and they did their best to help him. Like Mar, they felt that " it is children we want, the sooner they come the better, and their not coming at all would be ruin to us ".[5] A marriage could be security to him, satisfaction to his friends ; it would be confusion to his enemies, and render the remainder of his life prosperous.[6] Pope Clement also, and many who had the Roman Catholic interests of Europe at heart, encouraged the project. In 1716 an envoy of James Edward was staying in Lucerne at a time when the Catholic cantons were holding a meeting, and was frequently asked by the Auditor and some of the deputies why the King did not marry.

[1] *Ibid.* vol. v. p. 50 *seq.*
[2] *Ibid.* vol. iv. p. 332.
[3] *Ibid.* p. 396.
[4] *Ibid.* p. 332.
[5] *Ibid.* vol. v. p. 311.
[6] *Ibid.* vol. iv. p. 545.

The reason for the question is that the foreign princes next in blood will never have an interest in Britain equal to that which those descended of his body will have. I must confess I am of their opinion, therefore I only said that the King was very young and I did not doubt he would marry soon, and I heartily wish it may be so.[1]

But the sovereigns of Europe were more than hesitant about the marriage of one of their daughters to a landless Pretender, and about incurring the hostility of the powerful House of Hanover. It is true the Prince was not fastidious, and did not demand a beauty ; but his friends, who knew the temperament of the Stuarts, feared that if she were not young and handsome, it might be of as dismal consequence as it was to Charles II.[2]

More important, though not decisive, was the religion of the bride. Although personally James and his mother would have liked a Roman Catholic, a Protestant marriage would be more acceptable to England.

If a proper person of the name of Protestant could be found, it would be a matter of great joy to them [his friends] to hear of his being married to-morrow, for many strong reasons, particularly that it would in all human probability reconcile the discontented Whigs to his interest.[3]

In 1717 a marriage to the daughter of the Landgrave of Hesse-Cassel was desired by the English Jacobites. Ormonde, Mar, and Dillon advised James to propose the marriage, " even if it were sure that it would be rejected ",[4] because of the good impression this would create among his friends in England. But an offer of Peter the Great to marry one of his daughters to the Pretender was also seriously considered though she belonged to the Orthodox Church, and was only thirteen years old. James mostly sought the hand of princesses, but equality of birth was not indispensable. Mar expressed his opinion that " rather than he should delay it much longer, I wish he were married to some well-born gentle-woman, though much below his quality ".[5]

---

[1] John Carnegy to the Duke of Mar, *Stuart Papers*, vol. iii. pp. 357-8. The assertion that George I's Government also desired the Pretender's marriage cannot be taken seriously in the light of subsequent events. Stanhope's words, quoted by Haile, *James Frances Edward*, p. 241 [1], can only have been meant as a joke.

[2] *Stuart Papers*, vol. v. p. 537.   [3] *Ibid.* p. 328.

[4] *Ibid.* vol. iv. p. 323.   [5] *Ibid.* vol. iii. p. 256.

For full five years the Pretender was looking for a wife. On each occasion he showed himself more matter-of-fact than tactful. As soon as one negotiation failed he began another, and sometimes he conducted several at one time. He had not really the right to pride himself that he only made a new proposal when the last was off the *tapis*.[1] In 1715 a letter from Queen Mary, concerning a possible bride whose name is not mentioned, shows her anxious for her son's happiness, while he wants to postpone a decision because he is just occupied with another courtship.

At times his hopes soared high, and he sought the hand of an Archduchess. After the Peace of Utrecht the matter was seriously discussed. Even Louis XIV, his minister Torcy, and Marshall Berwick, a half-brother of James, were sympathetic.[2] One of the daughters of Joseph I was suggested, preferably the elder as she would have the larger dowry ; or else a sister of Charles VI. For the Emperor it was purely a question of policy, which appealed to him most during the period of tension between Vienna and London about the Triple Alliance of January 1717.[3] On the advice of the Marquis de Prié in Brussels and of the Imperial Envoys in Holland, James sent a request to the Emperor by Walkingshaw, who however had as little success in this matter as in others.

Particular significance attaches to the Pretender's efforts to win an Archduchess because of the problem of the Austrian Succession. The Princes of Saxony and Bavaria were courting the daughters of Joseph I, and Charles VI was afraid that these marriages might become a danger to the rights of his own daughter Maria Theresa, which he had tried to secure by the Pragmatic Sanction. This would provide another reason for considering the Stuart as a possible match for one of his nieces. It was even said that the Empress Amalia, the widow of Joseph I, had received the proposal favourably, and would bring the Emperor to it ; [4] also that one of the Emperor's people had promised that he would undertake to manage it.[5] Whether there was any truth in these assertions or not, fate willed it that Charles VI required the support of England in the Quadruple Alliance and against Spain, and James' plans of marriage with an Archduchess fell to the ground.

[1] *Ibid.* vol. iv. p. 433.
[2] *Ibid.* vol. i. in many letters.
[3] Stair to Methuen, Dec. 18, 1716, S.P. 78/160.
[4] *Stuart Papers*, vol. v. p. 81.   [5] *Ibid.* p. 92.

On a short visit to Modena in 1717, James met the daughter of his uncle, its Duke. He described her in such glowing terms that Mar believed there was a real attachment and for this reason, if for no other, hoped they would marry. The Duke begged time for reflection and pressed for absolute secrecy because of the Emperor, his powerful neighbour in Italy. In spring 1717, Charles VI was watching the Alliance of the Western Powers mistrustfully, and might have agreed to a marriage between the Duke of Modena's daughter and the Stuart Prince. Pope Clement XI pledged himself to do his utmost to remove all difficulties, and to manage the business with the Emperor.[1] But in the summer, after Spain's attack on Sardinia, the Emperor drew closer to the Western Powers ; and in the autumn there began the negotiations which finally led to the Quadruple Alliance. The proposed engagement might now have proved detrimental to the Emperor in London, and the Duke had to send a final refusal to James Edward in September. As was his wont, James gave vent to his anger in insulting words against the Duke,[2] instead of recognizing his difficult position.

At last, however, James Edward's efforts were crowned with success. It was of good augury that this time negotiations were begun by the family of the proposed bride ;[3] yet the difficulties to be overcome were such, the Great Powers so opposed to the match, the bride so badly treated before they were happily united, that the marriage was wrapped in a glamour of romance which could not have been expected in view of the prosaic nature of the bridegroom. The bride's family was by its origin and connexions one of the foremost in Europe. Her father, Prince James Sobieski, was the son of the famous liberator of Vienna, and had once tried, though unsuccessfully, for the throne of Poland on which his father had sat. Now he was living (as a wealthy private person) in the Emperor's territory at Ohlau in Silesia. Her mother was daughter of the Elector Palatine Philip William, and sister of the Empress Eleonore, widow of Leopold I. As early as 1716 Prince James

---

[1] *Stuart Papers*, vol. iv. p. 284.

[2] *Ibid.* pp. 547-8.

[3] Cf. Pauli, "Stuart und Sobieski" (1881), *Historische Zeitschrift*, 46 ; Head, *The Fallen Stuarts* (1901) ; J. T. Gilbert, *Narratives of the Detention, Liberation and Marriage of Maria Clementina Stuart* (Dublin, 1894). The account following is based on these and also on diplomatic correspondence, on the Gualterio Papers in London, and particularly on the St. Saphorin Papers in Hanover.

Sobieski had suggested to Queen Mary and James Edward that his youngest daughter, the Princess Clementina, should marry the Stuart heir ; at the same time he named the sum she would receive as dowry, apart from her future inheritance. He assured the Stuart Prince that, notwithstanding the condition to which Stuart affairs were reduced, he would rather choose to give the Prince his daughter in marriage than to any other in Europe.[1] Clementina was only in her fifteenth year, little of stature, but very agreeable in her person, having more wit and humour than her sisters. The Stuarts do not appear to have responded eagerly, but presumably James Edward kept in mind the possibility of this Polish match, together with his other plans.

In November 1717 Charles Wogan, an Irish Catholic who had escaped from Newgate prison and from punishment for his share in the Rising, was sent by the Stuarts on a special mission to Germany. Under a false name he was to appear as a man of standing who was travelling for diversion or curiosity and therefore desirous of seeing the German courts. Wherever he went he was told to look out for eligible princesses ; the Princesses of Baden and of Saxony were expressly named. If any other courts fell in his way through Germany, where there were young princesses, he was to see them and inform himself about them, " for there are many in that country, and in some of them there may be princesses as fine women as any of the two we have been informed of ".[2] Only in a postscript to his instructions was there mention of Prince James Sobieski :

Prince James Sobieski, son to the late King of Poland, has several daughters, who, I believe, are somewhere in Germany. You may inquire about them, and endeavour to see them all, if they fall in your way or be not much out of it.

Charles Wogan conscientiously studied all the young German princesses, and reported on their eyes, figures, characters, and dowries, till in February 1718 he could truthfully write that

upon the strictest inquiry I can find out no other Catholic nor indeed any other Princesses in this country, which generally has been pretty well stocked ; and that the expense of travelling is just double what it is in France.[3]

---

[1] *Stuart Papers*, vol. iv. pp. 74-5.   [2] *Ibid.* vol. v. p. 235.
[3] *Ibid.* p. 473.

Yet he was still willing to go to Ohlau if he could procure any recommendations. Though no further report from him is to be found, he must have fulfilled his mission ; for in April Gualterio could already congratulate his master on the prospects of his alliance with Clementina.[1]

The Jacobites tried to make it appear that the bride's virtues and political connexions had determined the Chevalier, when once he had decided on marriage, to choose her and no other. The zeal with which James Edward pressed forward the negotiations was genuine, but was due only to his former disappointments. Now at last he believed he had found the desired bride : Catholic, of high birth and connexions, and, last but not least, one who did not reject him.

Probably Wogan outlined the marriage agreement before his return to Urbino. James Edward decided at once to complete the marriage with all speed. It would have been dangerous for him to go in person to Ohlau, as it lay in Imperial territory. Even a marriage by proxy seemed unsafe, for

if the Emperor for his own private reasons should think fit to prevent the bride from coming into Italy and place her under some form of arrest, the King might be bound to the marriage without possessing his wife.[2]

So a second messenger was sent to sign the agreement, and a third to accompany the Princesses, mother and daughter, to Italy. Merely a betrothal was arranged, without any religious formality ; the future husband was only to be bound by it if the Princess really became his wife.

The necessity of these precautions was soon proved. The secret came out, and the London Court sent urgent instructions to St. Saphorin, the British ambassador in Vienna, to press the Emperor to prevent the marriage. As the arrangements had been made on Imperial territory, and as the bride's mother was a near relation of the Imperial family, the English Government would not believe that the matter had not been known in Vienna. To clear himself of suspicion, the Emperor had to give some mark of his good intentions, particularly as news had just arrived of the English victory off Cape Passaro, showing how essential to his rule in Italy was the help of England. Count Sinzendorff promised that

---

[1] Cf. Head, *l.c.* pp. 205-6.   [2] See Head, *l.c.* p. 206.

the Emperor would at once send a very sharp letter to Prince Sobieski. Meanwhile, in September 1718, came news that the marriage had been concluded by proxy, and that the Princesses were on the road to Italy. Sinzendorff himself had recently passed them on their way. Now only quick action could be effective. St. Saphorin became more pressing, and called for the arrest of the two ladies. When asked on what grounds, he pointed out Sobieski's breach of faith and the unfortunate effect the marriage would presumably have on Anglo-Austrian relations. The Emperor and Prince Eugene were consulted, and after heated discussions couriers were sent to the Governors of the Tirol, of Styria, and of Mantua, with orders for the detention of the travellers wherever they were found.

But even this harsh decision was not as dangerous as it looked. In Vienna there were friends of the Pretender, and many friends of the Sobieski family. The old Empress Eleonore was most indignant at the insult that was threatening her sister and her niece. She secretly intrigued with the courier who was going to Innsbruck, and he prolonged his journey so much that the Princesses ought to have left Imperial territory long before the orders for their arrest had arrived. Even the ministers expected this result. But the bride's mother was foolish enough to spend seven or eight days with her brother, the Bishop of Augsburg; and when the ladies at last reached Innsbruck the messenger had arrived with his orders, which had to be executed. The Princesses found themselves prisoners.

Their fate caused a great sensation throughout Europe. The British Court breathed freely again, and the Whigs were jubilant.[1] The Austrian Government did not quite appreciate the praise they received from England. In face of the rage of the Jesuits and the anger of the old Empress, the ministers admitted that they themselves had hoped the courier would arrive too late. The Jacobites everywhere were furious. In Ormonde's words, " It is sure the most barbarous action that has been done for many years ".[2] The Pretender was once more cruelly disappointed. He had only just written to Cardinal Aquaviva saying, " I expect at any moment to hear that the Princess Sobieski is on her way ",[3] and he had

---

[1] Hoffmann's Report from London, Nov. 4, 1718, Vienna Archives.
[2] Dickson, *The Jacobite Attempt of 1719* (Scot. Hist. Soc. 19, 1895), p. 2.
[3] Gualterio Papers, Add. MSS. 20292, B.M.

come to Bologna to await her. But instead of the bride came the news of her arrest. He was astonished and overwhelmed by the Emperor's action ; at first he would not believe it, but weeks passed and the bride was still detained. He sent fiery protests to his protector the Pope,[1] saying that one must have renounced religion and honour not to take up his cause and not to oppose such a monstrous and barbarous action. The Pope ought to act as befitted the Vicar of Christ on earth. But if the Emperor were resolved to sacrifice all honour and humanity in carrying the affair to its conclusion, his entreaties would have as little effect as those of the Holy Popes, his predecessors, on the tyrants of old.

Prince Sobieski seems to have taken the matter less tragically, and even to have suggested to James that since the marriage with Clementina had come to nought, he might have one of her elder sisters.

English action had delayed the marriage, but not removed the difficulties : and no one knew what was to happen next. The young Princess could not be kept a prisoner for ever, and as soon as she was set at liberty she would become James Edward's wife. There were heated scenes between the cautious Count Sinzendorff and the over-zealous St. Saphorin,[2] who proposed the simple solution that Clementina should be married as soon as possible to someone else.[3] He suggested the Prince of Parma ; but when difficulties arose, he named the Prince of Baden. King George was ready to approve any marriage, if only she did not become the wife of the Pretender.[4]

In Vienna St. Saphorin's plans were never taken seriously. Here the Dowager Empress Eleonore and the clergy represented to the Emperor that honour and religion made it his duty to release the prisoners ; Sinzendorff, the statesman, thought of the advantages of England's friendship, of the English fleet and of Sicily. Though he several times asked the King of England to consent to the liberation of Clementina, he only wanted to be able to show the old Empress King George's refusal and to tell her it was not his fault if the Princess were still a prisoner.

---

[1] To Albani, Oct. 19/20 ; to the Pope, Oct. 19, 1718, Gualterio Papers, Add. MSS. 20292, B.M.

[2] St. Saphorin's letters, Hanover Archives.

[3] St. Saphorin to Robethon, Jan. 28, 1719, Hanover Archives.

[4] Stanhope to St. Saphorin, Jan. 6, 1719, Hanover Archives.

When news came that the Pretender had gone to Spain and
seemed to have given up the idea of the Polish marriage, Vienna
saw no further reason for detaining the Princesses any longer, and
felt that now their return home could give no offence to England.[1]
But St. Saphorin was afraid that Clementina might escape from
Ohlau by way of Poland, and become the Pretender's wife after all.
In any case, Innsbruck was not a safe place, a fortress would be
better ; so he would like her taken to Olmütz, where she would
also be nearer to her father.   England would defray the expense,
for, as the Princesses had travelled with a large retinue, Vienna
was unwilling to incur it.   Sinzendorff felt that a formal agreement
to this effect would have been undignified, but accepted St.
Saphorin's promise that the money would be paid monthly, provided the world believed it came from Charles VI's treasury.[2]

In the prolonged negotiations between London and Vienna, the
reserved George I found it compatible with his dignity to approach
the Freiherr von Pendtenriedter, now Imperial Envoy to the Court
of St. James, with the suggestion that it must create a very bad
impression in England if the Princess should go to Spain now, as
the Pretender wanted to attack England from there.   With the aid
of Pendtenriedter's reports St. Saphorin had his way in everything,
especially as the odium of the disagreeable affair fell on the English
Government, and the Emperor appeared to act under the pressure
of circumstances.   Clementina was informed that she would be
allowed to return to Ohlau, but that she must make her way through
Imperial territory only.   While apparently free, she thus remained
in the power of the Emperor.   It was, moreover, arranged that
before she reached Moravia the Vienna Court should have received
an answer from George I to their latest proposals.   On the strength
of this the Princess was to be stopped and taken to Olmütz.   There
she would be safe till her father had formally denounced the
betrothal.   The Pope was to write to James Sobieski in order to
allay his scruples about breaking his word ; he was reported to
have agreed, and a letter from him was daily expected in Vienna.

But all these intrigues failed, and Clementina made good her
escape.   Admiration for the Pretender and pity for the noble
prisoner made a whole crowd of conspirators help her on her romantic
and adventurous flight.   The plan was as carefully and cunningly

[1] Charles VI to Pendtenriedter, May 10, 1719, Vienna Archives.
[2] St. Saphorin to Stanhope, May 7, 1719, Hanover Archives.

designed as it was cleverly and cautiously executed, under the direction of Charles Wogan, now acting for the bride's father. A young woman, not unlike the Princess in figure and appearance, was taken into her quarters. Clementina exchanged her noble attire for the other's poor clothing, and slipped out into the darkness. Through snow and rain she safely reached the place where a carriage was waiting for her. The flight, in company of only a few people, was not without dangers ; but the Princess surmounted them with the high spirits of youth and a sense for the dignity of her position. She displayed the heroism of her ancestor John Sobieski, said Charles Wogan. They travelled day and night, over the Brenner and down the valley of the Adige to Italy, not slackening speed till they had left behind them the Holy Roman Empire and the risk of pursuit. When they had reached the promised land of Venice, shortly after midnight of April 30, 1719, Clementina was roused by her companions, and they all sang a bright *Te Deum* in the darkness. Then they continued their journey at a leisurely pace.[1]

News of the successful flight sped over the whole of Europe. In Jacobite circles it was received with delight : the politicians of the Quadruple Alliance were dumbfounded. St. Saphorin wrote saying that his heart was filled with grief ; [2] and that he foresaw serious consequences. But he did not believe that the Emperor and his ministers were implicated. The council in Innsbruck sent a lengthy report,[3] signed by nine prominent gentlemen, which explained what had happened. One day the Princess had not been to Mass or to meals, no one had had access to her because of an indisposition, and the doctor who was in daily attendance was told he need not come. When an explanation was demanded, her mother was found in tears, claiming that she had known nothing of these plans, and holding a note from her daughter in her hand. A pursuit had been ordered immediately, but was not likely to be successful, as it was not even known in which direction she had fled.

Sinzendorff and St. Saphorin were together in Laxenburg, the summer residence of the Emperor, to decide on Clementina's fate, when the report of the dreaded escape reached them. St. Saphorin

---

[1] For the flight cf. Gilbert, *Narratives.*

[2] St. Saphorin to Stanhope, May 7, 1719, and similar letter to George I, same date, Hanover Archives.

[3] Enclosure with above letter to Stanhope, May 7, 1719, Hanover Archives.

straightway supposed James Sobieski to be the originator of the plan, and angrily demanded that the Emperor should send orders to Ohlau for his arrest, and keep him prisoner till he produced his daughter.[1] Charles VI was just amusing himself at target practice in a neighbouring village. The two statesmen hastened to him, and Sinzendorff submitted to him the harsh demands of the British ambassador. The Emperor desired time to inform Prince Eugene, who should obtain a decision from the Conference in Vienna. The Conference recommended the expulsion of Sobieski from Imperial territory, but not his arrest. Though St. Saphorin pointed out that King George would hardly be satisfied with such action, he did not press his demands : the game was lost, and the bird was flown for good. When some weeks later the English ministers heard that the Pope had offered the Princess help and protection, they again thought seriously of carrying out their threat of two years earlier. But the marriage was solemnized without the English fleet pouring the thunder of its vengeance upon the Civita Vecchia.

[1] This demand was repeated in a letter to Sinzendorff, May 4, 1719, Hanover Archives.

CHAPTER IX

THE STUART DANGER IN 1719

AFTER the suppression in 1716 of the Scottish rising, Jacobite hopes were at a low ebb, but soon began to rise again when Charles XII of Sweden adopted their cause. He hated George both because as Elector of Hanover he took part in the war against Sweden, and because as King of England he sent his fleet into the Baltic every year, professedly to protect English trade, but also to support by its mere presence the operations of Sweden's enemies. This led to the plot in which Gyllenborg, the Swedish ambassador, was involved, and which was to have upset the throne of George I.[1] Jacobite disappointment at the failure of the plot did not last long. In spring 1717 the Swedish invasion was still considered possible. The exposure had not been complete : " it's next to a miracle that our enemies know no more ", was Oxford's comment.[2] The Jacobites, who believed they could count on the Tsar's support as well, intended to execute the invasion as part of a larger enterprise. To this end they would have to bring about peace between Sweden and Russia. Actually the Tsar's relations with the Court of St. James were correct and friendly, as became an ally. He was just travelling from Holland to Brussels and Paris, and had sent to the Earl of Stair suggestions for an Anglo-Russian political and commercial agreement, which were readily taken up by the English Government.[3]

None the less Peter, who was less exact and formal in diplomatic matters than the princes of Western Europe, did not refuse to enter into negotiation with the Jacobites. In Paris he would have received Ormonde and Mar personally, had not the Duke of Orleans

[1] Cf. Vol. I. p. 304 *seq.*
[2] *Stuart Papers*, vol. v. p. 538.
[3] Norris' Instruction, July 2, 1717, F.O. 90/57A.

asked him to have no dealings with them.[1] Despite this request,
he paid a visit to Queen Mary, negotiated with the Jacobite leaders
through his physician Dr. Erskine, a relative of Mar, and accepted
graciously a miniature of the Chevalier. He sent a proposal to Mar
that Ormonde might go to the Court of Charles XII, where he could
represent both the interests of James III and those of Russia. The
Jacobites, who thought they had won the Tsar completely, desired
that Ormonde should appear in Sweden with formal instructions
from Peter. But the Tsar declared that before he agreed to that
he must know the attitude of France, which, as he hoped, would
guarantee to him, as well as to the Elector of Hanover, the
permanent possession of the territory gained from Sweden.

Charles XII showed no intention of accepting Peter's demands,
of which he was already informed ; and so there was no basis for
mediation by Ormonde. Peter advised him to go all the same ;
but now the Jacobites feared that it would create a bad impression
if a man of Ormonde's repute were received coldly, or not at all,
by the Swedes. Besides, England was just going to reduce her
army by 10,000 men, and news of Ormonde's mission to Sweden
would certainly prevent this reduction in the size of the already
small army. In these circumstances it was decided to send
Jerningham, a less important man, ahead of Ormonde. Mar tried
to obtain for him too some new proposals to be carried from the
Tsar, and likewise instructions to propose James' mediation betwixt
their Tsarian and Swedish Majesties, and an alliance amongst the
three.

How glorious a thing would it be for the Czar, who would be at
the head of this confederacy, not only to settle and secure to himself
a great part of his own acquisitions, but also by restoring an injured
Prince, settle in a manner all Europe, make himself a powerful fast
friend of that Prince, and they two together with those princes, who
would in that case sue for their friendship, give the law to the
European world.[2]

Jerningham was sent with instructions[3] to announce that
Ormonde was on his way to Sweden ; he was also to do his utmost
to get his Swedish Majesty to accept James' mediation and to bring
about the proposed confederacy. But in case of the King of Sweden's
refusing an alliance which included the Tsar, he was to press for an

---

[1] *Stuart Papers*, vol. iv. p. 249.   [2] *Ibid.* p. 295.
[3] *Ibid.* vol. v. p. 546.

alliance with James III alone. But Ormonde did not even dare to undertake the journey, and Peter the Great, who had suggested the attempt, was most reticent, refused to see Ormonde again, or, after returning home, to allow him to enter Russian territory. So Ormonde spent the winter and spring at Mitau in Courland, and returned to Paris in June 1718 sorely disappointed.[1]

As usual London knew something of these plans, and alarmist reports exaggerated the Jacobite danger. From Dresden came news in the spring of 1718, that the Pretender had arrived in Libau, and had been ceremoniously received there on behalf of the Tsar.[2] When in August Francis Palmes was sent as envoy to the Court of Augustus II, he was instructed to watch closely whether Sweden and Russia were trying to win Poland for any plans they might have in favour of the Pretender.[3]

The Jacobites meant to lose no time. A Manifesto was prepared, similar to those issued in 1715, proclaiming the accession of James III as rightful sovereign. It was composed under the supervision of Mar, as there seemed to be no time to have a draft sent from England. As the Jacobites in Paris expected Charles XII to land in England at any moment, they agreed that if necessary they would not even wait for James Edward's orders, but publish it on the authority of Queen Mary alone, who had given her approval.[4]

The Manifesto, dated Pezzaro, March 21, 1717, contains first and foremost a justification of the use of foreign help, and then the programme of James' future policy as seen by leading Jacobites ; it indicates his own ideas, as he had approved of the document and had probably added a few important alterations.

Nothing in this world could have given Us so great satisfaction as to have owed to the endeavours of Our own loyal subjects without the concurrence of any foreign aid, both Our and their restoration to that happy settlement, which can alone deliver this Church and nations from the calamities . . . of the present usurpation . . . true British hearts, animated with a natural love of their own lawful Sovereign and ancient constitution are an overmatch to the abettors of usurpation, even when supported with the public treasure and standing forces. The Usurper and his associates . . . found it at

[1] Cf. Dickson, *l.c.* p. xxiii.
[2] R. Vernon, Apr. 13, 1718, S.P. 88/25.
[3] Additional Instructions for F. Palmes, Aug. 9, 1718, S.P. 88/25.
[4] *Stuart Papers*, vol. iv. p. 196.

last necessary to make sure, by a new treaty, of new foreign auxiliaries, by throwing themselves into the protection of those very Powers who ever till then were reputed by them as being of an interest incompatible with that of Great Britain, and whom they had represented in so odious a manner that it was made a crime to Us, though they themselves had forced Us to do it, to have had Our education amongst them. The inhuman persecution of Our own person was made another main article of this new alliance. The Usurper . . . forced Us to remove from place to place, and at last to retire beyond the Alps, thinking by Our being at so great a distance to render Our restoration absolutely impossible . . . wherefore . . . we have accepted the more willingly the assistance of this generous prince (the King of Sweden) . . . to bring about Our restoration. . . .

We have thought fit by this Our Royal Declaration to renew and confirm Our offers of pardon and indemnity . . . promising to extend them in ample form by advice of Our first Parliament, which We hereby promise to call as soon as matters shall be so far settled as that a free Parliament can meet together. . . . We do, therefore, command and require . . . that . . . all officers whatsoever, civil or military . . . shall either declare for Us or resign . . . promising hereby that such as resign and withdraw in manner aforesaid shall be thereby entitled to Our Royal pardon. . . . And that such as shall . . . declare for Us . . . shall be continued by Us in their former commissions, and receive a reward. . . . We do also refer to the wisdom of Our said Parliament . . . to ease the nation of the intolerable burdens under which it now groans.[1]

Of special importance were James' promises to " the Church of England and Ireland ", which were carefully thought out by Mar to avoid offending anyone,[2] and which now placed the Church of Ireland beside that of England. He promised to maintain all the members of the Church in the full and free exercise of their religion, and in as full and peaceable possession of all their churches, universities, colleges, and schools as ever they enjoyed them under any of his royal predecessors of the Protestant Communion. To make his promises more convincing he added that his returning by the aid of a Protestant prince would wholly dissipate what might remain of jealousy in the minds even of the most biassed of his subjects of that communion. Even the " Dissenters from the aforesaid Church " were offered his protection : " as it is not Our intention that any of Our subjects shall be persecuted under Our Government merely for conscience sake, so We shall refer to Our

[1] *Ibid.* p. 128 *seq.*   [2] *Ibid.* p. 172.

first Parliament to grant such indulgence to truly tender consciences as shall be thought fit ". Here he anticipated the concessions made to the Dissenters in the Act for Strengthening the Protestant Interest in 1719, and made himself appear more tolerant than the hesitant Whig Government.

The version of the Manifesto approved by the Pretender significantly enough omits the word " Protestant " before " Dissenters from the aforesaid Church ", which other versions contain.[1] The intention was evidently to extend to Roman Catholics, who could be called Dissenters, the benefits of the promised tolerance, a step which might have led to a repetition of the conflicts that cost James II his throne.

In England nothing was known of the Manifesto ; but in November of the same year a letter from the Pretender, which threw light on his Church policy, was widely circulated, and greatly admired by his adherents. At a time when the prorogation of Convocation caused by the Bangor Controversy had not yet become equivalent to its abolition, he wrote to point out the dangers threatening the Church of England.

. . . the affair of Dr. Hoadley before the Convocation . . . with many other proceedings of the Elector's, seem to be designed by Providence to show the Church and people of England how little secure their laws and privileges are under the present government, for by the best information I can have the intrinsic spiritual power of the Church, or power of the Keys as exercised by the Apostles and most pure and primitive Church in the first three centuries has ever been thought an essential right of the Church of England, so that it may inquire into the doctrines of its own members and inflict ecclesiastical censures, not extending to any civil punishment. Now the civil government's putting a stop to such proceedings is in effect taking away that undoubted right of the Church, which, if it please God to restore me to my own just right, I am firmly resolved to maintain to it.

James draws the inevitable conclusion that " doing justice to me is the only solid foundation for a lasting peace and happiness to both Church and State ".[2]

More amateurish still than the northern policy of the Jacobites were their efforts to win the Duke of Orleans and France. Here

---

[1] *Stuart Papers*, vol. iv. p. 131, and Introduction, p. xix.
[2] *Ibid.* vol. v. p. 244.

they were faced with the hard fact of the Anglo-French alliance of
January 1717. They recognized the motives which drew England
and the Regent together. He, like Philip of Spain, hoped to succeed
to the French throne, and England's Government, whether Stuart
or Hanoverian, must unalterably be on his side, since it could
never permit one person to be master of Spain and of France at the
same time. Therefore the Pretender, as future King of England,
should seek to win over the Regent : for

is it not certain that England would have it more in its power to
secure the Regent's claim and at the same time its own interest, if
by the Regent's means the King was brought to it ? since that
incident would remove those divisions which at present make its
power contemptible, and which will make it impossible for it to assist
the Regent effectually. . . . If this matter was laid before him in its
true light, it must make impression upon him . . . if he is a man of
such understanding as he is reputed to be.[1]

The weakness of the argument is made obvious by the fact that
England's foreign policy was by no means paralysed by internal
conflicts, but was assuming a dominant position in Europe through
the Quadruple Alliance.

Another plan to break the Anglo-French alliance was put
forward by General Dillon, who said he was credibly informed that
Dubois, while he was negotiating the treaty, had gone so far as to
promise in the Regent's name that the French Protestants should
be recalled. In the next session of Parliament an address to the
Elector was to be moved, that he should press for the fulfilment of
the promise.

One of two things must follow : that the Elector will either refuse
it, and a refusal to propagate the Protestant religion may be usefully
employed against him ; or, if he complies . . . the Regent, though
ever so willing, will not be master to grant his request, and the motion
coming originally from the Parliament cannot be kept a secret, which
will so incense the French nation that perhaps they will not be appeased
till the Regent breaks off all manner of dealings with the Elector.[2]

In Mar's opinion the project was a masterpiece [3] and it was just
going to be put into practice by Shippen, when he was removed to
the Tower for a tactless remark about the King,[4] and no more was
heard of the plan.

---

[1] *Ibid.* p. 326.   [2] *Ibid.* p. 150.   [3] *Ibid.* p. 323.
          [4] *Ibid.* p. 325 ; and cf. Vol. I. p. 310.

In Austria Jacobite scheming met with as little success.[1]
Negotiations with Turkey were considered, but apparently never
undertaken. To Spain James was finally forced to turn by financial
difficulties. Relying on an offer from Rome, James had promised
£100,000 to Peter the Great and Charles XII for the armaments
required to invade England. When Rome withdrew her offer, and
it seemed unsafe to collect the money in England,[2] the Pretender
sent a cleverly worked Memorial, which he claimed to have written
himself,[3] to the Government in Madrid. His situation and prospects
were revealed with dangerous frankness, and even the distortions in
the picture were unintentional, and due to the characteristic Jacobite
illusions.

The knowledge that every one of these [the European] Powers has
of the injustice and instability of England's present government is
rendered useless and ineffectual by their excessive fear of this rather
imaginary than real power . . . for in effect its exhaustion and its
intestine divisions render it weaker and more exposed to be insulted
than any of the other powers of Europe. . . .

The King of Sweden's good intentions for his Britannic Majesty
have been but too well known by the unfortunate discovery that
was made of it last year. . . . The Czar's aversion for the Elector and
friendship for his Britannic Majesty is . . . yet more certain. . . .

These two princes . . . resolving to undertake his restoration,
find themselves destitute of an essential article . . . money. . . .

What is therefore proposed to his Catholic Majesty is that he would
be pleased to give . . . in writing an assurance to the King of England
that he has such a sum in his hands ready to be given him, whenever
these northern powers shall require it.[4]

The community of interests between Spain and the Pretender is
emphasized. Besides giving his usual assurances of gratitude and
goodwill, James could this time point to the real danger which
threatened Spain from the Western Powers, and could indicate his
own services.

. . . the true notion his Majesty has of the justice and great prudence
of his Catholic Majesty has moved him to recommend to them (his
loyal subjects in England) to do their best in Parliament to hinder
the sending an English squadron into the Mediterranean. . . . But,

---

[1] Cf. above, p. 145.   [2] Cf. above, p. 150.

[3] *Stuart Papers*, vol. v. p. 408.

[4] Memorial for Cardinal Aquaviva to be forwarded to the King of Spain ;
Jan. 27, 1718, *Stuart Papers*, vol. v. p. 616 *seq.*

unless his Britannic Majesty be enabled to send them at least some
general assurance of his Catholic Majesty's good dispositions towards
him, he fears it will not be any more in his power to render . . . the
like services for the future.

Gibraltar was not mentioned, though even as late as December
1717 an English correspondent of Mar suggested that if the
giving up of Port Mahon or Gibraltar would induce the Spaniards
to send over 6000 or 8000 men, one must think those ports advan-
tageously disposed of.[1] The Pretender did not care to name
Gibraltar, as it was not within his power to make such an offer
definitely.[2] Here he appears more conscientious than George I ;
but at the end of the Memorial he hinted at the possible cession of
the port : " a nation which he will have delivered from a cruel
slavery . . . cannot after that refuse anything to their King, when
it is to do a pleasure to a common benefactor ".

The Memorial must have made a good impression on Alberoni,
who would use any means to attain his ends, and had long toyed
with the idea of helping the Pretender in order to create a danger
for England. At this time the Spaniards had taken Sardinia and
were soon to send an expedition to Sicily. But the Quadruple
Alliance was not yet signed, and Passaro had not yet been fought.
Alberoni's reply was both disappointing and pregnant. " The time
is not yet ripe, a little while and . . . suitable steps will be taken
to serve him." [3] James was delighted. " The return [is] short and
sweet, which without giving a direct answer to the proposal gives
hopes of yet greater matters." [4]

Jacobite patience was not long put to the test. In March 1718
the Spanish Government was informed of the terms of the yet
unsigned Quadruple Alliance. News had also reached them of the
proposed English naval expedition to the Mediterranean. The
threat to the Spanish Government was felt to be serious.[5] At a
conference attended by the English and French ambassadors
Alberoni had several times repeated that either England or Spain
must perish, and had hinted at support for the Pretender.[6]

Nothing irritated the English ministers as much as the mention

---

[1] *Ibid.* p. 332.   [2] *Ibid.* p. 408.
[3] *Ibid.* p. 620.   [4] *Ibid.*
[5] Cf. Vol. I. pp. 352-3.
[6] W. Stanhope to Craggs, June 6, 1718, S.P. 94/88.

of this theme. Colonel Stanhope was told by Craggs to intimate their opinion to the Cardinal.

That is a subject which for several good reasons I think he ought not to touch upon, that if he attacks us in that violent manner, there is the Emperor, who is at least as dangerous a pretender to the crown of Spain.[1]

Alberoni seems to have avoided being so tactless a second time ; but instead of words came deeds, and from now on Spain worked for the restoration of the Stuarts.

The Jacobites had the pleasure of seeing their machinations become a part of the policy of Spain and form one episode in the war of 1719.[2] Alberoni was the more willing to co-operate, as he saw many of his other hopes come to nought. The war with Turkey, that was to have hampered Charles VI, was over, the Quadruple Alliance had been formed, the Spanish fleet defeated by the English. So the northern plans of the Jacobites were adopted by Spain and jointly developed. First and foremost Charles XII, who had just made his victorious advance into Norway, was to be enabled to use it as a base from which to attack Scotland.[3]

It must have been early in November 1718, when a plenipotentiary of Charles XII came to Paris to take counsel with the Spanish ambassador and Ormonde. He brought a memorial in which the King of Sweden desired to enter into a strict alliance with the King of Spain, the chief article being to depose the Elector. The plan was that the King of Sweden, as soon as he had taken Drontheim, should himself cross to Scotland with a few troops, on transport vessels but without warships, which were not available. There he would call upon the people to rise on behalf of James III, and Protestant suspicions of the Catholic Stuart prince would be allayed by the fact that the successor of Gustavus Adolphus, the protector of Protestantism, was supporting him. The alliance with Catholic Spain should not be a stumbling-block to English and Scotch Protestants, for Philip V would only be giving financial support. Sir Patrick Lawless was already on his way to settle this matter on the lines of James' recent Memorial. Concurrently with the attack from Scandinavia, Jacobites would rise in Scotland and England.

[1] Craggs to W. Stanhope, June 23, 1718, S.P. 104/138.
[2] Here unfortunately the *Calendar of the Stuart Papers* ceases.
[3] Stair to Craggs, Jan. 21, 1719, S.P. 78/163.

At the end of November Ormonde was expected in Madrid at
any moment.[1] He had left Paris, and despite a sharp watch by
the French Government, had managed to cross the border disguised
as the valet of a noble traveller.[2] On December 1 he announced
his arrival in Alcalá to the Cardinal, and a few days later discussions
began in Madrid between the famous Spanish minister and the
military agent of the Pretender.[3] The position in the Mediterranean,
the war in Sicily, the threatened invasion of Spain by two French
armies, and all that could be done to damage the Quadruple Alliance,
the conspiracy against the Duke of Orleans, Charles XII's help, the
mobilization of the Jacobites in England, who could only hope for
success if aided from abroad — all these things were taken into
consideration.

But success depended on the secret execution and favourable
outcome of too many separate actions. Everyone put his own ends
first. Charles XII declared that a landing in England could only
be considered after he had conquered Norway. Ormonde's disappointment over this loss of time was little allayed by the fact
that Alberoni had sent Lawless to induce Charles to change his
mind ; for he was unlikely to prevail against the notorious obstinacy
of the Swedish King.

Alberoni asked Ormonde what he demanded as necessary to
make an attempt to restore the King. Ormonde replied, 7000 or
8000 men, with arms and ammunition for 15,000. Alberoni answered
that since the greatest part of their troops were in Sicily, and since
they were threatened with an invasion from France in two places,
they could not spare a man, but that they would give arms and
ammunition, and money for the King of Sweden. Later Alberoni
agreed that

Spain would give 5000 men, of which 4000 are to be foot, a thousand
troopers, of which 300 with their horses . . . and two months pay
for them, ten field pieces, and 1000 barrels of powder, and 15,000 arms
for foot.[4]

Ormonde was pleased, but demanded further that, in order to
make a diversion in Scotland, he should send 2000 or 3000 arms
thither. Alberoni would only agree if there were a man of con-

[1] W. Stanhope to Craggs, Nov. 26, 1718, S.P. 94/88.
[2] Dubois to Stanhope, Mar. 15, 1719, Aff. étr. 323.
[3] For what follows see Dickson, *Jacobite Attempt of 1719*, Letter XIII.
[4] Dickson, *l.c.* p. 15 *seq.*

sideration to go with them. Ormonde named the young Earl
Marischal, who had led two cavalry squadrons at Sheriffmuir and
had been living since then in exile. Ormonde was to write to him
to come with all dispatch, and as privately as possible. In these
changed circumstances a second messenger was to be sent to Charles
XII, to press him to invade England before the spring, and to tell
him that otherwise no money would be given by the King of Spain.

The Chevalier was asked by Alberoni to leave Rome because of
the Emperor's spies, and to come to Spain with all expedition. He
ought either to embark with the troops if he could arrive in time,
or to follow as soon as possible, for the opportunity was not to be
lost.

But the greater part of Alberoni's plans was doomed to failure.
Once again bad luck dogged the Stuarts. The Cellamare conspiracy
was discovered; Charles XII fell on December 11 (N.S.), 1718, at
Friedrichshall. The Government of his successor, Ulrike Eleonore,
had no taste for military expeditions, and Baron Goertz, their chief
advocate, was executed a few months later. The relief of English
ministers was expressed by Craggs' words : " The death of the King
of Sweden . ... is a plain declaration, I think, that our cause is
a just one, since God has so visibly espoused it ".[1]

Alberoni and Ormonde did not at once realize what Charles XII's
death meant for their plans. " A very great loss," Ormonde
remarked, " but notwithstanding this misfortune we must follow
out our enterprise." [2] " If it is the Prince of Hesse who succeeds
. . . I think it will not be difficult to get him to hear reason on
this matter." [3] " A good sum ought to be offered to effect this
object." [4] Further messengers were to be sent to Sweden. Though
the Cardinal may have hesitated a moment to continue with the
now almost hopeless adventure, he pressed forward the preparation
of the expedition to England. To conceal their objective it was
said that the fleet was destined for Sicily, and Ormonde was not
allowed to come near Cadiz. He was to go to Corunna, where he
would be picked up by the fleet.

The expedition, which should have left on February 10, 1719,
was held up by winds and bad weather till March 7. Every lost
day diminished the prospects of success. Ormonde, waiting im-

[1] Craggs to Stair, Dec. 29, 1718, S.P. 104/30.
[2] Dickson, *l.c.* Letter XXVI.   [3] *Ibid.* Letter XLII.
[4] *Ibid.* Letter XXXVII.

patiently at Corunna, sent a small boat to lie off Cape Finisterre, which should give news of the approaching fleet. But then he decided that it would be more advisable that the admiral in command, Guevarra, should land in Corunna and discuss with him the route to be taken. What was good three weeks or a month ago seemed less good now ; he had heard that both France and England had been informed about the expedition, and had had time to take precautions ; so he thought it would be well to land in Scotland.

We could avoid a squadron which apparently is to be waiting for us at the mouth of the Channel by keeping well out to sea to the west of Ireland. We could defend ourselves and hold out in the Highlands. . . . I am assured that our friends will do what they can to join us, that is to say, those who are in the north of England. It is well to have a footing in the island ; accidents might happen to our advantage, and it is not impossible that the English troops in the country might desert.[1]

James' journey to Spain in February 1719 had to be made with all speed and secrecy ; for the English Government were trying by every means in their power to secure the arrest of the Pretender, whom they could now consider as an enemy in arms. To avoid this danger a cunning plan was devised. The Pretender left Rome in the direction of the Alps, as if intending to meet the Princess Clementina, while the Dukes of Mar and Perth in company of a third person set out with a large retinue, by way of Florence to Bologna. The bait took. When they reached Voghera on Imperial territory, they were stopped and taken to Milan. A general of the Emperor's forces came to see them, and told them that the King of England (for so he called him) had left Rome, nobody there knowing whither save the Pope. Mar asked him who they took them to be, and whether they by any chance took one of them for the Pretender. " God forbid ", said he, and then left them. But the world was surprised by the great news that the Pretender had been arrested near Milan. Stair reported the event to London with delight.[2] The mistake was soon discovered ; and the satisfaction at St. James' turned to disappointment ; the Emperor was furious, and sent orders himself that the travellers should be set at liberty.[3]

---

[1] *Ibid.* Letter LXXXVI.
[2] Stair to Craggs, Mar. 4, 1719, S.P. 78/163.
[3] Dickson, *l.c.* p. 206 *seq.*

Meanwhile the Pretender on his way to Spain had one adventure after another.[1] After he had embarked in the small papal harbour of Nettuno, he was pursued by two English ships. In Marseilles he lay ill with fever for three days, fled to Villefranche near Nice, and went for his health to the Iles d'Hyères ; here he landed in a miserable tavern, had to mix with vulgar people, and, as it was carnival time, he had to dance with the proprietress. At last he reached the Spanish coast at Rosa, and from here on he was under the protection of a friendly Government. King Philip and Queen Elizabeth sent him polite letters,[2] and greeted him as an ally. In Madrid he was received with royal honours, lodged in the Palace of Buen Retiro, and received a guard of honour of the King's bodyguard.

When he heard of Ormonde's change of plan, to which the Cardinal had already agreed,[3] James Edward showed himself obstinate and intractable, and would hear nothing of it. So Ormonde was forced to embark on an enterprise which, in existing circumstances, was doomed to failure from the outset. He obeyed the King's orders unhesitatingly and wrote apologetically that he had mentioned Scotland only as a *pis aller*.[4]

Your Excellency may rest assured . . . that I will think no more of Scotland, and that it will not be my fault if we do not land in England, for we shall do what is humanly possible to make the enterprise succeed. . . . I am bound by honour, which I value more than anything on earth.

But if Ormonde had made up his mind to sacrifice himself, his ships, and their crews, he would not agree that the person of the King should be exposed to such danger. He must not embark, though it would be embarrassing to find an excuse for the public, which judges with malice of the actions of princes as well as of those of persons of the humblest birth.[5] Ormonde's heroism is the more astonishing when one thinks of the man and the cause that it was to serve.

The surprise attack almost succeeded ; for in reality the English ministers only heard of it at the eleventh hour. A Jacobite travelling to Spain to join Ormonde was induced by agents of the French Government to tell everything they wished to know—the real

---

[1] Dickson, App. No. 17.   [2] *Ibid*. Apps. Nos. 15, 16.
[3] *Ibid*. Letter XCIII.   [4] *Ibid*. Letter XCIV.   [5] *Ibid*. Letter XCVI.

objective of the preparations in Cadiz, the number of ships, of
crews, and of weapons being taken. He told them that a landing
was to be made near Bristol, that Ormonde would lead the invasion,
and that the Pretender, who had already reached Spain, would
follow. Richly rewarded with gold the man was allowed to go on
to Spain, where he should serve the French Government further.

Dubois at once informed Stair, who forwarded the news to
England.[1] The danger was not considered serious, but precautions
had to be taken. Stair sent an urgent note to Craggs : " Press the
fitting out of your ships, raise as many troops as you [can], and
send to the Dutch to have their troops ready. The Spaniards
could not sail before the 7 or the 8 of this month. I hope our
squadron will be ready in time." [2] He thought the plan to be
absolutely in the style of Lord Oxford, who had not informed
Atterbury of it, because this prelate approved of no projects he had
not formed himself.[3] Stair had heard a report that Oxford considered about 6000 men sufficient for a landing in western England,
where, as they would be joined by the English soldiers who had
been dismissed the year before and by many of the gentry, their
numbers would soon reach 26,000. With this force they were to
march straight upon London. Though Stair saw the futility of the
whole project, he pointed out that it was only conceivable because
of the fundamental insufficiency of the English army, and pressed
for an increase. " It is a ridiculous thing for us always to be in
such a precarious situation as to be at the mercy of any prince
that will send 4 or 5000 men into England." [4] Because of the
English conception of freedom and distaste for a standing army,
even the few troops that the Government had at their disposal
had to be maintained by a sort of legal fiction.[5]

In England the ministers, despite the warnings they had had,
were surprised that the Spaniards could be so rash. Several
admirals had recommended that some men-of-war should cruise

[1] Dubois to Craggs, Mar. 8, 1719. (Dickson, l.c. App. No. 21) ; Stair to
Craggs, Reports and private letters of Mar. 1719, S.P. 78/163. Dubois to
Stanhope, Mar. 15, 1719, Aff. étr. 323.

[2] Dickson, l.c. App. No. 26.

[3] Stair to Craggs, Mar. 11, 1719, S.P. 78/163.

[4] Stair to Craggs, Mar. 12, 1719, S.P. 78/163.

[5] Cf. Hallam, *Constitutional History of England* (ed. 1850), vol. ii.
pp. 422-3.

off Cadiz in view of the preparations being made there. Had this advice been taken, said the fault-finders, the present danger would have been averted.[1] But no one was seriously perturbed ; " I cannot say ", wrote Craggs, " His Majesty is extremely alarmed about it " ; [2] and Hoffmann had heard say that the King was only worried about his plans for the summer, when he intended to go to Hanover.[3] As soon as the British coast was threatened by a Jacobite invasion, the Government could count on the active support of people and Parliament. George I attended Parliament in person for the reading of the King's Speech relating to the invasion, in which he expressed the hope that he would be enabled to make the necessary dispositions for the country's security. Both Houses assured him of their support, and the Commons in their Address promised to make good any increase of expense on that account. Even Robert Walpole, the only speaker for the Opposition, did not directly oppose the motion, but took the opportunity to find fault with the ministers. After he had been castigated by Craggs for unparliamentary allusions to the Peerage Bill, the Address was adopted unanimously.[4]

The preparations for the defence of the English coast were made without haste. Admiral Norris sailed from Portsmouth with a squadron of seven good ships to cruise off Land's End ; the ministers did not doubt that he would be able to give a very good account of a dozen Spanish ships, should he meet with them.[5] None the less the Earl of Berkeley, Lord High Admiral, wished to be commander-in-chief himself, and followed on March 29 with seven men-of-war. The two squadrons were to guard the approaches to the Channel. When the Spanish ships appeared, they were to use their utmost endeavour to come up with them, and either by taking, sinking, or otherwise destroying them, to prevent their landing in any part of the country.[6] These precautions seemed ample. The Duke of Orleans offered to lend 15,000 seamen for the English ships, and to post 20 battalions of infantry on the north coast of France. But the King in Council resolved to accept

---

[1] Hoffmann, Mar. 17, 1719, Vienna Archives.
[2] Dickson, *l.c.* p. 234.
[3] Hoffmann, Mar. 17, 1719, Vienna Archives.
[4] *Parl. Hist.* vol. vii. pp. 595-9.
[5] Dickson, *l.c.* p. 235.
[6] Instructions for Admiral Berkeley, Mar. 23, 1719, S.P. 44/220.

500 or 600 of the French seamen only as a proof that he could trust
them.   These men were never used, for the English navy prided
itself in doing its own service without any obligation to foreign
helps.   They were transported by English men-of-war from Havre,
Calais, and Dunkirk, and landed on the coast opposite.   But even
before the fate of Ormonde's expedition was known they were sent
home with a month's pay in their pockets as a gratuity for the
offer they had made to serve the King of England.[1]

On March 7, 1719, some thirty vessels sailed from Cadiz,[2] carrying about 5000 men and a number of horses.   Of this fleet only
five were men-of-war ;   the admiral's vessel had 64 or 66 cannon,
two others 50 each, the remaining two 20 or less.   This force was
absolutely inadequate to fight the two English squadrons which the
English Admiralty had easily been able to fit out, in spite of Byng's
fleet in the Mediterranean and preparations for an expedition to
the Baltic.   The crews were not equal to their task, some of the
captains had been pressed into service, and an English helmsman,
who had been taken prisoner and brought in chains on to one of
the vessels, was, after twenty-four hours, released and called upon
to steer his ship.   The delayed start of the fleet had been partly
due to such difficulties.

Water and provisions were taken for thirty days, which would
have been enough if they had taken the straightest route to England ;   instead they held W.S.W., apparently to accompany on a
part of the way a merchantman and a small mail boat that were
bound for the West Indies.   Only off the Canary Islands did they
turn N.N.E., but now the winds were unfavourable for a whole
month or more, and the English remarked with satisfaction that
they would probably be driven to the Azores.[3]   This the Spaniards
might have foreseen as well as Stair, who wrote without knowing
of their departure :   " The easterly wind which I have often seen
blow at this season of the year for a great while may do us great

---

[1] Stair to Craggs, Mar. 15, 1719, S.P. 78/163 ;   Craggs to Stair, Mar. 9,
12, Apr. 2, 9, 1719, S.P. 104/30.   This disproves the generally accepted view
that the transport of French infantry in English ships in the Crimean war
is unparalleled in history.

[2] Cf. Stair's Reports, S.P. 78/163 ;   Hoffmann's Reports, Vienna Archives ;
and Dickson, *l.c.*

[3] Hoffmann wrote that the wind alone would probably defeat this hostile
enterprise :   Apr. 4, 1719, Vienna Archives.

service ".[1] It was March 28 before they reached Cape Finisterre. Even if the weather had been good, their provisions would not have lasted, and the whole fleet would have had to put in to Corunna and re-victual.

Had the expedition actually landed in western England it would have had little prospect of defeating the English Government. For the 5000 foreign soldiers would hardly have inspired the English to rise in favour of the Pretender. But at one o'clock in the morning of March 28, when the fleet was in the latitude of 43°, about 50 leagues from Cape Finisterre, a violent storm sprang up, worse than experienced sailors could remember for the last twenty years. The ships were tossed about for three days and completely lost sight of each other. Cannon, horses, weapons, and provisions were thrown overboard to lighten them. When the gale abated, each captain tried to reach the nearest harbour ; one by one from about April 5 the ships appeared in the ports on the western coast of the Iberian peninsula, heavily damaged, often without masts and rigging, their crews exhausted, ill, and half starved.[2] The fate of the expedition recalls the famous defeat of the Spanish Armada, though the importance of the two catastrophes is in no way comparable.

James did not yet give up hope, and pressed King Philip to fit out another expedition. In the ensuing discussions Admiral Cammock (who had been dismissed from the English service for serious offences, had accompanied the Pretender across the Mediterranean, and was now an important member of the Spanish navy because he knew the English coasts so well), declared lightly that within eight days the fleet could be ready to sail again. Admiral Patiño, who had commanded the expeditions to Sardinia and Sicily, insisted that three months would be necessary for the preparations. Alberoni was of the same opinion, and felt that it would then be too late to repeat the experiment. The Pretender received empty promises that Spain would do all she could to carry out the project. Alberoni and the King and Queen assured him of their zeal for his cause, and King Philip wrote to him that they would work and work to refit the expedition,[3] but they pointed out the difficulties as well — the ships must be repaired ; new transport vessels must

---

[1] Stair to Craggs, Mar. 12, 1719, S.P. 78/163.
[2] Cf. Henry Worsley's Reports from Lisbon, S.P. 89/27.
[3] Dickson, *l.c.* p. 248.

be found ; weapons must be bought in Holland, and, though there was money enough, this would not be easy ; to procure the necessary supply of ship's biscuits two months would be needed ; finally, the fleet would have to be gathered at one place.

The refitting of the expedition was never attempted: the invasion of Spain by two French armies absorbed all the attention of the Spanish Government. Though James stayed on for several months, he received nothing but polite letters from the King and Queen. The escape of Princess Clementina was a welcome pretext to leave Spain in order to join his bride. His ambitions were buried again indefinitely, and the English Government could look on calmly if his Spanish benefactors sent nothing more than money to the landless Stuart prince.

The second expedition that was bound for Scotland left the bay of Los Pasajes on March 8.[1] Called upon by Ormonde, both Lord Marischal and his younger brother James Keith hastened to Spain. Marischal met Ormonde, but received instructions direct from Alberoni, who placed larger means at his disposal than was at first intended. The expedition consisted of two frigates with 300 Spanish soldiers and plenty of provisions.

Marischal had letters from Ormonde to several chiefs of the clans. It was expected that the Highlanders would join the Spaniards against the house of Hanover just as the English were to rally round Ormonde. The King himself would arrive in due time.

It was most important to win the participation of those Scottish nobles who had been living in exile since the last rising, and whose only hopes were centred on the Pretender. To this end the younger Keith was once more sent to France. Here he encountered numerous dangers. He set out with a few thousand crowns in his pocket and a note from the Duke of Ormonde which said : " Pray have entire confidence in the bearer ".[2] He visited his friends in Bordeaux, travelled to Orleans disguised as a servant, and attended a sort of Jacobite council of war in Paris, where the jealousy of the Scotch nobles, who grudged each other the leadership, was already visible. Yet all those who were able to travel joined him. They left the mouth of the Seine in a small ship on March 19, succeeded in slipping

---

[1] For what follows see letters given in Dickson, *l.c.*
[2] A Fragment of a Memoir of Field-Marshal J. Keith, written by himself (publ. of the Spalding Club, 5 ; Edinburgh, 1843).

through an English squadron near Land's End, and, after sailing round the west of Ireland, reached the Isle of Lewis, where they joined Marischal's expedition.

Meanwhile the English ambassador at Paris had learned from his spies that all those Englishmen and Scots, of whom they otherwise never lost sight, had suddenly disappeared, that they had embarked for Scotland, and, afterwards, that their ship had returned to Honfleur.[1] The English Government complained angrily

that such numbers of Jacobites are permitted openly to embark in the ports of France in order to disperse themselves over our provinces, when at such a juncture nothing should excuse France from publicly seizing and confining them.[2]

When the two brothers Keith and the foremost Scotch nobles held a council of war on the Isle of Lewis, opinions were already very much divided. The Earl Marischal wanted to cross at once to the mainland and to march with his Spanish soldiers and as many Highlanders as would join him straight to Inverness. The English garrison there of scarcely 300 men was to be overpowered quickly, and in possession of this place they could wait calmly for the spread of the rebellion, and would collect sufficient numbers of cavalry and infantry to advance southward. This was the course agreed upon with Alberoni, which, if Ormonde's forces and the English Jacobites co-operated, seemed to have some prospect of success. But suddenly the Marquis of Tullibardine produced a document in which he was appointed commander-in-chief of all the forces in Scotland by James III himself. The commission dated from the intended Swedish invasion of 1717, but Marischal at once made way for Tullibardine and only reserved for himself the command of the ships.

Now Marischal's firm determination was hampered by Tullibardine's cautious indecision. The crossing was made contrary to the wish of Tullibardine, and the march to Inverness was not attempted. In order to avoid every challenging action he would not even try to stir the masses of the Scotch people, and hoped the rebellion would spread underground till news arrived that Ormonde had landed in England. After they had waited for a few days in vain he despaired of everything and thought it best to sail

[1] Stair's Reports, Mar. and Apr. 1719, S.P. 78/163.
[2] Craggs to Stair, Mar. 16, 1719, S.P. 104/30.

back to Spain. The others, however, persuaded him not to give up ;
and to avoid any recurrence of such pusillanimity Marischal promptly
sent back his two frigates. For better or for worse they now had to
go on with their adventure.

Weapons and provisions had been stored in a fort on an island
near the coast, and left under the guard of forty-five Spaniards. A
few days after their frigates had left, several English men-of-war
appeared, and the old stone walls of the fort were not able to resist
their cannonade for long. Soldiers and provisions fell into the
hands of the English and the old fort was blown up. The small
force on the mainland was now in a desperate position, for there
was no hope of escape by sea, and the poverty of the countryside
offered little for the maintenance of the troops. To crown it all,
news arrived that Ormonde's fleet had been destroyed ; and though
it was said that another one would be fitted out quickly, no immediate help could be expected. Now Tullibardine was forced to call on
the Scots to raise the banner of the Stuarts. Only a small band of
about 1000 men could be induced to join in the hopeless struggle.

Because of the military conditions in Great Britain, the Government took a long time to send troops to crush the rebellion.[1] The
force under General Wightman, who had fought at Sheriffmuir,
was not even as large as that of the rebels. As troops and horses
arrived only slowly, he had to postpone his departure several times.
On June 4 he complained that " had the gentlemen of the civil
power performed their parts in the least proportion to my actions,
I should have been ashamed to have dated this letter from Inverness ". Next day he left with 850 infantrymen, 120 dragoons, and
about 130 Highlanders — for the Government too attempted to win
the Scots to fight for them. Even this force was not purely British,
but contained a regiment and four companies of Dutch troops
brought to fight for the house of Hanover in a remote corner of
Scotland against the Spanish troops of the house of Stuart.

The Jacobites had chosen the gorge of Glenshiel, near Kintail,

---

[1] For the fight at Glenshiel cf. the Reports of Wightman and others,
S.P. 43/61 ; Wightman to Carpenter, June 11/22, 1719, in Hoffmann's Report
of June 30, 1719, Vienna Archives ; Mar's " Distinct Abridgement " in
C. S. Terry, *The Chevalier de St. George* (1901), pp. 474-5 ; *Portland MSS.*,
vol. v. pp. 584-7 ; Terry, in the *Scotch Historical Review*, July 1905, with
two plans of the battle, one reproduced here.

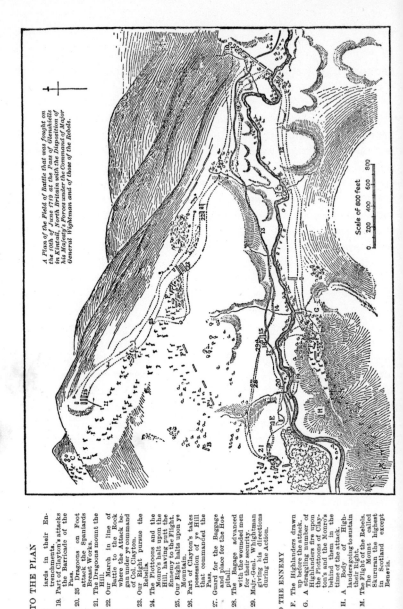

A Plan of the Field of Battle that was fought on the 10th of June 1719 at the Pass of Glenshiels in Kintail, North Britain with the Disposition of his Majesty's Forces under the Command of Major General Wightman and of those of the Rebels.

Scale of 800 feet

0 200 400 600 800

REFERENCES TO THE PLAN

1. A Sergt. and 12 Grenadiers.
2. An Officer and 24 do.
3. Main body of Grenadiers, 120 in Num.
4. Col. Montagu's Regmt.
5. Col. Harrison's Detacht Battalion.
6. Huffel's Regmt. and 4 Companies of Amerongen's.
7. Dragoons.
8. Col. Clayton's Regiment.
9. The Monro's Highlanders.
10. The Sutherland's Right.
11. The first march by ye Right.
12. Clayton's march by the Left.
13. The Dragoons march to the Plain.
14. The Dragoons Halt.
15. The Dragoons advance to the middle of the Plain.
16. Clayton's four Plottoons and the Monro's making ye First Attack on ye Rebels Right.
17. Cohorn Mortars throwing Granades at the Rebels where ye First Attack was Ordered.
18. Cohorn Mortars throwing Granades at ye Spaniards in their Entrenchments.
19. Part of Clayton's attacks the Barricade of the Pass.
20, 35 Dragoons on Foot attack the Spaniards Breast Works.
21. The Dragoons mount the Hill.
22. Our March in line of Battle to the Rock where the Attack began under ye command of Col. Clayton.
23. Our Right pursue the Rebels.
24. The Plottoons and the Monro's halt upon the Hill, having pitt the Ennemy to the Flight.
25. Our Right halts upon ye Mountain.
26. Part of Clayton's takes possession of ye Hill that commanded the Pass.
27. Guard for the Baggage and place for the Hospitall.
28. The Bagage advanced with the wounded men for their security.
29. Majr.-Genl. Wightman giving his directions during the Action.

REFERENCES TO THE ENEMY

A. Spanish Regiment posted on the Hill that commanded the Plain and the Pass.
B. Spaniards march to ye Mount and Halt.
C. The Spaniards retire to the Top of the mountain.
D. The Barricade that defended the Pass on the River Side.
E. The Breastworks on the Side of the Hill.
F. The Highlanders drawn up before the attack.
G. A straggling number of Highlanders fire upon the Plottoons of Clayton's and the Monro's behind them in the time of the attack.
H. A Body of Highlanders going to sustain their Right.
M. The Right of the Rebels. The Mount called Skurruan the highest in Scotland except Benevis.

to await the enemy.　The gorge stretches from west to east, and down it runs the river Shiel, skirted by a path which threads the Pass of Glenshiel.　On both sides are rocks and mountains which to the north rise to a height of 3505 feet.　Tullibardine expected that the enemy would march up the valley and deliver their main attack here.　He placed his best troops, the Spaniards, on a hill commanding the path, and fortified their position to the east, whence he expected the enemy, with entrenchments and ramparts. A barricade was built a little further east between the path and the river to hold up the advance of the enemy.　The left wing consisted of a few hundred Highlanders who had taken up positions in the hills, largely behind rocks.　Lord Marischal was here with Lord Seaforth, who had gathered 200 of his best men about him. The main body of the Highlanders, 500 strong or more, was posted between the Spaniards and the left wing.　To the south-east, and somewhat higher, 150 Highlanders under Lord George Murray, brother of Tullibardine, formed the right wing.　They were to be joined by 80 men, stationed on a more distant hill, but these failed to appear at the critical moment and did not take any part in the battle.　The enthusiasm of the Scots was probably just as lacking as their discipline.　They had come in obedience to their chiefs, especially Lord Seaforth, but their support was only half-hearted.

General Wightman marched as quickly as the nature of the Highlands would allow.　From Inverness he proceeded along Loch Ness, and at the far end of the loch he waited for a day, hoping to collect more pack-horses, but found none, so not much more provisions could be taken than the soldiers were able to carry.　In spite of this they overcame the difficulties of their way across the mountains with excellent discipline, and Wightman gave the credit especially to Major Robinson of the Grey Dragoons that not one horse had been left behind.　On June 10 at four o'clock in the afternoon they first caught sight of the rebels in their battle-array, and Wightman very much wanted to attack them the same day, as it was the birthday of the Pretender.

The centre of General Wightman's order of battle was formed by 120 dragoons, who were placed on both sides of the path behind four mortars.　To their right stood the main body of the infantry, consisting of the regiment and four companies of Dutchmen, the regiments of Harrison and Montague, and then 150 grenadiers under Major Milburn ; to their left, south of the river, stood Colonel

Clayton's regiment. The two extreme wings were formed by Highlanders, some 50 men of Lord Strathnaver's soldiers on the right, 100 men of Monroe's regiment on the left.

Wightman opened the battle by attacking with Clayton's regiment and Monroe's men the enemy's right wing, which was led by Lord George Murray. They resisted for some time — according to a Jacobite report for two hours — and not much damage was done to either side, till the four mortars fired the heath and woods so successfully that the Highlanders had to leave their positions. In vain Lord George and two other commanders drew their swords and ordered their men to follow them. They fled across a little brook to the steep slopes opposite, where for the moment the enemy could not follow them.

Meanwhile General Wightman had sent his men to the attack on the other side of the valley. Evidently he intended to drive back the main body of the enemy, the greater part of the Highlanders which he saw before him, by an onslaught from the right, and then to storm the Spaniards' position. Apparently the extreme left wing of the rebels under Seaforth had completely escaped his notice. Only when his troops had climbed a hill in order to attack the enemy's left did they see that there were still some hundred Highlanders high above them on the right. Colonel Clayton, who was in command of the Government's right wing, had to wheel to the right with the greater part, probably not the whole, of his troops and to climb the height occupied by Seaforth. The fight which Seaforth's men and the Mackenzies put up from behind rocks and bushes against superior numbers is loudly praised in Jacobite reports. It seems to have lasted for several hours. Again and again Seaforth asked for reinforcements from the centre ; but far too few men were sent, because it was feared that a weakening of the centre would attract the main attack of the enemy. At last Seaforth's men gave way, and he himself was carried wounded from the field. The reinforcements that were on their way hardly came into action. The Macgregors, the Mackinnons, the Camerons, all retired instead of fighting. The Spaniards, unwilling to bear all the weight of the battle, joined in the general retreat, and tried to reach the hill-tops before it was dark. Wightman's plan to roll up the enemy lines from their wings had proved a complete success. Only darkness prevented a pursuit.

The strength of the Jacobite band was broken. When next

morning the commanders met for a council of war, they could
hardly have any illusions about the hopelessness of their situation.
Though the Spanish commander recommended that they should
make an attack, and Tullibardine talked of a joint march across
the Highlands, where they should wait for an opportunity to renew
the struggle, both courses were impossible. So the humiliating
decision was taken that the Spaniards should surrender, and the
Scots should disperse in the mountains. Their flight was made the
subject of a biting satire :

> Not famous for one martial deed
> But that they run away with speed
> And nimbly skipped from rock to mountain
> And of their heels made most account on.
>
> The hardy Marshal I protest
> He ran as fast as did the best
> And Seaforth that great man of Mars
> Was glad like Mar to shew his arse.
>
> That doubly champion Tullibardine
> His honour valued not a farthing.
> But rather than stay to be taken
> Ran clean away to save his bacon.[1]

The battle of Glenshiel was the end of the campaign. General
Wightman made a short raid through the neighbouring Highlands
to burn the houses of rebel leaders and to spread fear of the
Government's strength. But twelve days after the battle he was
back in Inverness, and could report that the Jacobites were totally
dispersed.[2]

The leaders of the rising managed to hide till they found an
opportunity to leave Scotland. Thus the Government was spared
the unpleasant task of again making a bloody example of some
highborn rebels. Nor could the other Highlanders who had fought
at Glenshiel be punished. They had long been back at home, and
when Government forces approached they were either innocently
at work or, if they thought they had been recognized, had disappeared. " It is impossible to catch any rebell Highlanders with

---

[1] *An answer to the Hymn to the victory in Scotland.* By an Officer in
His Majesty's fleet (London, n.d.), B.M. 1872 a.1.

[2] Hoffmann, July 14, 1717, Vienna Archives ; Wightman to Carpenter,
June 11/22, 1719, in Hoffmann's Report of June 30.

party's of regular troops ", said Lord Carpenter ; " they are on the mountains with their cattle, and will be able easily to avoid any parties of the troops that might be sent to take them or their cattle." [1] It was impossible to draw up a list of the persons of note and the numbers of those who had been in the rebellion, as the Government desired ; [2] for prisoners, who could have been questioned, had hardly been taken, and the loyal Highlanders were unwilling to give evidence because of the ties of affinity and consanguinity that existed between them and the rebels.

The Spanish soldiers who had surrendered caused the Government some embarrassment. Wightman took them to Inverness, but no one knew what to do with them next. [3] It was suggested that they should march through Scotland and England to London and finally embark in Plymouth, in order to give the lie to those who asserted that the invasion was only a fable invented by the ministers in order to obtain grants from Parliament. [4] The Spaniards were, however, only taken to Edinburgh, where their confinement was mild but the money advanced for their subsistence was scarce. [5] The population liked the simple people, who had nothing of Spanish swagger about them. On October 27 they were put on board at Leith and sent to Spain, though peace was not yet concluded.

Once again the Protestant Succession had withstood an attack from the Jacobites. Without so much as waiting for the end of the campaign George I had gone to his beloved Hanover. For the next twenty years Jacobite activities consisted of nothing more than conspiracies that were nipped in the bud. Lord Seaforth made his peace with the English Government some years later, and was allowed to return home. The brothers Tullibardine and Lord George Murray fought and failed again in the 'Forty-five. The two Keiths acquired European fame in the service of Frederick the Great.

Queen Mary had not lived to see the disappointment of 1719. She died on May 7, 1718, in St. Germains, as devout as she had lived. [6] She was buried without royal pomp ; and when the Regent

[1] Dickson, *l.c.* App. No. 68.
[2] *Ibid.* App. No. 66.
[3] Craggs to Stanhope (in Hanover), July 3, 1719, S.P. 44/269A.
[4] Hoffmann, July 7, 1719, Vienna Archives ; Dickson, *l.c.* App. No. 66.
[5] See *Lockhart Papers*, vol. ii. pp. 23-4. Also Dickson, *l.c.* App. No. 74.
[6] Saint-Simon, *Mémoires*, vol. x. p. 41 (ed. 1878).

asked the English ambassador whether his Court would go into mourning, he was told that for the moment King George did not wish any notification in form.[1]

James Edward spent some years of private happiness with his wife Clementina and two sons in Rome, where his stay could now do no damage to a cause already lost. Rome and the Pope treated him as a foreign sovereign, calling him King and Majesty. Condemned to a life of inactivity which befitted his soft nature, he appeared to the world as a noble martyr.

An English traveller described a visit to Prince James Edward's stately palace, the Villa Ludovisi : [2]

> The Pretender was easily distinguished by his Star and Garter, as well as by an air of greatness, which discovered a majesty superior to the rest. . . . I was perfectly stunned and not aware of myself, when pursuant to what the standers-by did, I made him a salute ; he returned it with a smile, which changed the sedateness of his first aspect into a very graceful countenance.

The Prince said that English gentlemen were always welcome in his house, and the Princess added in the prettiest English that if they liked music, they should come to her concert that evening.

> We went and saw a bright assembly of the prime Roman nobility, the Consort [sic] composed of the best musicians in Rome, a plentiful and orderly collation serv'd . . . next day . . . the Pretender entertained us on the subject of our families as knowingly as if he had been all his life in England. . . . I was surprised at his perfect knowledge of our families in England. His answer was that from his infancy he had made it his business to acquire the knowledge of the laws, customs and families of his country, so as he might not be reputed a stranger, when the Almighty pleased to call him thither.

The traveller and his friends were then pressed to have lunch with James, who had every day a table of ten or twelve covers.

> It's supplied with English and French cookery, French and Italian wines, but I took notice that the Pretender eat only of the English dishes and made his dinner of roast-beef, and what we call Devonshire pye. He also prefers our March beer . . . to the best wines.

On post-day Englishmen commonly went to the Pretender's house

[1] Stair to Craggs, May 7, 1718, S.P. 78/164.
[2] A letter from an English traveller at Rome to his father of the 6th May, 1721 (O.S.), S.P. 35/26.

for news, largely concerned with the South Sea mismanagements. The Pretender

bemoaned the misfortune of England groaning under a load of debts, and the severest hardships, contracted and imposed to support foreign interests. He lamented the ill treatment and disregard of the ancient nobility. . . . Some may imagine, he continued, that these calamities are not displeasing to me, because they may in some measure turn to my advantage, I renounce all such unworthy thoughts. The love of my country is the first principle of my worldly wishes, and my heart bleeds to see so brave and honest a people distressed and misled by a few wicked men, and plunged into miseries almost irretrievable.

James also discussed the position of the Churches.

I have been told by several of the most eminent prelates of the Church of Rome . . . that it should never be my business to study how to be an apostle, but how to become a good king to all my people without distinction. . . .

He (James) was entirely of opinion, that all clergymen not authorized by the Statutes of a nation ought to be confined to the bare duties of their profession, and that if any of them should be found intermeddling with public concerns or creating disputes, to the prejudice of the good understanding, that ought to be cherished between the King and his subjects, it was his opinion, they ought to be removed out of the way of doing mischief.

The traveller was more impressed by the dignity with which James Edward bore his fate than by the poverty of his political ideas : " . . . were he not the Pretender I should like the man very well . . . he speaks with such an air of sincerity ".

CHAPTER X

IN the early eighteenth century there existed in Europe two blocs of states, which seemed to be almost completely disconnected. In the centre, west, and south were the Germanic and Romance states that had inherited and developed the classical and Christian tradition ; in the north and east the Scandinavian states had long been powerful, the Slav state of Poland, which had been influenced by western culture since the Middle Ages, had risen to political importance, and Russia, a complete newcomer to the scene, had been attracting universal attention.

Between these states of the north and east a war was being waged quite independently of the war of the Spanish Succession. It had been begun by the young Charles XII in order to anticipate the dangerous plans of Russia, Poland, and Denmark ; but in the end he was not even able to defend his old possessions against his enemies, who had been joined by Prussia and Hanover.

The scene of the Northern war remained distinct from that of the war of the Spanish Succession because a disunited Germany in the middle of Europe formed a neutral zone. But the rest of Europe was keenly interested in the outcome. France still favoured Sweden's presence on German territory, for since the days of Richelieu this had been considered a political necessity as a help against the House of Habsburg ; but as Sweden's power had been reduced by the war, France looked to Prussia for a substitute. England's interest on the other hand was mainly commercial. Sweden had till now held the *Dominium maris Baltici* ; but as she exploited it only politically and financially, allowing Dutch and English merchantmen to ply the Baltic without let or hindrance, England raised no objection. This trade was sometimes criticized in England because the imports by far exceeded the exports in value and quantity ; strict theorists of the mercantile system would have liked to forbid it completely. But it was indispensable because so much shipbuilding material came from this quarter. Through the annual expeditions to the Baltic England had incurred Sweden's hostility,[1] but by 1718 Sweden was so weakened that she could no longer be a danger to England. Charles XII's plan of invading Scotland would hardly have worried the English ministers, even if they had not heard of his death before they heard of the plan.

With the passing of Sweden's power no one knew who would assume the *Dominium maris Baltici*. If Peter the Great, the pupil of Dutch shipbuilders and the promoter of western trade and industry in Russia, were to keep the ports of Riga and Reval, taken from Sweden in 1710, he would gain the best part of the Baltic trade, which England could not allow. Though he had promised Queen Anne never to build a navy in the Baltic, the English politicians felt it safer not to allow him any footing on its coasts.

England's connexion with Russia had begun in 1553,[2] when an English merchantman was driven by a storm into the mouth of the Dvina. The captain, who had to winter on the Muscovite coast, obtained permission to visit the court of the Tsar, where Ivan Vassilievitch received him well. In the spring he was allowed to return, bearing a letter from the Tsar to Edward VI in which formal permission was given for English ships to visit the Russian coasts, and for English merchants to travel where they pleased, to bring their goods and to establish markets.

From that time dated England's domination of Russian trade. In 1555 the merchants who had been on the expedition of 1553 formed the Russia or Muscovia Company, the first Joint Stock Company in England.[3] The Company was able to sell Russian wares in England at high prices because of its monopoly ; and it obtained more and more facilities and exclusive rights in Russia. By the end of the sixteenth century England had established its

---

[1] Cf. Vol. I. Ch. XI.

[2] On Anglo-Russian relations before Peter the Great cf. the introduction by F. de Martens to the *Recueil des traités et conventions conclus par la Russie avec les puissances étrangères* : Traités avec l'Angleterre (1892), vol. i. pp. i-cvii. (First published in the Revue d'hist. dipl. 5.)

[3] Cf. W. R. Scott, *The Constitution and Finance of English, Scottish and Irish Joint Stock Companies to 1720* (1912), vol. i. p. 18 seq.

commercial supremacy throughout the Russian empire, while avoiding all closer political ties.

The English Revolution and Civil War led to the collapse of English privileges in Russia. The merchants of Moscow took advantage of the anti-English feeling and laid before the Tsar a written complaint about the domination of Russian markets by foreigners. The news of Charles I's execution did the rest. On June 1, 1649, the Tsar Alexis Michailovitch ordered the expulsion of all Englishmen from all towns in his Empire. Even in Archangel, at the mouth of the Dvina, they were only allowed to land and trade, but not to settle.

Anglo-Russian relations remained unfriendly till the reign of Peter the Great. At first he too was little inclined to satisfy the wishes of English merchants; but he was greatly interested in England's maritime achievements. In 1698 he spent three months in London, where the shipyards and docks attracted him more than political circles. When he left with his huge train of Russian nobles and hundreds of English craftsmen and technicians, William III did the right thing by presenting him with an old frigate. But there was little change in the relations between the two states.[1]

Peter's star was now in the ascendant, and in spite of his defeat at Narva he was able to establish himself on the Baltic coast, and even dared to found his new capital on Swedish territory. England watched his progress with anxiety, and became less and less inclined to offer him political support. In 1704 Charles Whitworth, an able young diplomat, was sent to the Russian Court. His chief duty was to protect and develop English trade; but he soon realized that if the English spoke of nothing but trading interests it would become evident to the Russians how much they needed their goods, and how indifferent they were to Russia's power and friendship.

The Tsar hoped to overcome England's mistrust and to press her into the role of mediator between Russia and Sweden. Matveyev, his ambassador at The Hague, was to go to London and to declare that if Russia kept the Baltic ports they would be open to English trade. He was to point out to the English how much more convenient and advantageous it would be for them to ship the Russian

[1] Cf. Collyer, " Diplomatic Relations between England and Russia in the First Half of the Eighteenth Century ", *Transact. of the Roy. Hist. Soc.*, N.S. XIV. (1900).

wares from these ports than by the dangerous route from Archangel. But in spite of Peter's clever appeal and the offers of huge bribes, Matveyev's mission was a complete failure.

Under George I Anglo-Russian relations improved, as the Elector was an ally of Russia.[1] By the Greifswald Alliance of 1715 between Hanover and Russia, the Tsar was to have Ingermanland, Karelia, Esthonia, and Reval from Sweden, and the Elector Bremen and Verden. In March 1716 Prince Kurakin,[2] who had signed on behalf of Russia, came to London to draw England into the alliance against Sweden.[3] The English again demanded that a commercial agreement must precede any political alliance ; but the aims of the two parties were so different that no agreement was possible. Kurakin left London in April with a draft alliance, given to him by Bernstorff and Bothmer. The English proposals were answered by Russian counter-proposals, in one of which, relating to the political alliance, it was only too clear that Russia intended to drive England into the war against Sweden. This was directly contrary to English wishes ; and the Russian offer of a commercial agreement was thought quite inadequate, as it did not so much as restore the old privileges for trading in Kasan and Astrachan.

Soon after Kurakin's mission had failed to bring about the desired *rapprochement* between Russia and England, the relations between the Tsar and Hanover also deteriorated. In 1716 the Russian fleet of galleys landed 10,000 men in Danzig, and still larger forces came overland through Poland. They were all to join in the siege of Wismar, and, after this last Swedish bulwark on German territory had fallen, they were to invade Schonen. Owing to a series of disagreements among the allies these troops were ordered back to Mecklenburg when they had reached Seeland on their way to Schonen. They then remained on German territory, and their presence was a source of general anxiety. In 1717 there were still some 40,000 Russian soldiers in Mecklenburg. It was feared that Peter the Great thought of following the example of

---

[1] Cf. Vol. I. p. 295.

[2] Cf. Waliszewski, *Pierre le Grand* (1897), p. 234.

[3] Cf. Appendix 7 ; also J. F. Chance, *George I and the Northern War*, p. 122 *seq.* ; Norris and Whitworth to Sunderland, Aug. 31, 1717, S.P. 84/257. Hoffmann, Apr. 7, 1716, Vienna Archives.

Gustavus Adolphus by establishing himself in Germany. A strongly worded letter from the Emperor Charles VI, in which he demanded the withdrawal of the Russian soldiers, was without effect. George I felt his German possessions threatened by the proximity of the Russians, especially as Frederick William I of Prussia was on good terms with the Tsar. Hanover began to arm, and Denmark was expected to help in raising a strong force to drive out the dangerous guests.

Peter the Great was at that time travelling in western Europe. He dropped hints to the French ambassador at The Hague about a close political union between their two countries. In May 1717 he went to Paris, where according to Saint-Simon court circles were amazed at the extraordinary mixture of majesty and barbarism in their distinguished guest, at his curiosity and at his clear, practical mind. Here, in an audience which he gave to Lord Stair, the Tsar agreed to the withdrawal of the troops from Mecklenburg,[1] and the necessary orders were given. His change of attitude was probably due to pressure from the Emperor, the threat of a combined attack, the advice of Prussia,[2] and the mediation of France. In this case England had honestly supported the policy of Hanover, not out of sympathy with Germany or even Hanover, but because she felt Russia's growing power to be a threat to her own interests in the Baltic.

The Tsar also told Stair that he was willing to conclude an Anglo-Russian treaty of commerce, and the British Government was able to look forward to a period of improved relations with the Tsar. They inquired politely where their plenipotentiary might find him.[3] As Peter had left Paris for Amsterdam, Sir John Norris was sent there with instructions that, after giving general assurances of friendship, he should in particular return thanks for the Tsar's willingness to evacuate Mecklenburg. He was to express the hope that the Russian troops would leave Mecklenburg and the Reich without committing any excesses ; and that the Tsar would push on the war against Sweden with the utmost vigour. Norris was

---

[1] Addison to Stair, June 9, 1717, S.P. 104/29 ; Instructions for Sir John Norris, July 2, 1717, F.O. 90/57A.

[2] Droysen, in "Die Wiener Allianz vom 5. Januar 1719", in the *Zeitschrift für preussische Geschichte und Landeskunde*, 5, pp. 639-40, maintains that Prussia's attitude was decisive.

[3] Addison to Stair, June 9, 1717, S.P. 104/29.

further to find out whether the Tsar was in a condition to make any enterprise upon Sweden that summer or the following year. England would be ready to employ her best offices to settle a true friendship between Peter and Charles VI, which might be of great use to the Tsar if he hoped to recover from the Ottoman Porte what he was forced to give up by the peace of the Pruth. Above all, England was very desirous to bring the negotiations for a treaty of commerce to a good end, and to take them up again where they were left off the year before, to which purpose she would expect the Tsar's answer to the counter-project which was delivered to Prince Kurakin by the British minister then at The Hague.[1]

England evidently hoped to embroil Russia in a new conflict with Turkey. Norris and Whitworth, now Ambassador in The Hague, stayed in Amsterdam from July till September 1717, in their attempt to attain their objectives. But though Peter received the Admiral as an old acquaintance, it was clear almost from the beginning that the British and Russian aims were incompatible. The discussions on political, military, and economic questions were only superficial.[2] When Norris and Whitworth mentioned the suggestions which the Tsar had made to Stair concerning a treaty of commerce, the High Chancellor Count Golovkin and the Vice-Chancellor Baron Shaffirov gave them the crushing answer that the Tsar had never proposed to conclude the treaty of commerce separately, but only in conjunction with, and subsequent to, a defensive alliance and a treaty by which Russia would be guaranteed her conquests and England her Succession. If this treaty were not to be had, at least the British fleet was to help the Russians in the Baltic till the end of the war. They also asserted that before concluding a commercial treaty they would have to consult their own merchants ; and the suggestions concerning Turkey were rejected, as the Tsar did not want to take any steps which might involve him in a new war before peace with Sweden was concluded. Then the Russian ministers enquired if the English had definite proposals to put forward, and if they could make an agreement for military operations.

Either the treaty of guarantee or the help of the British fleet would have led to war with Sweden, against which the Tsar would

[1] Instructions for Norris, July 2, 1717, F.O. 90/57A.
[2] For what follows see Norris' and Whitworth's Reports, S.P. 84/257. Cf. also Chance, *l.c.* p. 225 *seq.*

then have been able to do what he pleased, and so to develop and fortify his conquests. Norris and Whitworth retreated, saying that their instructions were only to assure the Tsar that His Majesty was ready to consult with him and wished to be informed of his intentions.[1]

The vanity of their efforts was brought home to the English negotiators when under their eyes a Russo-Franco-Prussian alliance was concluded in Amsterdam.[2] Prussia was guaranteed afresh in the possession of Stettin ; Peter, who when in Paris had offered to take Sweden's place at the side of France, obtained the French promise to cease sending the annual subsidy of 600,000 crowns or any other help to Sweden ; in return France was formally recognized by the other contracting parties as mediator in the coming peace.

The British diplomats were irritated at the secrecy with which this treaty had been concluded ; and especially upset by the intention expressed in the treaty of completing the political arrangements by a commercial and maritime agreement. Negotiations were to begin within eight months, on the basis of the principle of the most favoured nation. The Dutch also were apprehensive of the intended treaty,[3] which however never came into being.

If France should settle a commerce with the Czar, it might be of great prejudice to Holland, since whatever . . . commodities France has hitherto wanted from the Baltick they always bought in this country.

The Burgomaster of Amsterdam and other prominent Dutchmen conferred with Norris. As the Baltic trade had so far been completely in the hands of England and Holland, the two countries were to work together in the attempt to make peace for the King of Sweden, and to regain for him his possessions on the Livonian coast, the loss of which he would feel far more than the loss of those in Germany. This was the way to keep the Tsar and Prussia within the necessary bounds ; but it could only be done on the principle of *negligere pecuniam.*

Norris was already convinced that his mission was a failure,

---

[1] Norris and Whitworth to Sunderland, Aug. 6, 1717, S.P. 84/257.

[2] Cf. Löwe, *Preussens Staatsverträge aus der Regierungszeit König Friederich Wilhelms I.*, p. 169.

[3] Norris to Sunderland, Aug. 17, 20, 1717, S.P. 84/257.

when he received instructions that in case the Russians did not express themselves more frankly before the Tsar left Holland, he should follow him no further.[1] The tone of the discussions grew steadily sharper; the Tsar thought that the English gave many fair words, but offered nothing real or essential, and demanded written proposals for help in military operations. These the English declined to give, as not being in principle engaged in the war. Then the Russians offered their written proposals; but the English warned them that they must expect a pretty general answer—on which Shaffirov replied that he saw there would be no peace till England came into the war.[2]

Then written proposals were actually exchanged.[3] The Russians asked that the King of England should promise for the next campaign a squadron of not less than fifteen of the line, including some first raters, to join the Russian fleet and to be at the disposal of the Tsar. This granted, the latter would make a descent upon Sweden in proper strength. The British squadron was to come year after year until Sweden was reduced. In return, the Tsar would give every possible facility towards a treaty of commerce. The British insisted that the treaty of commerce must be put in the forefront, and that the Russian propositions would then be considered by the King.

The negotiations that ended thus were not even mentioned by Peter or his ministers when Norris and Whitworth took leave of them. The British diplomats were praised by their Government for having so cleverly avoided the traps laid for them.

Anglo-Hanoverian policy was now openly hostile to Russia. Negotiations began in Stockholm for peace between Hanover and Sweden. As Peter the Great was negotiating at the same time, Russia and Hanover were trying to forestall each other in concluding peace with Sweden.[4] But no peace was possible with Charles XII. In the summer of 1718, when Turkey had just concluded peace with Austria,[5] England tried to rouse her against Russia. The pretext was to be the fact that the Tsar had, contrary to the terms

---

[1] Sunderland to Norris, Aug. 2, 6, 9, 1717, S.P. 104/122.
[2] Norris and Whitworth to Sunderland, Aug. 31, 1717, S.P. 84/257.
[3] Their contents are given in Chance, *l.c.* pp. 228-9.
[4] Hoffmann, Mar. 25, 1718, Vienna Archives.
[5] Cf. Vol. I. p. 362 *seq.*

of the treaty of the Pruth, left his troops in Poland. St. Saphorin wrote to Sir Robert Sutton that he would crown his successes if, in addition to bringing about peace between Turkey and Austria, he should now bring about a war between Turkey and Russia. Sutton wrote to the Grand Vizier, warning him against the Russian danger. But Turkey was too much weakened to think of a new campaign.

The Tsar, whose diplomacy was as cunning as that of any of the old European Powers, followed the example set him and established contact with England's enemies, Spain and the Jacobites. James Edward and Alberoni were on friendly terms with Sweden on the one hand and Russia on the other. The son of Prince Kurakin went to Madrid, and leading Jacobites were given a friendly reception at the Russian Court.[1] Only a reconciliation between Russia and Sweden was needed to complete the circle of England's enemies ; but this was rendered impossible by the struggle for the Baltic provinces and the failure of the Aland conferences.

In these circumstances Peter preferred to keep up the appearance of friendship with England. In the summer of 1718 the Russian resident in London was instructed to suggest new negotiations for an alliance. As in England war with Spain now seemed inevitable, and as it was known how much Alberoni was counting on the Northern States, the suggestion fell on good ground. Though the English ministers doubted the Tsar's sincerity,[2] they decided to send Norris to the Russian Court.

You are so well acquainted with the situation of affairs in those parts [wrote Stanhope], as not to be ignorant, that his Majesty might very reasonably doubt of the truth and sincerity of what this Resident says. . . . But . . . your going . . . cannot fail . . . either to beget a real good understanding between us, . . . or . . . to make it notorious to the world that it doth not lye at our door, if there be not a good understanding between us.[3]

As Norris was away on the customary Baltic expedition, James Jefferyes was sent to bring him all the necessary material, to accompany him to St. Petersburg, and to stay there when the Admiral left after three or four weeks. James Jefferyes had been British minister to Charles XII from 1711 to 1715, first in London, then

---

[1] Memorial relating to the Court of Muscovy, S.P. 104/122.
[2] Cf. Appendix 7.
[3] Stanhope to Norris, Oct. 5, 1718, S.P. 104/122.

in Stralsund. His appointment as Resident in St. Petersburg was significant, as for years England had had no representative in the Russian capital.[1] Previously the Hanoverian Resident Weber had conducted the affairs of Great Britain. *Diplomatic amphibians* was the contemporary term for this kind of representatives, who spoke one day in the name of the Elector of Hanover, and the next for the King of England, but whose instructions all came from the German chancellery of George I. Peter the Great was said to dislike this arrangement, and to hate Weber as a creature of Bernstorff : the sending of two Englishmen to speak only in the name of Great Britain showed therefore consideration for the personal wishes of the Tsar.[2]

As Veselovski's statement that the Aland Conferences had been broken off was not believed in London, it was expected that by the time Norris and Jefferyes arrived at the Russian Court, the Russo-Swedish peace would either be concluded or on the point of conclusion. According to Norris' instructions, " If . . . the Peace be not already concluded, it may happen that you will be able to divert, or at least delay such a conclusion, than which you are sensible a greater service cannot be done to your King and Country ".[3] If, however, the peace were concluded, he should not believe that friendship and a good understanding between England and Russia had become impossible ; for though there could be no question of joint military operations, nothing could prevent Great Britain from cultivating practical relations with Russia. Jefferyes took with him the same proposals that had been given to Prince Kurakin at The Hague in 1717; and as Norris would hardly be able to finish the treaty of commerce during his short stay at the Court of Muscovy, Jefferyes was to carry on the work.[4]

The two English envoys were to complain of the hostile attitude of the Russian Court, instancing their help to the Jacobites. If England were accused of hostile intentions towards Russia, these

---

[1] Cf. Chance, " List of English diplomatic representatives . . . 1689–1762 ", in *Notes on the diplomatic relations of England with the North of Europe*, ed. Firth.

[2] Bonet, Oct. 17/28, 1718, Prussian State Archives ; Hoffmann, Oct. 28, 1718, Vienna Archives.

[3] Stanhope to Norris, Oct. 5, 1718, S.P. 104/122. See also the " Memorial relating to the Court of Muscovy " sent with this letter. Cf. the official instructions given in *Sbornik*, vol. 61. (B.M.Ac. 7886.)

[4] Instructions for Jefferyes, given in *Sbornik*, vol. 61, p. 453.

were to be denied. The truth of these statements can be judged
from their assurance that the Baltic expeditions were purely for
the protection of English trade, yet Norris' instructions of August
19 were to endeavour to prevent the Russians from joining the
Swedes, and thereby disappoint more easily and successfully any
attempts against the safety of England.[1] These instructions were to
be kept secret, and if there were no occasion to make use of them,
they should be buried in silence as though they had never been given.

Sir John Norris, who remembered his previous disappointment
with the Tsar and expected no better success this time, may have
hastened the return of the fleet more than necessary, and had left
Copenhagen some days before Jefferyes arrived. Jefferyes waited
for orders from the King before he continued his journey.[2]

The negotiations in St. Petersburg in 1718 were nothing but a
repetition of those in Amsterdam in the previous year. During his
first audience with the Tsar Jefferyes made a speech in German,
and the Tsar answered in Russian ;[3] only polite words were
exchanged, and the Minister was disappointed at the coolness of
his reception.[4] In the negotiations each party wanted first to
hear the other's proposals, and Jefferyes soon perceived that his
mission was hopeless. Baron Shaffirov asked whether Jefferyes
had brought any concert for the operations of the next campaign,
or whether he had power to agree with them about any. Jefferyes
answered him in the negative, and told him that he could not see
how any concert could be made with the Tsar against the King of
Sweden at a time when he was actually engaged in a negotiation
of peace with him. He added cunningly that he did not doubt,
if the Tsar would either wholly break off the negotiations at Aland
or let the English into the secret of what had been transacted, but
that his Majesty would take such measures with the Tsar and the
other allies as would oblige the King of Sweden to a peace. Shaffirov
replied that the Swedes were continuing the negotiations only to
distract them ; and therewith broke off the conversation. A week
later he handed Jefferyes and Weber a " resolution " of the Tsar,
which however was nothing but a project already communicated
to the British Government in 1716, and quite unsuited to the
existing situation.

---

[1] Cf. Chance, *l.c.* p. 271 ; see also Vol. I. p. 309.
[2] *Sbornik*, vol. 61, p. 459 *seq.*   [3] *Ibid.*
[4] *Sbornik*, vol. 40, p. 6.

When Jefferyes sounded Shaffirov about settling a treaty of commerce upon the basis of the plan of 1717, he seemed utterly averse to it, and spoke of it as an unreasonable request and very injurious to the Muscovite nation. As Jefferyes came back to the plan, the Russian replied with the old formula : first alliance or plans for the next campaign, then treaty of commerce. Even this treaty was to be concluded not upon the plan decided by the English nation, but upon a foot that regarded the mutual advantage of both.[1]

Jefferyes' attempt to disturb the Aland Conferences, to penetrate their secret, and place England in the position of arbiter, also failed. The situation seemed to have changed for the better when news came in quick succession of Charles XII's death and of the fall and execution of Goertz. But a new Swedish plenipotentiary went to the Aland Islands and the negotiations continued. Now Jefferyes thought out a desperate plan and submitted it to the Government in March 1719. England should

send a frigate or two to the place of congress, and bring the Swedish plenipotentiary away by force. The Danes being in open war with Sweden . . . will be the people most proper to put this into execution. . . . To carry it on more securely the vessel employed for this service may make use of Muscovite colours. . . . Should His Majesty think fit to interrupt this negotiation more effectually, the Muscovite plenipotentiary might likewise be carried away and afterwards be set on shore either at Dantzig, Koenigsberg or Riga, and some excuse may be invented to colour the enterprize. This enterprize will . . . give an opportunity to his Majesty of making his peace with Sweden, for a place of congress more secure and other plenipotentiaries must be chosen before they can meet again, which will take up the greater part of the summer.

Nothing further was heard of this scheme, which would have been a blatant violation of existing ambassadorial privileges. Jefferyes remained in St. Petersburg till the autumn of 1719 ; he only dealt with minor questions of British privileges and interests, but was an unwelcome observer who could report to London on Russian conditions at critical times.

Prussia was, like Russia, becoming more worthy of England's attention. The victory of Fehrbellin had made her independent of her powerful neighbours, Sweden and Poland. Frederick William I

[1] See Jefferyes' Reports of Jan. 1719. *Sbornik*, vol. 61, p. 459 *seq.*

of Prussia, after taking part in the war of the Spanish Succession, by which with England's help he gained Obergeldern, turned to the East ; and as he wished to gain Pomerania he was now among the enemies of Sweden.

Frederick William I had always been an unconditional supporter of the Hanoverian Succession, in spite of the old jealousy between Guelph and Hohenzollern, for George I was his uncle and his father-in-law. In February 1714 Bonet, the Prussian resident in London, was imprudent enough to discuss the risky theme of the Succession with the French ambassador, Iberville, without express orders from his King.[1] The Frenchman was reluctant to express an opinion, and recalled France's formal recognition of the Act of Settlement at Utrecht ; he categorically denied the widespread rumour that France intended to land troops in England in support of the Pretender. Bonet observed slyly that he had thought he was dealing with a friend and ally. None the less he pointed out the importance of the Succession for Franco-Prussian relations. For both powers a King of England, who was isolated by his religion as was the Chevalier, would be much more agreeable than an Elector of Hanover who, besides his British Crown, possessed large territories in Germany and alliances throughout the world ; and from the Whigs, on whom he would lean, not much good was to be expected. Iberville, growing somewhat more confidential, risked the statement that Louis XIV, in spite of his obligations at Utrecht, did not feel himself bound to forget an unfortunate Prince whom he had brought up and who was his close relative. The interest of the Crown and the principle of legitimacy pointed in the same direction. But the Chevalier ought to follow the example of Henry of Navarre and change his religion ; then he should marry a Protestant princess and entrust Parliament with the education of his children. France and Prussia could work together with England under such a King, and no other power could easily oppose their triple strength.

Bonet had heard what he wanted to hear. He tried to discuss the practicability of such plans, in particular the co-operation of foreign troops : but Iberville grew reserved again, and only asked whether he might report the conversation to his Government. This Bonet readily granted.

Frederick William was most annoyed. What would Hanover

[1] Bonet's Report, Feb. 5/16, 1714, Prussian State Archives.

say if it came out ? And the French would not even believe Bonet, for they knew of Prussia's sympathies for the Hanoverian Succession.[1] Bonet's excuse that he had only wished to find out France's intentions, and that unfortunately Iberville did not become talkative over a bottle,[2] was not accepted. He was constantly reminded to do nothing detrimental to the Hanoverian Succession, but rather everything calculated to realize and strengthen it.[3] Frederick William solemnly promised his father-in-law to support him actively ; [4] and Bonet was ordered to assure the Whig leaders that they could count on the King of Prussia in the hour of danger.[5] The Tory ministers and their followers watched Bonet askance, while the Prussian King came to dislike the Oxford-Bolingbroke ministry more and more. Whenever possible he avoided meeting Queen Anne's envoy,[6] who blamed Bonet's reports for the King's attitude :

Mr. Bonet never fails to give the worst turn he can to everything he writes. . . . All his letters have more of the style of a pamphleteer paid by the faction than of a foreign minister.[7]

Bonet's *faux pas* led to a French attempt to destroy the Protestant Succession by diplomatic means. Iberville asked Bonet the artful question whether in view of the existing strained relations between London and Hanover, due to Hanover's desire to see the Crown Prince in London,[8] it would not be advisable to offer the crown neither to Stuarts nor Hanoverians, but to the House of Prussia. The Hohenzollerns, too, were related to the Stuarts, he said, and as they belonged to the Reformed Church their religion was nearer to that of England than was the Lutheranism of the Hanoverians. Bonet, who had learnt his lesson, refused to be drawn, and reported the matter both to his King and to the Elector,[9] with the comment

---

[1] Instructions to Bonet, Mar. 3, 1714, Prussian State Archives.

[2] Bonet, Mar. 9/20, 1714, Prussian State Archives.

[3] Instructions to Bonet, May 15, 1714, Prussian State Archives.

[4] Frederick William I to George Lewis, Mar. 10, 1714, Prussian State Archives.

[5] Instructions to Bonet of May 15 and June 12, 1714, Prussian State Archives.

[6] Bromley to Breton, May 4, 1714, S.P. 104/53.

[7] Breton to Bromley, June 30, 1714. Cf. also same to same, May 29, 1714, S.P. 90/6.

[8] Cf. Vol. I. p. 15 *seq.*

[9] Bonet to the Elector George Lewis, Apr. 20/May 1, 1714, Prussian State Archives.

that France evidently wanted to start a quarrel between the two possible claimants to the throne, in order to play the crown into the hands of the Pretender. The Elector had Bonet's letter passed round among his London friends. Some of the Lords asked Bonet whether they might put Iberville's proposal before the House of Lords. Bonet cautiously refused ; but the French ambassador himself made his plan public. He argued that the Lutheran George Lewis was no better for the English than a Roman Catholic King, as for them there was no difference between consubstantiation and transubstantiation. An even greater stir was caused by the puzzling news published by an English paper in July 1714, and perhaps inspired by Iberville, that Prussia had been asked by France to remain completely neutral in the question of the Protestant Succession.

The peaceful accession of George I a few weeks later required no help from Prussia, but Frederick William openly renewed his promises to lend any necessary aid.[1] The Regency had only thanked him for his offer, but the new King intended to take him at his word.[2] Frederick William's attitude was in part determined by his sympathies as a Protestant, which now formed one of the ties between Prussia, England, and Holland. France was hostile to the Hanoverian Succession both for political and religious reasons, and even Charles VI, England's ally since 1688, did not dare to declare openly for George I out of regard for the Catholic religion.[3] He congratulated George I's representative in person, and instructed his envoys in London and The Hague to answer any questions simply by saying that the Emperor would " recognise as King of England anyone recognised as such by the nation ".[4]

After the accession of George I, Hanover and England had at first gone different ways in their northern policy. England was, however, soon pressed into the wake of Hanover, and George I used the British fleet for his own ends in the Baltic expeditions.[5] But Frederick William I could not understand that open participation

---

[1] *E.g.* the declaration of Sept. 13, 1714, delivered by von Borckenfelde in Brussels, Prussian State Archives.
[2] George I to Heusch, Aug. 25, 1714, Hanover Archives.
[3] Mörlin's Report of Sept. 1, 1714, Prussian State Archives.
[4] Instructions to Hoffmann and Heems, Aug. 25, 1714, Vienna Archives.
[5] Cf. Vol. I. p. 288 *seq.*

in the operations against Sweden was not possible for the British Government. He grumbled at the British squadrons, which only demonstrated, and demanded more active help in the fight against the common enemy.

Relations between London and Berlin were still under this cloud when in August 1716 Charles Whitworth, the first English envoy since George I's accession, appeared at the Prussian Court. The delay had occurred because the Earl of Forfar, who had been appointed in 1715, had been fatally wounded at Sheriffmuir ; his successor, Lord Polwarth, had been appointed for both Berlin and Copenhagen, and had remained in Denmark.[1]

In Russia, in Vienna, and at the Congress of Baden Whitworth had given proof of high talents. His instructions [2] were as vague as those for Forfar and Polwarth, and show that no serious negotiations were intended for the moment. He was simply to discover the Prussian views on the Northern war and to see that accounts of trade were transmitted from time to time from such factories of British merchants as were settled in any part of Prussia.

Whitworth took care not to give the impression of having any important political mission to fulfil.[3] On the advice of Townshend he decided not to seek a public audience of the King.[4] The simple Frederick William had no objection, for he did not care for the splendour which envoys to the French Court displayed at their public audiences. As Whitworth had only the usual compliments to make, he did not hasten even the private audience. First he paid his respects to the four-year-old Crown Prince and his sister Wilhelmine, aged seven ; then he went to Frederick William. He was in the anti-chamber when the King returned from Church later than ordinary, who, seeing him, came up to him very graciously. Whitworth presented His Majesty's letter with a short compliment, as was usual on such occasions. Afterwards he had the honour of dining with the Prussian King, who expressed the wish to see him more frequently. They spoke of their readiness to keep up friendly relations between the two Courts which were linked by the proximity of blood, the interest of religion, and the situation of their dominions

---

[1] The instructions for Forfar are dated July 3, 1715, those for Polwarth May 14, 1716, F.O. 90/52.

[2] July 6, 1716, F.O. 90/52.

[3] For what follows see Whitworth's reports, S.P. 90/7.

[4] Whitworth to Townshend, Oct. 9/20, 1716, S.P. 90/7.

in Germany. Frederick William stated expressly that he desired England's friendship, and wished to negotiate with King George.

As a result Whitworth discussed with the ministers Dönhoff, Printz, and Ilgen the renovation of an Anglo-Prussian treaty of 1704. But as Hanover and England wished the Russian troops removed from Mecklenburg, and Frederick William stuck to his friendship with the Tsar, co-operation was impossible. Again and again Whitworth warned the ministers against the Muscovite danger. When Frederick William desired to hear his arguments, he urged " that a thorough good understanding was particularly necessary . . . since the affairs of the North were ready to fall into confusion. . . . That it was His Majesty's opinion the Muscovites should not be suffer'd to fix themselves in the Empire." The King said that he meant in Mecklenburg, to which Whitworth replied, " both in Mecklenburg and the rest of the Empire ", adding that they ought to join in protesting, and at the same time consider measures to be taken in all events ; and that, apart from this question, King George had as much interest to keep up a friendship with the Tsar as any other Prince could have. Frederick William retorted that George I was not so much interested as he was. " Rather more, considering the English commerce ", replied the envoy. " But at the same time it was reasonable the Czar should act with his allies as Sovereign Princes likewise and not as bare dependents. . . . The design of taking his winterquarters in Mecklenburg . . . would certainly alienate the affection of the Emperor and the Empire from the Northern Allies . . . without their agreement the Northern Allies could never propose to themselves to be left in a peaceable possession of what they had gott." This the King immediately admitted as true. Whitworth continued that the Tsar could not possibly propose any advantage to the allies by persisting to winter in Mecklenburg ; for there could not be the least prospect of a descent on Schonen, in view of the feeble support given by Denmark. The Tsar's proceedings would even be prejudicial to the Duke of Mecklenburg, his nephew, whom he pretended to be helping. The King conceded that all Whitworth had advanced was very true ; but that as the Prussian dominions were more exposed to the Tsar than those of Brunswick or England, he was obliged to have a greater consideration for him.[1]

Frederick William avoided seeing his father-in-law, who had come

[1] Whitworth to Townshend, Oct. 9/20, 1716, S.P. 90/7.

to Germany in the summer of 1716, and refused an invitation to George's hunting-castle of Göhrde. In November he met Peter the Great, who was travelling through Germany. The Tsar wished the meeting to be at Lenzen, but as Lenzen was so near Göhrde that a visit to George I could hardly have been avoided, Frederick William arranged to see the Tsar in Havelburg. He also excused himself in a letter to his father-in-law, saying that he had been unable to avoid the meeting ; [1] and even sent an envoy to Hanover to explain why in the affair of Mecklenburg he could not go any further. [2] The military alliance between Hanover, Russia, and Prussia was still in existence ; but the close union between Russia and Prussia seemed so dangerous that England took up the more eagerly the negotiations with France which led to the Triple and Quadruple Alliances. [3]

Suspicion and estrangement grew between George and Frederick William. Frederick William complained to the Danish representative that the King of England intended to make himself arbitrator of the peace of the North ; and when asked if he were then desirous that the Tsar should be arbitrator of it, he replied, Why not ? [4] On the conclusion of the Triple Alliance Frederick William seemed disappointed that he was not asked to accede. Then, when news came of the arrest of the Swedish ambassador in London, it seemed that Prussia's suspicions about a secret understanding or negotiations between England, Hanover, and Sweden must vanish ; yet Frederick William continued to treat Whitworth civilly but coldly, like " a minister from a Court with which he is not oversatisfied ". [5]

In March 1717 there was a sudden change in Prussia's attitude. Ilgen paid Whitworth a visit, and urged the necessity of renewing a good understanding, in which all that was past should be forgotten. [6] But by now Whitworth had been given a temporary appointment at The Hague, as his further stay in Berlin was considered useless. [7] His luggage and personnel were to stay for the time being in Berlin, and a friendly tone was maintained at his departure. From The

---

[1] Frederick William I to George I, Dec. 5, 1716, Prussian State Archives.
[2] Instructions to Bonet, Jan. 19, 1717, Prussian State Archives.
[3] Cf. Vol. I. p. 320 *seq*.
[4] Whitworth to Methuen, Jan. 5/16, 1717, S.P. 90/7.
[5] Whitworth to Tilson, Feb. 5/16, 1717, S.P. 90/7.
[6] Whitworth to Stanhope, Mar. 16/27, 1717, S.P. 90/7.
[7] Bonet, Mar. 29/Apr. 9, 1717, Prussian State Archives.

Hague he sent a polite letter to Ilgen,[1] with the assurance that King George would do all he could to cultivate friendship with Prussia.

From Amsterdam Whitworth sent home a long report,[2] in which he described both the Government and policy of Prussia, and its ministers. He also gave a detailed account of his last audience with the King : he had begun with the usual remarks about the gratifying improvement in the relations between the two monarchs ; Frederick William asked bitterly if this were really true when, after his offers of help to King George on his accession, he had met nothing but opposition and chagrin from the House of Brunswick. Frederick William referred to the Russian troops, to unpaid subsidies, and to serious encroachments on his personal rights. Though he did not want to offend anyone, he declared that he could stand up to any attack, for he had troops and also a friend —meaning the Tsar—who, if he had no money, did at least not want for men. On Whitworth's remark that the King could have a more proper ally nearer to hand, Frederick William replied impatiently, that from that side he had received endless demands and no offers ; he still loved and honoured His Majesty personally, but he was tired of empty promises and of the tricks of ministers—he himself believed in the old proverb, " *Ein Mann, ein Wort* ".

Anglo-Prussian relations continued to grow cooler, although neither side had any reason or desire to provoke an open conflict. George I could not wish to make an enemy of a neighbour who had fifty odd thousand men, who was constantly augmenting his horse, whose magazines were well filled, whose artillery was in very good order, and who had at least five or six million crowns in his treasury.[3] Bonet remained in London even after Whitworth had left Berlin, and Frederick William frequently reminded him to try for a *bonne intelligence* with England, though he was not to press for it in a base or improper fashion.[4] Even the modest Bonet was sometimes roused to anger by the constant mortifications which he experienced ; he then advised his King to do all he could to develop industry and commerce in Prussia, for this would hurt England without giving

---

[1] Copy enclosed in Whitworth to Stanhope, Apr. 9/20, 1720, S.P. 84/256.
[2] Whitworth to Stanhope, Apr. 4/15, 1717, S.P. 90/7.
[3] Whitworth's Report, Apr. 4/15, 1717, S.P. 90/7.
[4] Instructions to Bonet, Mar. 30, 1717, Prussian State Archives.

cause for complaint, and would also put an end to the economic exploitation of Prussia by the English and the Dutch.[1] Frederick William evidently held the same view, for he was working towards these ends.[2]

Still, the near relationship between the two Courts was not forgotten. For two generations they had been linked by marriage, and now the plan was conceived of marrying the Prussian Crown Prince to Princess Amelia, second daughter of the Prince of Wales. The Crown Prince, later Frederick the Great, was barely six years old, the Princess about a year older, but was already proud of her future position as Queen of Prussia.

In spite of the material differences between England and Prussia, it was not without reason that Bonet blamed Bernstorff for the bad relations between the two Courts : for his insinuations were intended to make everyone suspicious of Prussia. Bonet complained that Court and City, Germans and English, the diplomatic corps and everybody else, were talking of " the great misdeed " of His Prussian Majesty ; all seemed united to disgrace him throughout Europe.[3]

Prussia's " great misdeed " consisted in her northern policy and her friendship with the Tsar. But even after the Russians had left Mecklenburg, England remained as cool as before, for Bernstorff opposed every *rapprochement*. Each side continued its complaints to the other. Bernstorff demanded that Frederick William should give up the Tsar, as his friendship was incompatible with that of England ; [4] he was afraid that Prussia would leave her allies in the lurch and make peace with Sweden. " I know nothing of such a peace ", was Bonet's reply.[5]

In spite of Bernstorff and Hanover, a *rapprochement* between the British Government and Prussia was sought in the autumn of 1718. Lord Stanhope was anxious about the Quadruple Alliance ; if the south of Europe were to be subdued, there must be no surprises in the north. The encirclement of Sweden was no longer effective,

---

[1] Bonet, May 24/June 4, 1717, P.S., *Sur le caractère de cette Cour*, Prussian State Archives.

[2] Droysen, *Preussische Politik*, vol. iv. pt. ii. p. 194 *seq*.

[3] Bonet, June 18/29, 1717, Prussian State Archives.

[4] Bonet, Sept. 2/13, 1718, Prussian State Archives.

[5] Bonet, Sept. 30/Oct. 11, 1718, Prussian State Archives.

but peace and order were not yet restored. The Aland Conferences
and the possibility of an alliance between the northern states, on
which Alberoni set great hopes, looked dangerous ; so the Western
Powers tried to entice Prussia, with her great military strength,
away from the threatened alliance and towards the Quadruple
Alliance.[1] But Prussia's relations with Austria were no better than
with England : for the Emperor still withheld his consent to
Frederick William's acquisition of Stettin. Bonet had repeatedly
asked that George I should procure this consent.

Between Prussia and France two treaties of alliance had recently
been concluded, but they had soon lost their importance. By both
treaties, dated September 14, 1716, and August 15, 1717,[2] France
had guaranteed Prussia in the possession of Stettin and of the mouth
of the Oder. The Tsar was a partner to the later treaty, but with
the change of circumstances in northern and southern Europe this
alliance was soon obsolete, and Frederick William was left between
two groups of powers.

In these circumstances France sent the Comte de Rottembourg
to Berlin, with instructions [3] to begin by attempting to bring about
a *rapprochement* between England and Prussia. Once their petty
quarrels were settled, England and France together would seek the
Emperor's consent to Prussia's accession to the Quadruple Alliance.
If Charles VI made difficulties, Prussia could at least join the
Triple Alliance of January 4, 1717. But Frederick William must
not be told of this possibility too soon, or he would never agree
to the alliance with the Emperor. However, when Rottembourg
reached Berlin in January 1719, his mission was already doomed
to failure. The death of Charles XII had completely changed
Sweden's policy, and George I as Elector had just concluded an
alliance which was clearly a threat to Prussia.

The idea of a partition of Poland was already current in Europe,
and after a Hanoverian envoy with full powers had, in January
1718, tried unsuccessfully to draw Prussia away from Russia, it
was feared that these two growing Powers might unite to swallow
Poland. To counter this danger Charles VI as Archduke of his
hereditary lands, George I as Elector of Hanover, and Augustus II

---

[1] Stair to Craggs, Oct. 24, 25, 1718, S.P. 78/162.
[2] Cf. above, p. 213.
[3] Of Nov. 29, 1718 ; given in A. Waddington, *Recueil des instructions
. . . Prusse*, p. 320 *seq.*

of Poland as Elector of Saxony sought to form an alliance.[1] The immediate aim was the defence of Poland, the basic idea the protection of the Empire against the Muscovite danger. The alliance could be turned against Prussia if she supported Russia's ambitions.

The negotiations for this treaty, which was a purely German affair, were carefully hidden from the English ministers, who just at that time were hoping for the success of Rottembourg's mission to Berlin. Stanhope and Bernstorff were working at cross-purposes, both in the name of George I, and the conflict between British and Hanoverian policy was more acute than ever. We must win Prussia, was Stanhope's maxim; of what use is Prussia to us, asked Bernstorff, when its only aim is the ruin of the Houses of Austria and Brunswick ? [2] To the German minister even the alliance with France seemed of little value : for he felt it would come to an end in three or four years, on the majority of the young King, or even earlier if he died ; and that in any case France was wooing Prussia only to use her later against the Emperor and the Elector.[3]

The negotiations for the Alliance between Austria, Hanover, and Saxony took place in Vienna. In a personal letter of July 1718, George I wrote to St. Saphorin that its conclusion was urgent ; but the accompanying draft treaty was found unsatisfactory by the Emperor, who demanded that George should sign the alliance both as Elector and as King, and that he should bring an effective fleet to its support. The Austrian attitude upset and angered Bernstorff intensely, as it meant telling the English ministers of the plan. Bernstorff's view of the position is clear from the answer given to the Imperial envoy in London, that for certain reasons His Majesty would not be able to join such a *foedus* as King ; but this would not prevent the British fleet stationed in the Baltic from co-operating in the work of the intended alliance ; it would do what was necessary, as it had done and still was doing against Sweden, although His Britannic Majesty had not as King declared war on the King of Sweden.[4]

[1] For what follows cf. the St. Saphorin papers, Hanover Archives. Cf. also W. Michael, " Ein schwieriger diplomatischer Fall aus dem Jahre 1719 ", *Historische Zeitschrift*, No. 88.

[2] Bernstorff to St. Saphorin, Nov. 25, 1718, Hanover Archives.

[3] Bernstorff to St. Saphorin, Nov. 25, 1718, P.S., Hanover Archives.

[4] Hampton Court, Aug. 22/Sept. 2, 1718, Hanover Archives. The contents and the use of German show clearly that the document came from the German chancellery of George I.

After this refusal negotiations were held up for some time in Vienna. But as Bernstorff kept pressing for a settlement, St. Saphorin himself drafted a plan which found approval both in Vienna and London, and formed the basis of the subsequent treaty. But the chief difficulty was to procure the co-operation of the British fleet, especially for the protection of Danzig and Elbing, which seemed to stand in particular danger, without approaching the British ministers. The Hanoverians in London thought this possible, and George I, Bernstorff, and Robethon were only anxious to find the right form. On September 9, Bernstorff declared rashly that the integrity of Danzig and Elbing would be guaranteed by England in a separate article ; [1] and Robethon wrote to St. Saphorin [2] that His Majesty was willing to engage himself, as King of England, for the defence of Danzig and Elbing and to use his fleet to this end, and that he hoped to persuade the Dutch to do the same. The allusion to the Dutch was clever, for it was just the participation of Holland in the recent Baltic expeditions that had given them a cloak of virtue.

St. Saphorin submitted to the Court in Vienna a written *exposé* of his master's point of view ; [3] after reiterating that George I could only engage himself as Elector, he added that Danzig and Elbing could none the less count on naval protection, and that even the States General might co-operate. To avoid any possible ambiguity, St. Saphorin added in the notes to two draft treaties which he submitted to the Court of Vienna that the King would undertake a separate engagement, as King of Great Britain, for the security and protection of Danzig and Elbing, to which end he would use his fleet in the Baltic. But in the treaty under consideration this promise was not to be mentioned.

Austria and Saxony were still not satisfied, and the negotiations came to a standstill. Meanwhile St. Saphorin was being pressed by his master to bring them to a conclusion. It had been rumoured in London that the Tsar would bombard Danzig and set fire to the country round it unless he were soon paid a large sum of money. George I reminded his ambassador that it was high time to create a real security against the dangerous Russian *desseins* and to close the door on them once and for all. The diplomatic activity began

---

[1] Bernstorff to St. Saphorin, Sept. 9, 1718, Hanover Archives.

[2] Sept. 9, 1718, Hanover Archives.

[3] *Éclaircissements sur le projet d'alliance*, etc. Vienna, Oct. 1, 1718, Hanover Archives.

again in Vienna, but the problem of Danzig and Elbing still seemed insuperable.

St. Saphorin now made a new proposal, that was at once approved by all parties. The treaty was to be made out and signed, but the Austrian and Saxon plenipotentiaries would make the reservation that they had signed only on the understanding that His Britannic Majesty would engage himself for the protection of Danzig and Elbing, and undertake to send a fleet for this purpose to the Baltic. St. Saphorin would formally confirm the receipt of this reservation ; he hoped to receive the royal promise very shortly, and he would immediately show it to the others, but would not let it out of his hands till the ratifications had been exchanged.[1]

Meanwhile Prussia and Russia had heard of the secret negotiations and suspected their hostile aim. " Their anxiety about our treaty ", wrote St. Saphorin, " is probably the best proof of its necessity." [2] France too, always well informed about diplomatic affairs, had heard of the matter, and was both offended and worried. The French ambassador in Vienna gave a warning against measures that might lead to a war in the north, when they were just preparing the joint struggle against Spain ; but he seemed to be appeased when St. Saphorin explained to him that they were on the contrary trying to exorcise the restless spirits in the north, in order to have a free hand in the south. France's intervention upset Bernstorff badly, for he believed France was trying to create firm ties between Russia and Prussia, and later Sweden, in order to carry out her own plans with their help. Only the nascent treaty in Vienna could restore the balance of power : " in short, our well-being, the well-being of the Emperor and of the whole Empire, depends on the rapid conclusion of this treaty ".[3]

On January 5, 1719, the treaty was signed, by Prince Eugene of Savoy and Count Sinzendorff for Austria, by Count Flemming for Saxony, and St. Saphorin for Hanover. The signatory Powers undertook the mutual defence of their territories and support in case of attack. Its 15 Articles appeared to be purely defensive in character.[4]

[1] St. Saphorin to Bernstorff and to Robethon, both Nov. 29, 1718, Hanover Archives.

[2] St. Saphorin to Robethon, Jan. 1, 1719, Hanover Archives.

[3] Bernstorff to St. Saphorin, Dec. 30, 1718, Hanover Archives.

[4] Printed in Dumont, *Corps dipl.*, vol. viii. partie II, p. 1 ; Lamberty, *Mémoires,* vol. x. p. 72.

But the aim and purpose of a treaty were often to be found rather in the secret and separate articles and the so-called Declarations, which were equally binding on the contracting parties. The secret articles to this treaty show that the allies also wished to strike a blow at the Duke of Mecklenburg. Hanover and Brunswick were to enforce the verdict of the Imperial Court in a quarrel between the Duke of Mecklenburg and his Estates ; the allies of January 5 wished to forestall the possible intervention of Prussia or Russia, which might have been expected but for the alliance. Furthermore, Poland was to be protected from attacks and the passage of foreign troops, and from the expansionist aims of its neighbours. The treaty succeeded in prolonging the life of the old Poland by half a century.

When St. Saphorin signed the Declaration 4 of the treaty, which contained the promise to protect Danzig and Elbing, he little knew what difficulties he was preparing for the German and English ministers in London. The question how far English ministers ought, out of consideration for their King, to pass over the essential requirements of national policy, led to the most awkward discussions.

The original of the treaty as sent to London [1] contains everything but the interesting Declaration 4. The treaty had been signed in the greatest haste and confusion ; the Declaration 4 had first been bound together with the other sheets, but was cut out because it was felt in Vienna to be superfluous in the London version. St. Saphorin wrote that it would be sent separately : but there is no trace of its ever having reached England.[2]

George I must have been relieved that the Declaration 4 was not included in the Instrument sent to London : for on the strength of this Declaration every Englishman could have accused him of a breach of the constitution. He wrote—apparently in his own hand —the required promise to protect Danzig and Elbing, and had a letter prepared for St. Saphorin, in which he announced that he would send him, together with the ratification, " two copies of our original Declaration concerning the fleet to be sent to the Baltic ". But the ministerial counter-signature was still lacking, and there could be no hope that Austria and Saxony would be satisfied with the signature of a Hanoverian minister, for in such a form the whole

[1] Now in Hanover Archives.
[2] Concerning the part that may have been played in this matter by diplomatic usage, see *Historische Zeitschrift* 88, p. 63.

Declaration would have become meaningless. The English ministers had to be informed, and the critical moment had come.

The negotiations between the German and English ministries of George I—the King himself remained in the background—lasted from February 7 till February 14, 1719. Luke Schaub, who could speak German with George I and his ministers just as well as English with the English, acted as mediator between the two camps. He had a great deal of tact, knew the weaknesses of both English and Germans, and was in the official service of neither England nor Hanover.

To Schaub Bernstorff handed the document containing the treaty of January 5, and a copy of Declaration 4, but the words " in fulfilment of the present treaty " (*ad sustinendam tractatus praesentis executionem*) were omitted : for how could the King engage the English fleet by virtue of a treaty concluded by Hanover ? Schaub somehow—probably through St. Saphorin—came to know of the passage ; [1] but the English ministers never learnt the full text of the Declaration.

Yet even without these words the English ministers could not possibly approve the Declaration 4. Annoyed at the secrecy with which the negotiations had been carried on by the Germans, they at first refused to have anything to do with the affair ; they objected that they could not face Parliament if without visible reason, without being asked, and without anything being done in return from any quarter, they undertook in black and white an engagement which might entangle England in a conflict with the Tsar. Nevertheless they had no desire to work against the wishes of the King, and wanted to be as helpful as possible. The English said they could turn a blind eye if the declaration were issued by the German chancellery and not the English. But Bernstorff declared that this would satisfy neither the Emperor nor the King of Poland. There was also talk of a treaty of union and mutual guarantee in perpetuity between George I as King and George the Elector. But for the moment nothing useful was effected.

In a last attempt to get out of the dilemma, Le Cocq, the Polish Resident in London, was asked to hand the King a formal Note requesting his protection for the two towns, on the ground that England had close commercial relations with them. To make the matter look still more innocent he was also to ask England to induce

---

[1] Schaub to St. Saphorin, Feb. 14, 1719, Hanover Archives.

the States General to help in the protection of the threatened towns. As there would be no mention of the treaty of January 5, the English ministry could hand over to the Polish diplomats the promise already written out by the King.

Le Cocq was at first willing to submit formally the Note that Schaub had rapidly composed ; but on seeing the Declaration 4 he declined to ask for something to which his country already had full rights by the treaty. He would however ask for instructions and put the matter before his Government in the best light possible. Then King Augustus himself would be sure to write to King George on the lines of Schaub's Note, and the difficulty would be solved with only the loss of a few weeks.

Augustus II never wrote the required Note, and nothing further was ever done in the question of the Declaration 4, which in a few months seemed forgotten. No more difficulties arose, because Saxony and Austria no longer pressed George I for the written promise. This had become unnecessary ; the treaty of January 5, which had meanwhile been ratified despite the lack of the required Declaration from George I, had had its effect, and Peter the Great withdrew his troops from Poland, even though on receiving news of the treaty he had foamed with rage and threatened to deluge Poland with Tartars and Kalmucks.

If anyone were to blame for the confusion, it was the King himself. St. Saphorin, who at most could be reproached with a mistake of form rather than of matter, received long epistles, dated February 14, 1719, from George I, Bernstorff, and Schaub, giving him somewhat fatherly advice. George I explained to him that the consent for naval operations, unlike the rest of the treaty, had to be given by the British Government, and so could not be promised " in execution of the aforesaid Alliance ". Schaub wrote that he knew perfectly well that St. Saphorin had not exceeded his instructions, but that the Declaration could be most damaging to him if the Milords of England were to see its full text. Bernstorff's comment was typical : the examples of Byng and of the Baltic would have made it clear that it was easier in England to do things than to discuss them in advance. There was no difficulty about giving help to Danzig and Elbing, but one had to be cautious with formal declarations.

CHAPTER XI

POLITICAL SUCCESS AND NAVAL DISAPPOINTMENT

WHEN the treaty of January 5, 1719, was signed, the diplomats in Vienna did not yet know that Charles XII of Sweden had died on December 11. His death left the Jacobites without their most valuable ally, Alberoni with one hope less, the English and their friends delighted. " If a good use be made of this accident ", wrote Craggs, " I think it cannot fail to extricate us out of all our difficulties both in the North and in the South." [1] Only Sweden's enemies did not at first know what it would bring them ; when the Tsar was asked if the death of the Swedish King was a cause of condolence or of congratulation, he shrugged his shoulders and replied that he did not know himself.[2]

In Sweden there was general satisfaction that at last peace would follow the calamitous policy of the royal adventurer, which the exhausted country had reluctantly accepted from their absolute King. Now the people were determined to end both the war and absolutism. At first the succession was uncertain. Ulrike Eleonore, younger sister of Charles XII, had quickly grasped the reins of government ; but then she had to agree to a declaration stating that a hereditary claim on the crown of Sweden no longer existed ; and she had to submit to election by the Estates. She was chosen Queen and solemnly crowned at Upsala, and the succession was fixed in her male heirs ; but the Estates were again to have the prominent role in the Constitution which had been theirs till the time of Charles XI, and thus to curb the military ambitions of royal absolutism.

The war in Norway was quickly ended. The siege of Friedrichs-hall was raised, and the army on its way back to Sweden suffered

---

[1] Craggs to Stair, Dec. 29, 1718, S.P. 104/30.

[2] *Sbornik,* vol. 40, p. 9.

severe losses although unmolested by the enemy. A second army, returning over the wintry mountains further north, lost one-third of its men, with all the artillery and baggage. The Swedes were so anxious for peace that many would have accepted it at any price.

Almost all Sweden's possessions were under foreign domination. Russia held large parts of Finland and Karelia, Ingermanland, Esthonia, and Livonia ; Prussia had seized Pomerania, Hanover the Duchies of Bremen and Verden. Only Wismar was still holding out. Which of these conquests were to be returned to Sweden, and whether by means of a general peace settlement or through separate agreements, were the main questions now to be decided.

The states directly concerned would probably have reached an early settlement but for the intervention of the great Powers, particularly England and France. These confidently began making their own plans of a peace for the north, plans which subordinated the interests of Sweden, Russia, Poland, Denmark, and Prussia to those of England, France, and Hanover. Although not fully realized, the plans of the Western Powers had a decisive influence on the character of the final settlement.

To exert effective influence, it was essential for London and Paris to reach complete harmony. As soon as Dubois heard of Charles XII's death, he sent a letter to Stanhope with his plan for a general peace.

> We must seize this chance that Providence has sent us to complete our task of giving peace to Europe. . . . We must forthwith make fair advances to the Czar . . ., let him hope that his claims will be respected, and that he would be best served by a general peace.[1]

Dubois intended that Sweden should, with the help of France, keep her footing in Germany ; and Peter the Great, who had recently become a friend of France, would keep at least part of his conquests on the Baltic. There would be a new balance of power in the north, which would be favourable to French influence. The cautious Dubois wrote to Stanhope direct, entreating him to let no one into the secret except Craggs and Sunderland ; if then Stanhope did not disapprove his suggestions, he would send someone to explain them more fully.

From the outset the English objected to the Tsar retaining Reval, as he then would soon have a fleet in the Baltic more powerful

---

[1] Dubois to Stanhope, Jan. 17, 1719, Aff. étr. 322.

than those of Sweden and Denmark combined.[1] Stair obtained
from the Regent a promise that he would fall in with King George's
wishes in the matter ; but Dubois naturally expressed himself with
much greater reserve.

Craggs wrote that clearly no peace was to be had which would
satisfy everyone. Something would have to be returned to Sweden,
and whoever was obliged to give up any part of his conquests would
be dissatisfied. Therefore England and France should agree which
of all the Powers who had stripped Sweden should be pressed to
give up the provinces they had gained, on the pretext that only in
return for these would Sweden enter into a peace. If France,
England, and the Emperor had different views as to whose interests
should be sacrificed, this might prove, instead of an opportunity
for a general peace, an occasion for new dissensions. In Craggs'
opinion Sweden's chief interest was the restoration of the provinces
of Esthonia, Livonia, etc., in the Baltic ; whereas he knew that
even a great many good Swedes believed the German provinces to
be only a burden to their kingdom, and a temptation to their princes
to make new conquests. "And as to the interest of Great Britain ",
Craggs concluded, ". . . it is visibly to put the trade to the Baltick
and the alliance with Sweden upon the ancient foot of treaties." [2]

In view of the friendship between France and the Tsar, Stair
was advised not to disclose the whole English plan at once, but to
dissuade the Regent from taking any decisive steps till he had concerted something with England ; this Stair was to do " in a friendly,
obliging manner, rather than by any pressing vigorous remonstrance ".

Dubois now declared that the Regent would accept the English
view, and if a general peace could not be made, France would support
a peace by separate agreements ; the interests of the Tsar would
be no obstacle, even if he were obliged to cede Reval or more.[3]

England could now take a stronger lead, and put forward

a plan, by which the Kings of Prussia, Denmark, and Poland may agree
with him (George I) in one measure and in some treaty to preserve to
each other what shall be agreed upon, satisfying Sweden at the expense
of the Czar, who should he retain Nerva, Peterbourgh and Cronstat
ought to rest satisfied.[4]

---

[1] Stair to Craggs, Jan. 30, 1719, S.P. 78/163.
[2] Craggs to Stair, Jan. 17 (O.S.), 1719, S.P. 104/30.
[3] Stair to Craggs, Feb. 11, 1719, S.P. 78/163.
[4] Craggs to Stair, Feb. 17 (O.S.), 1719, S.P. 104/30.

Orleans accepted, as he saw that it was impossible to satisfy both Sweden and Russia, and that the general interest required that the Tsar should not become master of the Baltic.

England's hostile attitude toward Peter the Great was intensified by Jefferyes' reports of his negotiations in St. Petersburg.[1] The Russians had produced afresh the draft treaty of 1716, demanding that England should guarantee all that Russia had conquered from Sweden, and put fifteen British men-o'-war under the Tsar's command. The English Government easily judged from this " that it would be in vain to pretend to make the Czar consent to such conditions as Sweden might accept, and that he will only do it . . . when measures shall be taken to reduce him to it ".[2]

. . . the King's thoughts . . . are in short, by an alliance to be contracted between Sweden, Denmark, Prussia, Poland, the Emperor and his Majesty to the content of these parties to recover to Sweden what the Czar has taken from her, and let him come into the Treaty *nolens volens* upon these terms.[3]

Craggs believed he was sure of the co-operation of France in this settlement of the future of northern Europe. Torcy and the other representatives of the Old System in France had nothing to say, for the concert of the Western Powers in the Quadruple Alliance dominated the policies of Europe. When France recalled that as guarantee of the peace of Westphalia she ought, in form at least, to be the mediator in the north, her suggestion was coolly turned down in London.[4] The Regent adopted the English way of speaking about the Tsar, and declared that Sweden must first make peace with all her enemies except Russia, and then ally herself with them. He and Dubois had so far given up their Russian leanings that they declared themselves ready to sacrifice the Tsar to the English.[5]

The happy unity of the Western Powers was interrupted when in April 1719 the French envoy to the Court of Sweden, Count la Marck, returned to Paris. He had been in Stockholm since 1717, had just witnessed the beginnings of the new government, and was familiar with the intentions and hopes of Sweden. He now

[1] Cf. above, pp. 217-8.
[2] Craggs to Stair, Feb. 17, 1719, Postscript, S.P. 104/30.
[3] Craggs to Stair, Mar. 9, 1719, S.P. 104/30.
[4] Craggs to Stair, Mar. 9, 1719, S.P. 104/30.
[5] Stair to Craggs, Mar. 12, Apr. 2, 1719, S.P. 78/163.

submitted to the Regent a comprehensive peace plan, intended as a panacea against the dangers in the north. Stair, who had been warned that la Marck was coming, soon found an opportunity for a detailed discussion with him, too detailed indeed for the liking of Orleans and Dubois.[1] Stair recognized at once that there could be no agreement between them. La Marck pointed out that Sweden was most anxious to keep her German provinces, and recommended that Hanover should renounce a part of Bremen and Verden. Stair absolutely refused. La Marck also proposed that a piece of Pomerania should be restored to Sweden. Stair asked what value a small part of Pomerania could have for the crown of Sweden, as France had already guaranteed Prussia in the possession of Stettin, and the rest would be nothing but an expense to Sweden. It would be better to regain Livonia with Reval, so that the Tsar should not become all-powerful in the Baltic. But la Marck retorted that Sweden was deeply attached to her German possessions, and that France was no less anxious that Sweden should retain a footing in Germany. Moreover the Prusso-Russian alliance was firm, as it was based on common designs against Poland ; and the Aland Conferences might still bring peace between Russia and Sweden. Stair expressed his dismay at the possibility of another war, more dangerous than the last. "*Mylord*," replied la Marck, "*j'en conviens, mais que faire?*"

The Regent soon changed his mind. Outwardly he seemed as obliging as ever and willing to sacrifice the Tsar. He told how in 1717 when the Tsar had been in France, he had refused Russia's offer to take the place of Sweden in counterbalancing the power of the Emperor, since he did not wish to bring the Muscovites into Germany. None the less he could not do without some foreign Power in the north of Germany, so Sweden must retain her footing ; but it mattered little to him how much she retained.

It was now obvious that the French aims ran counter to those not only of England but also of Hanover, which wished to retain Bremen and Verden, perhaps also to see German soil freed from foreign domination. Stair was beginning to mistrust the French heartily, especially the Abbé Dubois, whom he found inclined to foul play. He wrote privately to Craggs :

I have but one thing to say for the Abbé, . . . that he does not understand one single bit of the affairs of the North . . . he promised

---

[1] Stair to Craggs, May 6, 1719, S.P. 78/163.

me that he would study the map . . . I am afraid the Abbé has not found that time.

Stair could not even get from Dubois the peace plan proposed by la Marck.

When I pressed him a little he fell into a most violent passion, and raved for half an hour. . . . France has a mind to the mediation and sole management of this negotiation ; . . . they are desirous to keep us in the dark as long as possibly they can. . . . It imports us much to get out of this situation as soon as we can. As soon as that happens, that we see and hear with our own eyes and ears, and that we can speak for ourselves, France will act a fairer part with us.[1]

In his formal report of May 6, Stair put forward a plan by which England was without delay to dispatch an envoy to Stockholm, and another to Berlin, in order to ascertain the intentions of these two Courts.[2] Stair's proposals were tantamount to giving up concerted action with France ; they were approved in London and promptly executed.

With the alliance of January 5, 1719, the hostility between the Courts of London and Berlin had reached its highest point. Bernstorff, who dominated England's policy, had almost driven her into a war against Prussia. In his eyes the Prussians were thinking of nothing but conquest at the expense of their neighbours ; their rulers had become worse and worse.[3] Again and again he warned the English against their ambitions.

Bernstorff's hatred of Prussia was increased by personal motives and interests. He was lord of three villages in Brunswick-Lüneburg: Holtorf, Capern, and Gummern, which were under Prussian sovereignty. By a Convention of 1715 Prussia was to hand over to Hanover all fiefs which she possessed in Brunswick-Lüneburg as soon as Stralsund and Rügen had been conquered. Now in 1719 Frederick William did not refuse to fulfil this obligation, but the change of sovereignty entailed certain difficulties concerning military dispositions, the passage of troops, and customs. These questions complicated negotiations between Prussia and Hanover, and had later to be made the subject of a special treaty.

But the British Cabinet had begun to emancipate themselves

---

[1] (Hardwicke), *State Papers*, vol. ii. p. 561 *seq.*
[2] Stair to Craggs, May 6, 1719, S.P. 78/163.
[3] Bernstorff to St. Saphorin, Feb. 15, 1719, Hanover Archives.

from the domination of the German ministers. The alliance of January 5 with its underhand Declaration 4 had apparently opened their eyes. Bonet too was trying to win them from their Hanoverian colleagues, and he was completely successful. Instead of the sarcasms which he had previously had to listen to, he was now told that England and Prussia ought to be on good terms with each other, and pursue a common northern policy. Improved relations between England and Prussia were the first-fruits of the English ministers' victory over Bernstorff and the Hanoverian Junta.[1] Charles Whitworth was again sent to Berlin, as he knew better than anyone else Frederick William I and the peculiarities of his Court, and had parted in 1717 on good terms with everybody.

Stanhope had long wished for a *rapprochement* with Prussia. He had recommended it when on March 30, 1719, he sent his plan for the Spanish campaign to Dubois.[2] A treaty with Prussia would pave the way for English influence in the north, and with the completion of the Quadruple Alliance would make England predominant throughout Europe.

This time Whitworth's instructions were to reach an agreement with Prussia which would reconcile the differences, compose the troubles, and establish a good peace in the north. Frederick William was to guarantee the Protestant Succession in Great Britain, which in return would guarantee the King of Prussia's peace with Sweden and the treaty to be negotiated between Prussia and Hanover. Above all, however, no peace was to be made with Sweden unless commerce in the Baltic were restored to its former footing, in whichever hands the ports might remain.[3]

As proof of England's honest intentions, Whitworth was to hold out prospects that arrears of money due to Prussia from the French war should be liquidated. If Berlin insisted, this promise could be made a separate article in the treaty. In the spring of 1718, an Act of Parliament had authorized the Government to liquidate the arrears for foreign troops. Bonet had hastened to recall the claims of his master, but in vain.[4] A year later reference was made to the Act in the King's Speech,[5] and again Bonet asked[6] for the

---

[1] Bonet, Mar. 17/28, 1719, Prussian State Archives.
[2] See Appendix 3.
[3] Cf. Chance, *George I and the Northern War*, p. 310 *seq.*
[4] Bonet, Mar. 31, 1718, S.P. 100/46.
[5] *Parl. Hist.* vol. vii. p. 601.   [6] Bonet, Apr. 27, 1719, S.P. 100/46.

payment of the mere 1½ million Dutch guilders, which had been owing for seven years. He wished the matter settled before Whitworth's arrival in Berlin; but the English preferred to use it as a bait.

The German ministers in London followed the negotiations with ill will; [1] Bernstorff prophesied unhappy results, and that the only gain would be a salutary lesson for the English.

The reception accorded to Whitworth by Frederick William left nothing to be desired, and the Prussian King showed himself anxious for *une bonne et étroite union* with the King of England. Whitworth had been instructed to avoid the ministers Ilgen and Kniphausen till he had seen Frederick William, lest they should influence their master against him; also to bring the Hanoverian envoy Heusch into the conferences. The difficulties in the way of agreement became obvious in the first discussion, and were rooted in the difference of political groupings. England wished to draw Prussia away from Russia, in order to isolate the Tsar and force him to accept the English peace plan. In the concert of Powers for which England was working, Frederick William would have to make an agreement with the King of Poland, and together with him make his peace with Sweden. This the Prussian ministers, however, absolutely refused to do, saying they must keep their hands free. Already it seemed to Whitworth that this point might wreck the whole of the negotiations, [2] which were being carried on in a spirit of mutual suspicion.

Frederick William was anxious not to offend the Tsar, and openly informed the Russian envoy of the course the negotiations were taking: for a breach with Russia before the conclusion of peace with Sweden could have led to an immediate invasion of East Prussia by Russian troops. Despite England's assurances Frederick William could not bring himself to trust Poland: there had been too many frontier quarrels and other difficulties; and the Prussian King was worried by the possibility that the crown of Poland might become hereditary in the House of Saxony, which would have made his neighbour much too powerful. Nor could he easily have any faith in the allies of January 5. Though he had not yet seen the text of their alliance, he could not doubt that it

---

[1] Robethon to St. Saphorin, Apr. 25, 1719, and Bernstorff to St. Saphorin, May 5, 1719, Hanover Archives.

[2] Whitworth to St. Saphorin, May 23, 1719, Hanover Archives.

was aimed against Prussia and Russia and intended to protect Poland. Austria's attitude was uncertain. Till recently she had been determined no longer to suffer the Swedes on German territory ; now she found it more practical to let them have part or even the whole of Pomerania, in order to use their power, if need be, against both Russia and Prussia.[1] Frederick William would not believe that the present negotiations had been opened in a different spirit, and that they had been initiated not by Bernstorff but by Stanhope.

Whitworth's pride and obstinacy did little to improve the atmosphere. Whenever the conferences dragged, he would rise and ask when he might take his leave of the King.[2] None the less the attempt to reach agreement was not abandoned. The draft treaty which Whitworth had brought was sent to George I and Stanhope in Hanover to be recast in accordance with Prussian wishes.

Stanhope had followed the negotiations in Berlin with the keenest interest. He was striving for peace in the north in order to have a free hand in the south, and this time Hanover was to serve England as England had so often served Hanover.

Meanwhile France seemed to have dropped la Marck's peace plan and was again supporting England's policy. " If Mr. Whitworth succeeds ", wrote Stanhope, " we shall owe it to the Comte de Rottembourg." [3] The French Government thought it more important to exorcise the dangers in the north than to insist on their own plan. Dubois was afraid of a northern coalition which would threaten the Emperor and George I in Germany, and so detach them from France. Then Alberoni would be able to bring Philip V to France, where there was discontent enough, and a rising in Brittany would follow. Most probably a Spanish fleet held ready in Corunna would support the rising. To protect the coast of Brittany, France had had to ask for a British squadron. In this dangerous position it was of supreme importance for France that the hopes of Alberoni and the Spanish Party should be frustrated, and to this end the conclusion of the proposed Anglo-Prussian treaty was essential. Even if it were broken after two or three months, Alberoni would meanwhile have lost courage, and

---

[1] St. Saphorin to Whitworth, May 31, 1719 ; St. Saphorin to Bernstorff, same date, Hanover Archives.

[2] Cf. Droysen, *Preussische Politik*, vol. iv. pt. ii. p. 262.

[3] Stanhope to Stair, June 7, 1719 (N.S.), S.P. 78/164.

France and England would have won the game. A few months later, when the tension had relaxed, Stair declared scornfully :

> It is true, they helped us in our treaty with the King of Prussia : but when did they do so ? When they were apprehensive that the King of Spain was upon the point of breaking into France, and when they were very diffident of their own army, officers and soldiers.[1]

When the new draft treaty came back to Berlin, the diplomats managed to surmount most of the obstacles. Only the seventh Article, concerning Poland's share in the conclusion of peace, remained a stumbling-block. Whitworth and Heusch made certain concessions,[2] and the Prussian Government replied with a document entitled " *Nouvelles Remarques* ", based on notes made and signed by the King himself.[3] First it was demanded that Prussia and England should not conclude peace with Sweden unless Denmark, the Tsar, and Poland were also included. If this were refused, as it certainly would be, at least there should be no peace " *au préjudice des alliances faites par la ligue du Nord* ". Failing that, Frederick William's *Ultimatum*, as he called it, contained his consent in principle to Article 7, by which Poland alone, without Denmark and Russia, would be admitted. But Poland would first have to send Prussia a formal request to be allowed to participate ; further, King Augustus was to retract the Fraustadt letter, an open letter addressed three months previously to Frederick William, full of offensive accusations ; and lastly, all the frontier quarrels between the two states were to be finally settled in favour of Prussia.

Whitworth and Heusch found these demands excessive ; they felt that they were being asked either to place Poland at the mercy of Prussia, or to tie themselves to the Tsar for purposes unknown. Prussia would have Russia always at hand to worry the English and to serve Prussian ends.[4] On June 17 they formally broke off the negotiations ; each side blamed the other for the failure ; and Whitworth left Berlin for Hanover.

Bernstorff, whose demands concerning his three villages had been one of the causes of friction, was triumphant ; for he could interpret the failure of the negotiations as proof that Prussia had only intended

---

[1] (Hardwicke), *State Papers*, vol. ii. p. 592.
[2] Whitworth to St. Saphorin, June 18, 1719, Hanover Archives.
[3] See Droysen, *l.c.* p. 262 [2].
[4] Whitworth to St. Saphorin, June 17 and 18, 1719, Hanover Archives.

to break up his cherished Vienna Alliance of January 5. He believed that George I must now realize the true character of Prussia.[1]

In accordance with Stair's suggestion, diplomatic negotiations were also opened at Stockholm. For this task the British Government sent Lord Carteret, who had distinguished himself as a speaker in the House of Lords, and was now given his first diplomatic mission. He was well versed in questions of law, finance, commerce, and politics, and his knowledge of languages, both ancient and modern, was exceptional. He was one of the few Englishmen who could talk German with George I. By birth and by capacity he seemed marked out for a brilliant career. His reports reflect a strong temperament and a lively personality; they depict with dramatic force Swedish society and particularly the royal couple in their distress.[2]

The basis of Carteret's instructions [3] was the English plan by which Sweden should give up her former possessions in Germany, but receive back the territories lost to Russia. He was to impress on the Swedish Government that this was not only a good plan, but the only one possible. He was to remind Ulrike that even the late King of Sweden expected to retain but a very small portion of his territories in Germany; as the new Queen could not be expected to be more sanguine in her hopes, he was to convince her that what might remain to Sweden after such concessions would be a burden and an expense, and no advantage; and that the recovering of their losses towards Finland and Livonia was the only thing every true Swede should have at heart. This Carteret might

inculcate by representing that it is absolutely necessary for Sweden to have the friendship of the neighbouring powers of Denmark, Poland and Germany to strengthen her hands against the Czar, which friendship can probably be obtained upon no other terms than their being allowed to retain what they have taken . . . ; that the dominions which the Swedes have lost on the side of Finland and Livonia being a rich and fertile country and being situated towards those of the Czar . . . are necessary both for their subsistence and safety, for should the Czar remain possest of those acquisitions . . . the opportunity they give him of increasing his shipping and navigation and fitting out considerable fleets would not only enable him whenever he should please to land an army at the very doors of Stockholm, but would undoubtedly

[1] Bernstorff to St. Saphorin, June 20, 1719, Hanover Archives.
[2] S.P. 95/24, B.M. Add. MSS. 22511. [3] F.O. 90/65.

tempt him to extend his conquest even over the whole kingdom of Sweden.

Carteret was reminded that this would also make the Tsar master of the Baltic ; English commerce would be threatened, and even the nation's safety, which could not well be provided without the naval stores drawn from those parts.

The realization of this plan, which combined so perfectly the interests of Sweden and England, would certainly have been no worse for Europe as a whole than the settlement actually reached later. Stanhope's northern policy would have held back the power of Russia.

To encourage Sweden there were references to the common Protestant interest ; and more important, if she agreed to the English propositions, Carteret was empowered to employ for the security and interest of the Swedish crown the naval squadron which was again on its way to the Baltic under Sir John Norris. Politically the union might find expression in a treaty renewing the expired treaty of 1700. England, in addition to her own support, would try to bring the other states interested in the north to play their part in helping Sweden to " reduce the Czar to reason ".

Carteret arrived in Stockholm with a letter in George I's own hand, which he was to give to Ulrike Eleonore at his first audience. The Swedes complained that the Queen's title was incompletely given, and wished to postpone Carteret's audience ; but Carteret pointed out that such incidents as these were often made use of to break off negotiations, and he was hurriedly granted his audience. He delighted the young Queen by saying : " Providence, having shew'd in the late King the greatest example of military virtues that ever was, would shew, by calling her Majesty to the throne, that every sort of virtue was to be met with, in the highest degree, in the Royal family of Sweden ".[1]

The existing political situation in Sweden, though not exactly favourable to Carteret's plans, was not hopeless. A strong party, led by the Chancellor, Count Cronhjelm, was working for peace with Russia ; the Aland Conferences had been reopened, and the Swedish plenipotentiary was the Chancellor's brother-in-law. Peter the Great was prepared to make a number of concessions. If he agreed to evacuate Reval, there would almost certainly be a peace

[1] Carteret to Stanhope, July 3 (O.S.), 1719, B.M. Add. MSS. 22511.

which was the antithesis of that desired by Carteret. A second party, led by the Queen's husband, Prince Frederick of Hesse, and Field-Marshal Dücker, wanted to reach an agreement with England. But everyone was afraid of an attack by the Russian fleet. The Prince's first desire was that Carteret should have the English squadron come higher up the Baltic, a move which Carteret himself thought advisable.

> Unless we shew that we will screen them from him [the Czar], I believe they will conclude with him. And if our fleet does come up, it is more than probable that the Czar will not come out, and then we make a merit of what costs nothing.[1]

Ulrike Eleonore appeared ready to cede Bremen and Verden if George I would give more and engage himself to do more than these places were in fact worth. The Swedish demands made no distinction between George as King and George as Elector, and England would have paid for Hanover's gains.

> First the King is to renew the Treaty of 1700 . . . but that Treaty is to be extended farther, according to the present juncture, which extension is not specified. . . . Sweden is to be assisted with money, besides what the King gives as Elector, with troops and fleet, to reduce the Czar to his ancient limits, to oblige him to restore what he has taken, and to leave in good condition the houses, artillery and fortifications.

Carteret felt that Sweden would moderate these demands, but asked Stanhope how far he might go in acceptance.

Carteret's task was further complicated when a few days after his arrival the Russian danger became acute. He was told by Field-Marshal Dücker and the Hanoverian Bassewitz "that there was certain information that the Czar's troops were embarked, that he would land in all probability within four miles of Stockholm, that tho' it was true they had 18,000 good men ready to oppose him, yet they must, if he landed, make peace with him at his own terms, rather than suffer the fate of the nation to depend on the success of one battle ". As the King of Great Britain was the only Prince that could save Sweden, they desired that Carteret should write to Admiral Norris to approach beyond Gotland, which step might prevent the Tsar's attempt. Dücker promised that George's interests as Elector would then be settled entirely to his satisfaction in eight days. Carteret in his reply cleverly raised the main point

---

[1] Carteret to Stanhope, July 3 (O.S.), 1719, B.M. Add. MSS. 22511.

of disagreement : England would agree to the renewal of the treaty
of 1700, but not to the demanded extension. It was promised that
this demand should be dropped, if only Carteret would write to
Norris at once. Carteret wished first to have the promise from the
Queen herself ; an audience was immediately arranged, in which
Ulrike gave the desired promise in the presence of her husband,
together with fresh assurances that she would cede Bremen and
Verden, adding, however, that she must always reserve to herself
a footing in Germany. The Prince repeated everything that the
Queen had said ; and in return Carteret undertook to send a courier
to Norris and another to Hanover.

England had thus given up one important point in her northern
programme, the complete elimination of Sweden from German soil ;
but at least Sweden had been prevented from concluding a hasty
peace with the Tsar.

If the Muscovites land and beat the Swedish troops, there is an end
of Sweden ; if the Muscovites should be beat, which is most likely,
Sweden will then be so elated that there is an end of the King's business
that way ; but if they make a peace, which is the most likely of all,
Europe, especially the trading countries, will feel the consequences of
the Muscovite power in the Baltic.[1]

Our success is chiefly owing to the Czar's being at the gates of
Stockholm, this reasoned the best for us.[2]

Within a week the political results of these discussions had been
given a definite form. On July 11/22, 1719, a preliminary peace
between Sweden and Hanover was concluded by Bassewitz, and a
papier promissoire was given to the Swedes by Carteret. These
two documents[3] together were to be the basis of the future settlement between the three states, and nobody objected to the extraordinary confusion of English and Hanoverian interests inherent
in the documents, particularly in the preliminary treaty. In Article 2
Sweden ceded Bremen and Verden to Hanover in the same form
in which she had received them in 1648. In the next Article she
promised not to disturb English commerce any more, but to favour
it. In Article 4 George I as King of England engaged himself to
renew the old friendship and alliance with Sweden. In Article 5

[1] Carteret to Stanhope, July 4 (O.S.), 1719, S.P. 95/24.
[2] Carteret to Stanhope, July 12 (O.S.) 1719, S.P. 95/24.
[3] Included with Carteret's letters to Stanhope, July 12, 14, 1719, S.P.
95/24.

he spoke as Elector, promising to pay a million thalers to Sweden. Finally Article 6 expressed the general desire that, at a congress in Brunswick, a definite peace should be concluded between Sweden and Hanover, and Sweden be reconciled with Poland and Denmark. Carteret in his *papier promissoire* promised the renewal of the Anglo-Swedish Treaty of 1700 in a form adapted to the changed conditions ; he also undertook in writing to send another courier to Admiral Norris calling him to the defence of Sweden.

When the preliminary treaty was put before the Senate, there was deep dismay at the cession of Bremen and Verden. The *papier promissoire* was found utterly insufficient. Time was pressing. From nine in the evening till five in the morning a number of Senators sat in conference with Carteret, but without reaching an agreement. Carteret left them, saying that he would not go to bed, but wait at home till six o'clock to see if they would give him the ratification. Otherwise he would go to the Army. As the ratification did not come, he rode out to Dücker and the Prince. Dücker told him that he wished to conclude with England, even though they should be obliged to make a peace with the Tsar, knowing that his country would get better terms from every quarter when they were well with England. With a letter from the Prince to the Chancellor Cronhjelm in his pocket, Carteret rode back to Stockholm ; on the way he saw the evening sky lit by the glow of villages burning on the islands where the Tsar's soldiers had landed.[1]

The Prince's letter advised the Senate to conclude with the King of England without delay.

We have our enemies, the Russians, in a corner, so I believe there is no time to be lost, and ask Your Excellency to consider the situation carefully, since the welfare of the Kingdom depends on it.

Even so, the Senate was most unwilling to hand over the ratification. One of the Senators swore that he would rather pay 5000 crowns than put his name to the document ; but actually these people preferred receiving money to making sacrifices. When Carteret came to settle the details of the Anglo-Swedish Treaty he found that presents were the best way to attain his ends. " I believe for five or six thousand pounds sterling we may settle it almost our own way." [2] The ratification was only handed to Carteret when he had

---

[1] Carteret to Stanhope, July 14 (O.S.), 1719, S.P. 95/24.
[2] Carteret to Stanhope, July 12 (O.S.), 1719, S.P. 95/24.

signed a second *papier promissoire* concerning the alterations to be made in the treaty of 1700. He succeeded, however, in making the text of this document completely innocuous.

Carteret had achieved a diplomatic masterpiece. His Swedish friends felt as grateful as if they had already been saved by England. Prince Frederick wrote to George I : " This kingdom needs the magnanimous help of your Majesty. You can strike a blow here as in Spain, and thus gain immortal fame." [1]

The squadron with which Sir John Norris had sailed to the Baltic consisted of only 10 ships of the line (with 80 to 50 cannon apiece), 2 frigates, and a few smaller vessels. The war with Spain and the protection of the English coast against Jacobite attacks occupied the greater part of the English fleet. Norris himself had been engaged in coastal service till the spring. It had long been decided that a squadron should go to the Baltic, but when in May the King left for the Continent it had not yet been formed, nor had the instructions for its Admiral been drawn up. It was said that the arrival of some vessels from Port Mahon must be awaited ; [2] but in fact the Regency was reluctant to deprive England of all naval protection for the sake of the north. The expedition would have been postponed, perhaps even dropped for the year, had not Lord Sunderland used the full weight of his authority to obtain its immediate departure.[3]

As the Regents hesitated to draw up instructions for the Admiral in the absence of the King and Stanhope, they decided on Craggs' advice merely to repeat the instructions of the previous year and leave the rest to orders which he would receive from London and Hanover.

These instructions dealt with a situation that no longer existed. They spoke of the suppression of English trade by Sweden, and of the intended Swedish landing in England. Norris was to oppose the Swedish fleet with all his force if it tried to get through the Sound to the North Sea. But he knew that if force now had to be used it would be against the spreading power of Russia rather

---

[1] The letters of the Prince of Hesse to Cronhjelm and George I are enclosed with Carteret's letters, July 12-14 (O.S.), 1719, S.P. 95/24.

[2] Craggs to Stanhope, May 29, 1719, S.P. 43/57.

[3] Minutes of the Regency Council, June 2 (O.S.), 1719, S.P. 43/61. Also Hoffmann's Report, June 16 (N.S.), 1719, Vienna Archives.

than against enfeebled Sweden. Like most people in England he
expected a collision with the Muscovite fleet :

> My utmost endeavours shall not be wanting to the total destruction
> of the Russian naval force. . . . I think the Czar . . . to be the most
> dangerous enemy our country can have.[1]

Because his squadron was so small Norris tried to get reinforcements from home, and to win the support of the Danish and Swedish
fleets.   But the Danes, who had previously co-operated with
England, found war against Sweden more attractive than against
Russia. For several weeks Norris lay off Copenhagen, but did not
succeed in convincing the Danes that, although they might together
with Russia destroy Sweden, the Tsar would then be so powerful
that he would be a more dangerous neighbour than Sweden had ever
been.   Instead of joining him in the Baltic, the Danish ships were
sent to Norway, where they landed troops for an enterprise against
Sweden.   The Swedish Government, however, was most ready to let
its fleet co-operate against Russia ; but even so the allied fleets
would hardly have had definite superiority over the Russian. From
the naval history of the last two centuries Norris had observed that
approximately equal forces never gave decisive results.[2] So he did
not dare to sail further up the Baltic and openly to join the Swedes.
He only sent his couriers to the King, asking for reinforcements.
Stanhope wrote in the King's name to the Regency, requesting that
they should send every man-of-war that could be spared.

> . . . it would be a great misfortune if for want of some more ships
> we should lose the opportunity of awing the Czar, saving Sweden, and,
> by giving peace to the North, of defeating the greatest hope which is
> now left to Spain.[3]

The Regents once more voiced the old objections.

> Should all the ships we have go to the Baltick, it is certain we cannot
> get any more ships to defend our own coast or insult that of Spain.[4]

After consultation with the Admiralty, however, it was decided
to leave the coast almost without defence, since in view of the naval
offensive against Spain this seemed superfluous. In July five ships

---

[1] Norris to Stanhope, July 7 (O.S.), 1719, S.P. 42/75.
[2] Norris to Stanhope, July 7 (O.S.), 1719, S.P. 42/75.
[3] Stanhope to Delafaye, July 1 (O.S.), 1719, S.P. 43/2.
[4] Craggs to Stanhope, July 7 (O.S.), 1719, S.P. 43/57.

of the line were sent, in August a sixth, to strengthen the Baltic
squadron. In London great deeds were expected, as it was felt that

> though their [the Russian] fleet may be something more numerous,
> doubtlessly they are but sad wretches at the manœuvre of a ship ;
> and their case, if there is an action, will be like that of the Spaniards
> last year.[1]

The Admiralty also held this optimistic view.[2]

The Tsar rightly interpreted the appearance of the English
fleet as a threat to his success in the final stage of the war against
Sweden, and he hardly knew what to do. From Russia Jefferyes
reported :

> His Czarish Majesty is under great apprehension of our fleet, but
> what reason he has for it, unless his conscience accuses him of having
> deserved some ill treatment at His Majesty's hands, is more than I
> know.[3]

For the last four years the English squadron had been greeted as
a friendly force, and they had operated in concert with Sweden's
enemies. Now Norris was asked by the Tsar's envoy in Copenhagen
whether he had orders to hinder Russia's operations against Sweden.
The envoy also handed him a letter in which Peter the Great
demanded that Norris, before approaching the coasts and places
held by Russia, should give a written declaration that he had no
hostile intentions ; otherwise the Tsar must interpret his silence as
proof of the contrary and protect himself according to the rules of
war : for he himself had no hostile intentions against anyone except
the Swedes, with whom he was at war. In order to give the English
no pretext for hostilities, he formally accorded to Dutch and
English ships the right of free trade with all Swedish ports. This
declaration contained nothing that was not already allowed by the
existing law of nations, but was meant as a friendly gesture of the
Russian Government, and was sent together with a polite letter
from the High Chancellor to the British Admiral. Norris carefully
avoided a premature breach with Russia. He declared himself
astonished at the Tsar's apprehensions ; and pointed out that

---

[1] Sunderland to Stanhope, July 31, 1719, printed in Mahon, *History of
England*, vol. ii. (1853), p. lxxxi.

[2] Hoffmann, Aug. 11, 1719, Vienna Archives.

[3] Jefferyes to Craggs, June 25 (O.S.), 1719, *Sbornik*, vol. 61, p. 556. Cf.
also Jefferyes to Craggs, June 13 (O.S.), 1719, *ibid.* p. 551.

before leaving England he had informed the Russian Resident in London of his intended journey and had expressed the hope that the good understanding between England and Russia would not be disturbed.

The building of a Russian fleet[1] was begun by Peter the Great as part of his Baltic policy. After the capture of the first Baltic stronghold in 1703, Peter's small river craft attacked and took two Swedish ships that had approached the coast in the belief that without a fleet the Russians could do them no harm. The Tsar had the wounded Swedish commander nursed back to health, and took him into his own service.

Peter the Great's fleet was built up by English craftsmen on English models. By 1718 it comprised 27 ships with 64 to 14 cannon ; by 1724 it numbered 35 ships with 90 to 30 cannon. In construction and material these ships were as good as those of other Powers. When in 1715 Norris saw three Russian vessels of 60 pieces, he declared that he had seen none better in the English fleet.

But the excellency of this fleet ceased at the point where the Russian element came in. The builders of the ships and the flag officers were English and Dutch ; but the lower ranks and the crew were necessarily Russian. Most of them were people taken from the army, without training, knowledge, or naval experience. Often there were not more than 30 or 40 real sailors in a crew of 400 ; and performances corresponded to the quality of the crews.

If the Russian fleet is attacked in their own roads, lying at anchor in an advantageous posture, the water smooth and their bodies well secured from small shot, and their commanders are men of resolution, exposing their persons and seeming insensible of danger, then the common Russ, forming their judgment from the officers' intrepid aspect, apprehend the peril to be less than it really is, and will stand their ground, traverse the guns, and make a handsome defence, ever a Russian's masterpiece ; . . . (but) any man that has seen the condition their ships are in at sea, in a strong gale of wind, must readily allow a much inferior force might easily attack and destroy them, provided

---

[1] Cf. " History of the Russian Fleet by a Contemporary Englishman " (1724), in *Publ. of the Navy Rec. Soc.* xv. ; S.P. Russia ; Campredon's Reports in *Sbornik*, vol. 40, p. 282 *seq.* ; A. Stenzel, *Seekriegsgeschichte* (1910), vol. iii. p. 482 ; Kirchhoff, *Seemacht in der Ostsee* (1907), vol. i. p. 273 ; Nauticus, *Jahrbuch für Deutschlands Seeinteressen*, vol. v. (1900), p. 187 *seq.*

there was sea room sufficient to prevent their escaping into their harbours.[1]

Beside this first Russian fleet Peter created a second of peculiar character, especially suited to conditions in the Baltic. The coasts of Finland, Esthonia, Sweden, and Norway are lined with cliffs and reefs, and with numbers of rocky islands, which present the greatest difficulties to navigation ; these make it impossible for normal warships, with their deep draught and their sailing technique, to pick a way through them. The largest group of these islands, the Aland group, approaches to within 16 miles of the Swedish coast. Peter had flat-bottomed rowing boats built after the fashion of those seen in the Mediterranean, and likewise called *galleys*. They were built by Italians, and their officers were Italians and a few Greeks, the crews Russian soldiers, notorious for their brutality. On the larger vessels there were 200 men, on the smaller ones, called *lotkey*, 70 to 80, and all carried some cannon. In 1714 there were 126 galleys with five cannon apiece, and 60 lotkey, or Russian brigantines, with four ; in 1724 the galleys numbered 200, and it was said that 50 more could be built in three months. In 1719 there must have been some 150 galleys. The regular fleet and the galley fleet were two entirely separate entities both threatening Sweden. Norris might be able to destroy the regular Russian fleet, but could not possibly follow the galleys through the maze of islands.

After the signing of the preliminary peace between Sweden and Hanover, Carteret felt himself to be the saviour of Sweden and almost the master of the north. " The fate of this country and of the Czar too is humanly speaking in the King of Great Britain, our Master's hands." [2] Yet weeks of tension followed. As Sweden had scorned peace with Russia, the Tsar's galleys and transports entered the river of Stockholm carrying some 30,000 men ; troops landed to pillage and burn, and might have threatened the capital but for a hastily formed camp with 20,000 men who served as a garrison.[3] The Tsar's regular fleet was cruising off the coast.

In this emergency all eyes were turned on the English fleet. The Swedish Admiral Sparre informed Norris that his fleet of 11 ships, mounting 760 cannon, was waiting in Karlskrona ready to

[1] " History of the Russian Fleet ", *Navy Rec. Soc.* xv. p. 114.
[2] Carteret to Stanhope, July 12 (O.S.), 1719, S.P. 95/24.
[3] Chance, *l.c.* p. 338.

join the English squadron.[1] Carteret wrote to Norris that with this addition his fleet would be much superior to the Tsar's 26 ships ; if the communication between the Tsar's galleys and his fleet could be cut off, he would have to submit to England's terms.

> I am just come from the army. Everything is in good order, but it is from the English fleet and its conduct that Sweden expects its deliverance. If your instructions are sufficient, this is the time to act.[2]

But Norris remained with his fleet off Copenhagen. With orders from London, Hanover, and Stockholm, and without sufficient initiative of his own, he hesitated between a desire to strike and reluctance to risk the dangers and responsibilities of a bold decision, which would have embroiled England in a war with Russia. Reports about the efficiency of the Swedish ships were not encouraging, the promised reinforcements from England had not arrived, and Stanhope wrote warning him against precipitate action ; [3] for he felt that the behaviour of the Danes

> puts us under unspeakable difficulties and gives us too much reason to apprehend they will joyn what ships they have in the Sound to the Muscovite fleet in case we should joyn the Swedes . . . it behoves us to be very wary how we make any motion which might expose the King's arms to receive an affront which would only serve to raise the courage and heighten the demands of the Muscovites and Danes without procuring any real relief to Sweden.[4]

The Swedes were sorely disappointed at the hesitations of the English Admiral. In reply to their complaints and reproaches Carteret could only renew his promise that the fleet would come. He advised them to make peace with the Danes, but the suggestion was taken as an insult.[5] They re-opened negotiations with the Tsar, but without reaching agreement, for the Tsar's demands were high, and they were not prepared to give up Reval and the Livonians, who objected to being sacrificed. Also they still had some hope of help from England ; the Queen, Prince Frederick, and Dücker still put their faith in Carteret. The Prince declared that, if they made

---

[1] Sparre to Norris, July 12, 1719, S.P. 42/75.
[2] Carteret to Norris, July 13 (O.S.), 12 o'clock at night, 1719, B.M. Add. MSS. 22511.
[3] Stanhope to Norris, July 22 (O.S.), 1719, S.P. 42/75.
[4] Stanhope to Carteret, July 22 (O.S.), 1719, S.P. 95/24.
[5] Carteret to Stanhope, Aug. 3 (O.S.), 1719, S.P. 95/24.

a dishonourable peace with the Tsar, he would leave the country and serve in the English army.[1] The majority of the Senators, on the other hand, were ready to conclude with the Tsar any day.

One party must get the better of the other very soon : our fleet's coming or not will cast the ballance.[2]

In these circumstances Carteret wrote to Norris that he knew it was impossible to act in a matter of such consequence without positive orders from the King, but that he hoped these orders would arrive very soon.

If he [the Czar] makes his peace with this crown upon the terms that he is near doing, and which nothing can prevent but our assistance . . . he will begin a war with us. He already takes our merchant ships, writes to our Admiral in an extraordinary style, treats the King in his discourses with indignity, and his offers and propositions here tend all against our court.[3]

Meanwhile an important change had taken place in the King-Elector's relations with Prussia. After the failure of the negotiations in Berlin, Whitworth joined George I and Stanhope at Pyrmont, where the King was taking the waters. Stanhope regretted that Frederick William had let Whitworth depart *re infecta*, but did not believe that either Whitworth or Frederick William and his ministers were solely to blame ;[4] the fault seemed to lie with Bernstorff. Stanhope was deeply upset, as the failure in the north threatened the success of his work in the south. He was on the point of resigning.[5]

But before yielding to Bernstorff he made a last desperate attempt to win the King to the English side. Perhaps for the first time George I realized his duty towards England. Before the joint council of English and German ministers he twice condemned Bernstorff's attitude to the negotiations with Prussia, and even pointed out that it had been determined by his personal interests. Stanhope had triumphed ; the word of the Sovereign determined

---

[1] Carteret to Stanhope, July 27 (O.S.), 1719, B.M. Add. MSS. 22511.
[2] Carteret to Stanhope, Aug. 3 (O.S.), 1719, Private, S.P. 95/24.
[3] Carteret to Norris, July 27 (O.S.), 1719, B.M. Add. MSS. 22511.
[4] Stanhope to Whitworth, June 20 (O.S.), 1719, S.P. 44/269B.
[5] Craggs to Schaub, June 30 (O.S.), 1719, printed in Mahon, *l.c.* vol. ii. p. lxxix.

the policy of England and Hanover. On July 12, 1719, Whitworth set out once more for Berlin.

We have been in very great agitation here for some time, but have, at last, got a complete victory over the old man.[1]

George I and his ministers knew quite well that Frederick William was anxious to reach an agreement. The growing influence of England and the other Western Powers on the developments in the north was such that the Prussian King could not but realize the necessity of coming to terms with England. His wife urged George I, her father, with whom she was then staying, to conclude for both political and personal reasons. Whitworth was received in Berlin with warmth and candour by Frederick William, who asked him to assure his master that the agreement was as good as concluded. Whitworth considered the position promising, without giving way to optimism.[2]

In view of Frederick William's loyalty to the Emperor, it was of prime importance that Vienna had fully approved of an Anglo-Prussian agreement. For Charles VI it was decisive that England's fleet was required to help protect his Italian possessions. St. Saphorin had paved the way ; and the Austrian ministers showed themselves sympathetic, but made the reservation that Charles VI, as head of the Empire, could not possibly agree to England's guaranteeing Prussia in possession of Stettin.[3]

The French Government, still afraid of a Northern League which would occupy the attention of her allies, again instructed Rottembourg to support the negotiations. There were, however, delays in the conclusion of the treaty due to Frederick William's relations with the Tsar. Peter the Great had just sent Count Tolstoy to Berlin to find out what was to be expected of Prussia. This diplomat set himself to put all possible difficulties in the way of the negotiations, and he could be a real danger to their success, since Frederick William was still undecided, having just seen the text of the treaty of January 5. Even without knowing of the secret articles he felt that the treaty as a whole, as well as each one of the fifteen articles,

[1] Stanhope to Craggs, July 10, 1719, printed in Mahon, *l.c.* vol. ii. p. lxxx.

[2] Whitworth to St. Saphorin, July 18, 1719, Hanover Archives, "*Ante obitum nemo supremaque funera felix*", adapted from Ovid, *Met.* iii. 137.

[3] Whitworth to St. Saphorin, July 18, 1719, St. Saphorin to Whitworth, July 26, Aug. 5, 1719, Hanover Archives.

was directed against Prussia. On the margin of the document he wrote: " They mean no one but me; to be rubbed into Whitworth".[1]

Circumstances were now changed, but Frederick William could not easily shake off past impressions. With his heart he desired a treaty with George I ; his reason demanded that he should not give up the alliance with the Tsar. His wife was urging him to live in friendship with her father ; his ministers were warning him against a breach with Russia. In a marginal note[2] he complained that the English grudged the Tsar everything, that they wanted to hold down the *puissance qui naisse* ; he was not sure, but inclined to the belief that it was better for him if the Tsar were strong.

When Tolstoy realized that he could not prevent the conclusion of the treaty, he demanded that the Tsar should at least be a party to it. In a conference on July 18 the Prussian ministers favoured this plan. When Whitworth refused to consider it, Ilgen proposed that two treaties should be concluded : one for publication, to which Peter should be a party, and a secret one which Prussia and England would conclude alone. But the King-Elector would not hear of it.[3]

For a fortnight no progress was made. All the articles had already been discussed and formulated, and everything was ready for signature. Only details were still being debated. On August 2 Schaub wrote from Hanover that Herr von Bernstorff's three villages were the only remaining obstacle. But in the background there was still the question whether Frederick William would sign at all unless Russia were included.

Towards the middle of August the tension reached its zenith.[4] Whitworth declared that he must leave unless the treaty were signed within three days. Apparently he stated, boldly but untruthfully, that in the preliminary peace of July 11/22 with Hanover, Sweden had already agreed to cede Stettin to Prussia. He also gave a written declaration that he was ready to negotiate with the Tsar as soon as the treaty with Prussia was concluded, and that he hoped the initiative for these negotiations would come from His Prussian Majesty. Frederick William had withdrawn to Wuster-

---

[1] Droysen, " Die Wiener Allianz ", *Zeitschrift für preuss. Geschichte*, 5, p. 650.

[2] Droysen, *Preussische Politik*, vol. IV. pt. ii. p. 268.

[3] Schaub to St. Saphorin, July 20, 1719, Hanover Archives.

[4] For what follows cf. Droysen, *l.c.* p. 275 *seq.*

hausen, where his worries and doubts brought him to a sick-bed. Finally he gave his unwilling consent, remonstrating and threatening the ministers who had advised him to sign when, so he said, he was ill and irresponsible. The ministers accepted the responsibility, and on August 4/15 the treaty was concluded.

The treaty was of value to Prussia, but the superiority of England's diplomacy was evident. Whitworth however felt uncomfortable about what he had said concerning Stettin. He therefore desired that the treaty should be ante-dated to August 4 (N.S.), so that the English could say that it had been signed before news of the Anglo-Swedish agreement had reached Berlin. After the Anglo-Prussian treaty had been concluded on the assumption that Sweden had agreed to cede Stettin, the Swedes could hardly refuse, as this would badly expose England, whose help was indispensable.

On August 15, but dated August 4, three different treaties were signed in Berlin.[1] In the first Prussia and Hanover guaranteed each other their conquests, Bremen and Verden for Hanover, Stettin and the mouths of the Oder for Prussia. The second settled the question of the three villages belonging to Bernstorff. The third, concluded between England and Prussia, guaranteed the main treaty between Prussia and Hanover. This meant in practice that the King of England guaranteed Stettin and the mouths of the Oder to Prussia. In return Frederick William guaranteed the Protestant Succession, which he had already repeatedly promised to uphold.

The political friendship thus inaugurated between England, Hanover, and Prussia was steadily developed. Three months later England, Hanover, and Prussia made an agreement concerning the deportation of deserters. On January 17, 1720, Prussia and Hanover concluded a treaty by which they agreed to exercise in turn the leadership of the *Corpus Evangelicorum* in the Imperial Diet. Since Saxony, whose Elector and Crown Prince had become Roman Catholics, seemed no longer suitable for this office, Prussia and Hanover had both been striving for it. The significance of the agreement was not lessened by the fact that Saxony remained leader of the *Corpus Evangelicorum*, and that the treaty had no practical results. Finally on September 23, 1719, the Prussian and Hanoverian conquests were further guaranteed by France in a declaration signed by the Comte de Rottembourg.

---

[1] See *Publ. aus den königlich-preussischen Staatsarchiven*, vol. 87.

In November 1719 the King of Prussia paid a visit to his father-in-law in Hanover. Even now he mistrusted George I's political aims and thought of the ladies at his Court with horror. His reception was most friendly, but he found the life of the Hanoverian Court extraordinary, and had had enough of it within five days.[1]

The conclusion of a treaty with Prussia was an important step forward in England's northern policy. The Prusso-Russian alliance had been rendered innocuous, and with the position in Germany now secure England could risk a breach with the Tsar, which till now might have led to a Prussian attack on Hanover. The poor condition of the Swedish ships, the insufficiency of Norris' own squadron, and the possible co-operation of the Danish fleet with Russia—these facts remained unchanged. It was not even certain whether the five ships sent from England had joined Norris. Yet when on August 6/17 the news from Berlin reached Hanover, Stanhope at once sent decisive orders to Norris and Carteret.

These orders contained a wide plan of action : first Sweden was to be made England's ally, then England's relations with Russia were to be clarified, for better or for worse. Enclosed with Carteret's instructions were proposals for a preliminary agreement [2] which would implement Carteret's *papier promissoire* of July 11/22. The treaty of 1700 was to be renewed for the maintenance of peace and friendship between the two states and for the protection of the Protestant religion. England would again pay the old subsidies, would do her utmost to obtain the best possible terms for Sweden in the coming peace negotiations, and would seek to influence her allies in Sweden's favour. In return Sweden would do all possible to further English trade in the Baltic, and if because of this treaty one of her enemies should attack England or Hanover, she would only make peace with this state in conjunction with England or Hanover.

Here again, however, the main object of the treaty was to be in the separate and secret articles. England would guarantee the Swedish-Hanoverian agreement of July 11/22, and, more important, Sweden would agree to cede to Prussia Stettin, the district between

---

[1] Letters from King Frederick William I to Prince Leopold of Anhalt-Dessau. *Acta Borussica*, supplementary volume, 1905, Nos. 270, 271.

[2] Enclosed in Stanhope to Carteret, Aug. 6/17, 1719, S.P. 95/24.

the Oder and the Peene, and the islands of Usedom and Wollin. If Sweden would not accede to these demands, Carteret was to refuse to sign the treaty ; for without their fulfilment the King of Prussia would be driven back into the arms of the Tsar. Sweden must realize what Prussia's friendship meant to her, as well as to Hanover, whether she were first to make peace with Denmark or with Russia. To encourage the Swedes Carteret could inform them of the main points in the instructions being sent to Norris.

As soon as the English Admiral received news of the signing of this treaty, he was to sail with his fleet, which by then would presumably have been joined by the five ships from England, to the island of Hanö off Karlskrona. There he would keep in touch with the Swedish fleet, but not join it unless compelled to do so by the threat of a Russian attack. Otherwise he was to find out how strong the Swedes and Russians were, and whether the latter were likely to be joined by the Danes. If after weighing up all the circumstances he concluded that he together with the Swedes was a match for the Muscovites, he was to send an officer to the Tsar with a letter. In this he would point out that Great Britain was not a party in the war, and that George I had already offered the Tsar his mediation for peace with Sweden ; to lend weight to this offer he, the Admiral, had been sent to this coast. If the Tsar were ready to accept this mediation, which would be honourable and equitable to both sides, it was very necessary that there should be a suspension of arms during the negotiations, and that the Tsar should withdraw his forces from the Swedish mainland. If the Tsar refused to do this, the King of England would have to suppose that he designed to subdue Sweden. The interest of the English crown, the importance to his subjects of trade with the Baltic, and the interest of the Protestant religion made it impossible for George I to allow this. George was anxious to live in amity with the Tsar ; but if Russia were determined to destroy Sweden, he, Norris, had instructions to join with the Swedish forces in the defence of their country.

Norris was to wait off Hanö for the reply to this letter. If it were satisfactory, the King would attain his end of saving a brave people without any loss of his own subjects ; but if either an insolent or captious answer were sent, or none at all, Norris was to join the Swedes and act in the manner most effectual to destroy the Tsar's fleet, than which a greater service could not be done to England.

If you think you are likely to succeed, attempt, in the name of God, and be sure of all the support the King can give you, even though the event should not answer your expectations.[1]

To ensure Carteret's success in the initial stages of this plan, he was empowered to say that England would withdraw her fleet and perhaps also her envoy if Sweden were recalcitrant. He was also authorized to promise presents up to a total of £10,000, or even a few thousand more if the extra money were needed to secure the signature of the treaty in the desired form. To the Queen and the Prince of Hesse Carteret was to give the most definite assurances from the King of England that he would assist them if ever they were in any personal difficulties.

Carteret entered on the task with his accustomed zeal. He laid the draft treaty before the Prince of Hesse and the Senate, and offered England's mediation for the conclusion of peace with Russia. On the Prince's advice he did not make the same offer with regard to Denmark, as it would at present be inadvisable for England to suggest that Sweden should cede Rügen and Stralsund. He was also told that the conjunction of the fleets must be the *causa sine qua non* of the treaty. The cession of Stettin to Prussia formed the real stumbling-block. Carteret tried in vain to show the Swedes that they should not be too upset at ceding what was irretrievably lost. The Senate would not agree to this cession upon other terms than a guarantee of the recovery of Reval and Livonia. Their return to Sweden would have been welcome to England, but Carteret had no authority to guarantee it. The conference broke up, and he gave up all hopes of success.

Next day, August 18/29, Carteret received a letter from Sir John Norris, in which he said he was waiting only for the first fair wind to come to Hanö. This turned the balance, as the Swedes now saw that the King of Great Britain and his ministers were in earnest. The plenipotentiaries returned and told Carteret that the Senate was inclined to advise the Queen to conclude with England, if some small amendments were made. There was no more talk of guaranteeing the recovery of Reval and Livonia ; but Carteret had to give a written declaration that Norris should bring his fleet to Stockholm : for if the Tsar refused the mediation offered, he might

---

[1] Stanhope to Norris, Aug. 17 (N.S.), 1719, S.P. 44/269B. Extract printed in Mahon, *l.c.* vol. ii. App. p. lxxxvi *seq.*

reach Stockholm and they might be undone before the English fleet arrived.[1] The treaty was signed that very day, and Carteret could write : " I know thank God that I have prevented their making peace with the Czar ".[2]   Money had played its part in bringing about the success,[3] for the poverty of the high Swedish officials made them very susceptible to foreign gifts ; but there was nothing treasonable in their acceptance, as the Swedes yielded to Carteret's proposals only when they learned of Norris' approach.

After the treaty had been signed it was laid before the Queen for ratification. She spent the whole of the next day studying its text, and it was past midnight when she signed it and had it sent to Carteret.[4]   The English envoy deeply appreciated that the Queen had always trusted in George I's word, and some days later paid her the compliment that she had shown herself greater than Charles XII.

I told her . . . that her Majesty had equalled him, even in his courage : for I had heard . . . that the late King used to say, He would never make peace with the Muscovites 'till their army was at the gates of Stockholm ; that her Majesty had seen them there, and yet had not made peace.[5]

Sweden now grew so defiant in her negotiations with Russia that they were soon broken off. A heroic strain reappeared in Swedish politics, reminiscent of the spirit of Gustavus Adolphus ; the leaders of the nation would rather see some of their towns and villages burnt, than sacrifice the heritage of a great past by giving way to a powerful foe.

All eyes were turned to the Baltic, where the fleets of three Powers were converging. Carteret, now that the diplomatic work was done, was spurring the British Admiral to action.

It is now in your power . . . by the help of God, to do the most signal piece of service to your country, that any man has done this age. The scales of the North are in your hand. You can cast the ballance, as you please. . . . if the Czar refuses the King's mediation, as he probably will . . . you will by force of arms bring him to reason, and

---

[1] Carteret to Stanhope, Aug. 19 (O.S.), 1719, S.P. 95/24.
[2] See Ballantyne, *Lord Carteret* (1887), p. 49.
[3] Carteret to Stanhope, Aug. 19 (O.S.), 1719, Private Letter, S.P. 95/24.
[4] Postscript of Aug. 20, 2 A.M., to the above private letter.
[5] Carteret to Stanhope, Sept. 4 (O.S.), 1719, S.P. 95/25.

destroy that fleet, which will disturb the world, whilst it is steered by ambition and revenge.[1]

Norris, after receiving his instructions of August 6/17, invited the British and Hanoverian envoys in Copenhagen to a kind of council of war with himself and Rear-Admiral Hopson.[2] The instructions were interpreted as meaning that Norris might at once take his fleet to Hanö. All agreed on this course, although reports about the Swedish fleet were not encouraging. Norris, however, thought that the imminent arrival of five further ships from England would suffice to make not only the Swedes but also the Danes realize the great strength of England.[3] On August 15/26 he, in accordance with his instructions, sent a letter to the Swedish Queen saying that as soon as the treaty was signed in Stockholm he would obey her orders, that in conjunction with the Swedish ships he would seek out the Russian fleet, and do his utmost to destroy it. On August 16/27 he was joined by the five ships, under Rear-Admiral Hosier ; and next day the whole fleet appeared off Hanö. While here he received Carteret's letter asking him to come on to Stockholm.

Peter the Great had kept a close watch on the movements of the Swedish and English fleets. " I am afraid," wrote Carteret on August 21/September 1, " those two frigates, that hovered about our fleet, will have carried him advice of your disposition to sail, and he will run away."[4] First Peter called his galleys back to the Aland Islands, and Sweden was freed from the Russian invasion by the mere approach of the English force. But already 8 towns, 141 castles, 1361 villages, and 43 mills had been burnt down ; 70,000 or 80,000 bars of iron, which could not be shipped, were thrown into the sea ; the iron and copper mines were destroyed, and enough copper was taken to load most of the galleys.[5] The people must have been subjected to many cruelties, and a great number of young people and children were dragged off to St. Petersburg. An English report states that " the Tsar's commands were positive, and performed with reluctance by the Commander-in-Chief " ; [6] but a Russian report says that these cruelties were a just reward for what

---

[1] Carteret to Norris, Aug. 20 (O.S.), 1719, B.M. Add. MSS. 22511.
[2] Norris to Stanhope, Aug. 13 (O.S.), 1719, S.P. 42/75.
[3] Norris to Stanhope, Aug. 14 (O.S.), 1719, S.P. 42/75.
[4] Carteret to Norris, Aug. 21, 1719, S.P. 42/75.
[5] *Publications of the Navy Rec. Soc.* xv. p. 69 [1].
[6] See *Publications of the Navy Rec. Soc.* xv. p. 69.

the Swedes had done ten years previously at Smolensk and in the Ukraine, and for the burning of Altona in 1713.[1]

As soon as Carteret heard that the galleys were being withdrawn from the Swedish mainland he told Norris not to come to Stockholm after all.

The Muscovite galleys are retiring to Aland and the great fleet is supposed still to ly in the Le-Sund near that island. If that fleet retires to Reval, as probably it will upon the news of your approach, it must necessarily pass by Hangoe-ud, a point of Finland. In that case the Court thinks that the united fleet should not come up to Stockholm but go to the said Hangoe-ud, where there is good anchorage and sea room enough. But if the Czar's fleet should remain at Le-Sund and our fleet come up there, it is so much the better.[2]

But apparently the Swedish ships were short of food supplies and munitions, and by August 26/September 6 the united fleets lay at anchor outside Stockholm. Next day a council of war was held on the English flag-ship, and the following day on the Swedish, in which the Prince of Hesse, Carteret, and Field-Marshal Dücker took part. No definite decision could be taken, as it was not even certain where the Russian fleet was to be found. For two days they discussed the possibility of attacking the enemy in the Le-Sund if they were still there. But the Swedish officers and pilots who knew the place declared that there was no room to deploy the fleets, that there were too many reefs and other dangers, that there was no anchorage, and that the entrance to the sound was made impossible of approach by batteries on both sides, quite apart from the opposition that would be put up by the Russian fleet and the galleys. Nor was there much hope of intercepting the Russian fleet between Le-Sund and Reval, as it was now said that there was no suitable roadstead on this route where the united fleets could lie in wait. In the end the only decision taken was to send out a few Swedish frigates to discover the whereabouts of the Russians ; and as there no longer seemed any probability of an action that year, Norris began to think of his return to England.

When news reached Stockholm that one part of the Russian fleet had retired to Reval, and the other to Kronstadt, another council of war was held in presence of the Queen and her husband.[3]

[1] *Sbornik*, vol. 61, p. 579.

[2] Carteret to Norris, Aug. 21 (O.S.), 1719, Postscript, S.P. 42/75.

[3] Norris to Stanhope, Sept. 3 (O.S.), S.P. 42/75. Carteret to Stanhope, Sept. 2 (O.S.), 1719, S.P. 95/25.

Norris, Carteret, and Bassewitz were present, also the recently arrived French envoy Campredon, a strong supporter of Carteret's political activities. It was debated whether the joint fleets could still make an attack; but as both Reval and Kronstadt were well fortified by nature and also by great art and expense, the attempt seemed impracticable. To do anything with a reasonable prospect of success, they would have had to make a descent with good bodies of troops to possess themselves at least of the batteries on one side of the entrances to those ports. As they would never by naval operations alone force the Tsar to make peace, Norris actually proposed such a descent to the Queen, but only for the following year.

The annihilation of the Russian fleet was evidently out of the question, and the council of war turned to politics. Carteret now put forward the proposal for England's mediation between Sweden and Denmark. As respect for England had been much increased by the sending of her fleet, and even more because England and France were now agreed that the Danes must return Rügen and Stralsund to Sweden, England's mediation was accepted. England had in this adopted that part of the French programme which required that Sweden must keep a footing on German territory.

The return home of the English fleet was delayed for another two months. Its presence strengthened the Swedish Government both at home and abroad. As the season was good, and 120 Russian galleys were gathered in the Finnish harbour of Åbo, there were great apprehensions of another attack once the English had sailed. The mere presence of the English squadron encouraged Swedish shipping to venture once again into the Baltic. Norris was even asked if he would send six ships to join some Swedish frigates which were cruising between Danzig and Königsberg to keep the trade route open; he replied that he could not make any detachment, but that he was always ready, in any essential case, to move with all his force for Her Majesty's service.[1] In this way Norris avoided the risk of opening a war with Russia by small actions; the destruction of the whole Russian fleet must be the price of a breach with Russia.

If the English fleet had left early in September, fear of a renewed Russian attack would have strengthened the party in Sweden

---

[1] Norris to Stanhope, Sept. 22, 1719, S.P. 42/75.

desirous of peace with Russia. It was England's aim to delay
Russo-Swedish negotiations till after peace had been made with
Sweden's other enemies, and thus to reduce the Tsar's gains. It
was not till October 19 (N.S.) that Ulrike Eleonore agreed to the
departure of the English fleet; by the following evening it was
under sail, but owing to head winds and storms only reached the
high sea on November 27. On the way warships and merchant
ships were badly damaged. Before passing the Sound Norris again
called at Copenhagen, spoke of the Swedes' desire for peace, and
pressed the Danes to conclude with them.

On December 9, later than in previous years, the fleet arrived
back in England.

Despite the naval disappointment in the Baltic, England's
northern policy was progressing successfully. Friendly relations
had been established between Sweden and Hanover, and between
England and Prussia; the Anglo-Swedish preliminary treaty had
paved the way for peace between Prussia and Sweden. Now Sweden
finally made peace with Hanover on November 9/20, 1719, and with
Prussia on January 21/February 1, 1720; on the same day the Anglo-
Swedish treaty of alliance was signed; on June 3/14 peace was
made between Sweden and Denmark. All these treaties show clear
signs of English influence, which are also visible in the peace treaty
of January 7/18, 1720, between Sweden and Poland.

But the ultimate object of the Baltic expedition of 1719 had not
been attained. Russia's power was unbroken, and there was little
hope of wresting from her the territories she had taken on the Baltic.
England would have liked to treat the new maritime power as she
had treated the Spaniards off Passaro; but her position in the
Baltic was much weaker than in the Mediterranean, for she had no
bases like Gibraltar and Port Mahon where a fleet could winter,
and no ships like the Russian galleys which could operate amongst
the masses of small rocky islands. England's task had been further
complicated by the traditional hostility between Sweden and
Denmark. Norris had been held up for weeks off Copenhagen
through fear that if he helped the Swedes, the Danes might attack
him in the back or join the Russians.

Though for all he had done or omitted to do Norris could cite
Stanhope's orders, he was much blamed in England by the Regents
and the Admiralty, who thought it should have been easy to destroy

the Russians.[1]   After speaking with two experienced Admirals,
Jennings and Wager, who found Norris' attitude incomprehensible,
Sunderland wrote excitedly to Stanhope :

> I own I never did expect better from him, for he is one of those
> unreasonable, blustering men, that make a great noise, and are capable
> of doing nothing. . . . If Norris should persist in making his difficulties,
> the King should send express for Sir John Jennings to go and take upon
> him the command of the fleet.[2]

When Norris did not seek battle even after reinforcements had
arrived, indignation reached its climax.   Years later, after Norris
had led a few more expeditions to the Baltic, the old reproaches
still made themselves heard, and Norris was even accused of having
been bribed by the Tsar not to help the Swedes in time.   As late
as 1725 he had to defend himself by pointing out that as soon as
he had heard of Hosier's arrival in the Cattegat, he had sailed for
Sweden without even waiting for positive orders.[3]

Probably Norris could have forced the Tsar to fight if he had
followed Carteret's advice and lain in wait for the Russian fleet
off the coast of Finland.   When the Swedish Admiral was not to be
had for such a plan, a more dashing commander than Norris might
have acted alone—but woe betide him if he failed.   Even his critics
at the Admiralty finally saw that it would have been folly for him
to have taken the risk without definite orders.[4]

Carteret himself had fully approved of the Admiral's actions.
At times he had been very worked up about Norris' delays, and had
had to listen to many reproaches because of them.   Yet after a talk
with the Admiral, Carteret wrote privately to Craggs that " his
conduct from the beginning has been right. . . . He is a very
valuable man in his business." [5]

Few people in England felt any disappointment at the result of
the northern drama.   To the public, it was more important to
avoid war with Russia, and the consequent interruption of the

---

[1] See Hoffmann's Reports of the period, Vienna Archives.

[2] Sunderland to Stanhope, Aug. 4, 1719.   Printed in Mahon, *l.c.* vol. ii.
App. p. lxxxi *seq.*

[3] Norris to Poyntz, Nov. 29 (O.S.), 1725, S.P. 42/72.

[4] Hoffmann's Report of Aug. 25, 1719, Vienna Archives.

[5] Carteret to Craggs, Sept. 27 (O.S.), 1719.   (Private)   B.M. Add. MSS.
22511.

Baltic trade, than to deal a decisive blow to her growing sea power. The political success was plain to all, and all were agreed that it was due to Stanhope's diplomacy. The support given by France in no way lessened his merits, for none but Stanhope could have secured French co-operation while remaining complete master of the situation. His colleagues in the Cabinet ungrudgingly gave him his due :

> Your project of the preliminary treaty with Sweden, and the orders you have sent in all events to Lord Carteret, are the justest and rightest that ever were formed, and, . . . without a compliment to you, they are what nobody but yourself could have formed in so nice and just a manner.[1]

In September, when the diplomatic activity was over, the Regents sent a joint letter of appreciation to Hanover, to convey the thanks of the Government to the real author of the recent successes.[2]

The people of England learnt the importance of these successes from the King's Speech with which George I opened Parliament on November 23 (O.S.), 1719. The Speech proudly announced that " one Protestant kingdom has already been relieved by our seasonable interposition ", and that soon the peace of all Europe would be established by British arms and diplomacy. Stanhope himself may have written it ; he was not above dragging the successes of his foreign policy into the limelight : this was the best means for securing the position of the Government at home, and it seemed all the more necessary as the coming session was to decide its fate.

---

[1] Sunderland to Stanhope, Aug. 14, 1719, printed in Mahon, *l.c.* vol. ii. App. lxxxiv.

[2] Hoffmann, Sept. 29, 1719, Vienna Archives.

CHAPTER XII

INTERNAL DIFFICULTIES AND WALPOLE'S VICTORY

WHILE in foreign policy success followed success, at home England was drifting towards a catastrophe. The position of the Government was becoming steadily more difficult, and no one could foresee what would happen if it fell. As before the death of Anne, there was a general feeling of instability : for internal order was dependent on the Hanoverian Dynasty.

Hanoverians and Whigs — the two seemed to be inseparable — were faced with the same dangers. The split in the Whig party had so reduced the Government's majority in Parliament that if the Opposition under Walpole and Townshend could draw 30 or 40 more to their side, it would inflict a severe, and in the case of an important Bill, possibly fatal defeat on the Government. The quarrel in the royal family had become chronic, and it sometimes seemed as though internal politics were nothing but a duel between the King and the Prince of Wales. Most serious of all was the dual régime ; Hanoverian ministers so strongly influenced internal as well as foreign affairs that one is tempted to speak of a period of foreign domination in England.

After five years George I was still a stranger in England, knowing something perhaps of political practice, of English law, and of English society, but still unable to speak the language of his subjects. At Court chiefly French was spoken, and sometimes German ; in the Cabinet too, as long as George I presided, French was used ; perhaps also in the Privy Council whenever the Sovereign attended. He could converse in French with Stanhope and Craggs, in German with Carteret, and even in Latin with Walpole and Cowper ; in the first years of his reign he often used Robethon as an interpreter ; [1]

[1] See Memorial for Senneterre, Appendix 6. Cf. Bussemaker, *De Republiek der Vereenigde Nederlanden en de Keurvoorst-Koning George I*. Bijdragen voor

but though he overcame the language difficulty in this way, he never became conversant with English affairs. This defect was the more fateful because the King was still expected to direct the government of the country himself. So he was dependent on the advice and help of others. Before his arrival in London he had had memorials and expert opinions from Bothmer, Leibniz, and other sources. Then for five years English and German advisers had worked under him without a clear division of duties. Though the internal administration of Hanover was carried on locally by a college of so-called *Königlich Grossbritannische Geheime Räte*,[1] the most important decisions were made and the whole foreign policy directed from London.

The German Court in London consisted of several ministers with Bernstorff as Premier, of a political staff of twenty-three, of a large number of persons of estate, and of a numerous retinue, making about 150 in all. They were felt to be a foreign element in English society, and were the butt of malicious jokes. Many of them must have been disappointed when the Act of Settlement prevented them from holding English offices. Only Bernstorff and his political circle, however, the so-called Hanoverian Junta of St. James, are of any importance.[2] In 1718–1719, at the age of seventy, Bernstorff attained and passed the height of his power. Dubois described him as " a man of high merits, infallible in the affairs of the [German] Empire, untiring in his work, in appearance grave and wise, impeccable in his mode of life, in matters of state penetrating and suspicious, firm to the point of stubbornness, who has always been the most trusted minister of the King ".[3] Bonet called him firm in matters of business, and hard towards those who worked with him. Lady Cowper has recorded how Bernstorff came to her house to speak with her husband, and afterwards spoke to her in a tone never before used towards " an English Lady that had bread to put into her mouth ".[4]

Before George came to England he received a memorial from

Nederlandsche Geschiedenis IV, 1 (1900). On Robethon, cf. Chance, *Engl. Hist. Rev.* 1898, p. 55.

[1] Cf. Meier, *Hannoversche Verfassungs- und Verwaltungsgeschichte*, vol. ii. p. 41.

[2] Cf. A. W. Ward, *Great Britain and Hanover* (1899), esp. Lecture II; L. Melville, *The First George* (1908), vol. i. p. 232 *seq.*

[3] See Appendix 6.   [4] *Diary of Mary, Countess Cowper* (1864), p. 53.

Ker of Kersland warning him of the consequences of listening to
the advice of Hanoverian ministers in British questions : for the
British nation had always been jealous of foreigners. The same
Scotsman had corresponded on this subject with Leibniz,[1] who
agreed that the meddling of German ministers in British affairs
would necessarily lose the King all the affection of his people.[2]

Unfortunately the new King preferred to work with his accus
tomed helpers. Bernstorff and Bothmer became intermediaries
between the King and his English ministers, and it was said in
1715 that they had the first information in everything. As far as
France, Spain, Italy, and Austria, and the War of the Spanish
Succession were concerned, the Hanoverians pulled with the English.
In November 1717, at an important stage in the preparation of the
Quadruple Alliance, Pendtenriedter negotiated at times with Bernstorff and Bothmer, at others with Stanhope and Sunderland.[3]
Bothmer's history of the Quadruple Alliance, which is based on
documents,[4] is the best proof of how completely the Hanoverians
were versed in the secrets of English politics. In northern questions
the Hanoverian interest outweighed the English. The Baltic expeditions were intended to secure Bremen and Verden for Hanover,
rather than to protect English trade. In this way the German
Court drew profit from the expenditure of the English nation.[5]
Even in 1719, when England turned against Russia, Hanover's
interests still played an important part.

From the start there was no lack of friction between the German
and English ministries. In May 1716 there occurred a *collision
secrète*. The English were trying to emancipate themselves from
German influence, and refused to follow any interests but those of
their nation and party, much to the distaste of Bernstorff.[6] The
Hanoverian ministers were careful to tell no one, least of all their
English colleagues, of their influence on English policy in the Baltic.
But they could not prevent others from blurting out the truth.
In October 1716 came the Danish declaration[7] containing the reasons
why an expedition against Schonen, planned by Sweden's enemies,

---

[1] Ker of Kersland, *Memoirs*, vol. i. p. 97 (ed. 1727).
[2] *Ibid.* p. 101.
[3] See Pendtenriedter's Reports in the Vienna Archives.
[4] Ed. by Doebner, *Forschungen zur deutschen Geschichte*, 26.
[5] Bonet, Jan. 20/31, 1716, Prussian State Archives.
[6] Bonet, May 11/22, 1716, Prussian State Archives.
[7] Cf. Vol. I. p. 309.

had not been put into effect. Denmark blamed the Tsar for not having supplied the necessary forces ; and, to emphasize his dilatoriness, added that both the British ambassador at Copenhagen and Admiral Norris " had, on the express orders of their master, tried with all sorts of insinuations to dispose his Tsarish Majesty to this enterprise ".[1] The manifesto was published by the Danish resident in Hamburg, and immediately the full text appeared in the English newspapers. It was now evident that the King of England had used servants of the Crown to press the Tsar to invade Sweden, though England was not at war with her. The English ministers were as disagreeably surprised as was the public, which had always been told that the Baltic expeditions were only to protect English trade. The objection was not so much to the breach of neutrality as to the infringement of the Act of Settlement, by which England was not to take part in Hanoverian wars. The Government, expecting fierce attacks in Parliament, blamed the Danes for their unwise, unfriendly, and unnecessary manifesto ; but the real fault lay with the Hanoverians. Bonet was of opinion that the English ministry would probably be more careful in future about northern questions, and less willing to agree to the wishes of the German ministers.[2]

The First Lord of the Admiralty, the Earl of Orford, repeatedly wished to resign because of the instructions given to the Admiral in the Baltic. Early in 1717 he and several others, with Walpole and Townshend, were relieved of office,[3] and the ministry was now rid of all that were not pro-Hanoverian. George I, Bernstorff, and Bothmer had gained the upper hand, even over Stanhope and Sunderland. Bernstorff now became unbending and deaf to everything that did not suit his aims. His decisions were said to be the sure and infallible oracle which was obeyed and from which there was no appeal.[4] The pro-Hanoverian Government, however, had to face the combined opposition of the Tories and of the dissatisfied Whigs, now under the leadership of Townshend, Walpole, and other ex-ministers who knew the weaknesses of the Government better than the Tories.

On April 12, 1717, the storm broke in Parliament. The Govern-

[1] Lamberty, *Mémoires*, vol. ix. p. 626.

[2] Bonet, Oct. 23/Nov. 3, 1716, Prussian State Archives. Cf. also Hoffmann, Nov. 6, 1716, Vienna Archives ; and Whitworth's Reports of Oct. 9/20 and 13/24, 1716, S.P. 90/7.   [3] Cf. Vol. I. p. 331.

[4] Bonet, Apr. 16/27, 1717, Prussian State Archives.

ment asked for a credit of £250,000 for their policy against Sweden, and only obtained it after many hard things had been said about the Germans.   After Stanhope had put the motion there was for a minute or two a great silence in the House.   Mr. Pulteney, one of the ex-ministers, broke it first, and said that having resigned his place he acted with the freedom becoming an Englishman, and that he doubted not, but the resolutions of a British Parliament would make a German ministry tremble.[1]   Lord Finch, son of the Earl of Nottingham, attacked Bernstorff pitilessly.   He was certain that all that was said about the threatening position of the Tsar and about the money needed for the north was merely due to the fact that a certain German minister owned property in Mecklenburg.   Why had not the Government, instead of asking for £250,000, rather made the German ministers a present of £50,000 ?   This would have saved the nation £200,000.[2]   Other speakers stated bluntly that without Bremen and Verden, England would have had no difficulties at all in the north.

Stanhope had the difficult task of proving that the acquisition of Bremen and Verden was not merely an aggrandisement of Hanover, but was also most advantageous to England.   But he did not say one word in defence of Bernstorff.

In the next weeks the Opposition again poured its wrath over the German ministers.   In private circles there was already talk of driving the Hanoverian ministry from England ;   or, if this were not possible, other means of dealing with it were being considered. But the height of the storm had passed over Westminster, and did not return with such violence.

The Government remained at the helm, still under the influence of Bernstorff.   In his Reports Bonet likened Sunderland, Stanhope, and Cadogan to sovereigns in their several spheres, and said that they even infringed on the authority of the Archbishop of Canterbury by disposing of the bishoprics.   At the same time, however, he wrote that they had attained power by playing up to the Germans in Hanover in 1716, and by promising to help them acquire Bremen and Verden, even with the aid of English money ;   Townshend and Walpole had been dismissed only because they would not agree to this.

Bonet saw that Bernstorff's credit in British affairs was based

---

[1] *Parl Hist.*, vol. vii. p. 443.
[2] Bonet, Apr. 16/27, 1717, Prussian State Archives.

on the unlimited confidence which the King, his master, had in his abilities and his loyalty ; George I relied on him in everything, and because of this, and of the great difficulties which the English ministers had with their countrymen, they did not feel secure in their positions unless they possessed Bernstorff's confidence. To keep it, they followed his ideas punctiliously, and could not be brought to abandon them, except perhaps by the fear that this attitude might make a bad impression on the country. "This observation supplies the key to a multitude of events, which would otherwise involve one in endless errors." [1] Whether these details were correct or not, the fact remains that for some years Bernstorff was the true *maître des affaires.*

The conclusion of the Vienna Alliance of January 5, 1719, opens a new phase. The English ministers were henceforward determined to shake off the Hanoverian shackles. They looked upon the Vienna Alliance as an underhand blow at their policy, even at their security. France, their most valuable ally, was offended and threatened apostacy ; and the dangerous Declaration 4 was likely to bring upon them the anger of Parliament and of the public. Though France had been appeased and the Declaration had not been implemented, every day could bring a similar danger. The struggle which now began might look like a series of court intrigues for the making and overthrow of ministers ; but seen in true perspective it was a matter of national importance for England.

Within the Triumvirate Cadogan, now a Lord, was considered the most subservient to the Hanoverian ministers. He was also high in favour with George I. The attempt of 1717 to overthrow him by Parliamentary means had failed dismally.[2] Now a new attack came from within the Government. In 1718 Craggs had been appointed Secretary of State in place of Addison. The young politician, who had seen the world and had proved his ability in diplomatic missions, was a worthy colleague of the great Stanhope, whom he sincerely admired. His talents formed an excellent complement to those of his chief. As a clear-headed, practical politician he objected in principle to the influence of the German ministers, and worked systematically against it. Craggs became the driving force in a plot of which the first victim was to be Cadogan, whose

[1] Bonet, Oct. 17/28, 1718 ; cf. also Bonet, May 2/13, 10/21, June 7/18, July 16/27, Aug. 2/13, 1717, Prussian State Archives. [2] Cf. above, pp. 19-21.

removal would be an important step towards the overthrow of the German ministers. Cadogan, who was not even in the Cabinet, was acting as ambassador in The Hague. His failure to make the States General accede to the Quadruple Alliance was a serious stain on his reputation which his opponents exploited to the full.

When Craggs succeeded in gaining Stanhope's support, the Triumvirate became nothing but a name. When Sunderland joined them, these three formed in reality a new Triumvirate bent on the fall of Cadogan. They worked together to discredit him with the King. Their first success was the appointment of the Duke of Argyll as Lord Steward of the Household. The Duke was an old enemy of Cadogan from the days when they both claimed the glory of having suppressed the Scottish Rising. This success with Argyll was the more valuable to the hard-pressed Government as he controlled 7 votes in the Lords, and 14 in the Commons. In 1716 he had been dismissed from all his offices because of his close connection with the Prince of Wales. His reinstatement was an unusual step which seemed to foreshadow the fall of his enemy. In well-informed circles it was already thought that Cadogan's power was nearing its end.

George I was beginning to show more understanding for the principles and requirements of British politics; but Bernstorff still enjoyed his full confidence.[1] When the German minister heard what was in the wind, he hurried to the King and warned him against the ambitious intentions of certain English ministers. Bernstorff linked the affair with foreign politics, in order to increase its importance. He argued that England was allied with France and Austria, and that they were even waging a joint war. But their interests were not necessarily identical : Stanhope and Craggs were trying to make the King follow in the wake of France. The King was perturbed, the more so as Bothmer and even Pendtenriedter supported Bernstorff's case. Pendtenriedter even succeeded in breaking the coalition against the German ministers by winning over Sunderland ; nothing further was heard of Cadogan's disgrace, or of the Government's known intention[2] of making him innocuous by appointing him Commander-in-Chief of the Forces in Ireland. Instead the King gave a splendid reception to the returning ambassador in spite of the failure of his diplomacy ; and the reinstatement of Argyll was divested of all political importance by

---

[1] Destouches to Dubois, Mar. 9, 1719, Aff. étr. 323.
[2] Chammorel to Dubois, Feb. 9, 13, 1719, Aff. étr. 322.

making it a condition that he should refrain from taking part in any political, military, or Scottish affairs.[1]

Cadogan still took an active part in home and foreign affairs, but his influence depended on his close connexion with the German ministers. In March 1719 he did the King a personal service by obtaining Parliament's consent to the payment of arrears due to several foreign states, including Hanover. He urged vigorous action against Spain ; he also suggested to the Austrian envoy that Imperial troops should be sent by sea from the Netherlands for an attack on Cadiz or Seville, and declared that he was ready to lead them himself.[2] But meanwhile Craggs and Stanhope had won Sunderland back to their side. In addition to his office as First Lord of the Treasury Sunderland had just been appointed Groom of the Stole, an office which had been vacant since George I's accession, and which gave its holder the right of access to the monarch at any time.

Each side was striving to oust the other from the King's confidence. " My good Lord Cadogan ", Craggs wrote to Stair, " has a notion of being *premier ministre*, which, I believe, you will with me think a very Irish one." [3] Sunderland, Stanhope, and Craggs used to go into the King's closet together. One day as they were all leaving, Cadogan, who had gone in with them, " pretended to have forgot somewhat, . . . and so stayed behind half an hour, as if there was some secret only for his own use ".[4] His rivals were in despair, because they were convinced that he was undoing all they had just done.

Such a scene was typical of the permanent antagonism between the two camps. In the presence of their Master they could not speak their minds, but elsewhere they were at daggers drawn. In March 1719, for instance, the new Danish Envoy was seeking an alliance with England and Hanover against Sweden ; Cadogan and the German ministers were ready for anything, but the English ministers, who were expected to promise subsidies, were hesitant. They recalled the Act of Settlement by which any British minister who allowed British and Hanoverian policy to be confused was

---

[1] Cf. Robethon to Stair, Feb. 6, 1719, Hanover Archives ; Pendtenriedter, Feb. 17, 1719, Vienna Archives.

[2] Pendtenriedter's Reports, Mar. 24, Apr. 22, 1719, Vienna Archives.

[3] Craggs to Stair, Mar. 24, 1719, printed in Graham, *Annals of Stair*, vol. ii. p. 103.

[4] Craggs to Stair, Mar. 31, 1719, printed in Graham, *l.c.* p. 105.

exposed to the charge of high treason. The Germans answered scornfully that if the British crown was not allowed to help the Elector, it brought George I more trouble than pleasure, since for it he had to renounce the pleasure of living in his fatherland, and to deprive his German subjects of the solace of his presence. In reply the English pointed to the many millions which the nation had already spent for the King's foreign provinces, through loss of trade, the cost of sending a fleet to the Baltic year after year, and the payment of subsidies ; because of these expenses they had had to listen to many hard words in Parliament. To please the King, they declared, they would gladly do all that could be done ; but they must be given a chance to keep up appearances, and to avoid infringement of the Act of Settlement. Otherwise the nation would be roused not only against them, but also against the King himself, and there would be general confusion.[1]

Foreign governments kept a close watch on the dual régime in London and tried to take advantage of it. About the time when the Quadruple Alliance was concluded, France and Austria were each trying to carry more weight than the other at St. James ; Austria preferred to work through the German ministry, France through the English. This situation is visible in the memorial given to Senneterre when he went to London in 1719.[2] The description of the German ministers, and of their relation to the English, fills half the memorial. After an excellent portrait of Bernstorff, Bothmer is depicted, meek and subtle, sly and full of duplicity, an extreme partisan of the Emperor, and chief adviser to his representatives in England. Next Dubois describes Robethon, who, as an exiled Huguenot and the social leader of the refugees in England, hated France and was devoted to the Emperor. Dubois, as a French minister and a Roman Catholic, naturally disliked him, and doubted whether the Emperor would retain his loyalty, as there was no telling what he would do when stirred by his fanaticism. But he was to be treated with consideration, for his knowledge of languages and his capacity for work had given him a place between the German and English ministers. Sunderland and Cadogan esteemed him highly, Craggs and Stanhope made use of him, although they knew he was indiscreet and prejudiced.

Senneterre was to avoid carefully any sign of mistrusting Bern-

---

[1] Pendtenriedter's Report of Mar. 3, 1719, Vienna Archives.
[2] Cf. above, p. 134, and Appendix 6.

storff, Robethon, and their friends. Even on occasions when
Bernstorff was likely to be opposed to his wishes, he none the less
was to make a pretence of confiding to him those things which he
would in any case come to know. Above all, Senneterre was not to
take sides in disputes between the English and German ministries, but
rather to take advantage of these disputes for the benefit of France.

During 1719 two curious attempts were made to limit the rights
of the heir to the throne by Act of Parliament, of which one at
least was inspired by George I's hatred of his son.

The first follows the lines of a pamphlet secretly circulated in
England at the end of 1718 ; printed in Holland, it pretended to be
the translation of an English original, and was entitled : " *Lettre
écrite de Londres par le Chevalier N. à Mylord N.*" [1] The author
describes the foreign domination of England in extravagant terms ;
for him Stanhope, Sunderland, and Craggs are nothing but the distinguished underlings of the Hanoverians. As this state of affairs
must not continue, he proposes that both Houses of Parliament
should pass a Bill that would put an end to the personal union of
England and Hanover by forbidding the Kings of England to be
rulers of a State independent of the British realm. For the separation
of England and Hanover must be made as secure as that of France
and Spain, for which so much blood had been shed. The simplest
way would be if Hanover were given to the Prince of Wales' son
Frederick, who had so far been brought up in Germany, and England
to a younger brother if one should be born.

According to Bonet, the idea was not new : for the late Lord
Halifax had always considered it a gross blunder that the Act of
Settlement had not required the new Sovereign to renounce his
German possessions ; but so far no one had ever suggested raising
the matter in Parliament.

It is uncertain whether George I knew of the pamphlet ; but its
basic ideas recur in a carefully thought out plan for altering the
succession. If not composed by the King himself, it was certainly
written at his instigation and according to his ideas.[2] The male

---

[1] Not given in Halkett and Laing. It seems that no printed copy has
been preserved. A written copy is enclosed with Bonet's Report of Dec. 5/16,
1718, Prussian State Archives.

[2] See Stowe Collection, vols. 248 and 249 ; cf. also W. Michael, " Die
Personalunion von England und Hannover und das Testament Georgs I "

heirs were always to have precedence over the female, even if not so closely related ; female succession would only be allowed if the whole male progeny of George I had died.   The union between England and Hanover was to be maintained during the reigns of his son George and his grandson Frederick ; but then the separation was to be effected as soon as a Sovereign died leaving more than one male heir.   The eldest would become King of England, the second as Elector would inherit all the German possessions of his father. In the event of the English line being later without male heir, the Elector would, however, succeed to the English throne.   But such a re-union was to be ended again as soon as the joint ruler died leaving two sons, or one son and a more distant male relative to whom England or Hanover might be given.   Similarly, if Hanover were left without male heir, the English line would succeed, but in this case a second son, a brother, or a distant male relative of the King would have precedence over the King himself.[1]

(*Archiv für Urkundenforschung*, 6, 1918).   Recent research on the subject is summarized in " Das Testament König Georgs I und die Frage der Personalunion zwischen England und Hannover ", by R. Drögereit, in *Niedersächsisches Jahrbuch für Landesgeschichte*, 14 (1937).   The subject will be treated fully in vol. iii. (Translators' Note.)

[1] The following imaginary genealogical table was included with the plan by way of illustration ; but it is not clear why at the end Sophie should become Queen in preference to male relatives.

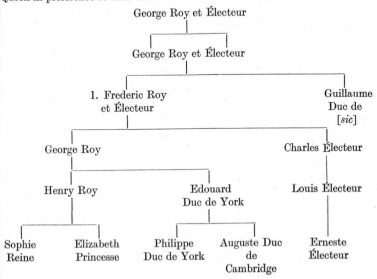

George Roy et Électeur

George Roy et Électeur

1. Frederic Roy et Électeur — Guillaume Duc de [*sic*]

George Roy — Charles Électeur

Henry Roy — Edouard Duc de York — Louis Électeur

Sophie Reine — Elizabeth Princesse — Philippe Duc de York — Auguste Duc de Cambridge — Erneste Électeur

Though the idea of altering the succession had been suggested to George I by the quarrel with his son, yet he managed to give it a purely practical form. His conception rises above the difficulties of any given moment, and like the Pragmatic Sanction of Charles VI, tries to create a lasting settlement.

The plan was put before a conference which was to examine it and make a report to the King. Thomas Parker (later Lord Macclesfield) was present as Lord Chancellor, but the names of the other ministers are not recorded. Evidently there were no Germans, for it was stated that as no one was sufficiently acquainted with the laws of the Empire, the discourse as to them was very lame and possibly based on false suppositions.

The ministers openly expressed their doubts about the plan, though they admitted Parliament's authority to regulate the succession. In this way the desired precedence of male heirs could easily be effected. The dissolution of the personal union, however, contained insuperable difficulties. Without going into the advantages or the disadvantages and dangers of so far-reaching a measure, the ministers only wished to discuss its practicability. The right of a King-Elector's eldest son to rule Hanover could not be annulled by the British Parliament, although Parliament could demand that in order to become King he should renounce his Hanoverian possessions. But it seemed equally impossible to enforce the renunciation either before or after the accession. Once King, he could easily have the Act repealed by Parliament before making the required renunciation. If he had to make the renunciation before becoming King, an interregnum would occur, to avoid which had been the main aim of the Act of Settlement. The proposed Act might thus become a source of troubles and domestic strife, and might lead to the putting forward of unjustified claims, even to the intervention of foreign powers.

George I apparently accepted the advice of his ministers and dropped the plan : for no more was heard of it. The Act of Settlement of 1701 still remains in force.

The second attempt to limit the rights of the heir to the throne is contained in the Peerage Bill.[1] The creation of peers had always

---

[1] Cf. Hatschek, *Englische Verfassungsgeschichte*, p. 564 ; Turner, in the *Eng. Hist. Rev.*, April 1913 ; W. Michael in *Historische Zeitschrift*, 107, p. 675, and 111, p. 674.

been part of the King's prerogative, but as early as 1642 the " Nine-teen Propositions " had contained the demand that no peers should be created without the consent of both Houses of Parliament. During the Revolution the House of Lords had been abolished, but Cromwell created a Second House, the members of which should be appointed by himself subject to the approval of the existing Parlia-ment. With the Restoration of the Stuarts the House of Lords was reinstated, but the Commons retained their priority. The country could not rid itself of the suspicion that the Upper House might one day become the tool of royal absolutism, as the King could create as many peers as might be required to secure the passage of any Bill he desired. At the end of the seventeenth century the idea was current that the Sovereign's right to create peers should be limited ; in 1681 Henry Neville proposed in his *Plato Redivivus* that " no peer shall be made but by act of parliament ".[1] Neville was, however, activated rather by respect for, than suspicion of, the Upper House, which he said

stemmed the tide, and made the waters quiet, giving the people time to come to themselves . . . if we had no such peerage now . . . we should be necessitated to make an artificial peerage or senate instead of it.[2]

Realisation of the need for an Upper House, and mistrust of the King's power to create peers, both lasted into the eighteenth century. To the Sovereign the right of creating peers was a precious part of his prerogative which enabled him to reward great services to the State. The general who had led the English and Dutch troops in the War of the Spanish Succession had been made Duke of Marlborough ; Robert Harley and Henry St. John, the famous Tory ministers of Queen Anne, had entered the Upper House as Earl of Oxford and Viscount Bolingbroke. These promotions were political measures only inasmuch as the party in power did all it could to have the honours bestowed on their supporters. William III neither intended nor effected any radical change in the relative strength of the parties when he created a number of new peers.[3] Even when Queen Anne created or promoted ten Lords on December 30, 1706, all of them Whigs, there could be no question of a direct political motive.

[1] See C. H. Firth, *The House of Lords during the Civil War* (1910), p. 287 [1].
[2] *Ibid.* p. 296.
[3] Cf. Turberville, *The House of Lords in the Reign of William III* (Oxford Hist. and Lit. Studies 3, 1913), p. 14 *seq.*

Not so with the notorious creation of peers in 1711. The pre-
liminaries with France had been signed, and the English Government
was on the point of concluding a peace which would have left Spain
and the West Indies to the Bourbon Philip V. The Queen's Speech
at the opening of Parliament had referred to the imminent opening
of the peace congress. In their Address of Thanks the Lords, on the
motion of Nottingham, inserted a clause that in the opinion of the
House no peace was safe or honourable if Spain and the West Indies
were to be allotted to any branch of the House of Bourbon.[1] In
the critical situation that followed the Queen seemed undecided,
and to save the situation the Government took a most unusual step.
The Whig majority in the Upper House was changed into a Tory
majority by the creation of twelve new peers.

The public took strong exception to the manœuvre, and Bolingbroke himself later admitted that it was hardly justifiable.[2] The
Queen's prerogative was not questioned, but the motive was objectionable. By such means the Pretender could be restored or Popery
re-established. Even the best friends of the Government realized
the inherent dangers of the measure, though they were glad the
situation had been saved.

The Whigs never forgot their opponents' use of so unfair a
weapon ; and when they impeached the Earl of Oxford, they
accused him of having led the Queen to abuse her prerogative.
None the less they themselves saw to it that they always had a
safe majority in the Upper House. There was no conspicuous mass
creation of peers, but on the coronation of George I the creation of
eight new peers [3] sufficed to destroy the Tory majority established
in 1711. By the end of 1717 more peers had been created, and the
Government could have no objection if the *status quo* in the Upper
House were perpetuated.

When in 1719 the Whigs introduced their Peerage Bill, they had
other reasons than the perpetuation of their majority : the hostility
between the King and his heir, the split in the Whig party, the
influence of women, and the eternal jealousy between the English
and German ministries. During the last years bribery of influential
courtiers had played an important part in the creation of new peers ;
a century previously the Stuart Kings had been reproached with

[1] *Parl. His.t,* vol. vi. p. 1042.
[2] Bolingbroke, *Letter to Sir William Wyndham.*
[3] Cf. vol. i. pp. 111-12.

selling titles ; [1] now male and female favourites received sums up
to £12,000 from aspirants to a coronet. The new peers seemed to
have no feelings of gratitude or duty towards the King, and were
detrimental to the dignity of the House and the reputation of the
Government. Further creations would only strengthen the influence
of the Germans, as they were worst at trucking with titles.[2] It
would be a service to the King if he were protected from the importunities of all those who from selfish motives wanted to procure a
peerage for this or that ambitious climber.[3]

Besides being intended to lessen the influence of the Germans,
the Peerage Bill was to punish the Prince of Wales for his opposition
by reducing the prerogative of the Crown he would inherit. He
would on his accession be unable to reverse the balance in the
Upper House and so bring the Tories to the helm. Sunderland was
animated by the desire of retaining his high authority even after
the death of George I.[4]

If the Septennial Act of 1716 encroached on the constitution
of the House of Commons in the interests of immediate policy, the
Peerage Bill would have made a still more fundamental change in
that of the House of Lords. The question how far a rigid Upper
House would continue to fulfil its legislative tasks had been completely ignored.

On February 28, 1719, a Bill to settle and limit the Peerage was
introduced in the Lords by the Duke of Somerset,[5] who in 1714
had done good work for the Hanoverian Succession. He represented

that the number of Peers being, of late years, very much increased
. . . it seemed absolutely necessary to fix the same, both to preserve
the dignity of Peerage, and to prevent . . . the creation of a great
number of Peers to serve a present purpose, of which they had a remarkable instance in the late reign. . . . That the number of English Peers
should not be enlarged beyond six above the present number, which
upon failure of male issue might be supplied by new creations : That
instead of the sixteen elective Peers in Scotland, 25 be made hereditary
on the part of that kingdom.

Even so, only a small fraction of the 156 Scottish peers would have

---

[1] Cf. Firth, *l.c.* ch. i.

[2] Chammorel's Report of Mar. 9, 1719, Aff. étr. 323.

[3] Bonet's Reports of Feb. 24/Mar. 7, Feb. 27/Mar. 10, 1719, Prussian State
Archives.

[4] Cf. *The Lockhart Papers*, vol. ii. p. 57.

[5] For what follows, see *Parl. Hist.*, vol. vii. p. 589 *seq.*

seats in the House of Lords; upon failure of heirs male their numbers would be supplied by others of the Scottish peerage. According to Bonet failure of male issue had occurred in England about 100 times since 1620.[1]

The Duke of Argyll, now Lord Steward of the Household, seconded the motion. As Earl of Greenwich he had had a seat in the House of Lords since 1705, and thus had no personal interest in the Bill, of which it has been said he was the real originator.[2] His speech is not preserved, but he must have had in mind the dissatisfaction among the Scottish nobles [3] who felt that the Union had deprived them of a seat in the Upper House. The Bill would remove the causes of dissatisfaction by giving the leading Scottish nobles 25 seats instead of 16, and making them independent of election.

Against the Bill spoke the Earls of Oxford and Nottingham, both declaring that such an Act would infringe the prerogative not only of the ruling King but of his successors. Among other things Oxford said

that as it tended to take away the brightest gem from the crown, it was matter of wonder to see it supported by those, who, by the great employments they enjoyed, seemed under the strictest obligation to take care of the royal prerogative; that therefore there must be a secret meaning in this motion; that for his own part, though he expected nothing from the crown, yet he would never give his vote for lopping off so valuable a branch of the prerogative, because this would put it out of the power of the crown to reward merit and virtuous actions.

Finally, on the Earl of Carlisle's motion, it was decided that the House should meet in committee two days later to take into consideration the present state of the peerage of Great Britain. Meanwhile the ministers decided on an unusual measure. As Oxford had adopted the role of defender of the King's prerogative, and had doubted whether the motion was consonant with the King's intentions, Sunderland and Stanhope induced George I to intervene in the pending debate [4] by sending a message to the House:

. . . that he has so much at heart the settling the Peerage of the whole kingdom, upon such a foundation, as may secure the freedom

---

[1] Bonet's Report of Feb. 27/Mar. 10, 1719, Prussian State Archives.
[2] Hoffmann's Report of Apr. 25, 1719, Vienna Archives.
[3] Cf. Bonet's Report, Feb. 27/Mar. 10, 1719. Prussian State Archives.
[4] Hoffmann's Report, Mar. 14, 1719, Vienna Archives.

and constitution of parliament in all future ages, that he is willing his prerogative stand not in the way of so great and necessary a work.

Oxford's accusation was refuted, but in the debate on the proposed Address of Thanks the Earl of Nottingham now pointed out that " it was unusual for the King to take notice of any thing depending in parliament, before the same was laid before his majesty in a parliamentary way ". Nottingham's objection was supported by Cowper,[1] the former Lord Chancellor, now a dissatisfied Whig. But it was overruled by the Duke of Buckingham ; " it could not be supposed ", he said, " that the King alone should be ignorant of what every body else knew ". The protagonists Sunderland and Oxford grew so heated that only Stanhope's intervention prevented a duel between them. The debate was adjourned to the next day, and the Address of Thanks was never mentioned again.

Theoretically the King had a right to refuse his consent to a Bill passed by both Houses of Parliament ; but as in practice this right was no longer exercised, it was a matter of political propriety to obtain his previous approval of a limitation of his prerogative. On this occasion his formal approval was obtained only during the debate and because of the criticisms of the Opposition. In 1868 and 1911 the originators of Bills which would limit the prerogative of the Sovereign asked his previous consent, not to the content of the Bill, but to its discussion in Parliament ; and the Sovereign formally declared his desire that the Crown's prerogative " should not stand in the way of the consideration by Parliament of any measure that might be introduced in the present Session on the subject of the constitution of the House of Lords ".

The ensuing discussion in the Upper House went not unfavourably for the Government. The records are very incomplete, but it is known that the Opposition attacked especially the part of the plan which concerned the Scottish peers. Earl Cowper called it a manifest violation of the treaty of Union, urging

that the Scots peers, who should be excluded from the number of the twenty-five hereditary, would be in a worse condition than any other subjects, since they would neither be electing nor elected, neither representing nor represented . . . the Scots peers ought to have been consulted, before any steps were made in so nice and so important an affair.

In reply it was weakly alleged that

[1] Cf. Bonet's Report of Mar. 3/14, 1719, Prussian State Archives.

as for those peers who for the present would be excluded, they would afterwards have a chance to come in, upon failure of any of the twenty-five.

From the records it might seem as if only the question of the Scottish peers had been debated; but to judge from the great number of speakers mentioned in the Parliamentary History, and from the Earl of Newcastle's argument that the Bill was intended to tie the hands of the future King in advance,[1] the debate must also have touched on English questions. When at last a vote was taken on the eleven points which the ministers wished to see in the Bill, the Government had a majority of 83 votes against 30, and the Bill was drafted accordingly.

In the House of Commons, however, feeling was against the principle of the Bill. Though it had not yet come regularly before them, they had, contrary to Parliamentary usage, taken notice of it; and they seemed resolved either to reject it, or to pass it only after making important amendments. It was urged that the Lords must never become more powerful than the Commons—for this they supposed would be the result of the Bill. Their jealousy of the Upper House, with its hereditary membership, had been roused. The unprecedented number of 507 out of the 558 Commoners came to London. It was rumoured that the Government's next Bill would be to exclude the Prince of Wales from the succession. To prevent this the Peerage Bill must be defeated, and then the King must be sent an Address in which the House of Commons asked him to dismiss those ministers who had advised him so ill and had compromised the dignity of the Crown.

The ministers could not but see how great was the danger. At their request the King enjoined his German advisers to do nothing against the Peerage Bill by word or deed. They also begged him to spend £60,000 in order to obtain the necessary votes for the Bill; he was, in Bonet's words, to spend this enormous sum in order to lose part of his prerogative. Meanwhile the Government gained time by delaying for weeks the final decision in the House of Lords. After the Second Reading had been passed, the House again discussed the Bill in Committee. On April 14, when the Bill was to be read the third time, and would have had to be sent to the Lower House, Lord Stanhope came to the Upper House and observed that the Bill

---

[1] Bonet, Mar. 6/17, 1719, Prussian State Archives.

had made a great noise, and raised strange apprehensions ; and since the design of it had been so misinterpreted, and so misunderstood, that it was like to meet with great opposition in the other House, he thought it advisable to let that matter lie still, till a more proper opportunity.

Thereupon the third reading was put off till the 28th of that month, by which time Parliament had been prorogued.

People thought that the ministers themselves had dropped the Peerage Bill. Yet Stanhope and Sunderland were determined to bring it before Parliament again in the coming winter. Their immediate concern was to restore their shaken position.[1] Because of the King it seemed advisable to re-establish for the present good relations with Bernstorff and the other Germans, who had been irritated by the Bill. A meeting took place in the house of the Duchess of Munster, the King's mistress, at which the two English-men tried to explain to the German the advantages of the Bill, and a superficial reconciliation was effected. From thence they went to the King, to assure themselves of his continued favour. Two days later 160 pro-Government Whigs from the House of Commons gathered in the house of Sir Hugh Boscawen, a Court official. The old arguments were repeated by Lord Sunderland : the Union would be rendered more secure, the leading Scottish peers preferred not to beg for their seats at every election, the Whig majority in the Upper House would be permanently assured by the newly appointed 25 Scottish and 6 English members, and the late abuse of the prerogative would be made impossible for the future. Sunderland added the hope that even if the Government and the party con-tinued to disagree on the Peerage Bill, agreement on other questions would not be disturbed. Of those present, 100 declared against the principle of the Bill, because it would make the House of Lords superior to the Commons ; but they were all ready to support the Government in other matters. The general belief that the Bill had been proved a failure found expression in April, 1719, in a lampoon on the meeting in the house of Boscawen.[2]

With the prorogation of Parliament the excitements of the session were over and the ministers could hope for a few months of political quiet ; society withdrew to the country, and the King went to Hanover.

[1] For what follows cf. Bonet's and Hoffmann's Reports.
[2] See Appendix 9.

George I had not been there since 1716 because of the dangers at home and abroad. This time his decision had been made months in advance, and it had long been known that the Prince of Wales would not again be entrusted with the regency.[1] As it would be least insulting for him if no Regent were appointed, a convenient precedent was sought. After the death of Queen Mary, William III had been represented whenever he went to Holland by a Regency Council consisting of the whole Cabinet. The instructions given then were now repeated almost *verbatim*.[2] This example was more appropriate than that of the Regency of 1714, composed of seven great officers of State together with nominees of the new King.

Once again the juridically non-existent " Cabinet " became the executive body, but the unpopular name of " Cabinet " was avoided. Among the 13 Lords Justices appointed were the Archbishop of Canterbury, the Lord High Chancellor and the Lord President of the Council, the leading Court officials, the Lord-Lieutenant of Ireland, the Duke of Marlborough, still Captain-General of the English forces but suffering from senile decay, the Lord High Treasurer and the Lord High Admiral, the two Secretaries of State, and the Secretary of State for Scotland. As in the Cabinet, so in the Regency Council most of the members, especially the courtiers, were usually absent from the meetings, Stanhope even having gone to Hanover with the King ; sometimes the number present did not exceed the quorum of four.

According to custom the Lords Justices waited for news of the King's arrival in Holland before they assumed office : for as long as he was on the sea the fiction held good that he had not left his dominions, which extended to the *Dominium Maris*. In their first session they agreed to meet every Tuesday and Thursday, and to sit down to business at ten in the morning, or as soon after as the quorum of four was reached.[3] Mr. Delafaye, the experienced secretary, was to keep the minutes : for these were kept as long as the Cabinet was acting as a Regency Council.[4] The Lords Justices

[1] Hoffmann, Jan. 27, 1719, Vienna Archives ; Bonet, Jan. 13/24, 1719, Prussian State Archives.

[2] Cf. Turner, " The Lords Justices of England ", *Eng. Hist. Rev.*, vol. 29, p. 453 *seq.* For details of the activities of the Regency Council of 1719 see S.P. 43/61-3, and the Reports of the foreign diplomats.

[3] Delafaye to Stanhope, May 19, 1719, enclosing Minutes, S.P. 43/61.

[4] Cf. W. Michael, " Walpole als Premierminister ", *Historische Zeitschrift*, 104, p. 517.

would only write to the King on special occasions ; but Delafaye
was to report to Stanhope, and send him the minutes. The more
important political correspondence was to be carried on between
Stanhope and Craggs direct. The Lords Justices also arranged that
their coaches should be allowed to pass through St. James' Park
and that the King's chair should not be placed in the Privy Council,
to show that they were the King's representatives.

As the Regency was neither to dissolve nor to summon Parliament, but to keep it in existence by short-term prorogations, important developments in home affairs were avoided ; and as Stanhope and Bernstorff had accompanied George I, foreign policy was
conducted from Hanover. Stanhope's secretary, Luke Schaub,
complained of having so much to do that he could scarcely find
time for private correspondence.[1] In London the Northern Department and the Southern Department in foreign policy had been
kept separate ; in Hanover they were combined, and Schaub wrote
that even home affairs were piled on his shoulders. In London
only Sunderland and Craggs were kept informed of the essential
facts. Schaub asked St. Saphorin to put in his official correspondence only what the Lords Justices might safely be allowed to
know, and to send a copy to Mr. Craggs. The rest was to be sent as
a postscript or in a private letter direct to Lord Stanhope or, better
still, to Schaub himself. Craggs would be confidentially informed
of as much as they thought fit.[2] So the " foreign letters " read in
the Regency Council [3] contained only carefully sifted news, and
decisions were only taken on minor questions.

In Hanover Bernstorff crossed Stanhope's work, disturbed the
negotiations in Berlin, and carried on his personal and his English
policy, never letting Stanhope know what was happening if he
could avoid it. Schaub complained that Bernstorff never showed
them any of St. Saphorin's letters or any document of importance
if he could help it, whilst Stanhope told him everything open and
honestly.[4] St. Saphorin then sent polite letters to Bernstorff,
suggesting that he might show more confidence in the ministers,
and saying that he sincerely hoped Bernstorff would not oppose
the treaty with Prussia, if only to avoid being blamed if the negotia-

[1] Schaub to St. Saphorin, June 19, 1719, Hanover Archives.
[2] Schaub to St. Saphorin, July 3, 1719, Hanover Archives.
[3] S.P. 44/279 and 44/280.
[4] Schaub to St. Saphorin, June 19, 1719, Hanover Archives.

tions should fail.[1] None the less the friction between English and Hanoverian policies was becoming more acute. The King had to decide between them, and as he was beginning to feel as an Englishman, he now put Bernstorff in his place.[2]

At the end of the summer George I's return to England was delayed by Frederick William's courtesy visit. He only reached London on November 25, and was received with illuminations and the requisite jubilation.[3] Soon everything appeared to have returned to normal, but Bernstorff's authority was undermined.

Before leaving Hanover Stanhope had written to the Earl of Newcastle :

I cannot promise that the old man will be left behind, but I may safely assure your Grace that tho' he should come the King will do whatever shall be proposed to him to make every body sensible that he is not to meddle in English business.[4]

George I had made this clear to his Hanoverian premier by word of mouth, to Count Bothmer in writing ; his Lord Chamberlain told the rest of the German Court. All were threatened with the monarch's deepest displeasure if they dared to speak a word to him about English affairs. The King himself told every visitor that his decision was irrevocable. The news was received in England with delight, the ambassadors' reports were full of it ; in Sunderland's words, the resolution the King had taken, not to suffer his Germans to meddle in English affairs, would contribute more to the King's and the public service than any other thing. It is surprising that the proud Bernstorff could bring himself to reappear in England under the gloating eyes of the public.

The English ministers looked forward in the highest of spirits to the coming Parliamentary campaign, which was to establish them permanently in their position. After their successes abroad, they hoped to carry through fundamental innovations at home : the Peerage Bill, the Repeal of the Septennial Act, and a University Bill.

Their University Bill was intended to remove the coming generation of English politicians from Tory influence. The details of their plan must be guessed from casual allusions. There was talk of a

[1] St. Saphorin to Bernstorff, June 28, July 15, 1719. Postscript à part. Hanover Archives.   [2] Cf. above, p. 255.
[3] Hoffmann, Nov. 28, 1719, Vienna Archives.
[4] Stanhope to Newcastle, Oct. 27, 1719, B.M. Add. MSS. 32686.

visitation of Oxford and Cambridge, the strongholds of Toryism, and of placing appointments in the hands of the King.[1] Investigations were made how far the King's power extended in this matter.[2] But in Oxford no one was worried. A young clergyman who had dared to preach a sermon in commendation of the Bangorian doctrine, and who refused to recant, was in 1718 formally suspended from preaching. A letter-writer records that the Bishop of Oxford assisted at the censure, and adds : " Does this look as though we were afraid of visitations ? " [3]

By the Repeal of the Septennial Act the ministers hoped to gain the same security in the Commons that the Peerage Bill was to give them in the Lords. Under the Septennial Act the next elections would only be held in 1722. But Stanhope and Sunderland wanted even this limitation on the life of Parliament removed, so that they could retain indefinitely the existing Parliament with its strong Whig majority. Why not, as once under Charles II, for seventeen years ? Such a measure might even induce, if not Walpole, at least some of his followers to return to the Government fold. *Do ut des :* if the Government helped the Commons to prolong their power, they expected the Commons to help them to gain permanent control of the Upper House by accepting the Peerage Bill. It was hoped that through these three Bills the great aim of re-uniting the Whigs would be achieved, if it could be achieved at all.

The plan is known only from the correspondence of Stanhope and of Sunderland, who had gone to Hanover in the autumn, and the Earl of Newcastle,[4] who had remained in London. Newcastle, who at the age of twenty-six was already Lord Chamberlain, was more sceptical than his older colleagues. He considered the University and the Peerage Bills well thought out, but could not bring himself to approve the Repeal of the Septennial Act ; he believed they would lose more than they would gain, and that it would in no way help the passage of the Peerage Bill. Nor was he afraid of new elections :

I cannot but think that by a new election Mr. Walpole and the few friends his party will be able to bring up, will be so incorporated with

[1] Bonet's Reports, Mar. 29/Apr. 9, Apr. 5/16, May 14/25, July 23/Aug. 3, 1717 ; Mar. 25/Apr. 5, 1718, Prussian State Archives.
[2] Hist. MSS. Com., *Portland MSS.*, vol. v. p. 574.
[3] *Portland MSS.*, vol. vii. pp. 246-7.   [4] B.M. Add. MSS. 32686.

the Jacobites, that we shall have but little difficulty in dealing with them.[1]

The cautious attitude of the young politician prevailed, and his colleagues unwillingly dropped the University Bill and the Repeal of the Septennial Act, but they still clung to the Peerage Bill.

Even after the Peerage Bill had in the spring of 1719 been temporarily dropped, the public continued to discuss the problem. Under the pseudonyms of the *Old Whig* and the *Plebeian*, Addison and Steele wrote a series of pamphlets and counter-pamphlets for and against the Bill.[2] The *Plebeian* pointed out that shutting the door of the House of Lords would exclude the frequent supplies which such a body requires, and it might in time become like a stagnant pool. The Commons must wish for the number of Peers to be increased, for the greater their number, the less considerable they become. For the Crown the right to increase their numbers was its natural weapon against the Lords if they should become too powerful, as dissolution was its weapon against the Commons. The *Old Whig*, on the other hand, represented that the triple division of the supreme power would be valueless if one branch of the legislature was liable on any occasion to be controlled by one of the others.

Addison's campaign on behalf of the Peerage Bill was his last literary act; he died in June 1719.

Among the pamphlets about the Peerage Bill was one by Robert Walpole himself entitled: *The Thoughts of a Member of the Lower House in relation to a Project for Restraining and Limiting the Power of the Crown in the future Creation of Peers*.[3] This pamphlet has often been called his most important literary production; it reflects his fundamental conception of King and Parliament in the days before he gave a new form to English constitutional life. For him the three legislative factors, King, peers, and representatives of the people, form a proper balance of power, so that each

can give some check to both the others; and two concurring have always the means in their power to bring the third to reason without recurring to force. . . . If the King had the prerogative of raising money . . . the monarchy would be absolute, but that privilege

[1] Newcastle to Stanhope, Oct. 14, 1719, B.M. Add. MSS. 32686, f. 153.
[2] Cf. Aitken, *The Life of Richard Steele*, vol. ii. p. 210 *seq.*
[3] Publ. London, 1719.

remaining in the people, the Crown must often recur to their assistance, and then they always have it in their power to do themselves right : which keeps the ministry in perpetual dependence and apprehension.

On the other side, if the House of Commons was fixed and indissolvable, the Government would soon devolve into an ill-contrived democracy. . . . The effectual remedy is a dissolution . . . which power always hanging over their heads must be a constant restraint upon their actions . . . the Lords are always at hand to screen the Crown, whose honours and dignities flow from it . . . yet never can have an interest to make it arbitrary.

A monarchy must subsist by an army or nobility ; the first makes it despotick, and the latter a free government. . . . An essential prerogative (of the monarchy) must be to add to, and augment their (the Lords') numbers in such proportion, as to render them a proper ballance against the democratical part of our Constitution. . . . With out this power in the Crown, they must be dangerous to it . . . the House of Lords will be a fixed, independent body, not to be called to an account like a ministry, not to be dissolved or changed like a House of Commons.

The Lords would then, said Walpole, be able to commit the ministry to prison ; or in case of a conflict with the House of Commons, compel the Crown to exert its authority to chose another. All the great employments of England would be theirs, and like the nobles of some other countries they would pay no taxes. Already they had all the property of Great Britain under their jurisdiction ; soon their position would be as impregnable as that of a big company of merchants or of the priesthood in some countries. To prevent such abuse of the King's right to create Peers as had recently been witnessed, there was always the possibility of impeaching the ministers — that is to say, there was no need to upset the constitution.

In all this there is no suggestion of Parliamentarism as understood to-day, of diminishing the sovereign's share in the legislature. The co-ordination of the three legislative factors is Walpole's dominant idea.

The Government determined to throw its full weight into the battle for the Peerage Bill which, dropped or delayed, must in Stanhope's opinion " be looked upon as lost for ever, . . . it will probably never happen again that a King and ministry will be for it ".[1] Bernstorff and Cadogan were considered to have been

---

[1] Stanhope to Newcastle, Oct. 27 (N.S.), 1719 ; B.M. Add. MSS. 32686, ff. 155-6.

the chief instigators of the intrigues against the Bill during the previous spring. Bernstorff's influence was broken, and Cadogan had to accept a diplomatic mission to Vienna.[1]

The support of the Lords was certain, and success or failure depended on the attitude of the Whigs in the Commons. The ministers supposed that the memory of the creation of peers in 1711 would bring even the dissatisfied Whigs to vote for the Bill. Walpole realized how important it was to reconcile condemnation of the happenings of 1711 with opposition to the present Bill. The dissatisfied Whigs of both Houses met to discuss their attitude towards the Bill. It seemed that the meeting was going to decide in favour of supporting the Government, the Lords perhaps because they favoured a Bill which would increase their importance, the Commoners because of the past experiences of their party. But then Walpole rose to speak. He maintained that this was their great chance to harass the administration, and declared

that he would place it [the Bill] in such a light as to excite indignation in every independent Commoner ; that he saw a spirit rising against it among the Whigs . . . that he had overheard a member of the House of Commons, a country gentleman, who possessed an estate of not more than 800 *l* a year, declare to another, with great warmth, that although he had no chance of being made a Peer himself, yet he would never consent to the injustice of giving a perpetual exclusion to his family.[2]

This declaration, urged with uncommon vehemence, occasioned much altercation ; but Walpole's powerful personality carried the day, and they agreed to oppose the Bill in the Commons, even if only because they found him resolved to do it, whatever they had said or should do upon it.[3] So the fate of the Bill was practically sealed before it was submitted to the two Houses of Parliament.

Most of the King's Speech [4] on opening the new session was devoted to the successes of foreign policy, but it also referred to the " many undeserved and unnatural troubles I have met with during the course of my reign", which was interpreted as hinting at the conflict between the King and the Prince of Wales.[5]

[1] Cf. Hoffmann, Nov. 28, 1719, Vienna Archives.

[2] *Parl. Hist.*, vol. vii. pp. 607-8, note.

[3] Onslow, *On Opposition*, ch. 1, in Hist. MSS. Com. Rep. 14, App. IX, p. 459.

[4] *Parl. Hist.*, vol. vii. p. 602 *seq.*

[5] Hoffmann's Report, Dec. 5, 1719, Vienna Archives.

The Peerage Bill was only indirectly referred to when the members of both Houses were admonished

to establish and transmit to your posterity the freedom of our happy constitution, and particularly to secure that part which is most liable to abuse . . . and . . . to complete those measures which remained imperfect the last session.

The Debates on the Addresses gave no definite clue to the attitude that Parliament would take towards the Bill. The Jacobite Shippen put a motion " to congratulate His Majesty upon his safe return, and to give him thanks for part of his Speech, and appoint a day to take the rest into consideration " ; but he soon waived it, and the Address of the Commons was as colourless as that of the Lords. When the Bill was brought before the Upper House, the Tories held back. Earl Cowper criticized the eagerness with which it was brought before them at the beginning of a session ; for such pre-cipitation in affairs of moment was, in his opinion, a sign of a secret meaning in the Bill. The Earl of Sunderland replied that he knew of none other than what his Majesty had intimated in his speech, namely to prevent " the abuse of one part of the royal prerogative, of which they had a fatal instance in the last reign ". The Bill passed the House of Lords without difficulty and was sent down to the Commons on November 30.

The debates in the Commons on the Peerage Bill brought the Government their worst defeat since the accession of the Hanoverians. Some contemporaries thought that the introducing the Bill in the Lower House, even before money matters were settled, was proof of the strength of the ministry ; but the Govern-ment only wished to use the time when many members of the Opposition had not yet come to London.[1] For the same reason they tried, when the Bill had been read for the first time on December 1, to have the second reading fixed for a few days later, but even in this they could not carry their point, and it was put off to December 18. Of those who had spoken against the Government only one was a Tory, the others all Opposition Whigs. One of these said that the reading ought to be put off till as many members as possible were present, in order to mete out to the Bill the fate that its infamous character deserved.

Meanwhile the dissatisfied Whigs meant to show that they

[1] Hoffmann, Dec. 12, 1719, Vienna Archives.

were sensitive to the true interests of the nation. The demands of the Government for the upkeep of a military force in the coming year and the usual land tax of three shillings in the pound were conceded without difficulty. But the outlook for the Peerage Bill was gloomy. Lord Stanhope consoled himself with the hope that even if it was rejected this time, the King would have it introduced again and again, and that in the end it would certainly be passed.

On December 18 some 500 members were present in the Commons. The speeches in favour of the Bill are imperfectly recorded, but they came from the best speakers in the Government benches. The speakers against the Bill were again with one exception Opposition Whigs. Walpole and his followers intended to inflict on the Government such a defeat that they would have to resign, and that Walpole and Townshend should then replace Sunderland and Stanhope. The Tories, however, did not want to look as though they were followers of the Opposition Whigs ; if the Government fell, the King might well prefer them, as they had been silent, to those who had loudly opposed him.

When a motion was made for committing the Bill, Sir Richard Steele spoke first against it, repeating the arguments used in his *Plebeian*. The Bill, he said, might change this free state into the worst of all tyrannies, that of an aristocracy. He strongly objected to any diminution of the King's prerogative, as the abuse of the right to create Peers could easily be prevented by the impeachment of those ministers who had been neglectful of their duty ; and, he asked sarcastically : " Can the gentlemen in present power reasonably think, that the consummation of the English glory and merit is to close and rest in their persons ? " He concluded with the sally : " I am against committing of this Bill, because I think it would be committing of sin ".

The Tory Sir John Packington severely criticized from the point of view of his party the whole foreign policy of the Government since 1714. He spoke of the alliance with France, by which that ancient and almost irreconcilable enemy of England was given an opportunity to retrieve the extreme low and desperate condition of their affairs ; and he referred to the strong squadron being sent into the Baltic to secure some acquisitions of the King in Germany, to the declaring war against Spain, by which His Majesty's subjects had been deprived of the beneficial trade to that country, and to sending a fleet into the Mediterranean to serve as ferry-boats for the Emperor's troops. After the good-natured Commons had approved " those wise counsels ", they were being rewarded by a Bill visibly calculated to exclude them from titles of honour, and to raise the dignity and power of the Peers. The King's conde-scension in parting with so valuable a branch of his prerogative ought to be acknowledged, if the measure reached no further than his lifetime ; but the House should never allow the Prince of Wales to be deprived of so bright a jewel of the Crown. After a panegyric of the Prince, praising the virtues which, during his regency, had gained him the hearts and affections of all true Englishmen, Park-ington closed with a reference to the unhappy difference in the Royal House, which might be rendered irreconcilable by this Bill.

In defence of the Bill Mr. Hampden declared appeasingly that it would rather diminish than increase the power of the Peers, since this was mainly due to the constant addition of riches through the ennobling of wealthy Commoners. Craggs, who is said to have objected strongly to the Bill in the Cabinet, now ably defended it in accordance with his conception of Cabinet solidarity. With no other view, said Craggs, than to procure the good and happiness of his subjects, the King had been magnanimous enough to consent to a diminution of his prerogative. It was only in the reigns of good princes, he exclaimed, that legislators had opportunities to remedy and amend flaws in the constitution.

After a few more speeches Robert Walpole rose and delivered his attack, which, it has been said, was the best speech ever heard in Parliament. He began by a reference to the Romans, among whom

the Temple of Fame was placed behind the Temple of Virtue. . . . But if this Bill is passed into a law . . . there would be no arriv-ing at honour, but through the winding sheet of an old decrepit lord. . . .

High titles, he declared, would no longer be derived from the will of the sovereign to reward signal services or conspicuous merit by a recompense which would survive to posterity. Referring to Stanhope he expressed his surprise

that a bill of this nature should either have been projected, or at least promoted by a gentleman, who was, not long ago, seated amongst us, and who, having got into the House of Peers, is now desirous to shut the door after him.

The creation of peers in 1711 was now termed only a temporary measure, whereas the mischief occasioned by this Bill would be perpetual, for there must be the intention of overthrowing the constitution behind it. " Is the abuse of any prerogative a sufficient reason for totally annihilating that prerogative ? " he asked. Under that consideration the power of dissolving Parliament and the prerogative of making peace and war ought to be taken away, as both had on occasion been abused. Then he repeated the argument, already used when he addressed the party meeting, that the Commons could not be expected to accept a Bill by which they and their posterity were to be for ever excluded from the Peerage. How would the Lords receive a Bill which should prevent a Baron from being made a Viscount, a Viscount an Earl, an Earl a Marquis, and a Marquis a Duke ? If something was to be done for the freedom of Parliament, many other steps could be taken, such as the discontinuance of bribes and pensions. This Bill would only form the peers into a compact, impenetrable phalanx.

In this way Walpole bore down everything before him,[1] and the Bill was rejected by 269 votes to 177. After this the Opposition, to signalize their victory, moved, and it was resolved without a division, " That the Bill be rejected ".

The position of the Government had become untenable. Though at that time a defeat in Parliament did not mean the automatic resignation of the Government, they could not remain if Parliament repeatedly refused them its support.

After the rejection of the Peerage Bill the ministers preferred to seek support from the ranks of the Tories rather than to make a conciliatory gesture to their *quondam* friends. Negotiations to this end seem to have been repeatedly tried since the split in the Whig party had occurred. Pendtenriedter reported in 1718 that the King would rather throw himself into the arms of the Tories than collaborate with the Whigs who had left him.[2] Meanwhile the Tories were biding their time ; they were courted by both Whig groups, as they were able to cast the balance to whatever side they

---

[1] *Parl. Hist.*, vol. vii. pp. 623-4, note.
[2] Pendtenriedter, Feb. 25, 1718, Vienna Archives.

joined.   Yet they were resolved to join entirely with neither,[1] for it was

the resolution unanimously taken by all the Tories to join with either one or the other by turns to depress them by turns until by their clashing they ruin both.[2]

As early as 1716 the ministers had tried to win Bolingbroke, after the Pretender had unwisely and ungratefully rebuffed him. Lord Stair was instructed to get in touch with " the late Lord Bolingbroke ", who was staying in Paris.   The Government had heard that he was ready not only to submit at any time to King George, but also that the Jacobites were most alarmed lest he should return and betray them all.[3]   This was what the ministers most desired ; but Bolingbroke, in a long conversation with Stair, declared honourably that though he would do all he could to disillusion those of the Tories who favoured the Pretender, yet he would not become an informer.   If he lost his good name, he could not give effective service to the King.[4]   The ministers had apparently not expected such strength of character ; and when the question of his pardon came before the Cabinet, Walpole and Townshend seem to have opposed it successfully.[5]   As a sign of some goodwill, however, his father, Sir Henry St. John, was raised to the peerage.

But Bolingbroke still nursed hopes of returning to England and to power.   In September 1716 he sent a letter to his Tory friend Sir William Wyndham, which was allowed to fall into the hands of the English ministers.   The letter seemed intended to convince the Tories of the hopelessness of the Stuart cause, but in reality it was meant to show the ministers how he could influence the Tories without exposing anyone.   The Government let the letter go on to the addressee, and nothing further happened.[6]

In November 1718 the question of pardoning Bolingbroke was again given serious consideration.   The ministers meant to use him against his old enemy Walpole, now in Opposition ; and they hoped to win through him a part of the Tories to the Government side.   They thought of introducing a Bill to repeal the Act of

---

[1] *Stuart Papers*, vol. iv. p. 291.   [2] *Ibid.* p. 300.
[3] Stanhope to Stair, Mar. 28, 1716, S.P. 78/160.
[4] Stair to Craggs, printed in *Letter to Sir William Wyndham*, Appendix.
[5] Cf. T. Macknight, *Life of Bolingbroke* (1863), p. 497 *seq.*
[6] Cf. Coxe, *Walpole* (1798), vol. ii. p. 307 *seq.*

Attainder by which Bolingbroke had been condemned in 1715. The other leading politicians of the days of Queen Anne were also to be restored to full favour in so far as this had not yet been done. The good intentions of the ministers were in themselves sufficient to influence the attitude of the Tories. This was clearly visible in the debate on the Address of Thanks in November 1718, when the measures being taken against Spain were to be approved, and the Government gained a large majority.[1]

Meanwhile Bolingbroke had frequently seen Stair, who used to ask his advice in political questions. It was rumoured that Bolingbroke would soon be in London, if he were not already there. Oxford's nephew, Edward Harley, hoped Bolingbroke would become Secretary of State again, so that the King's ministry might be entirely completed.[2]

All these hopes were rudely destroyed by Walpole's opposition. During the debate on the Bill for the strengthening of the Protestant Interest in January 1719, he dragged in the question of Bolingbroke. Without mentioning him by name, he pointed out that there were people enough to fill a vacant Secretaryship without fetching an exile from abroad, though he might be never so true a penitent.[3] Shortly after, in his pamphlet against the Peerage Bill, he bitterly attacked his old opponent who " presumes to expect an act of the legislature to indemnify him, and qualify his villainy ", and who probably expected once more to give laws to the kingdom.[4]

The Government withdrew before Walpole's threats, and for some years there was no talk of pardoning Bolingbroke, however much Lord Stair praised his loyalty.[5] When some months later Mar was trying to make his peace with the English Government, Stair was instructed to proceed with the utmost circumspection, as the news that they favoured the return of Lord Bolingbroke had already had such ill effect in England.[6]

Walpole opposed in Bolingbroke a rival leader who might return and stand in his own path to power, and who like himself hoped one day to hold supreme authority in the kingdom. He had believed that Bolingbroke's power had been destroyed for ever, while he

[1] *Parl. Hist.*, vol. vii. pp. 560-61.
[2] Hist. MSS. Com., *Portland MSS.*, vol. v. pp. 573-4.   [3] *Ibid.* p. 576.
[4] *Thoughts of a Member* . . ., see p. 292.
[5] Stair to Stanhope, June 17, 1719, S.P. 78/164.
[6] Stanhope to Stair, June 7 (N.S.), 1719, S.P. 78/164.

himself had become the dominant figure in the Opposition, able to sweep all waverers with him at the critical moment, to discover the weak spots of the ministers and to strike their best weapons from their grip. The Parliamentary records tell very little ; but his successes and the admiration of his contemporaries in their letters and reports are eloquent. Bonet describes him as the foremost expert in matters of finance, and the best debater in the Commons. His group, which included his brother Horace, followed his lead blindly. Together the two brothers thundered against the Address of Thanks for the King's Message on declaring war with Spain ; together they strove against the employment of foreigners in the service of the State. The Tories greeted Walpole smirkingly as their ally ; Shippen observed that Walpole seemed to fear the name of Jacobite as little as he feared it himself, and the ministers tried to brand Walpole and render him harmless with that name.

Walpole and the other leaders of the dissatisfied Whigs are neatly satirized in a little poem *On the seven wise men of England*.[1] Like the seven planets in the sky, there were seven wise men in England, four peers, and three Commoners :

> Which Peerless three they don't see why
> They mayn't be Peers before they dy.

The four peers were Oxford, Townshend, Cowper, and Devonshire, the three Commoners two unimportant names and the brothers Walpole :

> The Walpoles twain but one I count,
> For say whate'er they can,
> Altho' two wags they do amount
> But just to one wise man.

Spurred on by Walpole, the Opposition had frequently lost sight of the true interests of the nation in the heat of party strife. Alberoni hoped for a " *good* " Parliament, and the Dutch, when they refused to accede to the Quadruple Alliance, were confirmed in their resistance by the English Opposition. Without this influence the whole war with Spain might have been avoided. In June 1718, just after an English fleet had sailed to the Mediterranean, and before the Quadruple Alliance had been signed, Craggs told Pendtenriedter that the Government's difficulties were due not to the £600,000

[1] B.M., *Stowe MSS.*, 970, f. 58b.

which the fleet cost, not to Alberoni's defiance, but to internal dissensions. Walpole had publicly drunk Alberoni's health, and Craggs believed this was the true reason why Spain was so obstinate. The ministers' northern policy suffered from like criticism and suspicions, and Stanhope's great work had to be achieved in face of these obstacles at home.

The Government's difficulties in home policy were just as great. In February 1719, for the first time since the accession of Queen Anne, the Money Bill was defeated in Parliament. In the trial of Lord Oxford and in the debates on the Bill for the strengthening the Protestant Interest, as well as in the debate on the Peerage Bill, the weight and the stubbornness of the Opposition were always the same.

After the failure of the Peerage Bill the Government approached the Tories, but most of them were very reserved. Only Lord Harcourt, who had been Lord Chancellor under Queen Anne, busied himself on their behalf, perhaps because he had an assurance of being employed if he could prevail on any number of Tories to come in with him.[1] But the Tories wanted to form the Government themselves, and not come in one by one to a Whig ministry. The negotiations lasted for months.[2] It was suggested that Trevor, Atterbury and other Tories besides Harcourt were ready to enter the ministry. One project followed the other, and sometimes several were running concurrently. Lady Cowper recorded in her Diary that " there was not a rogue in the town that was not engaged in some scheme and project to undo his country ".[3]

In the spring of 1720 the Government found new difficulties added to the old. It was the year of the South Sea Bubble, when everything depended on the Government's credit. The opposition of the dissatisfied Whigs, and especially of Walpole, the expert in finance, made itself disagreeably felt, and might easily wreck all the plans made by the ministers. Another problem was the King's Civil List, which was exhausted and overspent. The ministers wanted to ask Parliament for £500,000, but feared, probably with good reason, that in face of the opposition of Walpole and his followers they would not be able to carry through such an unusual request for so high a sum. In foreign policy Spain and Russia

[1] Hist. MSS. Com., *Portland MSS.*, vol. vii. p. 266.

[2] *Ibid.* pp. 267, 273-4.   [3] *Diary of Lady Cowper*, p. 144.

presented them with serious difficulties.   Finally the ministers, after having had to drop the repeal of the Septennial Act, had to think of the coming election campaign, if they did not wish to lose their majority in the next Parliament.

These circumstances, however, would not have led to precipitate action without special motive.   In April 1720 a strange document was put into the hands of Lord Sunderland.[1]   It contained nothing less than a plan for the overthrow of the English ministry by the German.   Bernstorff had sent it to Vienna for Sinzendorff's informa- tion.   He was in league with the " disgusted Whigs ", who

have endeavoured to convince his Majesty that the Cabal designed to alter the constitution, to destroy the present establishment . . ., to run the nation into an Aristocracy . . . and be able for the future to give laws to the King and his son, and even remove them when they shall think proper.

To countermine these designs, the " disgusted party " laid before the King a scheme which would link him more closely with the Emperor than with France, which they supposed would undertake no new war during Louis XV's minority.   George I was to make friends with the Tsar, Augustus the Strong was to be helped to make the crown of Poland hereditary in his family, and Hanover was to be enlarged by the purchase of some country contiguous to its present territories.   This they said would enable the King to hold the balance between the northern Powers better than by sending a fleet yearly to the Baltic, which gave umbrage to the people. As large funds would be necessary, they should give good terms to Spain in order to improve the trade of the South Sea Company, thus enabling it to furnish the King with two or three millions independent of Parliament.

All this was to be achieved by a change of Government.   The dissatisfied Whigs would be given the chief offices — with Bernstorff, of course, pulling the strings.   The list of the proposed ministry included a few Tories, and it was suggested that six or seven more of the leading Tories should be added.   Of the existing political leaders Stanhope and Sunderland, but not Craggs, were to be included in minor positions.

[1] The German original seems to be lost ; English translations are printed in the *Townshend MSS.* 104 and the *Portland MSS.* vol. v. p. 594 *seq.*   A French translation is enclosed with Chammorel's Report of Apr. 29, 1720 Aff. étr. 31.   The three show minor variations.

The originators must have felt that the change could not be effected without risk, for at the end of the document stood the note : " His Imperial Majesty to assist the King with his troops from the Netherlands on any emergent occasion ".

Lord Sunderland was appalled by the document. He too had been hoping to draw Tories into the Government. Now he was afraid that the dissatisfied Whigs had stolen a march on him. He at once consulted Stanhope and Craggs ; after three days they decided to take the bull by the horns and draw, not the Tories, but the dissatisfied Whigs into the Government. At the same time the King and the Prince of Wales were to be reconciled. Of course everything had to be kept secret from the Germans, whose last attempt to regain their lost power was thwarted by the disclosure of their plan.

The negotiations lasted a fortnight.[1] Sunderland found the King exceptionally cool when he spoke of reconciliation with the Prince of Wales. Walpole was throughout the most important figure. He had frequent conversations with the Princess, he stated his conditions to the princely couple as well as to the ministers. The Prince and the Princess yielded to the force of his personality, though they felt, not without reason, that they were being sacrificed to the interests of Walpole and Townshend. They did not even get back their children. Walpole, Stanhope, Sunderland, and Craggs all turned to the Duchess of Kendall, who undertook the most difficult part of the work. She found the King almost inflexible, but succeeded finally in making him change his mind.

For the ministers the reconciliation between father and son was less important than the restoration of unity in the Whig party. The King would have preferred to regain the dissatisfied Whigs without making peace with the Prince. But it was the reconciliation which made the deepest impression on the people.

On March 4, when the whole Court was assembled, the King was handed a letter from the Prince in which he offered his full submission, and asked to be allowed to throw himself at his father's feet. When the King had granted this request, the Prince came to the Palace in a sedan chair, and as he was not yet to be received with military honours he entered the King's apartments by the

---

[1] Cf. the reports of Senneterre, Chammorel, and Destouches, Aff. étr. 331 ; of Wallenrodt, Prussian State Archives ; of Hoffmann, Vienna Archives ; also *Portland MSS.* vol. v. pp. 596-7, and the *Diary of Lady Cowper.*

back stairs. After letting him wait some time in the ante-chamber, the King admitted him to his closet, where they had a few minutes' conversation behind locked doors. Rising from his knees on a sign from the King, the Prince expressed his deep submissiveness ; the King, deeply moved, could only speak in disjointed sentences, and the Prince caught the words : *Votre conduite, votre conduite.* After leaving the King, he had himself carried across the courtyard, the guard saluted, the drums beat, a party of guards escorted him home, and a guard of honour was put before his house. The streets were filled with jubilation and shouts of approval. In the evening a few barrels of beer were distributed in the City, bonfires were lit in several quarters, and all London was decked with lights.[1]

The first act of reconciliation was followed next day by a second and more important one, of which the public did not hear. The leaders of the dissatisfied Whigs, among them Townshend and Walpole, were received by the King. The Duke of Devonshire, probably because he was the oldest of them, spoke on their behalf. The King replied vaguely and briefly that he was pleased to see them all reunited. Ten days later an important division took place in the House of Commons, when for the first time the whole Whig party voted in one bloc, and the Government gained a majority of nearly three to one. In the following weeks Townshend was made President of the Privy Council, Devonshire entered the Cabinet without holding an office, Methuen was given a position at Court ; Walpole was appointed to the lucrative post of Paymaster of the Forces, but he too remained outside the Cabinet. But whether in the Cabinet or not, his influence made itself felt in the ministry, and with the bursting of the South Sea Bubble he became the foremost man in the Government. Only Lord Cowper declined to return to the ministry, saying to his wife that he was old and infirm, and that his infirmities would not let him struggle with knaves and fools.[2] When in June the King again went to Hanover and the Cabinet was once more entrusted with the Regency, Hoffmann could report that all those who had gone out of office with Townshend, and had since attached themselves to the Prince of Wales, had been provided with new places.

The reunion of the Whigs brought about the final discomfiture of the German ministry in England. The preparations for the

[1] Limier, *l.c.* vol. iii. p. 388.   [2] *Diary of Lady Cowper,* p. 146.

great change had been so well hidden that no member of the German Court except the Duchess of Kendall had heard of it. In the King's ante-chamber, shortly before the arrival of the Prince, Stanhope came up to Bernstorff and Bothmer and exclaimed triumphantly, " *Eh bien! Messieurs, la paix est faite — la paix est faite*". Bernstorff, thinking of the coming peace between Russia and Sweden, asked in astonishment if important letters had arrived. " No," said Stanhope, " it is peace at home. We are going to see our Prince again." " Our Prince ? " " Yes, our Prince, our Prince. We are awaiting him for his reconciliation with the King." Deeply offended, Bernstorff said : " Sir, you have been very secretive in your affairs ". " Oh yes," Stanhope replied coldly, " secrecy is always necessary when good work is to be done." The two Germans completely lost control ; Bothmer burst into tears, and Bernstorff left the Palace without having entered the King's closet.[1]

During the next weeks Bernstorff tried hard to recapture his lost power.[2] Slowly he recovered from his shock and regained his confident attitude. He excused his ignorance of recent events with the bold assertion that he had had no desire to know of such things. He suggested that his help was already required in order to dissuade the King from going to Hanover, but said he did not want to interfere. He made complaints about the ministry, foretold its imminent fall, and was already looking for future ministers. " Baron Bernstorff ", wrote Lady Cowper, " will never cease till he has got the better." But it was clear to the initated that his day was over. The German ministers cut a *triste figure* in London ;[3] when George I went to Hanover in June, Bernstorff went too ; but when the King returned, Bernstorff stayed in Hanover. The public hardly noticed his absence and certainly did not regret it. The politicians, the diplomats, and the foreign Courts all noticed it and tried to find the reason.

Frederick William I, whose plans had so often been crossed by Bernstorff in London, demanded from Wallenrodt a detailed report of what had happened to the Hanoverian minister. Wallenrodt wrote that Bernstorff expected the ministry to fall during the

---

[1] *Diary of Lady Cowper*, p. 145 ; cf. also Hoffmann's Report of May 7, 1720, Vienna Archives.

[2] For what follows cf. *Diary of Lady Cowper*.

[3] Wallenrodt's Report of May 3/14, 1720, Prussian State Archives.

coming session, and that he then intended to return in triumph to play his old role beside a new English ministry.

The struggle between the English and German ministers had ended with an English victory. An English admiral would no longer have to ask Bernstorff before sailing to the Baltic what was the real aim of the expedition he was to lead. Hanoverian ministers and officials remained in London, but none of them ever tried to meddle in English politics. Count Bothmer reported to George I on the foreign affairs of Hanover, von Hattorf on home affairs, and Reich was head of the German Chancery. When in the years that followed English policy was allowed to serve Hanoverian interests, it was the English ministry which decided how much consideration was due to the German interests of the Sovereign.

Bernstorff retired to his large estates in north Germany, where he devoted his great energies mainly to their administration and improvement, and to the care of his family. He retained his titles of " Councillor to His Britannic Majesty, Prime Minister of Bruns-wick-Lüneburg, and Privy Councillor ", and remained closely linked with the fate of Hanover both by office and by inclination. In 1715 he had been created a Baron of the Holy Roman Empire, and he modestly refused the title of Count of the Empire, as he did not want to endanger the position of his family by wild aspirations. In order to secure the future of his house, he took the step, unusual in those parts, of turning his widespread possessions into three entails. Like a miniature Frederick William I, he worked for the future of his land and the well-being of his heirs, for whom he drew up a " Family Statute " with fixed rules for the administration of the estates, the education of the sons, and the provision of the daughters.

The dangers that threatened England had been removed, internal peace had been restored. Once again the public could see the King and his heir together at divine service, and watch whether they were standing in silence or speaking to each other. For the King the reconciliation had been an unpleasant necessity ; and when France wished to send an envoy to congratulate him, this was politely but firmly refused.[1] The Prince was heartily

---

[1] Pulteney's Reports from Paris, May 13, 14, 17, 1720, S.P. 78/166. Wallenrodt, May 17/28, 1720, Prussian State Archives.

thankful that he was no longer forbidden the Court. Amongst his friends he seemed even gay and high-spirited. When Lady Cowper congratulated him, he embraced and kissed her again and again, while the Princess stood by and laughed.

In the development of the English constitution the reunion of the whole Whig party was the last important step to party government. All plans for the formation of a mixed ministry had been dropped, and the Tories were left out. Robert Walpole himself became the most ardent advocate of a purely Whig ministry, and thus created the system of government by one party with the other in opposition. With the Hanoverian domination broken, and the ship of state in the care of the united Whig party, the hour had come for a great personality to lead the nation across the threshold of a new epoch.

APPENDIX

In the following letters or extracts the spelling has been modernized and corrected.

No. 1

THREE LETTERS FROM THE PRINCE OF WALES TO GEORGE I (cf. pp. 26-7)

Enclosed with Hoffmann's Report of Dec. 24, 1717 (Vienna Archives) in the original French form

[Their publication in print, due, it was said, to the Prince of Wales himself, greatly annoyed the King. No copy appears to have been preserved ; the English translation, published twenty years later and recorded by Lord Harvey in his *Mémoires*, was inexact.]

Première lettre du Prince de Galles au Roi du 30. nov. 1717

Sire,

J'ai reçu avec la soumission que je dois les ordres que Votre Majesté m'a envoyés de demeurer dans mon appartement jusqu'à ce que Votre Majesté m'ait fait savoir Ses volontés ultérieures.

Cette marque forte de l'indignation de Votre Majesté m'a infiniment surpris, n'ayant jamais eu d'autres sentiments à l'égard de Votre Majesté que ceux qui conviennent à un fils obéissant.

On m'avait fait croire que Votre Majesté avait paru assez facile sur le choix que j'avais fait du Duc de York pour être Parrain de mon Fils, et qu'il pourrait être représenté par le Duc de Newcastle sans qu'il le fût lui-même, et en étant persuadé, je ne pouvais m'empêcher de regarder comme un traitement inouï qu'il voulut être Parrain de mon Enfant en dépit de moi.

Mais lorsque Votre Majesté jugea à propos de l'ordonner je me suis soumis.

Le procédé du Duc de Newcastle m'a touché sensiblement, et j'en fus si indigné que le voyant dans l'occasion, je ne pus m'empêcher de lui en donner des marques.

Mais comme le respect que j'ai toujours eu pour Votre Majesté m'avait empêché de lui en témoigner aucun ressentiment, quand il était chargé de Vos ordres, j'espère qu'Elle aura la bonté de ne pas regarder ce que j'ai dit comme un manque de respect envers Votre Majesté.

Cependant si j'ai eu le malheur d'offenser Votre Majesté contre mes intentions, je lui en demande pardon, et je La supplie d'être persuadée du respect avec lequel je suis etc.

Seconde lettre du Prince de Galles au Roi du 1. déc. 1717

SIRE,

J'espère que Votre Majesté aura la bonté de m'excuser si dans l'état où je me trouvais quand je pris la liberté d'écrire à Votre Majesté j'ai omis de lui dire que je ne témoignerais aucun ressentiment contre le Duc de Newcastle, et je prends cette occasion d'en assurer Votre Majesté étant avec un très profond respect etc.

Troisième lettre du Prince de Galles au Roi du 2. déc. 1717

SIRE,

Je viens d'obéir aux ordres de Votre Majesté en quittant St. James. La princesse m'accompagne, et nos domestiques sortent du palais avec nous avec toute l'expédition possible. Je etc.

No. 2

THE SUPPRESSED PREAMBLE TO THE QUADRUPLE ALLIANCE (cf. p. 66)
(S.P. 80/36)

Projet du traité entre leurs Majestés Britannique et Très-Chrétienne et les Seigneurs États Généraux pour la paix entre l'Empereur et le Roi d'Espagne, et entre l'Empereur et le Roi de Sicile

. . . .

Sa Majesté Britannique touchée d'un objet si grand et si digne de ses soins, ayant communiqué au Sérénissime et Très-Puissant Roi Très-Chrétien, et à leurs Hautes Puissances les Seigneurs États Généraux des Provinces Unies ses vues pour y parvenir, ils ont embrassé avec zèle ce juste dessein, et ces trois puissances ont dès lors employé leurs soins de concert à en faire approuver les moyens par les parties intéressées. Mais le Roi Catholique ayant occupé par les armes l'île de Sardaigne, dont l'Empereur était en possession, sans que les offices les plus effectueux des dites trois puissances aient pu détourner, ni faire réparer ensuite cette entreprise faite contre la neutralité d'Italie, Elles ont vu le commencement de ce qu'elles avaient si justement prévu et appréhendé, et ont cru qu'elles devaient redoubler leurs efforts pour tâcher d'éteindre ce feu dans sa naissance, et de prévenir, pendant qu'il en est encore temps, les maux et les calamités dont l'Europe est menacée, et auxquelles Elle demeurerait exposée, tant qu'il ne serait pas supplée à ce que les traités d'Utrecht et de Bade ont laissé d'imparfait, et tant que les diverses prétentions sur les successions à écheoir en Italie ne seraient pas fixées.

Dans cette vue leurs Majestés Britannique et Très-Chrétienne et les Seigneurs États Généraux, qui d'ailleurs n'ont aucun autre intérêt que celui du repos public dans les différends qui subsistent encore, ou qui pourraient survenir entre les dits trois princes, ont jugé que le seul moyen qui restait pour tirer l'Europe de l'état d'incertitude où elle se trouve, et lui procurer une tranquillité générale et permanente, était, que les trois puissances contractantes réglassent entre elles avec une impartialité religieuse les prétentions réciproques que les parties intéressées peuvent avoir présentement et à l'avenir et qu'elles prissent des mesures pour faciliter l'exécution de ce qui leur aurait paru le plus juste et le plus convenable, pour anéantir tout prétexte de nouvelles guerres que les dits trois princes intéressés pourraient exciter, ou en repoussant des injures reçues, ou en revendiquant des droits réservés ou en voulant faire valoir des prétentions obscures.

A cette fin pour procurer une paix durable entre les dits trois princes, et pour assurer une paix générale et solide à toute l'Europe qui ne se ressent que trop encore du poids des longues et sanglantes guerres qu'elle a essuyées, leurs Majestés Britannique et Très-Chrétienne et les Seigneurs États Généraux des Provinces Unies, avec des intentions si justes et si sincères et sous les auspices de la Sagesse Divine, après une mûre délibération et en suivant la conduite qui a été heureusement pratiquée [1] dans plusieurs occasions importantes par les prédécesseurs de leurs Majestés Britannique et Très-Chrétienne et des Seigneurs États Généraux sont convenus que les articles suivants pourraient servir d'un fondement équitable pour établir une paix perpétuelle entre Sa Majesté Impériale et Sa Majesté Catholique, et entre Sa Majesté Impériale et le roi de Sicile.

[1] Traités conclus à la Haye le 21 mai, 24 juillet et 4 août 1659 : entre la France, l'Angleterre et la Hollande, pour porter, ou en cas de refus, forcer les rois de Suède et de Danemarc à faire la paix entre eux, avec les changements du traité de Roschil, dont les trois puissances étaient convenues, ce qui fut suivi du traité de paix entre ces deux couronnes, conclu à Copenhague le 27 mai 1660. Triple Alliance conclue à la Haye le 23 janvier 1668 entre l'Angleterre, la Suède et la Hollande, pour obliger le roi d'Espagne à faire la paix avec la France aux conditions concertées par les trois puissances avec cette couronne, ce qui donna lieu au traité de paix d'Aix la Chapelle conclu le 2 mai 1668.

No. 3

STANHOPE'S MEMORIAL (TO DUBOIS, MAR. 30 (O.S.) 1719)
CONCERNING THE WAR OF THE QUADRUPLE ALLIANCE
AGAINST SPAIN, AND THE POLITICAL SITUATION IN
1719 (cf. p. 89 *seq.*)

(St. Saphorin Papers, Hanover Archives)

MONSIEUR,

Je suis encore réduit à commencer cette lettre par des excuses mais
j'ai le plaisir de voir par celle que V. E. a écrite à M. Schaub, que vous
êtes d'avance disposé à les accepter, et que vous jugiez trop bien de
l'accablement d'affaires où les serviteurs de S. M. devaient être dans
ces circonstances, pour me savoir mauvais gré que j'aie tant tardé à
vous répondre. Aussi je m'empresse à le faire dès que l'ajournement
de notre Parlement me donne un peu le temps de respirer. Je ne
saurais assez vous dire, Monsieur, combien le Roi est sensible à la
vigilance et à l'attention de V. E. à nous avertir si promptement et si
exactement des desseins et des mouvements de nos ennemis, et à la
cordialité avec laquelle S. A. R. est allée au devant de tout ce que
S. M. pouvait désirer d'Elle à cet égard. Le Roi devait sans doute ne
se promettre pas moins de votre affection ; mais vous savez vous y
prendre à la faire sentir doublement à vos amis, et à redoubler aussi
leur reconnaissance.

Je ne m'étendrai pas sur les dispositions que nous avons faites ici
tant par terre que par mer, pour prévenir, ou pour repousser l'invasion
des Espagnols. My Lord Stair et M. Craggs en auront déjà amplement
informé V. E. Mais les soins de S. M. ne se sont pas bornés à la sûreté
de ses propres royaumes. Comme vous paraissiez soupçonner que
l'armement espagnol pût aussi être destiné à envahir quelque partie de
la France, le Roi a enjoint à ses amiraux d'y apporter toute l'attention
possible, et au cas que cet armement s'approchât de vos côtes, d'y
accourir incessamment, et de les défendre avec la même diligence et la
même vigueur que les nôtres. Et s'il arrivait que malgré toutes vos
précautions et les nôtres, les Espagnols fissent une descente en France,
S. A. R. doit compter sur tout le secours et sur toute l'assistance qu'il
sera dans le pouvoir de S. M. de lui donner, tant en vaisseaux qu'en
troupes.

De quel côté que les Espagnols puissent se tourner, j'espère qu'avec
l'aide de Dieu, nous parerons assez aisément au coup qu'il voudront
nous porter. Mais nous ne devons pas nous arrêter à nous garantir
seulement de leurs insultes, si nous ne voulons pas y demeurer exposés
continuellement. Il faut pousser le Cardinal Alberoni chez lui, pour
l'empêcher de porter ses vues au dehors ; et S. M. voit avec une satis-

faction singulière que Monseigneur le Régent entre dans ces sentiments, et se dispose si bien à les mettre en œuvre. Ce que Mylord Stair vient de nous mander à cet égard, me rappelle ce dont j'ai eu l'honneur d'entretenir et S. A. R. et V. E. pendant mon séjour à Paris. Et comme vous paraissiez le goûter alors, je vais vous le retracer présentement avec la même confidence, et d'autant plus librement, que les ordres du Roi me le prescrivent.

J'ai bien prévu dès mon retour d'Espagne, que si le Cardinal ne se rendait pas pendant le terme qui lui était fixé, il n'y aurait plus rien qui pût dompter son courage, ni lui faire perdre l'espérance de remplir ses vastes desseins, tant qu'il ne serait pas attaqué dans l'Espagne même, tant qu'on ne tournerait pas son application à sa propre défense, et qu'il se verrait à l'abri de toute entreprise de dehors, et de toute contradiction au dedans ; mais j'ai prévu en même temps, que l'on ébranlerait, bientôt, et son opiniâtreté et sa puissance dès que l'on se mettrait en devoir de perdre un ministre si inquiet et si dangereux, en relevant efficacement le courage tant des peuples qui souffrent impatiemment la perte de leurs privilèges, que des grands qui gémissent sous le mépris où ses maximes les ont fait tomber. C'est ce que le bien de l'Europe exigerait de nous quand le Cardinal ne nous en aurait pas donné l'exemple lui-même. Mais après toutes les injures atroces et indignes qu'il a employées contre le Roi, et contre Mgr. le Régent, après tous les attentats qu'il a formés contr'eux et leurs États, et après qu'il a voulu armer leurs propres sujets contr'Eux, leur honneur et leur sûreté exigent également, qu'ils lui fassent essuyer tout le poids de leur ressentiment. S. A. R. paraît être trop convaincue de cette nécessité pour que j'y insiste davantage ; mais afin que les opérations qu'Elle a résolu de commencer aussitôt que son armée sera assemblée, et que la saison pourra le permettre, produisent plus sûrement l'effet qu'Elle se propose, voici la méthode que S. M. croit devoir y être observée. Il lui semble qu'après l'expédition qui doit se faire au Port de Passage, et aux environs, S. A. R. devrait partager son armée en deux corps, pour pénétrer avec l'un plus avant dans la Biscaye, et avec l'autre dans la Catalogne ; non seulement afin de diviser par là les forces de l'Espagne, mais principalement pour faire espérer à tous les peuples qui confinent avec les Pyrénées une part égale à la restitution de leurs privilèges ; mais en même temps que l'armée sera prête à se mettre en marche, il faudra déclarer par un manifeste, que S. A. R. n'entre point dans l'Espagne pour y faire des conquêtes, ni pour s'y rien approprier, mais qu'au contraire quelque progrès que ses armes y puissent faire, Elle restituera tout à la paix, sans en garder un pouce de terre. Qu'Elle ne se propose d'autre but que d'affranchir le Roi Catholique et ses royaumes de l'oppression et de la tyrannie d'un ministre étranger, qui ne songe qu'à élever sa gloire particulière sur leur ruine et leur destruction ; qu'Elle invite tous les bons Espagnols à se joindre à Elle dans un dessein si salutaire ; qu'ils y trouveront une sûreté entière pour eux et pour

leurs biens, et qu'Elle ne posera pas les armes que les natifs du pays ne
rentrent dans le maniment des affaires, dont le cardinal les a exclus.
Outre ce manifeste général, il sera bon d'en faire un particulier, qui
regarde spécialement les peuples de Catalogne, d'Arragon, de Valence,
de Navarre, et de Biscaie, leur promettant que ceux qui recevront
l'armée de France sans opposition, et qui concourront avec Elle à
chasser leur tyran, le cardinal, de l'Espagne, jouiront tous également de
la protection de S. A. R. ; qu'ils seront immédiatement rétablis dans
leurs anciens privilèges, et qu'on ne fera la paix avec le Roi Catholique
qu'à condition qu'il les leur confirme. Et comme peut-être l'on gagnerait
plus facilement la confiance de ces peuples, si la garantie de leurs
privilèges leur était promise en même temps de la part du Roi, S. M.
offre à S. A. R. de tenir dans son armée un ministre muni de pleins pouvoirs
pour publier en son nom partout où il sera besoin, des déclarations
convenables pour cet effet, ou même de lettres de créance vers les dites
provinces, afin que de concert avec votre général il puisse traiter avec
elles, et s'engager formellement à cette garantie. Le choix en pourrait
tomber sur mon cousin Stanhope qui avec la connaissance qu'il a de
l'Espagne, y serait peut-être plus propre qu'un autre ; et Sa M^{té} le
dépêchera aussitôt qu'Elle en saura la volonté de S. A. R. de qui il
prendra ses instructions. De plus si Monsg^r le Régent jugeait qu'il fût
utile que de nos escadres parussent sur les côtes de Biscaie et de la Catalogne pendant que vos troupes y agiront, S. M. y ordonnera autant de
vaisseaux que S. A. R. trouvera nécessaires.

En s'y prenant ainsi, S. M. ne peut qu'espérer que l'on viendrait en
peu de temps à bout du cardinal, dont la perte lui paraît de plus en
plus essentielle et nécessaire pour votre sûreté et pour la nôtre. Car
avec les idées qu'il roule dans son esprit, et se jouant aussi ouvertement
des traités qu'il le fait, toute paix qu'on pourrait faire pendant qu'il
gouvernerait l'Espagne, ne serait pas seulement précaire, mais beaucoup
plus dangereuse que la guerre même.

Vraisemblablement S. A. R. trouvera peu de résistance dans des
pays où Elle ne paraîtra que comme leur ange tutélaire, et où tous les
peuples doivent naturellement être disposés à se jeter entre ses bras.
Or une infinité de raisons doivent porter S. A. R. à cette entreprise, à
occuper ces pays le plutôt qu'Elle pourra, et à les remettre dans leur
ancien état. S. M. ne conçoit pas d'autre moyen de procurer une paix,
et prompte et durable. Le grand dessein du cardinal est sans doute de
renverser Mg^r le Régent, et s'il nous envahit, ce n'est que pour en
venir plus facilement à bout ; mais il ne sera plus guère à craindre pour
S. A. R. dès qu'Elle occupera en Espagne la lisière depuis la Méditerranée
jusque à l'océan, car non seulement Elle le réservera, par là, et l'éloignera
de ses frontières, mais Elle lui ôtera l'une de ses plus grandes ressources,
en coupant les revenus si considérables qu'il tire de ces provinces.
Leur exemple animera les autres peuples de l'Espagne, et bientôt il
ne sera plus dans le pouvoir du cardinal de résister à leurs clameurs, ni

dans celui du Roi Catholique de se dispenser d'en faire la victime de la paix ; mais quand la perte du cardinal aura donné lieu à la paix, rien ne sera plus efficace pour la consolider, et pour mettre S. A. R. dans une sûreté réelle, que le rétablissement des privilèges dont ont joui ci-devant les peuples qui bordent les Pyrénées. Car là Elle se les attachera inviolablement, et Elle pourra faire d'autant plus de fond sur cette barrière (quoiqu'entre les mains de l'Espagne) que tout ce que le Roi Catholique tenterait dans la suite contre les droits de S. A. R. rejaillirait nécessairement sur eux, et mettrait en risque les privilèges dont ils lui auront eu toute l'obligation. Outre que ce sera un affaiblissement solide et permanent de la monarchie d'Espagne, laquelle étant privée des revenus immenses que ces provinces lui donnent depuis qu'elles sont dépouillées de leurs privilèges, sera réellement, et en tout temps, beaucoup moins redoutable à la France qu'elle ne l'est présentement, soit que votre jeune Roi vous soit conservé ou qu'il vienne à manquer. Cette diminution de finances laissera à tout ministre téméraire moins de tentation à bouleverser l'Europe. Et quand même l'Espagne viendrait à reprendre des vues pareilles à celles du cardinal, elle serait bien moins en état de les soutenir. Mais nous n'aurons guère à craindre, que des ministres espagnols mis à sa place puissent travailler sur ses plans, ni par rapport aux affaires étrangères en général, ni par rapport à la France en particulier. Ils savent très bien par l'expérience du passé, ce qu'il leur a coûté de posséder les Pays Bas et l'Italie, pour vouloir s'épuiser à les reconquérir. J'ai vu que les grands mêmes qui y gagneraient le plus, en pensent ainsi, et que s'ils en étaient crus, l'ambition de leur roi se bornerait uniquement à bien régler l'interne de l'Espagne et les Indes. Et quant à la France, ce qui porterait le cardinal au plus haut degré de sa gloire, ferait le comble de leur honte, et de leur malheur.

Votre Excellence ne regardera pas, j'espère, ce que je viens de déduire, comme le simple effet du juste ressentiment de Sa M^{té}. Quelque indignée qu'Elle soit de la conduite de la cour d'Espagne tant à son égard qu'à celui de Mgr le Régent, Elle ne vous propose que ce qu'Elle juge être indispensable pour notre sûreté commune, et pour le bien de la paix. Rien ne doit mieux vous en convaincre que les mouvements extrêmes qu'Elle s'est donnée pour obtenir de l'Empereur la prolongation du terme qui était fixé au Roi d'Espagne pour l'acceptation des expectatives. S. M. est confirmée en cela aux intentions et aux instances de S. A. R. Et pourvu seulement que les États Généraux se dépêchent de signer, les nouveaux 3 mois seront accordés à l'Espagne pour se résoudre à la paix.

Mais il est évident que ce surcroît de condescendance ne ferait que produire un effet contraire, et rendre le cardinal plus insolent, si elle n'était suivie de vigueur et de force.

V. E. jugera aisément avec quelle répugnance l'Empereur a consenti à ce nouveau terme. Aussi ne sommes-nous parvenus à le lui arracher, qu'à condition que ce sera le dernier, et qu'ensuite il ne puisse

plus s'agir des expectatives pour le fils de la reine, mais qu'immédiatement après la signature des Hollandais l'on convienne ensemble du
prince ou des princes qui devront lui être substitués au cas que le Roi
Cath. laissât encore écouler ce temps sans souscrire à notre traité. Et
c'est sur quoi M. de Pendtenriedter exige de nous des déclarations par
écrit. Nous voyons par la dépêche de Mylord Stair que S. A. R. ne
trouve pas seulement cette condition très juste et indispensable à
l'égard de l'Empereur, mais qu'Elle en comprend encore toute la
nécessité par rapport au Roi d'Espagne. Car sûr est-il que les expectatives ne seront pour ce prince un motif de paix, que quand il sentira
qu'il les perdra sans retour en continuant la guerre. Sans cela il pourrait
impunément tenter tout ce que son violent ministre lui suggère, et se
jouer de nous en attendant des conjonctures plus favorables à ses
desseins, si on lui laissait la liberté de revenir toujours aux mêmes
conditions, après qu'il aurait inutilement épuisé tous ses efforts, et
toutes ses tentatives. De sorte que le Roi et S. A. R. sont réellement
les plus intéressés à éviter cet inconvénient et à y obvier par la déclaration que l'Empereur demande. Mais S. M. a d'autant moins hésité à y
donner les mains, qu'autrement nous pourrions nous exposer encore à
d'autres inconvénients pas moins dangereux pour nous que celui dont
je viens de parler. V. E. a déjà eu quelque appréhension que l'Empereur
ne traitât séparément de l'évacuation de la Sicile, et d'un accommode-
ment particulier à cet égard. A la vérité nous avons pris toutes nos
précautions pour le prévenir ; mais l'on ne saurait pourtant répondre
de ce qui en arriverait si l'Empereur ne voyait pas de fin à nos ménage-
ments pour l'Espagne, surtout le Roi de Sardaigne ne se mettant de la
partie, comme il ne manquerait pas de le faire ; nous le connaissons
trop pour en douter. Et comptez, Monsieur, que ses menées à la Cour
Imp. ne tendent pas à moins qu'à renverser tout notre système. D'ailleurs
nous avons lieu de soupçonner que les ministres espagnols à Vienne,
depuis qu'il s'agit de leur amnistie, prennent à tâche de faire leur cour
au Roi d'Espagne. Vous savez le pouvoir qu'ils ont sur l'esprit de leur
maître. Et si une fois nous leur donnions une aussi juste prise contre
nous, que de faire les difficiles sur une déclaration conforme en tout à
nos engagements, après avoir poussé le premier terme de 3 mois jusqu'à près d'une année. Dieu sait où ces gens seraient capables de mener
l'Empereur qui déjà ne paraît que trop piqué de cette prolongation, et
de la chaleur dont nous l'avons sollicitée.

Quoique S. A. R. se soit montrée si prête à donner la déclaration
dont il s'agit, j'ai crû néanmoins qu'il ne serait pas tout à fait inutile
de m'étendre un peu sur ces considérations. Nous sommes présentement occupés à coucher cette déclaration, et nous vous en enverrons
copie dès qu'elle sera dressée.

Mais outre cette déclaration, les ordres de M. de Pendtenriedter
sont encore clausés par une autre condition. Comme les nouveaux
trois mois ne doivent commencer que la signature des Hollandais,

l'Empereur a aussi limité un terme pour cette signature, et M. de Pendtenriedter ne pourra plus y concourir si elle ne se fait au plus tard en 4 semaines à compter du jour qu'il a reçu son rescrit. Or comme ce terme s'écoulera avec la semaine prochaine, et que nous avons appris que le consentement des États ne tient plus qu'à l'échange des ratifications de la nouvelle convention pour la barrière, nous avons dépêché d'abord un exprès au Marquis de Prié pour le presser de faire incessamment cet échange. Aussi comptons-nous qu'il l'aura été fait actuellement, et que par ce moyen le ministre des États Généraux pourra recevoir à temps les ordres de signer ici les articles secrets avec le reste du traité. Nous comptons aussi que Votre Ex^{ce} aura soin de nous faire tenir pour ce temps-là la déclaration pour S. A. R. Cependant comme nous n'étions pas sûrs qu'elle pût arriver ici sitôt, et que nous avons crû ne devoir point arrêter à cela la signature des États, et mettre par là en risque leur accession si capitale pour nous, et pour laquelle le Roi, et S. A. R. ont tant sacrifié, nous avons enfin disposé M. de Pendtenriedter à signer en tout cas sur la déclaration de S. M^{té}, lui promettant qu'elle lui procurera celle de S. A. R. le plus promptement que faire se pourra, et qu'aussitôt après cette signature, l'on procédera à concerter ensemble à quel autre prince l'Empereur devra conférer les expectatives à l'exclusion du fils d'Espagne, si par l'obstination invincible du cardinal, le Roi Catholique laissait encore écouler ces derniers 3 mois sans se rendre à la paix.

Il me reste, Monsieur, à vous parler sur les affaires du nord. J'avoue à Votre Excellence que notre attention en a été un peu distraite, tant par l'équipement des Espagnols, que par nos occupations parlementaires ; mais quand même nous aurions été plus libres, nous sommes encore trop peu informés des dispositions présentes de la Couronne de Suède par rapport à la paix, pour avoir pu nous déterminer à rien de fixe à cet égard. Et nous en sommes encore à nos premières idées vagues et générales. Il n'y a qu'une chose sur laquelle le Roi ait pris son parti ; c'est de chercher en premier lieu à s'unir étroitement pour cet effet avec le Roi de Prusse, suivant ce que vous n'avez cessé de nous inculquer. S. M. comprend parfaitement combien il est important au repos du nord de faire envisager à ce prince d'autres à ses ressources que celles qu'il croit trouver dans le Czar, et de le fixer à ses vrais intérêts par des liaisons plus voisines. Mais comme nous n'avons d'autre ministre à employer à Berlin que M. Whitworth, il nous faut attendre à l'y envoyer, que les États Généraux aient pris leur résolution finale sur les articles secrets, et vous approuverez sans doute que nous ne le tirions pas plutôt de la Haye. Lorsqu'il sera à Berlin, il agira entièrement de concert avec le Comte de Rottembourg, et se prévaudra de son secours. Et quant à la pacification générale du nord, nous serons mieux en état d'en juger par les lumières que le comte de la Marck pourra vous fournir là-dessus. Je supplie V. E. de vouloir nous les communiquer avec les réflexions que vous y aurez faites, et je vous promets de même une communication exacte des avis que nous recevrons du Colonel Bassewitz. Nous le croyons présentement arrivé en Suède, quoique nous n'en ayons pas encore la nouvelle. Je suis, etc.

No. 4

A CONTEMPORARY'S OPINION OF THE VALUE OF GIBRALTAR (1716) (cf. p. 129)

Bonet's Report of Sept. 29/Oct. 9, 1716.   (Prussian State Archives)

C'est une acquisition bien onéreuse que celle que cette couronne a faite de cette dernière île[1] et de Gibraltar, les garnisons qu'elle y entretient lui coûtent 89,501. 15. 3 sterl. outre la dépense qui regarde les vaisseaux qu'on y envoye annuellement. L'intérêt du commerce fait qu'on soutient ces dépenses, mais si on est un jour bien assuré qu'on n'a pas à craindre une union de la France et de l'Espagne qui fermât le détroit de Gibraltar et interrompît le commerce de la mer Méditerranée, on cédera volontiers ces places à l'Espagne pour de bons avantages de commerce, ce qui sera un acte fort populaire, mais où la couronne trouvera aussi ses avantages.

No. 5

THE READING OF FULLER'S " MANIFESTO " (cf. p. 130)

Destouches to Dubois, Feb. 1, 1719.   (Aff. étr. 322)

Je ne puis me dispenser, Monseigneur, de vous rendre compte d'une aventure burlesque (car on ne peut nommer autrement ce qui vient de se passer) qui est arrivée aujourd'hui dans la Chambre des Communes. Un nommé Fuller qui passe pour l'âme damné de Walpole, s'est avisé de dire qu'il apportait à la chambre un libelle qui méritait toute son attention et qui était intitulé : Manifeste sur les sujets de rupture entre la France et l'Espagne, par lequel un particulier étranger s'ingérait de disposer du domaine de la Couronne d'Angleterre en se faisant fort d'avoir assuré la restitution de Gibraltar au roi d'Espagne. La Chambre a été si étonnée de cette étrange motion, pour me servir de termes de ce pays-ci, qu'elle est demeurée d'abord dans un profond silence. Mais celui qui a mis la matière sur le tapis a été plus étonné lui-même, car de dix ou douze membres qui lui avaient promis de l'appuyer, aucun n'a osé ouvrir la bouche, voyant l'indignation générale que ce discours avait

[1] Minorca.

causée, et le meilleur de l'affaire c'est que Walpole lui-même qui avait
détaché cet enfant perdu et qui s'était fait fort de le porter aux nues, ne
s'est pas trouvé à la Chambre ; en sorte qu'on a passé tout d'un coup
à une autre matière sans témoigner la moindre attention au discours de
Fuller. Mais il s'est vanté en sortant que quoique ceux qui l'avaient
animé l'eussent abandonné aujourd'hui, il aurait demain sa révanche.
On est persuadé que son impudence sera suivie du même succès.
Néanmoins ceci me confirme ce que M. Craggs m'avait dit il y a
quelque temps que ce que l'on avait jugé à propos d'insérer dans le
manifeste de France touchant Gibraltar causerait quelque tracasserie
dans la Chambre des Communes. Mais au surplus elle n'aura aucune
suite selon toutes les apparences et ne pourra produire qu'un bon effet,
puisque le silence des deux Chambres sur cette matière ou leur approba-
tion, rendra authentique cette clause secrète du Traité.

No. 6

THE ENGLISH COURT IN 1719 (cf. pp. 134 *seq.*, 277 *seq.*)
(Aff. étr. 323)

Mémoire contenant quelques observations dont il paraît nécessaire que M.
le Comte de Senneterre soit instruit avant son départ pour aller
remplir l'ambassade d'Angleterre

. . . . . .

Comme M^d Stanhope est celui des ministres anglais qui a le plus
de part à ces traités, cette raison seule suffirait pour assurer qu'il
voudra soutenir son ouvrage, mais ce jugement n'est plus une simple
conjecture, l'expérience a fait connaître qu'il s'y portait avec zèle et
avec vivacité et qu'étant persuadé de l'utilité réciproque d'une intelligence parfaite et d'une entière confiance, il n'a négligé aucun des soins,
ni aucune des attentions qui pouvaient contribuer à l'une et à l'autre ;
l'ambassadeur du Roi ne peut aussi rien faire de mieux pour le service
de S. M. que d'agir en tout avec ce Ministre sur les mêmes principes.
Il lui trouvera l'esprit net, décisif, et solide, avec un cœur droit, vrai et
même impatient de montrer la vérité se portant toujours avec vivacité
et avec courage à ce qu'il croit utile à sa patrie ou pouvoir concourir
avec qui serait avantageux à la nation anglaise. Il est simple, sans
faste, capable d'amitié et en même temps de quelque jalousie lorsqu'on
la partage. Il est intègre, sans aucun intérêt, sans détour et ne demande
que les soins nécessaires pour le tenir dans des préventions favorables,
et pour l'empêcher d'en prendre de contraires, à quoi, à la longue, des
gens appliqués quoiqu' inférieurs à lui en lumières et en connaissances
pourraient réussir, en sorte que ce ministre que les plus habiles ne
pourraient surprendre, et que nul intérêt et nulle considération ne
sauraient tenter, n'est pas incapable de se rendre aux continuelles

insinuations de son sécrétaire, ce qui doit obliger à attirer et à caresser le Sr Schaub pour le remplir des principes dont il est important que M^d Stanhope ne s'éloigne pas pour lui faire passer dans les occasions qui se présentent les principales choses auxquelles il convient qu'il fasse attention, et afin que les lettres, qu'il doit écrire soient plus fortes ou plus faibles suivant les circonstances. Le Sr Schaub se pique extrême- ment d'amour pour sa patrie qui est le Canton de Bâle et se regarde comme un ministre qu'il faut consulter. L'ambassadeur du Roi le gagnera en lui faisant espérer quelque protection pour la ville de Bâle, et en traitant avec lui comme s'il avait la principale part aux affaires, avec la précaution toutefois que comme il parle beaucoup, et qu'il est en grande familiarité avec les ministres allemands, il ne faut pas lui faire confidence de ce que l'on ne veut pas qu'ils sachent. Il est élève de M. de St. Saphorin, ministre du Roi de la Grande Bretagne à Vienne qui a beaucoup de capacité ; le Sr Schaub est un canal par où l'on peut le disposer aux choses qui conviendront au service du Roi.

M. Craggs, Sécrétaire d'État ayant le département de la partie méridionale de l'Europe, a un sens droit et beaucoup d'esprit sans en avoir l'affectation. Il est généreux, fidèle, droit, et penche plus à la hauteur qu'à la dissimulation et à la finesse. Il est sensible à l'amitié, et en est très capable ; on ne doit craindre de lui aucune infidélité ni aucune surprise. Il est susceptible cependant de prendre assez facile- ment de l'ombrage et de la défiance, mais il se rend aux éclaircissements vrais. Il est persuadé qu'une union parfaite entre la France et l'Angle- terre est nécessaire pour leur avantage commun, ce qui est le principal lien entre M^d Stanhope et lui. Il est blessé plus que personne de l'influ- ence qu'ont en Angleterre les ministres allemands, et le dissimule moins qu'aucun autre de ceux qui ont part aux affaires ; c'est aussi ce qui règle son affection et ses opinions sur le crédit que doit avoir en Angle- terre la Cour de Vienne. Comme il sait ce qu'on peut faire avec le ministère d'Angleterre et auprès du Roi son maître, pour les précautions que l'on peut prendre à l'égard de la Cour de Vienne, il n'y a personne dans le ministère d'Angleterre par qui l'ambassadeur du Roi puisse mieux sentir lorsqu'il sera chargé de faire quelques démarches contre les vues et les mouvements des Impériaux, ou lorsqu'il croira lui-même que le bien du service du Roi demandera qu'il les fasse jusqu'où il le faut porter et quelle doit être la règle et la mesure qu'il faudra garder dans chacune de ces occasions.

M. le Comte de Senneterre apprendra de ce ministre qu'il ne faut jamais parler au Roi de la Grande Bretagne de manière qu'il puisse penser que la France aurait en vue de le brouiller avec l'Empereur, mais seulement de l'aider à prendre les précautions convenables à un grand Roi contre les entreprises et les hauteurs de la Cour de Vienne.

La droiture de M. Craggs l'a conservé en liaison et même en amitié avec des personnes de mérite de différents partis à qui il rend service et qui ont confiance en lui malgré son principal engagement.

Celui qui tient le premier rang entre ceux avec qui M^d Stanhope et M. Craggs agissent pour les arrangements domestiques de l'Angleterre et pour ce qui regarde les intérêts de cette Couronne dans les pays étrangers est M^d Sunderland qui depuis longtemps a parcouru presque toutes les principales places du gouvernement d'Angleterre. Il a été Sécrétaire d'État, Viceroi d'Irlande, chef du Conseil, et il est présentement premier Commissaire de la Trésorerie. C'est l'homme du monde le plus actif, très instruit de tout ce qui regarde la chambre des Seigneurs et fort accrédité parmi eux et dans la cité. Il rassemble contre lui la haine des partis qui sont contraires au gouvernement, et celle des ennemis du Duc de Marlborough et de sa famille, et particulièrement celle du Prince de Galles qui le regarde comme le principal auteur de l'éloignement que le Roi son père a pour lui, les démarches d'éclat qui se sont faites pour le mortifier, et des obstacles à sa réconciliation.

M^d Sunderland est véritablement fort droit et très désintéressé. Ses goûts dominants sont les femmes et les livres, non pour les lire, car il est trop vif et trop occupé pour s'y arrêter, mais par curiosité pour en amasser et former une bibliothèque extraordinaire.

Sa principale correspondance est avec M^d Stanhope et M. Craggs, mais il est plus lié qu'eux avec M^d Cadogan, et surtout avec M. de Bernstorff dont il estime la droiture et sans lequel il ne pourrait pas soutenir les attaques qu'on lui donne auprès du Roi. Il n'a pas la même opinion de M. de Bothmer, et il ne le voit ni sincère ni bien intentionné pour lui.

L'on peut regarder comme l'un des points qui demandent le plus d'attention dans la conduite de l'ambassadeur du Roi, la manière dont il doit se gouverner contre les ministres anglais et allemands.

Il n'est pas douteux que les derniers n'aient une confiance de prédilection dans l'esprit du Roi de la Grande Bretagne. Ce Prince est lié par un intérêt capital aux affaires d'Allemagne, et il est obligé par la même raison de ménager l'Empereur. Ses Ministres allemands agissent dans le même esprit non seulement par les mouvements d'une affection née avec eux, et confirmée par d'anciens préjugés, mais encore dans des vues ou d'intérêt ou d'élévation.

L'attachement du Roi leur maître à ses États d'Allemagne, la violence qu'il s'est faite en les quittant et d'autres motifs encore lui donnent du goût pour tout ce qui a rapport à ces mêmes États, et ouvrent aux ministres allemands des voies faciles auprès de lui.

Le premier d'entr'eux est le Baron de Bernstorff, homme de mérite, consommé dans les affaires de l'Empire, d'une application sans relâche, d'un extérieur grave et sage, droit dans le commerce de la vie, profond et défiant dans les affaires d'État, ferme jusqu'à l'opiniâtreté et qui a toujours conservé la principale confiance du Roi s. m^{tre}.

M. de Bothmer second ministre d'Hannover, résidant en Angleterre, n'a ni l'estime du Roi son maître ni celle de M. de Bernstorff, mais il est attaché à son service depuis si longtemps et il a été employé dans tant d'affaires intimes qu'il se soutient et qu'il a toujours beaucoup de part aux affaires . Il a de l'esprit et des connaissances assez étendues, son caractère le conduit à être doux, fin, rusé et même double. Comme il a résidé longtemps à Vienne, et qu'il a reçu des grâces de cette cour, il est partial sans mesure pour tout ce qui la regarde, et il est le principal conseil des ministres de l'Empereur qui résident en Angleterre. Il est connu et méprisé des ministres dont il n'ignore pas les sentiments pour lui. Il aime la dépense et néglige aucune des occasions qui peuvent lui être utiles, ce qui le met dans la nécessité de ne se déclarer contre personne et d'aller à ses fins par des intrigues secrètes. Il est soupçonné d'entretenir des intelligences secrètes avec M^d Townshend, et avec M. Walpole, ennemis du ministère présent. Ses correspondances à la Cour sont particulièrement avec le secrétaire du Conseil d'Hanovre, avec le grand Maréchal et avec celui qui fait la charge de Grand Écuyer du Roi d'Angleterre. Il est aussi en relation avec Melle la Comtesse de Kilmanseck et il ménage Mehemet, premier valet de chambre de ce Prince. La jalousie que M. de Bothmer a de la supériorité de M. de Bernstorff est retombée sur M. Robethon qu'il traverse secrètement tant qu'il peut.

Quoique M. Robethon ait souvent donné des assurances d'un vif désir de faire connaître qu'il n'a pas oublié les devoirs de sa naissance, et qu'en effet il y ait eu lieu de le croire en plusieurs occasions, il faut cependant le regarder comme un homme entièrement livré à M. de Bernstorff dont toute sa fortune dépend.

Il est né Français, et il est sorti du Royaume pour la religion pr.

Il a été attaché en premier lieu au Duc de Zell, ensuite au Roi Guillaume. Il est revenu à Hanovre où M. de Bernstorff s'est servi de ses talents et de ses connaissances et l'a approché du Roi de la Grande Bretagne en lui procurant l'emploi du secrétaire du Cabinet, et la place de Con^{er} de la chancellerie ou Con^{er} d'État de l'Électorat d'Hanovre.

M. Robethon est homme d'esprit, il sait plusieurs langues et il a du goût pour les belles lettres, il est très instruit des affaires de la Basse Allemagne, et il est vif et laborieux. Pendant toutes les dernières guerres il n'y a eu aucun réfugié plus emporté contre la France que lui. Il est encore quelquefois très caustique contre elle, surtout en ce qui regarde les religionnaires qu'il protège, car il est dévot, et un des chefs du comité des réfugiés d'Angleterre. Il suit la pente de M. de Bernstorff pour l'Empereur. Peut-être en attend-il quelque distinction, et quelque titre, si le Roi d'Angleterre venait à mourir, ou que quelque disgrâce l'obligeât de se retirer en Allemagne. Si la Cour de Vienne lui a présenté quelque gratification secrète il ne l'aura pas refusée, mais il ne se tient pas lié par ces sortes d'engagements, et lorsque l'occasion ou l'humeur qui domine en lui, le rend quelque fois comme fanatique, lui inspirent des emportements, rien n'est capable de le retenir. Il parle même souvent involontairement et par humeur. La commission qu'il a eue d'abord de servir d'interprète au Roi de la Grande Bretagne lorsqu'il donnait audience à des Anglais qui ne savaient pas parler français ou allemand, l'assiduité qui le met toujours à portée l'a familiarisé avec M. de Bernstorff, diverses correspondances étrangères dont on s'est déchargé sur lui, et la nécessité de lui donner le soin de suivre beaucoup d'affaires auxquelles les ministres anglais ne peuvent vaquer qu'imparfaitement pendant les séances du Parlement, lui ont fait une espèce de ministère entre les Anglais et les Allemands qui demande qu'on le ménage malgré les inégalités et le peu de sûreté que l'on trouve dans son commerce, mais on apprendra moins et l'on ferait moins si l'on négligeait la correspondance avec lui. M^d Sunderland et M^d Cadogan ont assez de confiance en lui, M^d Stanhope et M. Craggs le croient indiscret et intéressé, mais ils ne laissent pas de se servir de lui. Il a un accès continuel avec M. de Bernstorff, et il est très bien venu auprès de Madame la Duchesse de Munster, il est haï de Melle de Kielmanseck, il est l'objet de la jalousie de Mme Bothmer et des Allemands de la chancellerie d'Hanovre ; aussi bien que de la haine de tout ce qui dépend du ministère allemand, et de Mehemet premier valet de chambre du Roi de la Grande Bretagne.

M^d Stanhope est celui d'entre les Anglais que l'on a cru le plus capable de concilier l'opposition naturelle des deux ministères, et en effet, il a su depuis quelques années se conduire de manière qu'en agissant selon les intérêts de la nation et du Roi, son maître, il est demeuré dans une assez grande liaison avec M. de Bernstorff.

Comme ses emplois dans le gouvernement ne lui ont pas ôté le goût de la guerre, et peut-être l'espérance de parvenir aux premières dignités militaires, on l'a regardé dans tous les temps comme l'un de ceux qui pouvaient prétendre le commandement général à la mort de M^d Marlborough. Cependant sa probité l'a porté à rendre justice aux talents de M^d Cadogan pour la guerre, et depuis qu'il a associé au gouvernement le Duc d'Argyle, il lui laissera disputer à M^d Cadogan le commandement des troupes, et il ne sera plus son seul compétiteur.

M^d Cadogan a de son côté plusieurs avantages. Il est étroitement lié avec les Allemands, son dévouement aux intérêts de l'Empereur lui donnera dans tous les temps de puissants appuis, et si la nouvelle entreprise des Espagnols lui donne lieu de rendre des services importants au Roi, sa destination pour succéder au Duc de Marlborough pourra être confirmée.

. . . .

Il doit avoir une attention très particulière à ne pas marquer de défiance des intentions de M. de Bernstorff, de M. Robethon, ni de ceux qui sont liés au même parti, et il faut même que dans les occasions où il pourrait croire que M. de Bernstorff serait opposé à ce que l'on désirait, il affecte de lui confier les choses dont il saura que la connaissance ne peut pas lui être dérobée, quand même il en attendrait le succès uniquement de l'intérêt et des bonnes dispositions des ministres anglais, afin qu'il ne puisse pas croire que l'on ait eu intention de les lui cacher et qu'il ne puisse pas supposer au Roi, son maître, que l'on n'affecte de la réserve à son égard que dans la vue de se ménager des moyens d'aliéner l'Empereur de ses intérêts. Mais soit que l'ambassadeur du Roi croit avoir des raisons de prévenir le Baron de Bernstorff sur les affaires dont il serait chargé, soit qu'il juge à propos de ne lui en point parler ou de différer de le faire, il faut qu'il concerte sa conduite à cet égard avec les ministres anglais qui pourront, lorsqu'il se sera attiré leur confiance, lui donner de bons avis sur le temps et sur la manière d'agir auprès des autres ministres.

Sur toutes choses l'ambassadeur du Roi doit éviter avec beaucoup de soin de prendre ouvertement un parti dans les différends qui peuvent s'élever entre les deux ministères et s'il marque dans le particulier plus de confiance aux Anglais dont il tirera le plus de secours, il faut que les dehors soient observés de manière que les Allemands ne puissent pas en prendre d'ombrage, en telle sorte que profitant de ce qu'il il saura des défiances qui naîtront entre les ministères pour régler sa conduite il en tire avantage pour le service du Roi, et c'est ce qu'il ne peut faire avec succès qu'en évitant de s'attirer des confidences qui pourraient lui ôter les moyens de ménager l'un et l'autre parti, mais en s'instruisant cependant par d'autres voies des causes de leurs démêlés.

Il est bien important que M. le Comte de Senneterre ait une attention très particulière à sa conduite à l'égard du Prince de Galles, et c'est le principal écueil qu'il ait à éviter. Il doit faire en général des vœux en toutes occasions pour la réunion de la Maison Royale, mais il faut qu'il évite avec soin de donner la moindre défiance sur ce sujet au Roi d'Angleterre et à ceux de ses ministres qui ont le plus d'intérêt que cette réunion ne se fasse pas.

Les principaux objets de l'aversion du Prince sont M^d Sunderland et M^d Cadogan. M. de Bernstorff est le plus ferme à l'égard du Prince, mais c'est cependant celui à qui on s'adressera toujours lorsqu'il s'ouvrira quelque moyen de conciliation.

M. de Bothmer et Mad^{elle} de Kielmanseck sont soupçonnés de conserver des liaisons secrètes avec le Prince et avec la Princesse.

.   .   .   .

M. le Comte de Senneterre recevra des instructions plus particulières[1] sur le compte qu'il rendra par ses dépêches des dispositions qu'il aura reconnues par lui même et S. A. R. a seulement voulu lui faire remettre ce mémoire pour ne lui pas laisser ignorer le caractère et les affections de ceux qui ont le plus de part aux affaires à la Cour d'Angleterre.

Fait à Paris le 13e avril 1719.

Dubois.

[1] To be found in Aff. étr. Corr. Pol. Angl. Suppl. 6.

No. 7

ANGLO-RUSSIAN RELATIONS, 1716–1720 (cf. pp. 210, 215)

From a memorial signed by Stanhope and given to the Russian Resident
Veselovsky, dated Whitehall, Feb. 11/22, 1720. Enclosed in
Hoffmann's Report of Feb. 23, 1720 (Vienna Archives)

.   .   .   .   .   .

Il est vrai que le Prince Kurakin se rendit ici pour cette négociation
au commencement de l'an 1716, mais au lieu de répondre aux avances
de Sa Majesté on mit en avant plusieurs difficultés qu'il serait trop long
de rapporter ici, et en particulier on refusa aux sujets du roi la liberté
de trafiquer à Casan ou à Astrachan, privilège qui leur avait été accordé
par les prédécesseurs de Sa Majesté Czar. Mais ce qui fit principalement
échouer la négociation, c'est qu'on ne voulut jamais entendre de la
part du Czar à conclure le traité de commerce sans conclure en même
temps une alliance à laquelle on donnait une telle étendue qu'elle
n'aurait pu manquer d'engager la couronne de la Grande Bretagne dans
une rupture avec la couronne de Suède, son ancienne alliée, dont la
destruction serait également incompatible avec le repos et la balance
de l'Europe et avec le soutien de la religion protestante auquel Sa
Majesté par tant de raisons de conscience et d'État se trouve obligée de
contribuer de tout son pouvoir.

.   .   .   .   .   .

Quoique dans une telle situation des affaires Sa Majesté eût lieu de
croire que le mémoire qui lui fut présenté par le Sieur Résident l'été de
l'an 1718 dans lequel on faisait mention du penchant du Czar à vivre
en amitié avec elle, n'était qu'un artifice déstiné à cacher les négociations
et les intrigues dont on vient de parler, cependant pour n'avoir aucun
reproche à se faire, Elle en prit occasion d'envoyer le Sieur Jefferys à
Pétersbourg en qualité de resident, et même Elle ordonna à l'amiral
Norris de s'y rendre avec lui ; mais cet amiral ayant déjà fait voile de
la mer Baltique pour retourner en Angleterre, lorsque le Sieur Jefferys
arriva à Copenhague, celui-ci poursuivit son voyage. Il ne négligea
rien pour profiter des bonnes dispositions dans lesquelles on l'avait
assuré qu'il trouverait le Czar, mais il parût bientôt que ce n'était
encore qu'un amusement, puisque au lieu de lui faire des propositions
on lui en demanda et que lorsqu'il parla de rétablir l'ancienne amitié
et de conclure un traité de commerce on lui dit qu'il fallait auparavant
songer à une alliance et à un plan d'opérations de guerre contre la
Suède ; propositions qu'on savait bien ne pouvoir pas être admises par
un ministre de la Grande Bretagne.

Enfin lorsque le entreprises concertées à Ahland avec le Baron de
Görtz eurent été entièrement renversées par la mort du roi de Suède,
le Czar ne trouvant point dans la princesse qui lui a succédé d'inclination

à poursuivre des plans si injustes et si dangereux, forma le dessein de l'y réduire par la force et par des excès dont il se trouve peu d'exemples. Occupé de cette idée il s'allarma de la flotte que Sa Majesté etait obligé d'envoyer tous les ans dans la mer Baltique pour protéger le commerce de ses sujets. Il demanda d'une manière impérieuse et menaçante à quoi elle était destinée ; et il écrivit à l'amiral Norris en des termes auxquels la couronne de la Grande Bretagne n'est point accoutumée.

Cependant à tout ceci le roi n'a opposé que les voies de la douceur et de la médiation, l'ayant fait offrir au Czar par le Lord Carteret et par l'amiral Norris, mais le Czar trouva à propos de ne pas recevoir leurs lettres, sous prétexte qu'ils n'étaient point accrédités auprès de lui, prétexte sur lequel les autres puissances en guerre contre la Suède n'ont fait aucune objection quoiqu'elles fussent dans le même cas.

Comme on ne cherche pas à aigrir les choses, on ne parla point ici des mauvais traitements faits aux sujets de Sa Majesté dans les états du Czar, des matelots anglais forcés à servir sur la flotte russienne, des artisans à qui on refuse la liberté de retourner dans leur patrie, des marchands arrêtés sans cause, et des vaisseaux saisis et confisqués injustement avec leur cargaison.

No. 8

TWO JACOBITE SATIRES

From Bonet's Reports of 1718 and 1719. (Prussian State Archives)

1

Satire apposée à la statue du Roi à la bourse en octobre 1718

Behold th'usurper on Great Britains throne,
At Court mere wax and in the city stone.
To Tories steele, to Whigs a log of wood,
None but his whores ever felt him flesh and blood.

2

Satire publiée en juillet 1719

The Whigs would the Tories all devour.
They the King do now possess :
In his folly lies their power,
Wisdom soon would make it less.
The Prince with raging passion heated
Vows to have his will obeyed :
Like King James he will be cheated
And by Walpole soon betrayed.

Whilst the Princess all things knowing
Laughs at all without disguise,
Labours at her own undoing
And late or never will be wise.

No. 9

AN EXCELLENT NEW BALLAD TO THE TUNE OF " WHICH
NOBODY CAN DENY ", MADE IN APRIL 1719 AGAINST
THE BILL OF PEERAGE (cf. p. 287)

I sing of a meeting which happend of late
Where Bos: has the honour to live by a gate
And a hundred wise heads mett in wise debate,
    Which no body can deny.

Twas touching a Bill the Peerage to fix
By twenty five Scotch and the English but six
But the Wiggs thought it some what like Robins old tricks,
    Which no body can deny.

When Bos: had thus spoak up Sunderland rose
And said the K . . . values not which way it goes,
But wishes you still would be led by the nose,
    Which no body can deny.

He wonders how they could find fault with so clever
A schem to keep Whiggism in the House ever
Which already has made Whigs of Harcourt and Trever,
    Which no body can deny.

He tould them you know the K. has a son
Who should he succeed we are surely undone
But the game had been ours had we made thirty one,
    Which no body can deny.

Then Stanhope with eloquent fury bespoak
The audience and told them the Unions a joak
And cared no (by god) how soon it was broak,
    Which no body can deny.

Though in this they might differ he begg'd they'd maintain
The King in his quadruple project in Spain
Where he heretofore so much honour did gain,
    Which no body can deny.

As soon as Aisleby found the Bill it was lost
Though before he had sett as dull as a post
He begged they consider how much it had cost,
    Which no body can deny.

In discharge of his office he tould them he hop'd
That since they agreed the Bill should be drop'd
They'd think it but just further payment be stop'd,
    Which no body can deny.

Then he call'd to their minds the Bill about Treason
Which at first was thrown out for many a good reason
But reviv'd like fresh flowers and pass'd the next season,
    Which no body can deny.

Then God bless the King, and may he long live,
Though he loves not, its true, his money to give,
He cares not a figg for his prerogative,
    Which no body can deny.

GENERAL INDEX

INDEX TO APPENDIX

THE END

Printed in Great Britain by R. & R. CLARK, LIMITED, *Edinburgh.*